ALSO BY NICHOLAS A. BASBANES

On Paper
About the Author
A World of Letters
Editions & Impressions
Every Book Its Reader
A Splendor of Letters
Among the Gently Mad
Patience & Fortitude
A Gentle Madness

Cross of Snow

Cross of Snow

A Life of
Henry Wadsworth Longfellow

NICHOLAS A. BASBANES

ALFRED A. KNOPF   New York
2020

Library of Congress Cataloging-in-Publication Data
Names: Basbanes, Nicholas A., [date] author.
Title: Cross of snow : a life of Henry Wadsworth Longfellow /
Nicholas A. Basbanes.
Description: New York : Alfred A. Knopf, 2020. |
Includes bibliographical references and index.
Identifiers: LCCN 2019028002 (print) | LCCN 2019028003 (ebook) |
ISBN 9781101875148 (hardcover) | ISBN 9781101875155 (ebook)
Subjects: LCSH: Longfellow, Henry Wadsworth, 1807–1882. |
Longfellow, Fanny Appleton, 1817–1861. | Poets, American—19th century—
Biography. | Authors' spouses—United States—Biography.
Classification: LCC PS2281 .B37 2020 (print) | LCC PS2281 (ebook) |
DDC 811/.3 [B]—dc23
LC record available at https://lccn.loc.gov/2019028002
LC ebook record available at https://lccn.loc.gov/2019028003

Jacket image: *Henry Wadsworth Longfellow* (detail), 1868,
by Julia Margaret Cameron. The Art Institute of Chicago / akg-images.

Jacket design by John Gall

For Connie,
my companion on the highway of letters,
non clamor sed amor

The Cross of Snow.

In the long, sleepless watches of the night,
A gentle face, the face of one long dead,—
Looks at me from the wall, where round its head
The night-lamp casts a halo of pale light.
Here in this room she died; and soul more white
Never through martyrdom of fire was led
To its repose; nor can in books be read
The legend of a life more benedight.

There is a mountain in the distant West
That, sun-defying, in its deep ravines
Displays a cross of snow upon its side.
Such is the cross I wear upon my breast,
These eighteen years, through all the changing scenes
And seasons, changeless since the day she died.

July 10. 1879.

Contents

Author's Note

Quotations from Henry W. Longfellow's journals are drawn from my examination of the manuscript copies in the Longfellow Papers (MS Am 1340) at Houghton Library, Harvard University, which I photographed during multiple research visits, in tandem with an unpublished partial transcription of the journals prepared in the 1990s by the late Stanley Patterson for the National Park Service, custodian of Longfellow House–Washington's Headquarters National Historic Site. Longfellow's manuscript journals are contained in numerous volumes, each with its own call number. Quotations from letters Longfellow wrote to others are taken, for the most part, from Andrew Hilen's indispensable six-volume edition, *The Letters of Henry Wadsworth Longfellow* (Cambridge, MA: Belknap, 1966–1982). Letters to Longfellow are quoted from unpublished correspondence in Houghton Library (bMS Am 1340.2), which I also photographed and transcribed, and identify in the notes with their individual folder numbers.

Quotations from the journals and correspondence of Frances Elizabeth Appleton Longfellow (FEAL) are drawn from my examination of digitally photographed copies of the unpublished documents, in tandem with verbatim transcriptions recently compiled by professional archivists at Longfellow House. In the interest of readability, and in conformance with the *Chicago Manual of Style*, Fanny Appleton's lifelong use of the ampersand (&) for "and" has been replaced uniformly by me with "and." All quotations, word usages, and spellings distinctive to the nineteenth century are as they appear in the original documents. Quotations from

Longfellow's poetry and prose writings are drawn, for the most part, from the earliest published editions, as available electronically through Google Books in full-text facsimile copies. Otherwise I have relied on *The Complete Writings of Henry Wadsworth Longfellow,* eleven volumes (Boston: Houghton, Mifflin, 1904), known as the "Craigie Edition."

Cross of Snow

Introduction

O ye familiar scenes,—ye groves of pine,
That once were mine and are no longer mine,—
Thou river, widening through the meadows green
To the vast sea, so near and yet unseen,—
Ye halls, in whose seclusion and repose
Phantoms of fame, like exhalations, rose
And vanished,—we who are about to die,
Salute you; earth and air and sea and sky,
And the Imperial Sun that scatters down
His sovereign splendors upon grove and town.

—from "Morituri Salutamus," poem for the fiftieth
   anniversary of the class of 1825 in Bowdoin College

$\mathcal{B}$eloved by millions of readers worldwide through much of the nineteenth century, the poet Henry Wadsworth Longfellow was in every respect a man for all seasons, discreet, loyal, and principled to a fault. Total strangers wrote him letters by the hundreds, an estimated twenty thousand during his lifetime, and he answered as many as he could, always gracious, always thoughtful. When admirers arrived unannounced at his home in Cambridge, Massachusetts, which they did by the droves, he was the person who opened the front door, occasionally inviting them inside, readily dispensing autographed cards kept nearby for just that purpose. And he was a soft touch, too; when asked for financial help, as he frequently was, he freely gave, even sent money on several occasions to Maria Poe "Muddy" Clemm, the destitute aunt and mother-in-law of his most abusive antagonist, Edgar Allan Poe.

One activity the Bard of Brattle Street routinely shunned, however, was speaking in public. Longfellow had the deepest admiration for those able to captivate multitudes with the spoken word—the Britons Charles Dickens and Fanny Kemble being two in particular, the French tragic actress Rachel Félix another—but the written word was how he preferred to communicate with the world at large, and there was no ambiguity on the point. On the day in 1854 that he gave his final lecture as a professor of European languages and *belles lettres* at Harvard College, he vowed that it would be "the last I shall ever deliver here or anywhere else." He was forty-seven years old at the time, and had been teaching for twenty-five of them—eighteen at Harvard, and seven before that at his alma mater, Bowdoin College, in Brunswick, Maine. He already enjoyed an international reputation, and had more than sufficient means to live in comfort and provide for his family. It was time, he had decided, to become a full-time writer.

For his final lecture, Longfellow spoke, with intended irony, on Dante's *Inferno,* and for the next twenty-one years he gave no public readings, and composed no "occasional poems" to commemorate specific milestones or events. When his dear friend and college classmate Nathaniel Hawthorne died in 1864 at the age of fifty-nine, he wrote a poignant elegy to mourn his loss and served as a pallbearer at the funeral, but did not speak formally at the services. When deeply depressed after suffering a grievous personal loss, he declined an invitation to visit the Bowdoin campus for a few undemanding days of rest and relaxation. "Too many ghosts there," he explained simply, and stayed at home.

Why, then, after vacillating for weeks, he agreed to address his classmates on the occasion of their fiftieth reunion in 1875, he never said, but from the moment he accepted, he threw everything he had into composing a lengthy poem he would deliver before eleven hundred people in First Parish Congregational Church. As a title for the 285-line ode, he echoed a cry shouted centuries earlier by Roman gladiators as they were about to engage in mortal combat: "Morituri salutamus"—We who are about to die salute you. Press accounts of the greatly anticipated oration—including full texts of the poem—appeared everywhere his work was read. The triumphant day, everyone who attended agreed, had belonged entirely to him.

FROM THE TIME he was a boy growing up in Portland, Maine, Henry Longfellow's driving ambition had been to fashion a form of literary expression distinctive to his time and place, one that celebrated America not only for Americans, but for readers around the world; and it was these twin attractions—accessibility and inclusion—that would earn him recognition as a "poet of the people" and a "fireside poet" whose verses were appreciated, understood, loved, and memorized by young and old alike, and from all demographics and social classes, a point often lost on those who would dismiss his work as being out of touch with a rapidly changing world.

Along with fame and celebrity came criticism, most of it into the 1900s positive, though there certainly were detractors, the troubled Poe by far the most hostile example, a more restrained Margaret Fuller another, though both expressed their generally dismissive views well before Henry wrote his most accomplished works. Poe died in 1849 from a variety of physical and emotional ailments, Fuller drowned the following year in a shipwreck—both at the age of forty—precluding what over time could have been more balanced evaluations.

That said, fashion and renown are slippery slopes in the best of times, and all writers have their ups and downs. Longfellow stands apart in that he did not meet his critical demise as the result of natural causes. Put another way, his fall from favor did not come about through general apathy or the purported transience of what he wrote, as the continued use in daily discourse of phrases and images he introduced makes abundantly clear. Instead, he was the victim of an orchestrated dismissal that may well be unique in American literary history—widely revered in one century, methodically excommunicated from the ranks of the worthy in the next. "In the repudiation of much of the old culture, Longfellow, not surprisingly, was targeted by a new generation of rebels and iconoclasts as the embodiment of the genteel spirit, the poet of purity, cleanliness, ideality, respectability, and conservatism, and as the relic of a defunct transition," the late Daniel Aaron, founding president of the Library of America and a distinguished professor of English and American literature at Harvard for many years, wrote in a trenchant examination of the poet's problematic legacy.

In ancient Rome, a condemned person's identity and accomplishments were subjected to *damnatio memoriae*— literally "damnation of memory"—a systematic banishment to oblivion carried out through the shattering of statues and the erasure of stone inscriptions. For Longfellow's sin of failing to satisfy the implacable demands of modernism and New Criticism, the punishment was expulsion from the literary canon, his work no longer deemed worthy of being read in classrooms or studied seriously in scholarly journals, regardless of how many people in the wider population might have felt otherwise. "Anthologists create the canon," is the way Joel Myerson, professor emeritus of American literature at the University of South Carolina and an authority on nineteenth-century American literature, explained the dynamic to me. "A writer who is not in the anthologies will not be read in the classrooms. It's as simple as that. How can you possibly be in the canon if you aren't being read? You can't."

Once the assault started, it rattled along like rolling thunder on a stormy summer night. "Longfellow is to poetry what the barrel-organ is to music," Van Wyck Brooks infamously proclaimed in 1915. Seventeen years later, Henry's standing was such that the now-obscure but then prominent critic Ludwig Lewisohn could propose, with undisguised contempt: "Who, except wretched school children, now reads Longfellow?" For young scholars with dreams of securing tenure and respectability among their peers, the message was clear: serious study of Longfellow would be done at their professional peril.

A rejoinder to the sort of scorn that became so prevalent at this time came in 1902 from Theodore Roosevelt during his first year as president of the United States. With forty-five published books to his credit on a wide variety of subjects by the time he died, and to this day America's most prolific author-president, TR was moved to write a fan letter to Martha Baker Dunn, author of an article that had just appeared in *The Atlantic Monthly* on the merits of the English poet Robert Browning. "Just one word about Longfellow," he added in seeming afterthought.

"Don't look down on him because he is so utterly different from Browning; so different that he might belong to another world. For all his gentleness he strikes the true ring of courage, the ballad-like ring of courage, in many pieces." He cited in particular "The Saga of King Olaf"—"only a translation, to be sure," but "like Julia Ward Howe's battle hymn" containing within it an almost ineffable quality "to which an appeal for brave action can be made. When Olaf strikes his sails and with his doom upon him makes ready to fight until the certain death overwhelms him, I think you can hear the clang of the weapons and the crash and splinter of the oars."

But the tides of dismissal could not be stemmed, the wishes of an erudite sitting president notwithstanding. On the occasion of Longfellow's centennial year in 1907, the eminent critic, writer, and educator Bliss Perry took sober note of the situation. "He is already thought negligible by some clever young men of over-educated mind and under-educated heart, who borrow their ethics from the cavemen, their philosophy from the raft-men, and who, in the presence of the same material from which Longfellow wrought delightful poetry,—the same landscape, the same rich past and ardent present and all the 'long thoughts' of youth,—are themselves impotent to write a single line."

Seventy-five years after that, another sympathetic scholar, Professor Steven Allaback of the University of California, Santa Barbara, reported dolefully at a professional symposium that "in the eyes of most critics" Longfellow was "very dead," with "no resurgence in sight." While other nineteenth-century poets were then being studied in college classrooms, Allaback lamented that "Longfellow gets laughed at," and he minced no words as to the root cause: "For years readers have been taught to regard Longfellow as an enemy of true poetry and authentic emotion, innocent of life's mysteries and complications."

Yet for all the slings and arrows directed his way, Longfellow is still the only American writer to have a bust of his likeness displayed in Poets' Corner at Westminster Abbey, and the monumental statue erected near Dupont Circle in Washington, DC in 1909 remains securely—almost defiantly—in place. And while he may well have been "very dead" "in the eyes of most critics" for much of the twentieth century, there were an important few who felt otherwise. Robert Frost drew the title of his first book, *A Boy's Will* (1913), from a key line in the Longfellow poem "My Lost Youth." During a reading at Bryn Mawr College in 1926, Frost delivered some selections of "new poetry" he said he had recently come across, three in all, each one enthusiastically received by his young audience. When the applause died down, Frost revealed—to the groans and gasps of everyone in attendance—the identity of his "discovery" to have been none other than Henry Wadsworth Longfellow.

The poet Howard Nemerov—winner of every literary prize of consequence America has to offer—edited a slim selection of Longfellow's poetry for a Dell paperback edition in 1959, explaining in an unapologetic introduction that "gentle" as Longfellow may appear on the surface, "beneath his gentleness" lies "a fair share of that unyielding perception of reality which belongs to good poetry wherever and whenever written." Lawrence Buell, professor emeritus of American literature at Harvard and renowned authority on the antebellum period, offered a similar justification for having edited a selection for a Penguin edition in 1988, calling the treatment of Longfellow then in vogue an egregious example of "critical overkill." In an interview with me, Buell said he felt a kind of obligation to do something at that time. "I never was ill disposed towards Longfellow. There were parts of his canon that always drew me. And Longfellow meant a great deal to my late father, which mattered a great deal to me—especially his love for *Tales of a Wayside Inn*. When I was deciding back in the 1980s what to include in my selection, I conferred with him on what he thought I should choose."

In his 1987 essay, Daniel Aaron counseled that "American literature isn't all that rich and various that we can afford to discredit or forget so good a poet," a caveat sufficiently prescient that three decades later, Harold Bloom, whose dozens of influential works over seven decades included *The Western Canon* (1994), could say, in an interview with me, that "all that silliness is over now—finished—done." Long regarded as the dean of American literary critics, and a lifelong champion of Longfellow, Bloom died on October 14, 2019, at the age of eighty-nine, having taught his final class as Sterling Professor of the Humanities at Yale just four days earlier.

The renaissance in Longfellow studies can be said to have begun in 1993 with the publication in *The Columbia History of American Poetry* of "Longfellow in the Aftermath of Modernism," a lengthy essay by the California poet and educator Dana Gioia, who would later serve as director of the National Endowment for the Arts. Gioia's spirited testimonial amounted to a clarion call for reconsideration; among prominent scholars to take the lead in the effort was Christoph Irmscher, today the provost professor of English at Indiana University and director of the Wells Scholars Program, and author of an exhaustive monograph, *Longfellow Redux,* that appeared in 2006. A well-attended exhibition he curated at Harvard University to commemorate the bicentennial of Longfellow's birth the following year occasioned publication of another important work, *Public Poet, Private Man.* These early efforts also included *Longfellow: A Rediscovered Life* (2004), a general biography by an independent scholar then based in Maine, Charles C. Calhoun, that is notably strong in tracing the arc of the poet's literary career.

A representative selection of Longfellow's writings edited by J. D. McClatchy and issued in 2001 by the Library of America, meanwhile, remains in print after close to twenty years as of this writing, and does respectably well in annual sales, according to figures provided to me by the publisher. In January 2020, the National Park Service, custodian of Longfellow House–Washington's Headquarters National Historic Site in Cambridge, reported having welcomed more than sixty thousand visitors in 2019 for the second consecutive year, record numbers for the property. Further validation of his comeback is to be found in recently issued anthologies of American poetry, and in college syllabi and curricula, where his name appears with increasing frequency.

In 2014, Fairleigh Dickinson University Press and Rowman & Littlefield jointly published in the United States and the United Kingdom *Reconsidering Longfellow,* a collection of ten scholarly essays based on fresh research that a dozen years earlier would have been inconceivable, let alone green-lighted by a reputable publishing house. "He is back in the anthologies; dissertations are being written about him," Irmscher wrote in the introduction. "Younger scholars especially have embraced" the poet's "documented love of foreign languages, his lifelong interest in translation, and the work he did to establish what we now call comparative literature in the universities." In another essay, for *Oxford Bibliographies Online,* Irmscher declared flatly that "Longfellow is back roaming

Ambrotype portraits of Henry and Fanny Longfellow, 1860, taken in the Boston studio of C. T. Sylvester, acquired by Bowdoin College in 2017 and previously unrecorded

the halls of academe," and that the once-stereotypical image of a white-bearded Fireside Poet had been replaced by "a multiculturalist, a speaker and a reader of many languages, a bold experimenter with poetic form, and an innovative translator"—all fueling study of his vast and various body of work.

In 2019, a group of academics and independent scholars calling themselves the Henry Wadsworth Longfellow Society gathered in Boston at the annual convention of the American Literature Association. The panel—"Fleshing Out Longfellow: New Directions in Longfellow Studies"—was organized by Professor Andrew C. Higgins, chairman of the English department at the State University of New York (SUNY) at New Paltz, and one of the "younger scholars" singled out by Irmscher who has made the study and teaching of Longfellow a top priority.

Higgins shared with me his thoughts on what he believes has contributed to the renewal of interest among his colleagues. "The United States today is undergoing a period of reflection on what it means to be an American. Longfellow played a major role in shaping middle-class American culture in the 1800s. One side of him often overlooked in the late 1800s and early 1900s is that he had a cosmopolitan vision, and was skeptical of extreme forms of nationalism. He was seen by many as just the author of 'Paul Revere's Ride' and *The Song of Hiawatha*. But he was also the translator and champion of Dante, and the editor of the thirty-one-volume anthology *Poems of Places*, which covered the whole world. So as we rediscover Longfellow—the whole of Longfellow—we have a chance to learn a lot more about America in the 1800s, while at the same time reflect on America in the 2000s."

All of this, it bears emphasizing, reflects the *public* side of Henry Wadsworth Longfellow, which by itself justifies a fresh look at where he stands in the grand continuum. Just as compelling, in my view, is the *personal* side, much of which has gone unexamined, and is possible now by a wealth of untapped archival and artifactual materials, many of them domestic objects that add flesh and substance to the account.

Long overdue, too, is a full consideration of Frances Elizabeth Appleton Longfellow, whose marriage to Henry during the momentous years leading up to the Civil War is at the core of the dual narrative that follows. For Henry, the union was transformative, giving him a second chance at a happiness he feared had been lost forever with the untimely death of his first wife eight years earlier, and it was a relationship that thrived on intellect as much as romance. Rigorously educated by private tutors from an early age, Fanny was multilingual, remarkably well read, highly skilled as an artist, diarist, correspondent, and conversationalist, and as the charming wife of an international celebrity, the perfect complement for all occasions.

My interpretation of their relationship was enriched by the availability of Fanny Longfellow's complete body of surviving correspondence—some 812 extraordinary letters—and her equally remarkable diaries, notebooks, and journals, all freshly transcribed by the National Park Service in anticipation of her own bicentennial, which was observed on October 7, 2017. What emerges is a love story of uncommon power, poignance, and significance, one that Longfellow celebrated in fourteen lines of poetry set down on a single sheet of paper toward the end of his life and tucked away among his private papers. At the bottom he had written the date, July 10, 1879; at the top, the title, "The Cross of Snow."

I

The Wind's Will

March 29: At night, as I lie in bed, a poem comes into my mind,—
a memory of Portland,—my native town, the city by the sea.

March 30: Wrote the poem; and am rather pleased with it, and with the
bringing in of the two lines of the old Lapland song,
> A boy's will is the wind's will,
> And the thoughts of youth are long, long thoughts.

—Henry Wadsworth Longfellow's journal, March 1855

Henry Wadsworth Longfellow gloried in the knowledge that he was a son of New England, born of solid Colonial stock with roots that traced back to the first permanent settlement at Plymouth in the seventeenth century. His maternal grandfather, General Peleg Wadsworth, was a direct descendant of *Mayflower* passengers John Alden and Priscilla Mullins, both of whom figure prominently in *The Courtship of Miles Standish*, and fought with honor in the American Revolution. He later served as a seven-term Massachusetts congressman representing the District of Maine, living a full eighty-one years, much of it in the foothills of the White Mountains on a seventy-five-hundred-acre estate granted to him in recognition of his distinguished service. "His grandchildren looked with a kind of awe upon his upright form, in the cocked hat and buckled shoes which he continued to wear," Henry's younger brother and first biographer, Samuel Longfellow, recalled of the old patriarch. "As they sat in the spacious and breezy hall, they never tired of hearing him tell the thrilling story of his capture by British soldiers, his imprisonment in Fort George at Castine, and his adventurous escape."

Peleg was born in 1748 in Duxbury, a coastal community thirty-five miles south of Boston that had been founded by his Pilgrim ancestors. After graduating from Harvard College at the age of eighteen, he taught school in Plymouth for three years, and married a local woman, Elizabeth Bartlett, said by a family historian to have been "a lady of eminent piety and uncommon intellectual qualities." Active in the growing movement toward independence, Peleg formed a regiment of minutemen in 1774 and was given the rank of captain. His participation in a succession of actions earned him command of a six-hundred-man detachment charged with protecting the entire coast of Maine, where he would take up permanent residence at the conclusion of hostilities. Active for many years afterwards in regional politics, he was a leading advocate of statehood, which would be granted in 1820 as part of the Missouri Compromise.

In 1785, Peleg began building a house near the waterfront of the seaport community known then as Falmouth and, befitting a man of his stature, had several tons of brick shipped up from Philadelphia expressly for the purpose. The town later took the name Portland, and the avenue where the sturdy dwelling still stands was designated Congress Street in 1823. One of Peleg's eleven children, Navy Lieutenant Henry Wadsworth, served heroically on the USS *Intrepid* in the Battle of Tripoli during the Barbary Wars, the republic's first foreign conflict after gaining independence from Britain, and prosecuted under the motto "Millions for defense, but not one cent for tribute."

A marble cenotaph erected in Portland's Eastern Cemetery records how the nineteen-year-old junior officer "fell before the walls of Tripoli" on September 4, 1804, "by the explosion of a fire-ship, which he and others gallantly conducted against the enemy," the sailors choosing "death and the destruction" of their foe "to captivity and torturing slavery." The last entry in the lad's shipboard journal—written a few days before their "torpedo attack" on the pirate fleet went disastrously awry—was upbeat: "We are in daily expectation of the Commodore's arrival from Syracuse, with the gun-boats and bomb-vessels, and then, Tripoli, be on thy guard." Washed ashore and dragged through the streets of Tripoli, the thirteen dead Americans were tossed in a pit outside the city, the precise location of their burial site not reliably determined until 1949, when memorial markers were installed by a contingent of naval officers from the USS *Spokane*.

In a death notice published in Portland on January 11, 1805, the recently married Zilpah Longfellow lamented how in "one moment, in the twinkling of an eye," the beloved brother called Harry by his siblings had "passed from time to eternity, from earth to heaven," his remains buried in a common grave thousands of miles from home. "Never! O never more, shall my eyes behold him! Never again shall my ears hear the sound of his voice. Oh! My Brother! Thou art laid low. No funeral rites for thee! No afflicted mourners consign thee to the grave. But thou, alone, unheeded, unprepared, was in one moment, slain, and buried. Thou fell the fairest flower that e'er has bloomed: so soon, so suddenly cut down." Later that year, Zilpah gave birth to her first child, a boy she named Stephen for his father; her second son, born on February 27, 1807, was named Henry Wadsworth Longfellow, in honor of his heroic uncle.

Another uncle, Commodore Alexander Scammell Wadsworth, Peleg's firstborn child, made numerous overseas deployments in a distinguished naval career of his own. As a gunnery officer aboard the USS *Constitution* during the War of 1812, he directed fire in a fierce broadside battle in the North Atlantic with the British frigate HMS *Guerriere*. Hewn by its Boston shipwrights with the sturdy, seemingly impenetrable timbers of live oak trees, the American warship rendered its much larger foe dead in the water, earning for itself the nickname "Old Ironsides." In recognition of his valor under fire, Alexander was presented with an engraved silver sword.

When Peleg moved forty miles west of Portland to an isolated village on the Saco River, the dwelling on Congress Street was taken over by Zilpah and her husband, Stephen, an up-and-coming lawyer from nearby Gorham. Henry would occupy a corner room upstairs overlooking the bustling waterfront to the southeast, "the beautiful town that is seated by the sea" that he celebrated years later in his poem "My Lost Youth." The vibrant community of Henry's childhood—the "shadowy lines of its trees," the "black wharves and the slips," the "bulwarks by the shore," the "breezy dome of groves"—is evocatively recalled, with a steady stream of "Spanish sailors with bearded lips" strolling the waterfront, firing his imagination of exotic places.

A moment of historical import that took place when the poet was a boy of six, the deafening face-off on September 5, 1813, in Casco Bay of the brig USS *Enterprise* and HMS *Boxer*, remained with him for decades. The two opposing skippers, Commander Samuel Blyth of the Royal Navy and American Lieutenant William Burrows, perished during the forty-five-minute encounter off Monhegan Island, which ended with the crippled British hulk being towed into Portland as a prize of war. In an extraordinary gesture of mutual respect among active combatants, the fallen commanders of both ships were buried side by side with full military honors in Eastern Cemetery at the base of Munjoy Hill. American and British seamen marched together near the Longfellow home in "one of the most imposing and impressive scenes ever witnessed in Portland," according to one account, summoning this reflection in "My Lost Youth":

> I remember the sea-fight far away,
> How it thundered o'er the tide!
> And the dead captains, as they lay
> In their graves, o'erlooking the tranquil bay,
> Where they in battle died.

Wedged between a cluster of commercial buildings in an otherwise modern quarter of the state's largest city, the Wadsworth-Longfellow House became a museum in 1901 following the death of Henry's sister Anne Longfellow Pierce, a widow from the age of twenty-three and a resident there for the remainder of her life. It is the oldest standing structure on the Portland peninsula. On the third floor—added seven years after Zilpah and Stephen moved in—faint traces of nineteenth-century graffiti can still be read on the walls and fixtures. One frame bears the inscriptions "How dear is the home of my childhood" and "Friday eve'g July 14th 1837—a magnificent sunset of golden clouds." Among the dozens of original furnishings and artifacts on display

Wadsworth-Longfellow
House, 489 Congress Street,
Portland, Maine, c. 1933

inside are images of family members executed by professional artists and
sculptors in the years before photography became the dominant medium
of portraiture. Silhouettes of Peleg and Elizabeth Wadsworth, Stephen
and Zilpah Longfellow, formal oils painted on canvas of Henry and his
father as young men, a lovely portrait of Anne Longfellow Pierce, and
a marble bust of Henry are among the likenesses that decorate every
room. Not on display, but included in the Maine Historical Society's
off-site collections, is a miniature painting depicting an adolescent boy
with an assured smile and a mane of wavy hair. Painted in 1845 by the
noted miniaturist Ann Hall, and based on a sketch from life rendered
when Henry was twenty-two, it parallels precisely a physical description of the budding poet as a young man. "Henry is remembered," Sam
Longfellow wrote, "with brown or chestnut hair, blue eyes, a delicate
complexion, and rosy cheeks; sensitive, impressionable; active, eager,
impetuous, often impatient; quick-tempered, but as quickly appeased;
kind-hearted and affectionate,—the sun-light of the house."

THERE WERE EIGHT CHILDREN in the Longfellow household, four
sons and four daughters, with Henry the most motivated to succeed on
a grand scale, and the one most empowered by his parents to achieve
his ambitious goals. In the numerous letters exchanged with his second-

born son, Stephen Longfellow—the third of five Longfellows in as many generations to have that first name—emerges as an upright and caring man, practical and clear-headed in the way he comported his life, and in the moral precepts he impressed upon his family. Though firmly rooted in Maine, he had the wisdom to accept Henry's eagerness to spread his wings and take flight. After graduating from Harvard in 1798, Stephen practiced law and dabbled in local politics, representing the District of Maine in the General Court of the Commonwealth of Massachusetts; and after statehood was realized, he served single terms in the United States Congress and the Maine State Legislature. In 1825, he formally welcomed the Marquis de Lafayette to Portland during the general's two-year tour of the United States to celebrate the fiftieth anniversary of American independence.

On the cultural front, Stephen Longfellow was a founding member of the Maine Historical Society and an enthusiastic supporter of the Portland Athenaeum. "In the home, there were books and music," Sam Longfellow tells us, noting that while their father's library was not large, it "was well selected for the time," and that Henry had full access to "Shakespeare, Milton, Pope, Dryden, Thomson, Goldsmith; the *Spectator*, the *Rambler*, the *Lives of the Poets, Rasselas*, Plutarch's *Lives*; Hume's, Gibbon's, Gillies's and Robertson's Histories, and the like," a reading list rich in literature, history, the humanities—all of the liberal arts. Their grandfather Peleg Wadsworth's home in Hiram, too, was well provisioned with books, and Henry drew eagerly from these springs of enlightenment during frequent summer stays. In 1813, when he was six, his schoolmaster wrote his parents that "Master Henry Longfellow is one of the best boys we have in school. He spells and reads very well. He also can add and multiply numbers. His conduct last quarter was very correct and amiable." We also know that Henry enjoyed playing the flute, and carried the instrument with him to Europe on his first trip abroad.

When it came time for college, Stephen and Zilpah chose nearby Bowdoin, chartered in 1794 and located twenty-five miles away in Brunswick. One of the school's first overseers had been Henry's grandfather Judge Stephen Longfellow, of the Court of Common Pleas in Gorham. Henry's father also became an overseer, and later was a trustee as well, so

The desk at which Henry wrote his first poems

legacy certainly figured into the decision. But the clincher seems to have been a desire to have their eldest sons together in the same class, and close by, the idea being that Henry—a model of probity and purpose—would keep a watchful eye on his older brother, a personable young man prone to careless behavior. For their freshman year, they did their studies with a private tutor at Portland Academy near their home. They took up residence in Brunswick as sophomores the following fall while their father was in Washington, leaving Zilpah to manage the household affairs; Henry was fifteen and Stephen, seventeen. Still at home with their mother were the six younger Longfellow siblings: Elizabeth (1808–1829); Anne (1810–1901); Alexander (1814–1901); Mary (1816–1901); Ellen (1818–1834); and Samuel (1819–1892), who would become a Unitarian pastor remembered best today as his brother Henry's first biographer, and with his devoted friend and collaborator of many years, Samuel Johnson, the author and anthologist of many spiritual and devotional hymns.

"IF YOU DESIRE the whole truth I must not conceal it," Henry wrote in response to Zilpah's demand for precisely that—"the truth and the whole truth"—made urgent by the number of fines Stephen was racking up for campus infractions. "He is absent from his room most of the time, and I do not know how much he studies, although he does not appear very well at recitation." Henry then confessed discomfort at finding himself in the middle of the crossfire. "You see in what a very unpleasant situation you have placed me, by setting me as a spy upon him. If I do not tell you the truth of the matter, I shall not be doing my duty, and yet when I tell you the truth, I am afraid you will interpret things worse than they really are. Don't write to papa about it for I am certain he will be more apt to do so than you are. I cannot say any more." But Zilpah, of course, did broach the subject with her husband, whose own attempts at long-distance intervention were proving equally futile. She declared "indolence" to be their eldest son's most "besotting sin," and that "only being subjected to the strictest discipline" would "rouse him from it." She acknowledged to her husband that they, as a couple, had "a severe trial" ahead of them to bear. "But we must not cast off our son, though his errors were greater than they are; we must endeavor to reclaim him, for who will be his friend if his parents are not."

Stephen's behavior did not improve, and before the year was out Bowdoin administrators suspended him for conduct deemed "disturbing to the quietness and dishonorable to the character of a literary institution," and in particular for "introducing spirituous liquors into the college." He was a regular visitor at a place on the outskirts of campus called Ward's Tavern, a favorite hangout of another Bowdoin classmate, Nathaniel Hawthorne, who would admit years later to having been better acquainted with Stephen during their student days than with Henry, both of them laid-back members of the Athenaean Society of undergraduates. Henry had joined a more academically focused group, the Peucinian Society, which included the most accomplished students. After a mandated stay of four months in the home of a Kennebunkport minister active in the temperance movement, the suspension—known as a "rustication"—was lifted, and Stephen resumed his studies, only to be sent home to Portland for further misbehavior. Allowed back in June, he took his examinations and graduated with Henry in the class of 1825.

In the years ahead, Stephen worked without enthusiasm in his father's law office, dabbled as a civil engineer, and spent a year abroad as secretary to Judge William Pitt Preble, a Portland neighbor whose daughter, Marianne, became his wife and the mother of his five children; she, too, became exasperated with his irresponsibility and filed for divorce a few months before he died in 1850 at the age of forty-five. "After life's fitful fever, he sleeps well," Henry wrote in his journal upon learning the news, quoting a line from *Macbeth*. Henry had never wavered in his solidarity, or in the support he extended to his brother's children, including a son, also named Stephen, who like his father was a lifelong alcoholic, embarked on a similar path of self-abuse that did not end well, either.

An in-house history of Bowdoin College published in 1882 on the occasion of the institution's eightieth anniversary gave Henry the superstar treatment, a generous discussion of his many accomplishments featured prominently along with a full-page engraved portrait. Stephen was gently described as having yearned for a naval career, but had "sacrificed his cherished inclinations, to the wishes of his honored father, who earnestly desired that his eldest son should share the burdens and transmit the honors of a profession to which he was himself devotedly attached and which he had highly adorned." The root cause of young Stephen's failure—demon rum—was never mentioned, the explanation given a classic exercise in Victorian circumlocution: "It cannot be disguised that Longfellow in the profession of his life was in a false position. He was unsuited by taste and temperament to the rude conflicts of the forum. He was amiable, exceedingly sensitive, diffident of his own powers, and of a fine literary taste. His mind was 'quick and forgetive,' his memory excellent, and he had a far greater ease in acquiring knowledge than in applying it or turning it to account. His fine disposition and gentlemanly manners endeared him to his ends in life. Had his lot been cast in a more favorable sphere, a different fate and a higher fame would have awaited him."

"WHAT CAN HAVE MADE the difference between our two sons, educated as they were together and alike?" an exasperated Zilpah had asked her husband. "Your plan for the education of your sons was liberal and judicious, and as it respected one of them perfectly right. But our sons are different, very different. I think they are so naturally, and it cannot, I think be imputed as a fault that he is not like the other."

That Henry's intellectual development had been "perfectly right" from the start was apparent to Zilpah on a number of levels. Well-read and astute in her own right, she maintained a lively dialogue with her gifted son that went well beyond the superficial, the first of many such intellectual relationships Henry would have with women throughout his life. One exchange began with a letter Henry wrote home from Brunswick, inspired, he told Zilpah, by a reading that very evening of "a few pages" of the eighteenth-century English poet Thomas Gray's odes. "I am very much pleased with them," he had determined, citing several as being notably "admirable," though he found "many passages" to be "quite obscure to me" in that they "seem to partake in a great degree of the sublime. *Obscurity* is the greatest objection which many urge against Gray. They do not consider that it contributes to the highest degree of sublimity; and he certainly aimed at sublimity in these Odes."

Zilpah thought long and hard before crafting a response, one we can pleasantly imagine the sixteen-year-old took to heart when composing his own verses in the years to come. "I am not very conversant with the poetry of Gray, dear H., and therefore cannot tell whether I should be as much pleased with it in general as you are," adding that she had read the poet's "Elegy Written in a Country Churchyard," his best-known work, "frequently, and always with pleasure," while also admiring it for "its truth and simplicity"—qualities she greatly appreciated. "I presume you will not allow it any sublimity. Obscurity, you think, is favorable to the sublime. It may be so, but I am much better pleased with those pieces which touch the feelings and improve the heart than with those which excite the imagination only and raise perhaps an indistinct admiration,—that is, an admiration of we know not exactly what."

In a follow-up letter, Zilpah asked Henry to bring a volume of Gray's odes home next time he visited. "I have a strong inclination to read the poems, since you commend them so highly. I think I should be pleased with them, though Dr. Johnson was not. I do not think the Doctor possessed much sensibility to the charms of poetry, and he was sometimes most unmerciful in his criticisms." Henry pointed out that Samuel

Johnson's severe criticism of Thomas Gray's poetry "is condemned by all of candid minds," and that the "cause of his severity is generally believed to be the difference of their religious and political opinions." That said, he backpedaled a bit on his earlier position. "I know and acknowledge that I am not a competent judge in this matter, and I only advance such opinions as suggest themselves to my mind, that you may know, not embrace, them. I am in favor of letting each one think for himself, and I am very much pleased with Gray's poems, Dr. Johnson to the contrary notwithstanding."

These wonderful exchanges, it bears repeating, came at a time when Henry was being required to report on his brother Stephen's unsettling deportment at Bowdoin. Henry's undergraduate years, by contrast, were both exemplary and stimulating, not only as a fully engaged student who would finish fourth in a class of notably high achievers, but in his literary endeavors outside the classroom. A knack for penning verse had first asserted itself in 1820 with publication in the *Portland Gazette* of "The Battle of Lovell's Pond," a piece of juvenilia inspired by stories Henry had heard from his grandfather, making him, at thirteen, a published poet well before he arrived on the Brunswick campus. A number of other poems he wrote at this time reached print in various outlets, and while these pieces are unremarkable—he would exclude most of them from his first collection of verse—he was testing his mettle in public forums, and enjoying the exposure enormously.

Henry dared, even, to consider becoming a professional writer—a fairly preposterous aspiration for a young American with limited means to nurture in the early decades of the nineteenth century, but that did not stop him from dreaming. A week after bringing his mother up to date on his brother's continuing misbehavior, he broached the subject of his future with his father, easing into it by mentioning how a series of "Chemical Lectures" he had recently attended convinced him that "Medical Science" would not be one of his driving aspirations.

"I feel very glad that I am not to be a Physician, there are quite enough in the world without me," he stated, and then moved directly to the point at hand. "And now, as somehow or other the subject has been introduced, I am curious to know what you do intend to make of me! Whether I am to study a profession or not? And if so, what profession?

I hope your ideas upon this subject will agree with mine, for I have a particular and strong predilection for one course of life, to which I fear you will not agree. It will not be worthwhile for me to mention what this is, until I become more acquainted with your own wishes." With that, a delicate dialogue got underway, Stephen responding that Henry should consider joining him in the practice of law. "In thinking to make a Lawyer of me, I fear you thought more partially than justly," he wrote back. "I hardly think Nature designed me for the bar, or the pulpit, or the dissecting-room. I most eagerly aspire after future eminence in literature."

As 1824 drew to a close, and with nothing between them resolved, Henry began floating the idea of spending a year doing graduate study at Harvard. "I would attach myself to some literary periodical publication by which I could maintain myself and still enjoy the advantages of reading," he reasoned, which then led to this stunning, oft-quoted declaration: "The fact is, I most eagerly aspire after future eminence in literature; my whole soul burns most ardently for it and every earthly thought centers in it." But with commencement looming, Henry declared himself open to compromise. "Whatever I do study ought to be engaged in with all my soul," he affirmed, "for I will be eminent in something."

Stephen Longfellow's reply to this plea came a few weeks later, tinged with sarcasm. "A literary life, to one who has the means of support, must be very pleasant," he began. "But there is not wealth enough in this country to afford encouragement and patronage to merely literary men. And as you have not had the fortune (I will not say whether good or ill) to be born rich you must adopt a profession which will afford you subsistence as well as reputation. I am happy to observe that my ambition has never been to accumulate wealth for my children, but to cultivate their minds in the best possible manner and to imbue them with correct moral, political and religious principles, believing that a person thus educated will, with proper diligence, be certain of attaining all the wealth which is necessary to happiness."

A bittersweet coda to this pragmatic stance of Stephen's would be apparent twenty-four years later when Henry, by then a top-tier educator and affluent man of letters respected on both sides of the Atlantic, returned to Portland to be with his ailing father, who died early one morning in August 1849, "very quietly without pain," after a lengthy illness, the cause never stated, but possibly in the aftermath of what would be diagnosed today as Alzheimer's disease. "Went to my father's law-office," the grieving son would write in his journal a few days after the funeral, "the dusty, deserted, silent place. Here he toiled on day after day. The ledger showed his reward, in page after page of unpaid charges. Alas for a lawyer in a little town!"

But that touching realization was still a quarter-century in the future; during this crucial time, when life-shaping decisions were being made, Stephen Longfellow's counsel carried weight, and Henry took it seriously. He continued to write for various newspapers and journals, placing a number of items in *The American Monthly Magazine*, a Philadelphia-based periodical, and fourteen poems, signed only with his initials, in *The United States Literary Gazette*, leading the owner and editor, Theophilus Parsons Jr., to solicit him for more submissions. "Will you permit me to add," Parsons wrote, "that your literary talents are of no ordinary character, and that they have not received their highest culture?"

In August 1825, William Cullen Bryant, coeditor of *The New-York Review and Atheneum Magazine*, and at the time America's leading poet, praised three of Henry's poems in a general commentary he wrote of the *Literary Gazette*, which he was pleased to report was turning out some excellent material. Bryant wrote that "of all the numerous English periodical" magazines being published at the time, none was introducing "as much really beautiful poetry as may be found, and still continues to be found in the columns of this *Gazette*. We might cite in proof of what we advance, the 'April Day,' the 'Hymn of the Moravian Nuns,' and the 'Sunrise on the Hills,' by H.W.L. (we know not who he is)."

With graduation rapidly approaching, Henry queried Theophilus Parsons about possibly coming aboard in some way as a paid employee of the Boston-based *United States Literary Gazette*. Parsons did not make ends meet by being the publisher of a shoestring publication, however; he was first and foremost a Harvard Law School professor, and an editor on the side. He wrote how "exceedingly difficult" it was for "any one to earn a living by literature." An "aspiring author," he maintained, "plays with his books, and thinks he is working when he is only playing hard."

His best advice: "Get through your present delusion as soon as you can," and consider the practice of law. But Henry was determined, and a consensus finally was reached between father and son: a year of graduate work at Harvard would be coupled with a summer studying case law in his father's Court Street office.

Invited to give an honors oration, Henry decided at the last minute to change topics from "The Life and Writings of Chatterton," already listed in the printed "Order of Exercises," and advocate instead the nurturing of a homegrown, distinctively American literary movement. A copy of the program in the Bowdoin College archives shows the original title of his oration crossed out with a single stroke of the pen, replaced above by "Native Writers." "But as yet," Henry declared in his remarks, "we can boast of nothing farther than a first beginning of a national literature: a literature associated and linked in with the grand and beautiful scenery of our country,—with our institutions, our manners, our customs, in a word, with all that has helped to form whatever there is peculiar to us, and to the land in which we live."

Commencement week was filled with other triumphs, including an invitation to compose and deliver the class poem. But most far-reaching was a vote taken by the college's board of trustees to establish a chair for the teaching of modern European languages, "particularly French and Spanish," as provided for by a bequest from the widow of the college's first great benefactor, James Bowdoin III. Only three other colleges in the United States had such a program at the time—Harvard, William and Mary, and the University of Virginia—and there was a dearth of people available who knew these languages, let alone had the qualifications to teach them.

Henry's name was put forth formally by Benjamin Orr, an oral-examinations supervisor on the board who recalled a Horatian ode the eighteen-year-old had translated and delivered with particular assurance during his sophomore year. Being the son and grandson of Bowdoin trustees must have weighed just as heavily in his favor. But there was a catch: Henry would be obliged to spend an unspecified period of time in Europe learning the very languages he was being asked to teach, and to do so at his own expense. The trustees also agreed that the appointment would be for a full professorship, and that it would pay a thousand dollars per annum. Board member Stephen Longfellow graciously offered to finance what turned out to be a three-year excursion abroad, with the understanding that the money being provided—precisely calculated afterwards to have totaled $2,604.24—was an advance on his son's eventual inheritance.

Though Henry was not by any means the first American scholar to study in Europe, he was among the vanguard. One of the pioneers, George Ticknor (1791–1871), was the Smith Professor of Modern Languages and Literatures at Harvard, and about to become an immensely influential figure in Henry's life, with a personal narrative that parallels in many ways his own. Sixteen years his senior, Ticknor, too, had been advised as a young man to become an attorney, had even passed the Massachusetts bar after graduating from Dartmouth in 1807 and taken a position in a Boston office. Uninspired by the work, he began, at the age of twenty-three, a course of independent study under the tutelage of John Sylvester John Gardiner, the rector of Trinity Church on Summer Street, who imbued him with "a love for ancient learning which I have never lost," he would say years later. A chance reading of the French historian Madame the Baroness de Staël-Holstein's *De l'Allemagne* (Of Germany), persuaded Ticknor that the University of Göttingen, home at the time to a library of more than two hundred thousand volumes, was where he wanted to pursue his studies. He borrowed German grammars and dictionaries where he could find them, one from the library of John Quincy Adams, which had been on temporary deposit at the Boston Athenæum during a lengthy diplomatic mission to France. "There was no one in Boston who could teach me," he explained of his method of inspired self-instruction.

Before sailing for Europe in 1815, Ticknor decided to see a bit of his own country first, visiting cities in Connecticut, New York, Pennsylvania, the District of Columbia, and Virginia. In Charlottesville, he was received at Monticello by Thomas Jefferson, a letter of introduction from John Adams paving the way. Jefferson was in the early stages of planning the University of Virginia at the time, and a close relationship between the two humanists ensued; their erudite correspondence reveals

George Ticknor, Dartmouth
College Museum of Art

a pair of kindred spirits, both of them unrepentant bibliophiles, with Ticknor happily buying books for the Sage of Monticello during his travels on the Continent.

In the fall of 1816, word came from America that a magnanimous businessman and Harvard alumnus, Abiel Smith of Boston, had bequeathed twenty thousand dollars to establish a chair for the teaching of the French and Spanish literatures, and the position was his if he wanted it. Ticknor accepted with the assurance he could complete his studies in Europe, and that he live in Boston, not Cambridge, as required then of other Harvard faculty. The annual salary of one thousand dollars was acceptable; not even an offer from Thomas Jefferson to become a professor in "Ideology, Ethics, Belles-Lettres and Fine Arts" at the University of Virginia—a post "you would splendidly fill"—with a salary of twenty-five hundred dollars a year and a fully provided house to live in, could dissuade him. Ticknor assumed the position in 1819.

Six years later, when Henry began thinking about his own European agenda, he secured a letter of introduction from Charles S. Daveis of Portland, a lawyer and acquaintance of his father, and trusted confidant of the Harvard professor. Whatever Henry may have expected when he called on Ticknor, what he did not find was a low-energy academic living in modest faculty quarters on the fringe of a quiet campus. By the time Henry appeared at his front door, Ticknor was a force with international clout, and a very wealthy one at that, having married especially well four years earlier, and living quite comfortably in a beautifully appointed house near Boston Common, his private library teeming with handsomely bound books brought back from his European travels. Ticknor's bride, Anna Eliot, was the daughter of Samuel Eliot, a banker and merchant from a distinguished Boston family whose numerous luminaries over the years would include the author and art critic Charles Eliot Norton, the historian Samuel Eliot Morison, and the poet T. S. Eliot. Another Eliot daughter, Catherine, married Professor Andrews Norton of Harvard; both of them would become important Longfellow intimates in the years to come.

One of Ticknor's most celebrated attainments was his having managed to become well connected, his friendship with Thomas Jefferson being "the first noteworthy instance of an extraordinary ability to make and keep friends among the most notable people of the day, old and young, American and foreign, noblemen and commoners, statesmen, scholars, men of science, poets, novelists, and artists," according to the scholar and educator Henry Grattan Doyle in a biographical essay. When the Ticknors moved to 9 Park Street on the corner of Beacon Street, facing the golden-domed State House on one side, Boston Common on the other, they became legendary for their soirees, their houseguests over the years including Sir Walter Scott and the Marquis de Lafayette. "The fortune he inherited from his father—together with that of his wife—enabled him to live at ease, with unpretending elegance," George Hillard wrote in an edition of Ticknor's letters and journals. "His disposition and tastes found their full exercise and expression in his home, and that home was thenceforth, for many years, a brilliant and genial centre of the most cultivated society of Boston."

My sense is that Ticknor took to Henry instantly, his vibrant mind, his passionate ambition, the very cut of his jib—handsome, nicely dressed, respectful of his elders, articulate, courteous, excellent references. When Henry left Ticknor's house on May 2, 1826, he had secured advice that helped define the rest of his life. "I dined to-day with Mr. Ticknor," he informed his mother immediately thereafter, judging the professor "exceedingly kind and affable," and strongly recommending a year in Germany. Ticknor also provided letters of introduction to Washington Irving, Robert Southey, and others "useless" for Henry "to enumerate," what with him being in a rush to board a coach for Northampton to meet with George Bancroft and Joseph Cogswell, founders of the Round Hill School, who also would urge study at Göttingen. "Stage has come—good bye," he scribbled in closing. "Love to all."

The four-week passage across the Atlantic was long and tedious; but once he arrived in "this great Babylon of modern times"—Paris—Henry wasted little time getting himself acclimated. "I have not yet forgotten what I came to France for," he assured his parents, but he was not about to deny himself the opportunity of a lifetime, either. "I have settled down in something half-way between a Frenchman and a New Englander," he crowed to his brother Stephen, having "decorated my outward man with a long-waisted thin coat—claret-colored—and a pair of linen pantaloons:—and on Sundays and other *fête* days—I appear in all the glory of a little hard French hat—glossy—and brushed—and rolled up at the sides—it makes my head ache to think of it. In this garb I jostle amongst the crowds of the Luxembourg, which is the favorite

Stephen Longfellow, Henry's father, portrait made during his term as a Member of Congress representing the State of Maine, 1823–25

promenade in St. Germain." His brother wasted no time sharing this with the family, as an unamused reproach from their father makes stingingly clear. "You will allow me to doubt the expediency of conforming your dress to the fashion of the country in which you may reside for a short time," the elder Stephen retorted. "You should remember that you are an American, and as you are a visitor for a short time only in a place, you should retain your only National Costume."

Henry was staying at this time in the boardinghouse of a Madame Potel, who made him feel "perfectly at home," "happy as possible," and altogether "delighted with Paris," a city, he assured his father, "where a person if he pleases can keep out of vice as well as elsewhere, tho' temptations are multiplied a thousand fold if he is willing to enter into them." A month and a half into his stay, he went off exploring on his own and visited Limoges, Orléans, Rouen, Anteuil, and Bordeaux, finding new quarters when he returned to the capital. The lengthy letter he wrote his mother describing these adventures was signed "Henri."

Another letter, written to his father on the same day—and signed simply "H."—pushed for a change in strategy, and what he now thought should come next. "The question then will be which is the most important for me as a scholar: the German language or the Italian? All those who have spoken to me upon the subject in America told me by all means to become a German scholar—and that no student ever regretted a years residence at Göttingen. Mr. Ticknor said, 'give up the Italian for the German'—and moreover urged me very strenuously to go first to Germany—tho' for my own part I am well satisfied with learning the French first." Should he, then, forgo Spanish entirely and focus on German and Italian, or should he spend more time nailing down French? "I had rather give up the Spanish and the Italian for the present," he proposed, "than leave the French half-acquired and miss a glorious opportunity of acquiring it." Arguing against Spain were reports that the country was unsafe to foreigners in the aftermath of a French invasion in 1823 to support the embattled monarchy, leading him to ask "which is the most important for me as a scholar, the German language or the Italian?"

Stephen Longfellow was not at all pleased with this waffling, and insisted that his son be mindful of the big picture. "If the state of Spain is such that it is not safe to visit it, you will undoubtedly find instructors in France or Germany. If you neglect either of these languages you may be sure of not obtaining the station which you have in view. And I should never have consented to your visiting Europe had it not been to secure that station." A serendipitous meeting with Pierre Irving, the nephew of Washington Irving and recently arrived in Paris, persuaded him that conditions in Spain were not nearly as dangerous after all. "I shall leave Paris for Spain on Wednesday," he thereupon announced, and he was feeling pretty good about the past eight months, too. "Setting all boasting aside, I must say that I am well satisfied with the knowledge I have acquired of the French language."

2

Awakening

A restless spirit prompted me to visit foreign countries. I said with the Cosmopolite, "The world is a kind of book, in which he, who has seen his own country only, has read but one page." Guided by this feeling I became a traveler. I have traversed France on foot; smoked my pipe in a Flemish inn; floated through Holland in a *Trekschuit*; trimmed the midnight lamp in a German University; wandered and mused amid the classic scenes of Italy; and danced to the gay guitar and merry Castanet on the borders of the blue Guadalquivir.

> —Henry Wadsworth Longfellow,
> "The Schoolmaster," *The New-England Magazine,* July 1831

Tell me, ye who have sojourned in foreign lands, and know in what bubbles a traveler's happiness consists,—is it not a blessing to have your window overlook a scene like this?

> —Henry Wadsworth Longfellow,
> *Outre-Mer: A Pilgrimage Beyond the Sea,* 1835

*F*undamental to everything young Henry Longfellow ultimately became in life was the unaccompanied trip he made abroad as a teenager fresh out of college, with an eagerness to experience and to learn that at times can be inspiring. The people he met, the relationships he made, the remarkable landmarks brimming with historical and cultural nuances he so hungrily absorbed, enriched a keen and inquisitive mind. Identifying himself at such an early age as a "cosmopolite"—a person, in essence, who strives to be a citizen of the world—anticipates by decades the concept of "multiculturalism," a word that does not even enter the English language until the 1930s.

Writing from Italy, Henry asked his sisters if they were studying French or Spanish. "If not, you should lose no time in commencing, for I assure you that, by every language you learn, a new world is opened before you. It is like being born again; and new ideas break upon the mind with all the freshness and delight with which we may suppose the first dawn of intellect to be accompanied." He would stress the same point some years later in one of his Harvard lectures: "As many languages as a man knows, so many times he is a man."

If any single word best describes the image the young scholar had of himself during these fruitful months in Europe, it is that of a "traveler" in the literary mold of Johann von Goethe (1748–1832), Lord Byron (1788–1824), and Sir Walter Scott (1771–1832). Writing his mother from Rome on Thanksgiving Day in 1828, he quoted a line from the Oliver Goldsmith poem "The Traveler" (1764) to describe his state of mind while on the Continent. "Like all other people, the traveler has his cares and sorrows:—sometimes he is gay—at others sad:—sometimes he feels like a bird engaged:—and then again he seems to 'drag at each remove a lengthened chain.'"

Another writer Henry looked up to as a model at this time was Washington Irving (1783–1859), a fellow American he got to know personally in Spain, who passed on advice that stayed with him for the rest of his days—that he should master the literatures of the countries he was visiting, not just the languages. Years later, Henry acknowledged his debt in a memorial tribute prepared for the Massachusetts Historical Society. "Every reader has his first book, I mean to say, one book among all others which in early youth first fascinates his imagination, and at once excites and satisfies the desires of his mind. To me, the first book was the *Sketch Book* of Washington Irving." Irving's *Sketch Book*—the full title is *The Sketch Book of Geoffrey Crayon, Gent.*—was a collection of thirty-four tales and essays set for the most part in Europe. Published in seven installments between June 1819 and September 1820 in the United States, and shortly thereafter in England, the quasi-travelogue was a best seller on both sides of the Atlantic. The sketches based on Irving's European travels were narrated by the fictional Geoffrey Crayon, a pen name he used periodically in later years. Two set in the Catskill region of upstate New York—"Rip Van Winkle" and "The Legend of Sleepy Hollow"— were ascribed to a fictional Dutch historian, Diedrich Knickerbocker.

"Europe was rich in the accumulated treasures of age," Irving had written in his preface, words that resonated deeply with Henry. "Her very ruins told the history of times gone by, and every mouldering stone was a chronicle. I longed to wander over the scenes of renowned achievement—to read, as it were, in the footsteps of antiquity—to loiter about the ruined castle—to meditate on the falling tower—to escape, in short, from the commonplace realities of the present, and lose myself among the shadowy grandeurs of the past." Just as influential was Lord Byron's *Childe Harold's Pilgrimage*, which came along with Henry to Europe in his knapsack. A delightful self-portrait in pencil and water-color Henry executed with considerable skill in his Spanish journal— one of at least five likenesses he would sketch of himself during this European trip, each outfitted in native garb—pictures a dapper young man on horseback headed to Granada from Malaga, his back straight, his head held high, his top hat tilted back at a jaunty angle, the animal being whisked along by a confident rider. The caption underneath uses two lines improvised from *Childe Harold:*

> To horse—to horse! If he quits, forever quits
> A scene of peace though soothing to his soul.

One minor calamity Henry would bemoan was to have unwittingly left his *Childe Harold* with an acquaintance in Rome, prompting him to prevail on a new friend he had made a year earlier in Marseilles—George Washington Greene of Rhode Island—to fetch it and bring it to Venice, where they planned to meet up again. One of the great highlights of Henry's stay in Venice, he would later tell his mother, was having met a gondolier who had worked as Lord Byron's private chauffeur nine years earlier, regaling him with stories of ferrying the poet back and forth on his many assignations. Henry sketched a nice portrait of the gondolier, Toni Toscan, in his journal; on the opposite page, in Toscan's handwrit-

To horse - to horse - he quits, forever quits
A scene of peace though soothing to his soul."
Byron.

Self-portrait of Longfellow on the road from Malaga to Granada, November 1827, in one of his travel journals

ing, is a poem he composed for Henry, identified underneath by him as a "famoso poeta"—famous poet.

Being allowed as a teenager to go off on his own to Europe involved considerable trust, and while Henry had certainly earned the confidence of his parents, he was braced with admonitions from them to be cautious. "I will not say how much we miss your elastic step, your cheerful voice, your melodious flute, but will say farewell, my dear son, may God be with and prosper you," Zilpah Longfellow wrote as her son was about to set sail for France. "May you be successful in your pursuit of knowledge; may you hold fast your integrity, and retain that purity of heart which is so endearing and interesting to friends. I feel as if you were going into a thousand perils. You must be very watchful and guard against every temptation." Stephen Longfellow was more direct in his bon-voyage letter. "It is impossible, with all my solicitude, to give you all the instructions which your youth and inexperience require, but permit me to conjure you to remember the great objects of your pursuit. Keep them constantly in view, and let not the solicitations of pleasure, nor the allurements of vice lead you from the path of virtue. Your tour is one for improvement rather than pleasure and you must make every exertion to cultivate and improve your mind."

Stephen's concerns notwithstanding, there is nothing to document one way or the other any serious romantic interest Henry might have had before going abroad. That said, he nurtured a healthy respect and high regard for women that is apparent throughout his life. His journals are replete with mentions of those he regarded as "pretty" or otherwise attractive, but also for those who impressed him with their demeanor and intelligence. Spain would prove to be an awakening for him in more ways than one.

When they met in Paris, Pierre Irving had recommended to Henry that his first order of business in Madrid should be to seek out Alexander Slidell, an American naval officer from New York then on extended leave in Spain helping Washington Irving research his biography of Christopher Columbus. Four years older than Henry, Lieutenant Slidell was staying in a private home in the heart of the capital, at the foot of the Calle de la Montera. Henry arranged to board in the same house himself; but since the room would not be available for another fortnight, he joined Slidell on a trip through the countryside, traveling to Segovia, San Ildefonso, and the Escorial, "all of which," he told his father, "a stranger should make it a point to visit."

The two Americans traveled through the mountains on horseback, by foot, in one instance aboard "a huge covered wagon drawn by six mules." Once returned to Madrid, Slidell said his goodbyes and left for Gibraltar, his time in Spain at an end; Irving's book, *A History of the Life and Voyages of Christopher Columbus*, would appear the following year in four volumes, and include a generous acknowledgment to Slidell. Henry, meanwhile, found the accommodations very much to his liking. "The family with whom I reside is a very kind and attentive one," he duly reported home. "It consists of an elderly gentleman and lady, with their daughter, a young lady about eighteen, who has already become quite a sister to me. Under her attentions I hope to find the acquisition of the Spanish a delightful task."

In a follow-up to his mother, he described his tutor as "one of the sweetest-tempered little girls that I have ever met with. The grace of the Spanish women and the beauty of their language makes her conversation quite fascinating. I could not receive greater kindness than I receive at the hands of this good family. I shall feel the most sincere regret in bidding them farewell." Writing to his sisters, Henry identified the young woman as "Florence." Her full name was Florencia González; she is mentioned several times in Henry's Spanish diary, which is more fragmentary than his later journals, this one serving basically as field notes for the travelogue he would call *Outre-Mer, A Pilgrimage Beyond the Sea.*

The first entry, under the heading "Madrid," is dated May 15, 1827: "A year today since I left New York for Europe, in the ship *Cadmus.*" Henry described attending a religious festival that night "at the chapel on the south side of the river." The next entry has him taking a "walk to the canal with Florence in the storm," and taking "refuge in the chapel. Overtaken by the rain on entering the city—the café." They were in the village of Villanueva del Pardillo, in the Guadarrama Mountains, on May 28, and still there on June 6, preparing their return to Madrid the next day. "Thus I have seen a little of Spanish rural life and am much delighted with it," Henry summarized of the past week, all the while channeling his inner Washington Irving: "I like to see things in reality—not in paintings—to study men—not books."

The arrival of funds from home occasioned a letter of gratitude to his father, "for although I live with all decent economy, yet I must confess that European economy would be extravagance in New England, and in residing in Madrid my expenses would have been greater than they would have been in a Provincial town. But unfortunately it is only in New and Old Castile, that the language is spoken with purity, and if I had gone to Barcelona or Valencia I should have learnt a jargon fit for the tower of Babel, and not the language of Cervantes."

We could leave Henry's friendship with the lovely Florencia at this point and move along, if not for the otherwise inexplicable decision he made to stay in Spain considerably longer than originally planned—a full eight months—and for the goading he received in the months to come from Alexander Slidell, the American who had introduced him to the González family, and prodded him for details of his relationship with the young woman. A career naval officer, Slidell would soon be known as Slidell Mackenzie, his surname lengthened to satisfy the wish of a bachelor uncle anxious to preserve the patronymic, in return for which he secured a substantial inheritance. A published writer in his own right, Slidell Mackenzie and Henry corresponded periodically over the next twenty years, meeting up on at least three occasions in the United States; in a circuitous way to be documented later, he figured indirectly in the writing of Henry's 1849 poem "The Building of the Ship."

Issued anonymously in 1829, Alexander Slidell Mackenzie's first book—*A Year in Spain by a Young American*—was a memoir of the time he spent in Madrid working for Washington Irving. In a chapter devoted to seeing Old and New Castile, he told how a "young countryman, who had come to Spain in search of instruction"—not named, but unquestionably Henry Wadsworth Longfellow—had in a "happy moment" provided companionship on a side trip he would otherwise have made by himself. "He was just from college, full of all the ardent feeling excited by classical pursuits, with health unbroken, hope that was a stranger to disappointment, curiosity which had never yet been fed to satiety. Then he had sunny locks, a fresh complexion, and a clear blue eye, all indications of a joyous temperament. We had been thrown almost alone together in a strange and unknown land; our ages were not dissimilar; and, though our previous occupations had been more so, we were, nevertheless, soon acquainted, first with each other, then with each other's views, and presently after we had agreed to be companions on the journey."

Elsewhere, Slidell Mackenzie recalled how he had come to live at 16 Calle de la Montera. "I did not like the look of Don Valentin, nor did I care to live under the same roof with him," he wrote of the first meeting he had with his prospective landlord. "So, when we rose to depart, I said I would think of the matter, secretly determining, however, to seek lodgings elsewhere." But as he was leaving, he encountered, on the narrow landing at the door, "Doña Florencia," the disagreeable man's daughter, who had just returned from Mass. "She might be nineteen or thereabout, a little above the middle size, and finely proportioned; with features regular enough, and hair and eyes not so black as is common in her country, a circumstance upon which, when I came to know her better, she used to pride herself for, in Spain, auburn hair, and even red, is looked upon as a great beauty."

Slidell Mackenzie continued along in this vein for another page and a half of text, paying special attention to the young woman's style of dress. "She had a mantilla of lace, pinned to her hair and falling grace-fully about her shoulders, and a *basquina* of black silk, trimmed with cords and tassels, and loaded at the bottom with lead, to make it fit closely, and show a shape which was really a fine one." She invited him to come back inside, "and I at once accepted the invitation, without car-ing to preserve my consistency." The nub of it all is that Alex changed his mind on the spot and decided to rent the room, having determined "to be pleased with everything," and "to look only at Florencia."

Henry showed no vacillation at all about moving in with the González family, and wasted no time making himself at home, develop-ing an approach to study that would be short on structured instruction but long on intense conversation with this talented young woman, who was also, he informed his family, an accomplished musician. In *Outre-Mer*, he described his garret "in the hired house of Valentin González, at the foot of the Calle de la Montera" at length. "My apartments were in the third story, above the dust, though not beyond the rattle, of the street; and my balconies looked down into the Puerta del Sol, the heart of Madrid, through which circulates the living current of its population at least once every twenty-four hours."

From this vantage point he would compose little vignettes of what he saw, his attention in one instance drawn to "a beautiful girl, with flaxen hair, blue eyes, and the form of a fairy in a midsummer night's dream" who had "just stepped out on the balcony beneath us! See how coquett-ishly she crosses her arms upon the balcony,—thrusts her dainty little foot through the bars, and plays with her slipper." The young woman was an Andalusian from Malaga, he informed the reader knowingly—he described just such a young neighbor on a lower floor, a friend of Flor-encia's named Anita, in a letter to his family—as the sister of a "bold dragoon" who "wears a long sword; so beware!"

As attached to Florencia as Henry may have been—how deeply can be no more than speculation, though the evidence we have suggests that it was deep enough—it paled by comparison to the candle Slidell Mackenzie burned for the young beauty. He made two return trips to the old neighborhood in 1834, which he recounted in *Spain Revisited*, a sequel. There he described Florencia's figure "as light and graceful as ever," her face "altogether the same." Her features in general "were of the

Two pages from Henry's Spanish journal

sort which owe everything to an amiable expression; a kind heart shining magically in the countenance, and conveying to the beholder the reflection of something yet more beautiful within," a woman, in sum, still "decidedly attractive." Dropping by her apartment one last time, he sat transfixed while Florencia played the guitar and sang some songs "in the soft Castilian which she so gracefully uttered" for a gathering of friends. "The whole scene, indeed, was so familiar, that when I took possession of a vacant chair," the years that he had been absent "were effaced from my memory."

In a number of the early letters he wrote to Henry over the next twenty years, Slidell Mackenzie confided the woman's hold on him with even greater candor. Their correspondence began in June 1828 when the young lieutenant was back on naval duty; Henry, meanwhile, had moved on to Italy. Slidell Mackenzie opened with a synopsis of their time together, recalling "the mules, and the mountains, the adventures of the snow-bank, the dread of robbers and the weary ride to Madrid, our room and balcony overlooking the Puenta del sol"—but "above all," he added, "the watchful eye of Florencia, best and greatest of her sex."

Eight months later, Slidell Mackenzie responded to news that Henry had been under the weather in Rome. "I hope you were not without some kind nurse of the more gentle sex, some Florencia to smooth your pillow or qualify the bitter doses of the doctor. Tell me if in all your wanderings you have anywhere met with a damsel whether of high or low degree so gentle, so kind, so affectionately amiable as that Florencia?" As for himself, he added, "if chance should ever throw in my way one like her in character, and otherwise suitable in country and condition," he would "buckle to" and "pop the question at her."

Though Henry responded graciously to these letters, he did not, to his everlasting credit, rise to the bait, and avoided engaging the matter, at least in writing. The two men met briefly in New York shortly after Henry's return to the United States, where apparently the subject did come up, but with little elaboration, as the next letter from Slidell Mackenzie implies. "My Dear Don Enrique," he began teasingly. "I like to call you by that old Madrid name of yours that used to sound so sweet from the lips of Florencia. How long is it since you have heard from our amiable Andalusian? I saw so little of you here in September that I had no time to hear at all about her." In his reply, Henry shared a few stories about several of the other people they both knew in Madrid, but still offered nothing about the young woman, which brought yet another prodding, this one written from the USS *Brandywine*. "You say little of Florencia in your letters, and I did not have time to ask you much about her. You told me I believe that she had been near marrying a man going to Cuba. I am sorry she did not do so; for independent of the great chance I should then have had of seeing her again, I hold that an indifferent husband is better than no husband at all. If she does not marry she will run a great risque of becoming either a nun or a prostitute, two evils between which there is little choice."

Of the fifteen surviving letters Slidell Mackenzie wrote to Henry between 1827 and 1847, four at the beginning make mention of Florencia; after that it stops. The seasoned veteran of salty belowdecks banter had apparently decided, finally, that enough was enough. To that, moreover, Henry in 1831 had become a married man, which may have persuaded Slidell Mackenzie to let the past remain securely in the past; four years later, he took a wife of his own. When he learned in June of 1843 that Henry, a widower of close to eight years, was engaged to marry "a very intelligent, amiable and attractive lady to whom you have been long attached," he extended his best wishes. "Having myself found married life most truly of increased and increasing happiness, contentment and enchantment, I can very heartily congratulate you on so auspicious an event, and have nothing better to wish you than that your happiness may be equal to mine."

Among the thousands of other letters Henry received and now in the Harvard collections, one, from Don Valentín González, responds cordially to an introduction Henry had sent his former landlord on behalf of George Washington Greene, who was planning to travel through Madrid. In a brief addendum at the end is a warm note from Florencia, in Spanish, polite and discreet, but redolent with nuance nonetheless.

The letter was translated from the Spanish for me by Iván Jaksić, director of Stanford University's Bing Overseas Studies Program in Santiago, Chile, and the author of numerous monographs of Latin American history. One of these, *The Hispanic World and American Intellectual Life, 1820–1880*, examines the introduction of Spanish literature in nineteenth-century America, with close attention given to Longfellow, George Ticknor, and William Hickling Prescott. Professor Jaksić quoted sparingly from the Florencia González addendum in his monograph, and offered to translate it in its entirety for me when I contacted him by email. He noted that Florencia also corresponded with Henry through a mutual friend in Spain, José Cortés y Sesti, who later—with Henry's help—spent some time in the United States hoping to find a career in teaching, even staying with him for a period in Brunswick.

"Florencia's *modus operandi* was to piggy-back on the letters by others," Professor Jaksić explained in one of our emails. "Cortés, in particular, would paraphrase what she said and, if I recall correctly, let her write PSs at the end. I looked for Cortés's records all over Spain and never found out about his whereabouts. He must have kept some very important letters from Longfellow." The Houghton Library has fifty letters Cortés wrote to Longfellow, all of them in Spanish; there are none there that Henry sent to him. Florencia's addendum to her father's letter is gracious, written, she began, "with pleasure," and "to tell you about the true friendship I feel for you. I will never forget you no matter how many years pass. I will keep this friendship as strong as the first day,

A sketch from Longfellow's
first trip to Europe, c. 1828

whether you reciprocate it or not, and with the same keenness as when I had the honor to meet you. I will always appreciate you." She added how she had been working on improving her singing. "If we ever have the joy of meeting again you will enjoy my useless musical skills. But if this hope turns out to be in vain, we will have patience and accept the will of God regarding our fate."

Aside from Florencia, there had been other inducements keeping Henry in Madrid and muddying up what had been a carefully planned itinerary worked out closely with his father. He was also having the time of his life mixing with a tight-knit group of Americans in the diplomatic community, who, to a person, had grown very fond of him. The head of the American legation, Alexander H. Everett, had brought with him as aides several people who were involved in literature and the arts, and they stuck very close together. Henry's letter of introduction to Everett was written by Charles S. Daveis of Portland, the same person who had directed him to George Ticknor. A Harvard graduate and member of a prominent Boston family, Alexander Everett was a distinguished man of letters, appointed minister to Spain in 1825 by John Quincy Adams;

he was also the brother of Edward Everett, diplomat, governor, senator, secretary of state. Later, as owner and editor of *The North American Review*, Alexander Everett became a champion of Henry's work in the years that followed.

Working as an attaché to Everett was another Massachusetts native, Obadiah Rich, an expatriate bookseller credited by the bibliographer Nicholas Trübner with having single-handedly created the field of Americana in many stateside libraries, most spectacularly those of James Lenox in New York, whose fabulous holdings became the core collection of the New York Public Library, and John Carter Brown in Providence, Rhode Island, now a stand-alone rare-books library at Brown University. Rich was doing double duty in Madrid, supplying his well-heeled clients and working for Everett; he also gave Henry a lot of hands-on instruction in the skills of antiquarian book hunting, which he was doing on behalf of Bowdoin College. It was Rich, too, who had arranged a diplomatic assignment for Washington Irving to keep him financially afloat while doing research in Spain, and provided him with lodgings.

The very first letter Henry received from Everett was delivered by courier to his rented rooms within days of their introduction. It was brief and to the point: "I have a box at the opera for tonight," and Henry was welcome, if so "disposed," to come along. Lucretia Orne Peabody Everett, Minister Everett's elegant wife, wrote Mrs. Daveis to tell her "how much satisfaction we felt at the introduction of your young friend Mr. Longfellow." She noted approvingly how "his countenance is itself a letter of recommendation," and that "we are much pleased with this addition to our little American circle." She concluded with words that proved prophetic—that the polished young traveler "bids fair to be a great light in your State, if you can keep him there."

Mrs. Daveis passed this praise on to Zilpah Longfellow, who, in turn, paraphrased it for Henry. Zilpah had been leaving the management of Henry's foreign adventure to her husband, but she did offer a bit of guarded advice in response to her son's previous letter. "I think it a very good sign," she wrote Henry, "when a young man retains his love for home, and for the friends of his childhood, we feel assured that he will do nothing to grieve them, and that his conduct will be such to deserve their approbation," leading her to ask, ever so delicately, for more information. "I have felt some curiosity to know how you parted from your Spanish friends with whom you lived, the mother and the daughter and her friend who resembled your sister Anne, you have not even told us whether you continued to be as much pleased with them, on a longer acquaintance."

However unconventional Henry's approach to learning Spanish may have been, it was not without its rewards. A few years later, George Ticknor, whose knowledge and expertise in the history and dialects of Spain was without parallel in the United States, paid the highest compliment possible to his young protégé. "I thought Longfellow's knowledge of the language and literature of France, Italy and Spain quite extraordinary," he wrote in a general letter of recommendation. "He writes and speaks Spanish with a degree of fluency and exactness, which I have known in no other American born speaking the English as their vernacular."

SPAIN WAS WONDERFUL, but it was time, finally, to move on. "I am traveling through Italy without any enthusiasm, and with just curiosity enough to keep me awake," he wrote to his mother on January 23, 1828. "I feel no excitement,—nothing of that romantic feeling which everybody else has, or pretends to have. The fact is, I am homesick for Spain. I want to go back there again. The recollection of it completely ruins Italy for me." His mood was mollified somewhat by having made the acquaintance in Marseilles a few weeks earlier of a traveling scholar from Rhode Island, George Washington Greene, grandson of the Revolutionary War general Nathanael Greene, one of George Washington's ablest and most trusted commanders. They had hooked up with a party of American naval officers from the schooner *Porpoise* on shore leave, and traveled as a group along the Riviera, arriving in Genoa on Christmas Eve. Parting with the naval officers there, Henry and Greene continued on to Livorno, a seaport community known to English travelers as Leghorn, where they split up, agreeing to get together again in Rome.

In Florence, Henry dined in the home of Princess Charlotte, the daughter of Joseph Bonaparte and wife of Prince Napoleon, who was sufficiently impressed by the confident young American that she drew a flattering sketch of him in her journal. At another event the next day,

Princess Charlotte "played 'Yankee Doodle' for me!" Henry arrived in Rome on February 11, 1828, "under the bright rays of a noonday sun," as he would write in *Outre-Mer*. George Washington Greene set his new friend up in the same house that he had used as a base of operations, the home of Innocenzo Persiani, a druggist once "very rich," but fallen on difficult times. Persiani and his family lived on the second floor of an old palazzo in the Piazza Navona section of the city, a focal point for foreign students, artists, and musicians, and a beehive of cultural activity. It became heaven for the twenty-year-old American called "Enrico" by his new friends, as he would attest in *Outre-Mer*. "We breakfast at noon and dine at eight in the evening. After dinner comes the *conversazione*, enlivened by music from every quarter of the globe."

He picked up on this in a letter to his mother. "There are three young ladies, who have all been excellently educated and speak, besides their native tongue, both English and French. They are great musicians also; one plays the harp with great perfection, the other the piano with the skill of a professor; and both sing. But the family is so very kind, we see so much good society in the evening, and I have so good an opportunity for practicing French, Spanish, and Italian, that I shall make my residence in Italy something longer than I had intended on leaving Florence."

Almost overnight, Henry's education took on yet another new dimension, one that persuaded him to stay in the Eternal City for close to a year, far longer than he originally intended. Once again, we tiptoe on delicate ground, relying on information that is sketchy at best; but what we do have—circumstantial as it may be for the most part, though haltingly acknowledged years later by Henry himself in several letters to Greene—points rather convincingly to another romantic liaison that had a lasting impact, this time with one of the Persiani daughters, Giulia. Years later, Henry would identify her to Greene as having been his "antiqua flamma," his old flame—fairly candid talk for a person who was typically circumspect in matters of such sensitivity.

Sam Longfellow paraphrased sparingly from a long letter his brother wrote home to explain why he had extended his stay in Rome, and not proceed as planned directly to Germany, where his Bowdoin classmate and Portland neighbor Edward "Ned" Preble was waiting at the University of Göttingen. Sam wrote that in the beginning of July, Henry came down with a "violent cold, which ended in a fever, that grew high and dangerous." The "crisis," which had him bedridden, "passed favorably, thanks to the devoted attentions of the kind family—the Persiani—in whose house he was living." Sam told how Henry "felt that he owed his life to the care of the eldest daughter, who, having the freedom of a married woman, was his especial nurse. She administered to him a healing medicine as he lay gasping for breath, and prevented the surgeon from bleeding him a fourth time." Helped along further by a therapeutic interlude in the mountain air of Ariccia, Henry's strength was restored, and they returned to Rome.

But he still put off going to Germany, preferring instead the hospitality of the Persiani family, and stayed another four months. As for Giulia (to whom Henry always referred in his letters as Julia) having had "the freedom of a married woman," what Sam Longfellow did not point out—and what Henry had failed to mention in his own letters home, for that matter—was that while the twenty-four-year-old woman was "Mrs. Julia," as he called her, she was a widow, having lost her husband not long after her marriage at the age of thirteen. When Henry took up residence in their home, she was living as an unattached woman with

Self-portrait of "Enrico" (so titled in the margin) in his Italy sketchbook

her parents and siblings, two sisters and a brother. Going beyond the circumstantial to the actual are the little asides Henry shared with Greene. A full decade after the Persiani relationship had become a distant memory, he mentioned to Greene, then serving as American consul in Rome, how a mutual acquaintance recently returned from Italy "brought the story of my romantic passion for Madame Julia in days gone by," and how the mere mention of her name "revived the past rather too vividly," which led to this: "I sometimes wish myself in Italy again. You have so much freedom there."

He picked up on the same theme once again three months later with a long, ruminative letter penned one night after a "solitary supper of Sardines, and wishing myself where they came from, in the Mediterranean." Headed playfully "Dearissimo George," the main thrust was a discussion of Henry's recently released book, *Hyperion*, and the reception it was receiving from critics. He closed with a plaintive paragraph in which he pressed Greene for what he knew about acquaintances from the old days. "Why don't you write me some of the gossip and scandal of Rome," he asked, and "How are the Persianis," then added, almost as an afterthought, "and that *hot* daughter, with the pale sister?—and old Magrini, who amuses every American he can get hold of with my *amour* with Julia? No one returns now from Rome without *that* story. I am glad of it. How is Julia, do you hear? What did you say her name was?" Whatever the adjective "hot" may have suggested in the nineteenth century—it did not have the same erotic connotation it does today— Henry mindfully used it to characterize an old flame from his past. And he followed that with a sly query seeking information on the current name of his old "amour," which can be read as code for marital status, telling us pretty much all we need to know about his thoughts on that episode, recalled at a time when he was feeling deeply sorry for himself.

Another intimate from those days was the Swedish poet Karl August Nicander (1799–1839), a boarder in the Persiani household when Henry moved in, and for a while also involved romantically with the young widow, at one point describing "Signora Giulia" in his journal as being a woman of "imperishable beauty." On Christmas Eve 1827—two months before Henry arrived in Rome—he confessed of wanting "to be her Romeo." A week later—New Year's Day 1828—Nicander wrote a sonnet dedicated to her, "Il primo sonetto, alla Signora Giulia Persiani." His journal entries, in Swedish and translated for me by a colleague in Stockholm, make several references to this alluring woman of "learning and charisma." January 6: "Near midnight I took a walk with the Persianis. I held Giulia under her arm, and gave her a small Christmas gift." On February 19, he asked: "Why does Giulia own such a magic power over me, without making me less free, if not because, in her whole person, appears a Nordic deep feeling, together with the southern beauty's best flowers?" If there was any competition with Henry, it does not show in the surviving documents—if anything, just the opposite. They all seem to have gotten along splendidly, exploring rural villages and Roman ruins together, and writing about their adventures in their travelogues and poems.

Nicander described one such excursion, naming Giulia and "the American called Enrico" as being in the party. "We wandered over the Capitol and the Forum, gloriously illuminated by the full moon, and past the Temple of Peace to the Colosseum." A generous gratuity to the guard enabled them to go inside the ancient arena after hours and take in the "beauty of memory and art" by themselves. "The moon sat right above in full clearness, pouring forth its richest rays over the mural crown." Henry would recall the same outing in *Outre-Mer*, with a lengthy recollection that is remarkably similar.

Henry's journal for the time he spent in Italy is shallow on primary research but deep on enjoying the company of his newfound friends. "Europe had done much more for him than merely make him an accomplished scholar," Charles Eliot Norton astutely noted on the occasion of Henry's centennial observance in 1907. "It had enlarged his view of life, fertilized his mind, and given him a social cultivation which he could not have gained at home. These three years abroad did much to give color to his future." Stephen Longfellow, however, did not take such a sanguine view, and became increasingly concerned that certain distractions might be hindering his son's commitment to unsupervised study. A letter he wrote at this time, which unfortunately does not survive, elicited an unusually defiant response. "I have only to assure you that whatever suspicions my stay in Italy may have occasioned you, they are wholly without foundation, as you will be satisfied of, in reading my last

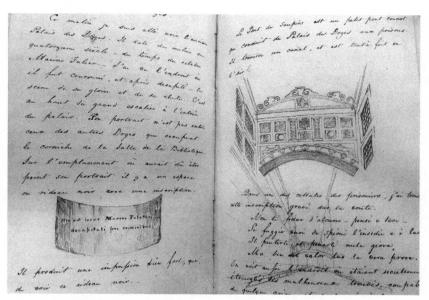

Two illustrated pages from Longfellow's Italian journal, in Venice

letters," Henry wrote, leaving the precise nature of his father's qualms vaguely unspecified. He then informed his father that he was "writing a book" as "a kind of *Sketch-Book* of scenes in France, Spain, and Italy," the work he would call *Outre-Mer*, the motivation starkly stated: "I hope by it to prove that I have not wasted my time."

Of more immediate concern, though, was a bit of jolting news contained in that now lost letter from his father: the Bowdoin trustees had decided not to give him a full professorship, and were now insisting that he agree to be a tutor with an annual salary of six hundred dollars. Henry's response speaks forcefully for itself: "I assure you, my dear father, I am very indignant at this. They say I am too young! Were they not aware of this three years ago? If I am not capable of performing the duties of the office, they may be very sure of my not accepting it. I know not in what light they may look upon it, but for my own part, I do not in the least regard it as a favor conferred upon me. It is no sinecure; and if my services are an equivalent for my salary, there is no favor done me: if they be not, I do not desire the situation."

And he held his ground, ultimately securing the professorship, but at a lesser salary of eight hundred dollars. For an additional one hundred dollars a year, he agreed to assume the collateral position of college librarian. Even more consequential, in the short run, was that he wasted little time leaving sunny Italy and moving on to Germany. Nicander, by then living in another boardinghouse, wrote in his journal how the "young, lovable Longfellow, my friend, whom I acquired in Rome, and with whom I have spent so many pleasant hours," had come by to visit him one morning with "tears in his eyes," explaining that he "suddenly had to leave the dear Rome and the kind Persiani family, in whose circle he had lived." Henry asked for a letter of reference "when we meet to say farewell," but when Nicander arrived at the appointed hour, "Enrico" had already left.

Arrived at Göttingen by way of Munich, Henry met up finally with Ned Preble, who had been waiting patiently for him to arrive, and enrolled in the university. He attended lectures regularly, kept long and detailed workbooks of his studies, and documented the books he was reading. His lingering resentment with the Bowdoin hierarchy is apparent in the tongue-in-cheek newspaper he and Preble cobbled together for the amusement of family back home, and called *The Old Dominion*.

A self-portrait made at the University of Göttingen in 1829 with Henry's friend from Maine Edward Preble

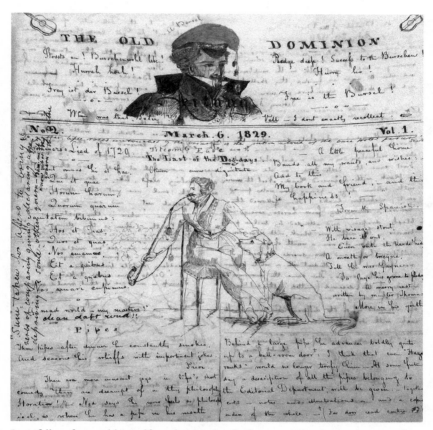

Longfellow featured himself on the masthead of a tongue-in-cheek newspaper he and Ned Preble fashioned while studying in Göttingen, *The Old Dominion,* dated March 6, 1829.

Quite cleverly drawn on the first page of the number dated May 22, 1829, is the caricatured image of a butcher about to slaughter a pig, the caption identifying the man as "Professor of the Dead Languages." On the back are other cartoons of similar disposition, one picturing the rear end of a load-bearing donkey identified as "The March of Mind in the East." On its back, the animal carries two buckets filled with books, one captioned "Northern Darkness." Being trampled beneath its hooves are several volumes bearing the titles "Rights of Man," "Human Under-standing," "The Law of B. College." Beside them is a kicked-over bucket, spilling out its contents, labeled "Professorship of Mod Languages."

Placing the matter in further perspective is this accompanying text: "We have been creditably informed that a professorship being offered to a young man by the government of Bowdoin College on condition of his passing two years in Europe *at his own expense*—at the expiration of which time the situation of Tutor was offered him at little more than half a professor's salary! *We are happy to add* that such a proposition has been treated with all the contempt it deserved!" But after three years in Europe, it was time, nonetheless, to go home. Though Henry had learned a good deal of German, it would be necessary for him to acquire more—he knew as much—but that was all in the future. In the meantime, he returned to Brunswick, assumed his new professorship, and taught his first classes in September 1829.

Many years later, and with Henry's financial backing, George Washington Greene published a biography of his esteemed grandfather Major General Nathanael Greene. That Greene would dedicate the book to Henry is no great surprise, as their friendship had spanned decades, and included material support in times of need. What is noteworthy is the four-page dedication to their long friendship, with a special reminder of the time they enjoyed together in Naples. Greene recalled a day when they viewed a magnificent sunset from the "flat roof of the house" where they were staying, a vista that looked out "upon the wonderful bay, and across the bay to Ischia and Capri and Sorrento, and over the house-tops and villas and vineyards to Vesuvius," talking until the stars came forth. "It was then that you unfolded to me your plans of life, and showed me from what 'deep cisterns' you had already learned to draw."

Ten years after the publication of Greene's book, and in the sunset years of his own life, Henry compared his experiences in Italy with those of his recently deceased friend Charles Sumner, whose correspondence he had been editing. "What a devourer of books he was! It amazes me to see the amount of his reading in four Summer months. He brought away from Italy a vast amount of knowledge, while I brought away little more than memoires and impressions,—a kind of golden atmosphere, which was always illuminated by life. Perhaps we were both wiser than we knew. Each assimilated to himself what best served his purpose afterward."

3

The Holy Ones

I think I have formed a just estimate of the excellence of Mary's character. I can say to your ear, what I would not often say to hers—that I have never seen a woman in whom every look, and word, and action seemed to proceed from so gentle and innocent a spirit. Indeed, how much she possesses of all we most admire in the female character!

> —Henry W. Longfellow, letter to Judge Barrett Potter, confirming proposal of marriage to his daughter Mary, September 26, 1830

Yesterday I was at Mount Auburn, and saw my own grave dug; that is, my own tomb. I assure you, I looked quietly down into it without one feeling of dread. It is a beautiful spot, this Mount Auburn. Were you ever there?

> —Henry W. Longfellow letter to George Washington Greene, reflecting on the burial of Mary Longfellow, in Cambridge, May 21, 1837

The final days of Mary Storer Potter Longfellow's brief life were fraught with uncertainty. Confined to an upstairs suite at the Hôtel des Pays Bas in Rotterdam with a variety of unspecified health issues, the twenty-three-year-old first wife of Henry Wadsworth Longfellow felt strong enough occasionally to sit up, take nourishment, and listen intently while her husband read a letter or two from her family in Maine. On other days she would lie in bed for hours on end, complain mildly of a headache or lingering fever, but otherwise endure in silence the anguish of having lost a child born prematurely on October 5, 1835.

Holland was an improbable place for the fragile daughter of a rural New England judge to be stricken with what modern physicians surmise to have been "an infected incomplete miscarriage." Just six months earlier, Mary was living contentedly as the adoring spouse of a dynamic young professor on the Bowdoin College faculty, and agreed to cross the choppy Atlantic only because the trip augured well for her ambitious husband's future as the newly appointed Smith Professor of Modern Languages at Harvard College, and on condition that two of her closest friends come along to keep her company. The addition to the traveling party of Mary Goddard, a Potter family cousin, and Clara Crowninshield, an independently provided-for acquaintance and former classmate at Miss Cushing's School for girls in Hingham, Massachusetts, had the advantage also of reducing costs on what was expected to be a year and a half abroad, as both women were paying their own way.

While still mulling whether she should make the trip, Clara confided her own reservations to a close friend. "I have a great desire to accompany the Longfellows, but it would be very essential to my enjoyment to have another female companion of a different sort from Mrs. Longfellow. She is very *sweet* and amiable, but she is so absorbed in her husband that she only lives in him. She has not much physical energy and if her husband only goes and sees what is worth seeing, she is satisfied to have it *second-hand* thro' him. Now I want to have somebody go who will *excite* instead of check any desire I may have to go about and improve myself." Once Mary Goddard signed on, Clara agreed to join them on the journey.

The first leg had passed uneventfully, beginning with a satisfying month in England. As he had done on his first trip abroad, Henry carried letters of reference, his introduction to Thomas and Jane Carlyle eased by one from Ralph Waldo Emerson, whom he did not yet know personally, but who wrote it as a favor for a mutual friend. Henry and the Carlyles hit it off from the start, with Mary and her friends being included in several of their get-togethers. "Mr. and Mrs. Carlyle have more genuine worth and talent than half of the nobility in London," Mary wrote approvingly to her mother-in-law. "Mr. Carlyle's literary fame is very high, and she is a very talented woman—but they are people after my own heart—not the least pretension about them. Mrs. Carlyle has a pin with Goethe's head upon it, which that great author sent her himself. She is very proud of it, I assure you. They live very retired, not wishing to mix with fashionable society, which they regard in its true light; still they have some friends among the nobility who know how to value them."

At a fancy soiree in the home of Charles Babbage, designer of the world's first mechanized calculating apparatus, Henry saw a model of the revolutionary device in action. Babbage's son, "a young and rather raw lad, who is said to be like his father a good mathematician," demonstrated its workings to the American, "which I cannot describe, for I do not understand it," he admitted, unaware that he had just seen the forerunner of what in time would be known as the computer. He was far more impressed that night by having met Ada Byron, the daughter of Lord Byron, "with a countenance like her father's, though rather too red to be handsome. Her figure and manner lady-like and engaging."

Henry was making progress on a number of other levels, too, acquiring books for the Harvard library, an assignment he had carried out admirably during his earlier trip to Europe on behalf of Bowdoin College, where his collateral duty was school librarian. According to one historical overview, Henry was personally responsible for having transformed "an unused repository of Scripture" at Bowdoin "to a more functional one that reflected in its collection contemporary European culture and the trend in American education toward the study of modern languages and literatures." Using the books he brought back then as sources, he produced a series of texts and translations for his classes, in one instance prevailing upon Gray & Bowen, his Boston publisher, to supply forty unbound copies of an Italian reading book he had prepared for immediate use by his students.

An examination I made of the Bowdoin library catalogue from that period contains numerous entries in Henry's distinctive hand. Of these, two are for his own textbooks, *Elements of French Grammar* and *Syllabus de la Grammaire Italienne*—the book that had been shipped up in proof to Maine from Boston. The text, it bears noting, was written entirely in French. A publisher's notice Henry included is instructive as

Portrait of Longfellow
as a twenty-two-year-old
Bowdoin professor, 1829,
by Thomas Badger

to why: "This compendious Italian Grammar has been prepared, not so much for those who wish to speak the language (however useful it may prove to such), as for those, who, having already some knowledge of the French, desire to learn to read the language of modern Italy in order to [facilitate] an acquaintance with its literature." Such a structure, George Lowell Austin wrote in 1882, served a "double" purpose—"it keeps fresh the knowledge of one language while teaching the elements of another. The methodology is certainly plausible and advantageous."

On the personal side, Henry's long-range strategy at that time included a desire to find a suitable companion. "His heart was always ideally sensitive to feminine attractions, his domestic affections always warm," Sam Longfellow explained of his brother's temperament; he was "no mere bookworm or dry-as-dust scholar." His interest turned to a daughter of Barrett Potter, a probate-court judge and widower whose reputation for running a tight ship was a staple of family lore. "Portland young men called the house where Mary Potter's girlhood was spent 'the nunnery,' because her stern father kept such a strict watch and ward over his three beautiful and motherless daughters," Mary Thacher Higginson, the niece and namesake of Mary Potter, wrote in a 1903 essay for *Harper's Monthly Magazine.* "Rumor said that Judge Potter had sown his share of youthful wild oats, and that this was one reason why he was so suspicious of all mankind." Samuel T. Pickard, a family friend, had a similar recollection of the judge, "a rather forbidding old Puritan," he would recall in a letter now in the Longfellow House archives.

Henry was sufficiently cowed by the judge's reputation that he asked his sister Anne, a friend of the young woman's, to deliver a note of introduction one Sunday after church. A traditional courtship followed, with Henry assuring the judge of his worthiness in a formal letter of proposal. "I most ardently hope, my dear sir, that you may never have the slightest occasion to think that your confidence has been misplaced. I certainly believe you never will: and this belief is founded upon the attachment I feel for Mary, in whom I find the inestimable virtues of a pure heart and guileless disposition—qualities which not only excite an ardent affection, but which tend to make it as durable as ardent." Mary was similarly enthralled with Henry. "I certainly never imagined that I could find in this world so good and affectionate a person, and one who would love me so much," she assured Anne Longfellow. "He answers much better to a being of my imagination than one of real life."

They were married on September 14, 1831, and moved into the cramped boardinghouse where Henry had been renting as a bachelor, the first of several apartments they would occupy over the next three and a half years. "Her character and person were alike lovely," Sam Longfellow wrote more than fifty years after Mary's death. "Under the shadow of dark hair, eyes of deep blue lighted a countenance singularly attractive with the expression of a gentle and affectionate disposition. She was also well educated at a time when Greek and Latin were less commonly included in the studies of girls than were the mathematics." Alpheus Packard Sr., a distinguished professor of Latin and Greek and a colleague of Henry's on the Bowdoin faculty, recalled Mary just as warmly. "My first impression of her is of an attractive person, blooming in health and beauty, the graceful bride of a very attractive and elegant young man."

As a teacher, Henry gave his alma mater the best he had to offer. The noted missionary and educator Cyrus Hamlin would assert years later that it was Professor Longfellow's reputation for excellence in the classroom that first attracted him to Bowdoin. "His intercourse with the students was perfectly simple, frank, and manly. He never sought popularity nor repelled it. He always and evidently enjoyed having students come to him with any reasonable question about languages, authors, literature, medieval or modern history,—especially the former. They always left him not only with admiration, but guided, helped, and inspired."

But Henry also was restless, and determined to find an exit strategy. Alexander Slidell Mackenzie, his friend from Spain, hit the nail on the head when responding to one of his earliest grousings. "I am sorry to find that you do not seem to be very happy in your new occupation. It may, perhaps, be natural that one accustomed for several years to roam at pleasure from city to city in the old world with no other object than to enjoy pleasures and gather a harvest of polite information, should find his situation at first uneasy and irksome, when suddenly called back from these poetic wanderings to the dull and prosaic pursuits of active life." Henry complained to James Berdan, a friend of Pierre Irving's he had met in Paris, of being mired in "this miserable Down East," and being made to feel like he was "living in exile."

A month before his wedding, he vented his frustration to his ever-sympathetic sister Anne. "You call it a dog's life," he wrote. "I do not believe that I was born for such a lot. I have aimed higher than this: and I cannot believe that all my aspirations are to terminate in the drudgery of a situation, which gives me no opportunity to distinguish myself, and in point of worldly gain, does not even pay me for my labor. Besides, one loses ground so fast in these out of the way places: the mind has no stimulus to exertion—grows sluggish in its movements and narrow in its sphere—and that's the end of a man." In the spring of 1832, Henry asked George Washington Greene to inquire on his behalf about a possible opening at New York University. "I have been laboring on in this little solitude" for close to three years, "and I now feel a strong desire to tread a stage on which I can take longer strides and spout to a larger audience." He would even accept the position for no pay providing he could secure a job editing a New York literary journal, he added, if anything of the sort were possible—but nothing materialized.

News that the secretary of the American Legation to Madrid had recently died encouraged him to ask Alexander H. Everett, by this time returned from his tour as minister to Spain and editing *The North American Review* in Boston, to put in a good word for him with his old diplomatic contacts. "You will excuse me for importuning you so much," Henry wrote, "but here I am in a corner, beyond the reach of almost everybody, and with only one or two friends, to whom I must apply in every emergency." Everett wrote back that the position had already been filled, and added that the likelihood of his being favored with an appointment from the new administration of President Andrew Jackson, which did not look favorably on New England politicians, was highly unlikely in any event.

Undeterred there, Henry asked a colleague at Harvard, Charles Folsom, to see if William Cullen Bryant, editor of the *New-York Evening Post*, might want to underwrite a school for young women in Manhattan that he would happily operate for him. Folsom wrote an effusive letter

Bowdoin College campus, Brunswick, Maine, c. 1822, possibly by John G. Brown, Bowdoin College Museum of Art

for Henry, but once again the response was negative. A flurry of excitement came in the wake of a proposal from Joseph Cogswell and George Bancroft to purchase a controlling interest in the Round Hill School. Henry made an exploratory visit to Northampton during the depths of winter to take a look, only to come up empty once more, the asking price too steep, the facility in disrepair. "I suppose you think I am dead," he wrote Greene. "But it is not so; I am only *buried*—in Brunswick, again, after a most fatiguing and almost useless journey *west*ward ho!" Another prospect—to teach at the University of Virginia—was similarly fruitless.

Henry did not lose his sense of humor through all this, at least, as a satirical tale of prose fiction he wrote in 1834 under an assumed name makes amusingly clear. Though deservedly obscure on its literary merits, "The Wondrous Tale of a Little Man in Gosling Green," as he titled the short piece, is noteworthy for the circumstance of its publication, and for its jocular setting, identified in a prefatory remark as "a village so far Down East as to be beyond sunrise." He named the lead character of the tale John Schwartkins after an actual Brunswick resident, an eccentric shopkeeper from Holland, who wore gosling-green clothes.

"Upon the margin of one of the blue rivers that pour their tributary waters into the broad lap of Merrymeeting Bay," it began, "stands the village of Bungonuck,—a drowsy land, where the rush of a waterfall lulls the inhabitants into a dreamy state of existence, leaving them neither quite asleep, nor quite awake. The village is intersected by a wide street, which yawns to receive the weary traveler; while around it are pleasant woodland walks, and groves of pine, that perfume the air, and cheerful with the bark of the squirrel and the twitter of birds." Bungonuck— so named, presumably, for Bunganuc Landing, a coastal village five miles from downtown Brunswick and within the municipal limits—is described elsewhere in the tale as a place of "uninterrupted tranquility," where excitement is defined by simple pleasures. "Indeed, the only event that breaks in upon its repose is the daily arrival and departure of the mail." During the summer, "a puppet-show, or a caravan of wild animals, or some distinguished foreigner with a hand-organ" fills the "little world" of the community with "uproar and misrule." And there is, too, "the occasional arrival of a strolling company of circus-riders. Their canvass palace rises as if by enchantment in a single night, and disappears as mysteriously the next."

The tale appeared in the November 1, 1834, issue of *The New-Yorker* under the name of George F. Brown, selected for publication on the strength of having been named cowinner of a hundred-dollar writing contest announced by Horace Greeley, founder of the recently established weekly magazine. Henry had submitted his entry under a pen name through Lewis Gaylord Clark, editor of *The Knickerbocker Magazine* in New York and an early supporter of his work. It was through this association that the Longfellow scholar James Taft Hatfield was able to identify Henry as the actual author almost a century later. While searching through a mass of miscellaneous materials in the Longfellow archives in 1931, he ran across some incoming correspondence, including a curious letter to one "George F. Brown, Esq., Boston," forwarded on to Longfellow by way of Clark, the intermediary, who had also served on Greeley's contest selection board. "At the suggestion of our friend, L. G. Clark, Esq., I herein enclose you a Fifty Dollar Note, being the amount of the award of the Literary Committee for your capital 'Little Man in Gosling Green.' Trusting that, in your future literary efforts, you will not entirely overlook the *New-Yorker*, I remain, Yours truly, Horace Greeley."

For all the angst and all the whining about being buried in the boondocks, it was Henry's stellar job performance that finally led to his liberation. His textbooks and translations were respected by his peers, and his long-awaited travelogue *Outre-Mer: A Pilgrimage Beyond the Sea,* had finally seen the light of day, issued first as a pamphlet in 1833, and in two volumes by Harper & Brothers in 1835. Though published anonymously, its authorship was not a secret for long, as an appreciative notice in *The American Monthly Review* attests, the critic confiding that it came "from the pen of a gentleman, whose reputation as an elegant scholar, an easy and graceful writer, a poet of no little celebrity, and a distinguished professor in one of our colleges, is already widely spread through our country."

Henry had also resumed writing poetry during this period, a return to original composition that Thomas Wentworth Higginson suggested may have been influenced by his marriage to Mary. "It is not unreasonable to recognize something of his young wife's influence in this rekindling of poetic impulse, and it is pleasant, in examining the manuscript lectures delivered by him at Bowdoin College and still preserved there, to find them accompanied by pages of extracts, here and there, in her handwriting."

As for the immediate dilemma at hand—how to escape the numbing tranquility of Down East Maine—deliverance finally came from Harvard president Josiah Quincy with a stupendous offer to succeed George Ticknor as Smith Professor of Modern Languages. The salary would be fifteen hundred dollars a year and residence in Cambridge was mandatory. One small condition, however—essentially the same one presented to him in the Bowdoin proposition a decade earlier—was that he spend some time in Europe securing "a more perfect attainment of the German," precisely what Ticknor had urged when they first met, and essential now. "Mr. Ticknor will retain his office until your return," Quincy assured him. Henry was ebullient. "Good fortune comes at last, and I certainly shall not reject it," he enthused to his father, leaving no wiggle room this time for compromise. As for the additional stipulation that he must spend more time in Europe? "I think I shall accept that also."

For Ticknor, the decision to step back at the age of forty-three and take what today we would call early retirement followed the wrenching death of a five-year-old son. "While my little boy lived, I looked only to the future, and considered him only as a bright hope, that was growing brighter every day," he explained to Charles Daveis in Portland. "But now that he is gone I look at the past and the present, and, yielding all the future, in a spirit of resignation, to God, I feel the immediate loss, the pressing want of something that was so dear to me, and that was associated, without my knowing it, to everything around and within me." Aside from the personal loss, clinching the decision was Ticknor's exasperation with Harvard's reluctance to fully embrace the European models of interdisciplinary teaching he had been advancing which were decades ahead of their time—problems Henry also would experience there. "I have substantially resigned my place at Cambridge, and Longfellow is substantially appointed to fill it. I say *substantially*, because he is to pass a year or more in Germany and the North of Europe, and I am to continue in the place till he returns, which will be in a year from next Commencement or thereabouts."

In the years ahead, Ticknor would devote himself to travel, writing, good works, and social networking of a scale that made his Beacon Hill dinner parties the talk of the town. He would also produce *History of Spanish Literature,* a magnum opus in three volumes that in 1849 "became the standard work on the subject as soon as it appeared," according to Thomas Hart Jr. in an essay for the Modern Language Association. For source material, he drew heavily on his Harvard lectures and on the Spanish sections of his fourteen-thousand-volume personal library. With more time on his hands, Ticknor took the lead in creating the Boston Public Library, wrote the planning report, and galvanized financial support for its opening in 1854 as the first institution of its kind in the United States. At his death in 1871, his preeminent collection of Spanish and Portuguese literature went to the BPL—not Harvard, as many had expected. He was, withal, a towering figure in the Boston-Cambridge cultural corridor; and the person he had handpicked to succeed him as Smith Professor was the same young man who had called at his door ten years earlier, now impressively accomplished, but requiring polish in a few of the areas he had been urged to master the first time around.

But getting everyone to agree was not a simple task, beginning with Stephen Longfellow, whose response to the news was anything but jubilant. "With respect to the idea of going again to Europe we all think you must not indulge it," he informed Henry, mincing no words. "Your compensation at Cambridge will not be better, considering the expenses there, than it is now at Brunswick." And then he added this: "Mary was here day before yesterday. She seems delighted with the prospect of change, but not with the idea of going to Europe." But Henry wanted out of Brunswick in the worst of ways, and despite what Mary may have said to her father-in-law, she was unstinting in support of her husband. If that meant leaving her comfort zone, so be it—but not without misgivings. "How often I recall you as I saw you the sad morning that we parted," she wrote in a long letter to her father from Sweden. "It could not be otherwise than a very sad parting to us all, for we felt that it was very possible we were saying our last farewell to some dear one." Judge Potter underlined that sentence in pencil, and read it repeatedly in the mournful years that followed, according to his granddaughter.

Once arrived in Hamburg, the Longfellow party left by steamer for Copenhagen, a city they initially found dark and unattractive, instilling such "a feeling of gloom and loneliness" that Henry decided they would not dawdle in Denmark, at least not then, and moved on to Sweden, planning to return later. Unable to make steamer connections in Gothenburg, they traveled three hundred jostling miles over deeply rutted dirt roads to Stockholm, an arduous five-day journey that could only have aggravated Mary's delicate state. In the capital, they encountered several setbacks, most disappointingly the unavailability of Karl August Nicander, the lyric poet Henry had befriended in Rome, and the person who had urged him to visit Scandinavia in the first place. But "Enrico" had not informed his old *paisan* about the trip in advance, and when he arrived in Stockholm on June 28, he learned Nicander had left the city for the summer months. Reached finally by letter, Nicander put Henry in touch with a number of artists and literary men, including the novelist Gustaf Henrik Mellin, who introduced the young American to the Finnish epic *Kalevala*, which in time would provide a model for *Hiawatha*.

Writing to her in-laws, Mary declared Stockholm "far different" than anything she had expected. "While in England I imagined myself only in another part of our own country." She described the shabby accouterments and furnishings of the dreary second-floor flat they had rented and the "unsightly room," where "Henry has ensconced himself": he "nearly filled it with his books." It was in this room where her husband was tutored in Swedish by a professor from Uppsala University. Henry began to establish a rhythm in his studies, all the while buying books for the Harvard library. After two months, they returned to Copenhagen, which he found far more agreeable this time around, and got some excellent work done on learning Danish.

After the travelers left Stockholm in August, Gustaf Mellin sent a gossipy letter to Nicander. "Thank you for the acquaintanceship with Longfellow," he wrote, calling him "an exceedingly agreeable young man," and offered his impressions of the three women in the entou-

Mary Storer Potter Longfellow,
portrait made in Stockholm
by Maria Röhl, August 1835

rage. He called Clara Crowninshield "a pleasant little thing, not exactly beautiful but with an expression of kindness that was very pleasing," and Mary Goddard "a large Juno-like figure with a beautiful face and a fine skin," her complexion "as white as a slice of fresh, boiled ham." The most flattering assessment he saved for last: "Mrs. Longfellow, who was pregnant, was the most beautiful and the most agreeable of all three of Longfellow's ladies," an observation notable for being the earliest documented confirmation of Mary's condition.

There is very little in the surviving documents to reconstruct the progress of Mary's pregnancy, or to indicate, even, when she may have determined she was with child. Purely speculative, too, is the outside possibility that the two female companions may have been asked to come along on the trip to be with Mary while she was expecting. One document that could conceivably answer many of these questions—Mary Potter Longfellow's personal journal—was destroyed in 1842, more than six years after her death, by Henry just prior to going abroad for a program of emotional and physical rehabilitation, an acknowledgment he made when asked by one of her sisters to see it. "Just before I sailed for

Europe, being in low spirits, and reflecting on the uncertainties of such an expedition as I was then beginning, I burned a great many letters and private papers, and among them this," he explained to Margaret Potter Thacher. "I now regret it; but alas! too late."

Henry's first recorded use of the word "miscarriage" appears in a letter to his father several weeks after the mishap. Writing to Judge Potter two days after Mary's death, Henry recounted how he had held out hope to the very end. "Though her sickness was long, yet I could not bring myself to think it dangerous until near its close. Indeed, I did not abandon all hope of her recovery till within a very few hours of her dissolution, and to me the blow was so sudden that I have hardly yet recovered energy enough to write you the particulars of this solemn and mournful event." Henry described Mary as calm, without pain, and at peace, her only regret for the sadness of her family when they received the horrible news, noting in particular how her "dear Father" would lament her loss.

Henry then described what followed next: "A short time afterwards she thanked Clara for her kindness, and clasping her arms affectionately round my neck, kissed me, and said, 'Dear Henry, do not forget me!' and after this, 'Tell my dear friends at home that I thought of them at the last hour.'" By the time a minister arrived, Mary had lost consciousness, and at half past one in the morning she stopped breathing. "Thus all the hopes I had so fondly cherished of returning home with my dear Mary in happiness and renovated health, have in the providence of God ended in disappointment and sorrow unspeakable." Even Mary herself, it appears, chose not to mention her pregnancy or the illness that followed her miscarriage. A month before losing the child, she focused on their constantly changing itinerary. "Henry has given up the idea of going to Berlin, and will probably pass the winter in some little town on the Rhine. I hardly know his plans yet, but he wishes to live cheaper than we could in Berlin."

Of the two women who had joined the traveling party in the United States, Clara Crowninshield commands our attention for the three-volume journal she kept throughout the trip, now in the Harvard collections. Named Clarissa at birth, Clara, as she was known throughout her long life—she died at ninety-six—was the "natural" daughter of George Crowninshield Jr. and his "kept mistress," Elizabeth Rowell, of Salem,

Massachusetts. Clara's mother had wisely insisted that the child take her father's surname, as the Crowninshields were a prominent Essex County shipping family, deeply involved in state and national politics. George Crowninshield was quite a character in his time, a flamboyant eccentric remembered as the owner of an opulent yacht known as *Cleopatra's Barge,* a great sensation when launched in 1816, and destined a few years later to be the royal yacht of King Kamehameha II of Hawaii. Shortly before his death, Crowninshield acknowledged paternity of six-year-old Clara and made provisions for her security. A guardian managed the child's modest inheritance well, enabling her to attend a private boarding school, and embark ten years later on a European adventure.

Clara's diary covers sixteen months, May 25, 1835, to September 26, 1836, and touches on time spent in England, Sweden, Denmark, Holland, Germany, and France, not all of it pleasant, particularly after the other female companion on the trip, Mary Goddard, returned home unexpectedly in September 1835. "How everything seems to have conspired to vex and pain me since I undertook this journey," Clara complained at one point. "What a prisoner's life I lead of it," she noted plaintively at another, when unable, because of Mary's worsening con-

Clara Crowninshield, portrait made in Stockholm by Maria Röhl, August 1835

dition, to leave the rooming house unescorted. "I am more confined even than I was on board the ship for then we had a larger party and we could walk the deck by way of exercise. But here I have no occasion to go downstairs from morning till night."

Like Henry, she, too, failed to mention Mary's pregnancy with any specificity in the early stages, only noting the days when she was not feeling well—periodic bouts of "ague," for instance, "rheumatism," fatigue, and general malaise—or not up to going out on any excursions. Modern physicians have speculated that the "worst symptom" euphemistically referred to by Clara was bleeding, described in one instance as "alarming." Mary's agony was prolonged over fifty-four days, from the time of the miscarriage—or stillbirth, possibly, depending on how far along the gestation may have been—to the early morning of her death on November 29, 1836.

For Henry, the response through most of the ordeal was a classic case of denial bordering on cluelessness, with good days giving him hope that the worst had passed and everything would soon return to normal. "Little Mary is slowly recovering," he wrote on Sunday, November 1, "but alas! How slowly." On November 25—four days before she died—his spirits were lifted: "Mary is better this morning. Father who art in heaven, I thank thee!" The entry he made in his journal for November 29 has an air of dark gravity to it, two paragraphs followed by five lines of small crosses, arranged geometrically so they themselves make a cross across the middle of the page, under which he recorded the devastating news. "This morning between one and two o'clock, my Mary—my beloved Mary—ceased to breathe. She is now, I trust, a Saint in Heaven. Would that I were with her." After kneeling and kissing "her cold lips," Henry prayed "that hereafter in moments of temptation I might recall that solemn hour and be delivered from evil."

While Clara's account supports Henry's factually, it is more detached, and with more detail. She told how Henry prayed with Mary as the end drew near, how he closed one of her eyes after she had lost consciousness, and invited Clara to close the other. "Her face was already cold and she breathed but a few more times." After Mary died, Clara noted this: "I was glad that Henry was able to command his feelings so entirely whilst he was with her, because if she had seen him distressed it would have lent a pang to those last moments which for herself had no bitterness. Happy as she was in life, I could not have believed she would have quitted it with such entire resignation."

After the body had been arranged by the attending nurse, Henry and Clara came back into the bedroom for a final viewing. "She was very much changed, so emaciated and old that no one would have known her. Henry kissed her cold lips and drew the rings from her lifeless hand and placed them on his own. I gave him some wine and prevailed upon him to lie down on my bed. I wrapped a cloak round me and reposed as well as I could on two chairs. Now that there was no longer cause for constraint he gave vent to his grief and wept bitterly till sleep came to his relief." Arrangements were made to have the body embalmed and shipped back to the United States, where it remained in storage until Henry's return. Clara informs us that two coffins were purchased, an inner one of lead, an outer one of oak.

Mary's deathbed words for her husband—"Henry, do not forget me"—remain heartbreaking to this day, yet touchingly ironic when set against the vast accumulation of everyday artifacts that have been preserved in the Longfellow House in Cambridge, and the paucity of objects there that can be traced definitively to her. Shortly after taking up his new duties at Harvard, Henry sent two steamer trunks with Mary's clothes and personal belongings off to one of her sisters in Maine. A good number of these materials later came into the possession of Mary's niece Mary Thacher Higginson, the wife of Thomas Wentworth Higginson, who made good use of them in a biography he wrote of Longfellow in 1902.

A few letters in Mary's hand are preserved, along with several books on language, grammar, and religious doctrine bearing her ownership signature, and two obscure images thought conclusively to be of her by Henry Wadsworth Longfellow Dana (1881–1950), the poet's grandson, and for thirty-three years the resident curator of the archives and contents at Longfellow House, known when Henry moved in as Craigie House. One of the images is a small pencil sketch, unsigned and not labeled, but likely drawn by the Swedish portrait artist Maria Röhl during the third week of August 1835, as confirmed by Henry in his diary and Clara in hers. Röhl sketched Henry and Clara as well—those are

Longfellow portrait
made in Stockholm
by Maria Röhl,
August 1835

signed, dated, and identified—though none were ever displayed, possibly because they were not received with approval. "It was not a fortunate one," Clara wrote of Henry's likeness, which Röhl offered to retouch. "She was so indefatigable in trying to please Mary with hers that she would have kept altering all day if we had persisted in calling it unlike."

The other presumed likeness of Mary, an unsigned oval portrait done on paper in crayon and chalk and housed in a gilt frame, has been kept in basement storage since the 1940s, there by way of a curious journey in which it resided outside Longfellow House for close to a hundred years. Rendered in stylistic elements that date it to the early 1800s, it pictures a young woman in her teens or early twenties. Harry Dana's accession notes identify the painting as being of Mary, drawn "when she was 15 to 19 years old," and that it was in Henry's possession when he arrived in Cambridge in 1836. Dana's notes state further that Henry gave the portrait to Elizabeth Craigie, his landlady, not long after he became a boarder in her house the following year, and that she bequeathed it to a cousin, the jurist Lemuel Shaw, at that time chief justice of the Mas-

Portrait of Mary Storer
Potter that Henry gave to
his landlady Elizabeth Craigie.
It was returned to Longfellow
House in the 1930s.

sachusetts Supreme Judicial Court, who kept it at his home on Beacon Hill until his death in 1861.

Drafted shortly before her death in 1841, Mrs. Craigie's will, which I examined at the Cambridge Historical Society, contains an inventory of many personal items, including a number of unspecified "paintings and engravings," one of them identified as "a female face," another simply as a "portrait." As sole executor of her estate, Judge Shaw knew who lived on the second floor of the house. I can assert this with certainty because the name "Professor Longfellow," who paid his rent in advance, appears in Shaw's compilation of his cousin's assets. Henry also bought at her estate sale; he acquired her seventy-five-volume set of the works of *Voltaire* for sixty-five dollars, and the copy of *Outre-Mer* she owned when they first met for another twenty-five.

The portrait eventually came into the possession of Judge Shaw's great-granddaughter Elizabeth Melville Thomas Metcalf (1882–1964), a name that should be familiar to textual scholars as the person who facilitated publication in 1924 of *Billy Budd,* the final manuscript of her paternal grandfather, Herman Melville, which had reposed for decades after his death in a tin bread box. She also edited for publication Melville's European journal, wrote several monographs of his work, and donated his manuscripts to Harvard University. Mrs. Metcalf ensured that other important materials found proper custodial homes, too, the Berkshire Athenaeum in Pittsfield and the Museum of Fine Arts in Boston among them. Once returned to Craigie House "about 1935," according to Harry Dana's notes, the portrait hung in a downstairs washroom, later on a pantry wall, before going into a vaulted alcove that once served as Henry's wine cellar, and where it remains today. Dana wrote that "Mrs. Metcalf remembers this picture in the dining room" of the Shaw residence at 49 Mount Vernon Street, which remained in the jurist's family through 1915. "In entering the hall one saw this picture on the back wall of the house, between the dining room window on the right side and the pantry on the left."

A cover letter Henry wrote to Eliza Ann Potter in the fall of 1836 to accompany the two trunks of personal items "which once belonged to your sister" he was shipping up to Maine by steamboat the following day offers some insight into what he was feeling at that time. He apologized for not tending to the matter sooner, but the mere handling of these intimate objects, he explained, brought on episodes of anguish that "I cannot begin to describe." What he then confided gives context to what undoubtedly motivated him to give Mary's portrait to his landlady, my guess with the provision that she keep it safe—but out of his sight:

The world considers grief unmanly, and is suspicious of that sorrow, which is expressed by words and outward signs. Hence we strive to be gay and put a cheerful courage on, when our souls are very sad. But there are hours, when the world is shut out, and we can no longer hear the voices, that cheer and encourage us. To me such hours come daily. I was so happy with my dear Mary, that it is very hard to be alone. The sympathies of friendship are doubtless something—but after all how little, how unsatisfying they are to one who has been so loved as I have been! This is a selfish sorrow, I know: but neither reason nor reflection can still it. Affliction makes us childish. A grieved and wounded heart is hard to be persuaded. We do not wish to have our sorrow lessened. There are wounds, which are never entirely healed. A thousand associations call up the past, with all its gloom and shadow. Often a mere look or sound—a voice— the odor of a flower—the merest trifle is enough to awaken within me deep and unutterable emotions. Hardly a day passes, that some face, or familiar object, or some passage in the book I am reading does not call up the image of my beloved wife so vividly, that I pause and burst into tears,—and sometimes can not rally again for hours.

If we know anything at all about Henry Wadsworth Longfellow, it was his conviction that life is precious and must be treasured. In the early spring of 1839, a watershed year in his development as a professional writer, Henry completed "Footsteps of Angels," a special kind of poem he called a "psalm." Begun several years earlier—but impossible to "rightly close and complete till now"—it would appear that December in *Voices of the Night,* his debut collection of poetry. He showed the poem to Cornelius Conway Felton, a Harvard colleague, hours after finishing it. Later that night, Felton called on Henry in his rooms to tell him his wife had "cried like a child" when he read it to her. "I want no more favorable criticism," he responded. The poem reflected on the deaths of two people: his brother-in-law and Bowdoin classmate, George Washington Pierce, and the "Being Beauteous," the woman "who unto my youth was given, more than all things else to love me." Three stanzas invoke an evening visitation that Mary makes to a table where the narrator sits, alone and disconsolate:

> With a slow and noiseless footstep
>   Comes that messenger divine,
> Takes the vacant chair beside me,
>   Lays her gentle hand in mine.
>
> And she sits and gazes at me
>   With those deep and tender eyes,
> Like the stars, so still and saint-like,
>   Looking downward from the skies.

Uttered not, yet comprehended,
Is the spirit's voiceless prayer,
Soft rebukes, in blessings ended,
Breathing from her lips of air.

In the hot summer days leading up to the writing of "Footsteps of Angels," Henry had been staying with his family in Maine. Unable to sleep one night, he made a few scribblings in his journal, commenting on a long letter just received from his friend Charles Sumner, a bit too garrulous for his taste, he thought, at least on this occasion. "Oh, give details of thy life, dear friend! and not generalities, which nowise satisfy," Henry wrote. His mind wandered a bit, as inevitably it did, to deeper thoughts. "It is raining now, late at night; raining gently,—a most Christian rain. Calm and holy quiet is around, and thoughts of the departed, the ministering angels who so soon unfolded their immortal wings. How well they lived and died,—the holy ones!"

4

Child of the Tempest

Those trackless deeps where many a weary sail
Has seen above the illimitable plain,
Morning on night, and night on morning rise
Whilst still no land to greet the wanderer spread
Its shadowy mountains on the sun-bright sea.

—Percy Bysshe Shelley, *Queen Mab:* epigraph to
Fanny Appleton's European journal, November 16, 1835

*N*ovember was not the most favorable month of the year to be making a long ocean voyage to Europe, when North Atlantic seas can be especially treacherous, but the Massachusetts merchant and textile manufacturer Nathan Appleton had made up his mind almost on impulse—he could not wait until spring. The devastating death from tuberculosis on October 26, 1835, of his twenty-year-old son and presumptive successor in the family business, Charles "Charley" Sedgwick Appleton, had quickened his resolve. A widower by that time of two and a half years, and dealing now with the sorrow of a double loss, he craved some private time with his grieving daughters, eighteen-year-old Frances Elizabeth, the future Mrs. Longfellow everyone called Fanny, and Mary, four years her senior.

Appleton had never forgiven himself for failing to be with his beloved wife, Maria Theresa Gold Appleton, in the winter of 1833 as she lay dying from the same disease that had just claimed Charley, the "white plague" that accounted for more fatalities in the United States in the nineteenth century than any other sickness, and was commonly known then as consumption. Serving at that time as a Member of Congress, he had traveled nonstop to Boston from Washington by fresh teams of posthorses hired in haste along the way, only to be informed upon arrival that he was too late. Maria Theresa had struggled mightily to remain conscious, refusing any medications that might have put her to sleep. "She kept her eyes anxiously fixed on the clock," her daughters wrote in a journal they kept jointly at this time, "to watch for the hour of my Father's arrival, whom she expected to see, until the last moment!"

Fanny and Mary described deathbed gatherings of children and household staff, complete with goodbye wishes for everyone to be virtuous and upright and to keep the faith. Their mother died on February 10, 1833, at the age of forty-six. "This evening Father arrived, having heard that all was over, just before arriving in town," Mary wrote the next day. "He was much agitated, and fatigued, after travelling day and night." It was partly in response to his wife's protracted illness that the fifty-three-year-old patriarch of the family had already chosen not to seek a second term in the House of Representatives; he would formally leave office a month after she died, and take his family on a two-month excursion to upstate New York, traveling variously by steamboat, railroad, and stagecoach to Niagara Falls and into Canada, then meandering back home through Vermont and New Hampshire. For part of the journey they traveled on the Erie Canal, which had opened the western interior of the region up to more expeditious travel just a few years earlier.

Joining Appleton's daughters on that adventure were Emmeline Austin, Fanny's lifelong friend from Beacon Hill and a key correspondent throughout her life, and their brother Charley, already determined to follow in his father's footsteps, and eager to see the exciting uses of water power along their routes of passage. Older brother Thomas Gold Appleton skipped this trip; he was traveling on his own in Europe, an affection he would indulge in the decades to come as an affable Boston wit and full-time bon vivant, making numerous voyages to the Continent, a good number of them to buy art masterpieces for the family collections, and later for the Museum of Fine Arts in Boston, an institution

Frances Elizabeth
Appleton, at seventeen,
oil, by G. P. A. Healy, 1834,
in the Longfellow House
dining room

he helped found in 1870, and for which he wrote the first guide to its holdings.

Many of the sketches fifteen-year-old Fanny drew of the landmarks they observed survive, including lovely views of Niagara Falls made from both sides of the border, and one of the Old Man of the Mountain at Franconia Notch in New Hampshire that the art historian Diana Korzenik has asserted to be the earliest known representation of the famous rock formation by an American artist. The trip was deemed most agreeable, a tonic, really, for everyone's tattered emotions, so much so that it persuaded Nathan Appleton to undertake an even bolder adventure in the aftermath of Charley's death. "We are now so desolate, with nothing to anticipate, and one loss making the few left more anxious for each other than ever, that Father has actually sent to N[ew] York to engage our passage to sail for Europe in a fortnight," Fanny informed a close family friend just three days after Charley died. "The slightest thought of it staggers and bewilders me so that I dare not yield to the excitement— and the indifference with which it now is viewed would have seemed last year incredible."

While grand tours of the continent were rites of passage generally reserved for young men in the early decades of the nineteenth century, this ambitious undertaking was intended for the primary benefit of Appleton's handsomely turned-out daughters. To complete the traveling party, three male members of the family were included: twenty-four-year-old big brother Tom and two cousins, Isaac Appleton Jewett, son of Nathan Appleton's sister Emily, and the consumptive William "Willy" Sullivan Appleton, brought along with faint hopes of restoring his failing health. They boarded the packet ship *Francis Depau* off lower Manhattan on November 16, 1835, joined on deck by some relatives and friends who had come to bid them adieu. Instead of departing as scheduled, the captain announced that calm winds would force them to wait until daybreak before weighing anchor, a mild annoyance for Fanny, the spirited "rogue" of the group, as Charley had once called her in a playful letter, who was eager to get the big show on the road.

"Flowers and kind wishes were showered upon us in equal profusion," she wrote in one of six notebooks she kept through the course of the two-year journey, "and if the latter could fill our sails with breezes, as they do our hearts with thankfulness, short would be the passage that wafts us to other shores!" Fanny had begun the journal that day with a five-line quotation from Percy Bysshe Shelley's *Queen Mab*, followed by a succession of thoughtful observations that reveal a poised young woman exuberant about the adventure that lay ahead. Along with the crew and fifteen passengers, the *Francis Depau* carried a complement of pigs, sheep, and squawking birds in the "caboose," as Fanny called the section back aft where they were kept, and a substantial cargo of cotton in the hold. This latter circumstance suggested the nickname "Lowell" for the captain's pet bulldog, a nod to the textile-manufacturing city Nathan Appleton had established north of Boston in the 1820s along the banks of the Merrimack River, the primary source of the family's great wealth.

To prepare for the thirty-five-hundred-mile voyage, Fanny had brushed up on her history and grasp of European cultures, and brought along plenty of paper, pens, pencils, and assorted sketching supplies, which she began putting to good use during the irksome standstill in New York Harbor. "The wind has died away, and the sea and sky are grey and commonplace, decidedly, but I sketched a pretty view of the opposite shore—a dark, picturesque wind-mill—houses and ships—this, for a last link to American ground." The lovely scene she drew appears on the first page of a large-format album containing much of her artwork from the trip, one of several Fanny would have mounted and bound in elegant albums after her return. The volume containing this sketch is encased in dark green leather with blind-stamped gilt borders along the edges, and marbled endpapers inside. Embossed on the front cover in gold gilt is the word "SKETCHES"; the initials F.E.A. appear alone on the rear cover and on the ribbed spine with the date 1835–1836. Inside are twenty-six full-frame drawings, some of them accented by watercolor, each one individually identified in pencil, all dated in her hand.

"Reclined on a coil of ropes and became mum," Fanny wrote as the afternoon wore on, her boredom beginning to show, "and take immense interest in the motions of the sailors and the feeding of the chickens." She noticed warily that her uncle William Appleton "hovers round Willy, as a hen with one chicken," breaking away only when it was time for him to head back to shore, having said what he may well have feared was a final goodbye to his ailing son. On the morning of departure, Fanny was still taking everything in, missing nothing. "We are off Sandy Hook, have now the broad and boundless Ocean before us," she recorded at ten o'clock. "There is a most piratical-looking character at the helm, whose shaggy locks, wild eyes and picturesque cap are tempting for a sketch." The first full night at sea was "beautifully calm," with a "magnificent dash of crimson beneath a dusky cloud" that "gave promise of a fair tomorrow. The holy stars were watching brightly over us, and a mysterious light which was neither of the sun, moon or stars but which seemed shining thro' the sky, spread its pure radiance over the happy waves."

Fanny quickly became fast friends with the captain, taking leisurely arm-in-arm walks with him about the main deck, picking up the lore and lingo of maritime life. "We are agreeably disappointed and fancy him vastly," she wrote of the stylish commander, who gave her "a most delicious promenade for two hours" the first night out, introducing her to words and phrases that she shared with her companions. Over the next eighteen days the captain would teach her how to box a compass, determine longitude and latitude on a nautical chart, understand the basics of celestial navigation, tack against the wind, and steer a proper course. "Studied thro' my vocabulary of nauticalities today," she would write of her progress, coining a new noun in the process. "I am now 'ready for service' if other amusements fail."

Fanny does not tell us the name of the *Depau* skipper, but logbooks and crew lists of the 595-ton full-rigged schooner deposited at the Mystic Seaport Research Library in Connecticut identify him as Captain Cleaveland Alexander Forbes, master of the ship from the time of its launching in 1833 until 1846. Born to a New Jersey seagoing family in 1780, Forbes sailed as a privateer in the War of 1812; he had to have been dazzled by this extraordinary young woman who had arrived with such spunky enthusiasm on his quarterdeck. She was a fountain of energy, eager to see and know everything, bright, irascible, witty, refined, and strikingly attractive—five feet ten inches tall with perfect posture, thick black hair coiled at the sides in corkscrew ringlets, and deep brown eyes that impressed everyone she met with their piercing intelligence.

As the ship continued along its heading off Labrador, the ocean turned angry, and for ten days there was a steady pattern of gales and squalls.

On board the *Francis Depau*, bound for France, dated November 13, 1835, in Fanny Appleton's sketchbook

The waves, she marveled, were "truly 'mountain high' and crested with foamy white caps, flashing with rainbows when breaking"—an unforgettable sight, "but I will not rhapsodize about the sea, for it is beyond words." After being "called upon deck" from below one night by the captain, she witnessed "the most magnificent Aurora Borealis" imaginable. "There were pillars of light shooting up from the sea and gradually an arch of the deepest most brilliant rose-colour glowed across the sky, relieving the sails with magical distinctness and making the bright stars dazzling as diamonds in a ruby ocean." A few days later, she savored a sunset, the sky "radiant with a clear and pearly light—opal tinted and transparent as a fairy's wing."

Fanny would flaunt her newfound expertise in a letter to Robert Apthorp, a family friend from childhood, written at "latitude 47, longitude 15," she noted helpfully in her salutation. "I have longed very much for a genuine *storm*, but some of these squalls have been terribly heavy, carrying away our 'main-topsail' and 'jib' and washing completely over both decks. We have been sailing, today, under double-reefed mainsail and topsail, fore and aft, which the Captain thinks a very charming style, as far as appearance goes but I like to see those winged beautiful 'studding sails' out, so delicately poised in the air—as if by invisible cords."

Finally getting her wish, Fanny "crawled up to the slippery deck" one afternoon to witness the relentless pounding of the ship, the other passengers prudently huddling in their staterooms, many of them suffering from the "*mal de Coeur*" that eluded her throughout the voyage. With the wind "rushing like the blast of a thousand trumpets," she "remained clinging to the toprail mast, awed, bewildered—till a monstrous wave broke over my head drenching me to the skin, —what an exulting thrill of fierce delight! To be baptised by such a priest, at such an altar—a child of the tempest!" It was altogether a "majestic scene" for the ages, one she left "reluctantly" only when her "sage Papa" came topside and "insisted upon my retiring to disrobe my dripping garments."

The *Francis Depau* was a modern vessel for its day, only two years old when it made this voyage, destined to ply the Atlantic trade routes into the 1850s before ending its career in San Francisco Bay, abandoned by its crew during the California Gold Rush and left to rot along the wharves of the Embarcadero. Though the age of steam was just beginning to hit its stride, sail still ruled the waves, and deepwater ship handling involved art as much as skill. However romantic the tradition, three weeks at sea is nonetheless a long time, as Fanny wearily acknowledged: "The lovely, the graceful, the gentle Earth! My heart yearns with filial love toward thee!"

Among the hundreds of material objects preserved in the Longfellow House storage vault are two portable traveling desks with folding, sloped tops, both the property once of Fanny Appleton. The one she likely brought along on this trip is tooled with brass fittings and mother-of-pearl decorations inlaid on the hinged lid; it was handcrafted in London by T. Dalton of Great Ormond Street, Queen Square, and purchased in Boston at E. V. Ashton & Co., an exclusive specialty shop on Washington Street, according to lithographed labels still affixed inside. Carved in the wood under the drop-down lid of the other, less elaborate desk— the one she had with her on the earlier trip to upstate New York and Canada—is the signature "Frances E. Appleton, Boston" and the year 1832. Documenting things visually, and in words, mattered to Fanny Appleton—and these were her tools of choice. "Today we surmise is Thanksgiving in New England, and we are going to celebrate it on venison and plum-pudding," she wrote on December 3, 1835, a day, gratefully, of peace and calm at sea, with soft swells gently swaying the ship, and landfall still a week away. "I wonder what the folks are about in old Boston?"

PRECOCITY SEEMS to have been a part of the Appleton DNA, apparent on both branches of the ancestral tree, and just as remarkable for Maria Theresa Gold Appleton (1786–1833), Fanny's mother, as for her father, Nathan Appleton (1779–1861), the self-made merchant and textile manufacturer who led the effort to introduce the water-powered weaving loom to the United States in the early days of the Industrial Revolution.

Nathan Appleton began life as a farm boy in New Ipswich, New Hampshire, a rural community on the Massachusetts border, one of twelve children born to a hardworking couple with roots that went back to the first settlements in the English colonies. Bright enough to gain admittance to Dartmouth at the age of fifteen, Nathan eschewed a formal education in favor of working with his older brother Samuel in Boston. A virtuoso in mathematics, he perfected a form of double-book accounting that proved useful in managing inventory for what became a lucrative import-export business with headquarters near the teeming waterfront. By the time Nathan was twenty-one, the firm was known as the S. & N. Appleton Company, and he was a full partner. He made his first trip to England in 1802, and kept a journal of his voyage with observations that at times foreshadow the wonder his daughter would record thirty-three years later under similar conditions. That notebook, along with numerous other Appleton family papers, are preserved in the Massachusetts Historical Society.

Appleton's first wife, Maria Theresa Gold, was a native of Pittsfield in the Berkshire Hills of western Massachusetts, the daughter of a respected attorney and Yale graduate who was described in an 1876 town history as "a man of elegant culture and refined tastes." A country lawyer by trade, Thomas Gold was regarded as "able and shrewd to a marked degree," noted for being "entertaining, discreet, and clear-headed." Politically, Gold had been a supporter of a regional protest movement of the 1780s known as Shays' Rebellion, which called for reform of the Articles of Confederation, "but growing years had taught him conservatism," the town history continued, so that by 1800 "he ranked with the most decided federalists." Gold ensured that all of his ten children got top-notch educations, which for his five daughters meant sending them a good distance away from home. When Maria Theresa was twelve, she studied at a private boarding school in Hartford, Connecticut, followed by enrollment in 1802 at the exclusive Berry Street Academy in Boston, which placed a heavy emphasis on Western culture, music, drama, and the arts, along with mathematics and geography.

Berry Street was located in a once-vibrant section of downtown Boston rich in history and throbbing with artistic activity. A good deal of the goings-on there centered around the Long Lane Meeting House, where state leaders led by Governor John Hancock met in 1788 to ratify the United States Constitution, resulting in a renaming of the road as Federal Street, and the old meeting house as Federal Street Church. Led by the charismatic minister William Ellery Channing (1780–1842), the church became a center of the spiritual, artistic, literary, and philosophical principles articulated by the Unitarian movement. A classmate of Stephen Longfellow's at Harvard, Channing became Maria Theresa Gold's spiritual adviser. It was in this neighborhood, too, where the Federal Street Theatre, the city's first public playhouse, opened in 1794. All of these buildings are long gone, many destroyed in the Great Boston Fire of 1872, and since replaced by what is today the city's financial district.

In 1805, the famed portrait artist Gilbert Stuart moved to Boston from the nation's capital at the behest of US Senator Jonathan Mason with assurances that some high-end business would be steered his way, and opened a studio on the corner of Summer and Otis Streets. Several of Senator Mason's daughters had been classmates of Maria Theresa Gold at the Berry Street Academy, one of whom, Susan, married the man who would become her physician. It may well have been through that friendship that two of Stuart's earliest clients in Boston were Maria Theresa Appleton and her entrepreneurial husband, Nathan, whose portraits hang today in the formal dining room of Longfellow House.

Another friend of Maria Theresa's was Eloise Richards Payne, daughter of the school's owners, William and Susanna Payne, and destined to be one of the most prominent art teachers of her generation; her brother John Howard Payne would achieve eminence as an actor, playwright, and lyricist of the song "Home, Sweet Home." John Payne also assisted his parents, and in 1804 wrote to Thomas Gold extolling Maria Theresa's writing skills. "The sentiment, the diction, the penmanship," he enthused, "are worthy of each other, and combine to form a brilliant model." Yet another Berry Street student was Catharine Maria Sedgwick (1789–1867), Maria Theresa's cousin from western Massachusetts, and soon to be one of the best-known writers of her time.

When Nathan met Maria Theresa, he had the clear stamp of an energetic young man on the rise, a savvy businessman with cosmopolitan tastes, and not timid about enjoying the emoluments of his success. How the two met is not recorded, but the proximity of Nathan's office to Federal Street in the bustling Cornwall neighborhood nearby—today the location of City Hall Plaza—and his early embrace of the Unitarian church she also attended, undoubtedly were factors. Maria Theresa

Maria Theresa Gold Appleton and Nathan Appleton, portraits by Gilbert Stuart, in the dining room, Longfellow House, 1806

never kept a diary, but she did write a number of letters to her family that have survived, including one to her father that mentions "Mr. Appleton" in a parenthetical nature, interesting only for the fact that it assumes a tone of familiarity. The couple exchanged marriage vows on April 13, 1806, and moved into a modest Boston apartment. Two years later, Nathan bought a spacious town house at 54 Beacon Street designed by the architect Asher Benjamin, a mirror copy of an adjoining home that in later years was the residence of the historian William Hickling Prescott, today a museum with authentic furnishings and appointments typical of the period.

Maria Theresa's affliction with tuberculosis dated to when she was thirteen, a circumstance that found her often in the Berkshire Hills with her relatives taking in the crisp mountain air. Medical wisdom of the day often prescribed travel as a therapy for illness, persuading Nathan and Maria Theresa to sail for Europe in 1810. The temporary change of scenery seemed to work wonders for her delicate condition, which to that point had included several miscarriages. The couple's first child, Thomas Gold Appleton, was born in 1812; Mary was born the next year, Charley followed in 1815, and Fanny, the youngest of the brood, arrived on October 7, 1817. As the family grew, the Appletons moved to a bow-fronted town house at 39 Beacon Street designed by Alexander Parris, a follower of Charles Bulfinch, whose masterpiece—the golden-domed landmark that Oliver Wendell Holmes would anoint "the hub of the solar system," the Massachusetts State House—is just a few blocks away.

Though Nathan Appleton never secured a college degree of his own, he and his wife instilled a spirit of intellectual curiosity among their children. He became a generous patron of philanthropic causes that promoted learning and achievement, including major support for the Boston Athenæum, which in the absence of a formal art museum or public library in the early years of the nineteenth century was a nexus of cultural activity, including major exhibitions of paintings his daughters were allowed to view in an adjoining art gallery, a considerable privilege, as women were not allowed use of what was then a men-only private library. Among Fanny's journal entries is a notation for August 11, 1832, when she was fourteen: "Went to see Audubon's original drawings of birds at Athenæum."

While traveling through Scotland with his wife in 1810, Nathan Appleton had occasion to meet with Francis Cabot Lowell, a distant cousin of his from the United States, and like himself a successful Boston merchant embarked on an extended journey to Europe. Lowell was determined during his stay to learn what he could about the textile-manufacturing companies centered in Edinburgh and Manchester, in particular the mechanics of the intricate looms they had developed to weave cotton yarn into finished cloth. Years later, Appleton recalled the fateful conversation they had about Lowell's bold plan to create a new industry in New England where the region's abundance of rivers could be harnessed to power the looms. "I urged him to do so, and promised him my co-operation." The enterprise Lowell had in mind would hinge on his cunning ability to replicate the proprietary processes he was grudgingly permitted by his hosts to see during tours of their factories. How the brilliant Harvard graduate accomplished this—no note-taking was allowed—is a fascinating story of industrial espionage and reverse engineering that has been studied by historians of numerous disciplines, and one I have discussed in my book *On Paper*.

Once returned to America in 1812, Appleton assembled a group of investors known latterly as the Boston Associates. With their financial backing, Lowell established the nation's first water-powered textile factory on the Charles River in Waltham. Their stunning success there led to Appleton's crowning achievement: the creation, in 1826, of a fully integrated industrial city twenty-five miles north of Boston on the Merrimack River, with a workforce of young women recruited from throughout New England and cared for in company-owned boarding-houses. Appleton named the new city in honor of Francis Lowell, who had died in 1819, all the while establishing himself as a captain of industry a full two decades before Thomas Carlyle coined the phrase. A true wonder of the age, the "Spindle City," as it became known—and where I was born and raised, the grandson of Greek immigrants who moved there in the early years of the twentieth century to work as weavers in the textile mills—would be visited and praised by such dignitaries as President Andrew Jackson and, in 1842, the famed novelist from England Charles Dickens during his first American tour.

Appleton's special genius in this enterprise, of which he was a controlling stockholder, was his development of sophisticated strategies for financing and marketing. A director of numerous banks and a principal in thirty key firms, he emerged as a leading spokesman for New England trade and industry, writing incisive articles, letters, and pamphlets in support of the region's economic interests, and serving six terms as an articulate representative in the Massachusetts state legislature. He was elected to Congress in 1830 as an anti-Jacksonian National Republican, and returned to Boston after the death of Maria Theresa on February 10, 1833, to be with his children.

AN INQUISITIVE GIRL from an early age, Fanny Appleton was spared nothing in the way of intellectual stimulation, with an intensive program of private instruction tailored to her individual needs and interests. Unlike Tom and Charley, who were sent to Round Hill School for Boys in western Massachusetts, Fanny's early education was entrusted to Elizabeth Palmer Peabody (1804–94), the pioneering educator, writer, and lifelong champion of women's rights who in 1869 would establish the first English-speaking kindergarten in the United States. A protégé of Ralph Waldo Emerson and confidante of William Ellery Channing, Peabody opened her first school for girls in the suburban town of Brookline in 1825, taking under her wing the daughters of well-to-do parents, assisted for a time by her younger sisters, Sophia, later to be the wife of Nathaniel Hawthorne, and Mary, who would marry the reformer Horace Mann.

In 1827, Peabody moved her operation to Franklin Place, a crescent-shaped development in downtown Boston, limiting enrollment at first to thirty girls, ten-year-old Fanny Appleton being one of her earliest pupils. Though mindful that a fine line separates candor and discretion, especially when dealing with the parents of her privileged young students, Peabody minced few words when evaluating each girl's performance, progress, and potential. Two evaluations she prepared for Nathan Appleton survive, and give a good sense of Fanny's willingness to learn subjects she found interesting, and her indifference to those she deemed boring.

Peabody's first letter was written, she made clear at the outset, at the behest of Maria Theresa, with whom she had already discussed Fanny's instruction, allowing us to conclude that it was Mrs. Appleton, *not* Mr. Appleton, who had engaged the brilliant young educator to teach their daughter. One initial point of contact could have been Catharine Maria Sedgwick, a first cousin three years Maria Theresa's junior, and like her a former student at the Berry Street Academy. Sedgwick attended meetings in the home of William Ellery Channing, a mentor to Elizabeth Peabody, and Maria Theresa's pastor at the Federal Street Church. In a letter to another cousin, written at the same time Fanny was enrolling in the school, Sedgwick recommended Peabody as "a very intelligent and highly improved young woman" who employed a distinctive method to her teaching. "She reads to them—and talks with them. She begins with Homer as the earliest history, and in order to give them the best notions of mythology—she then follows the stream—reads Herodotus and Thucydides."

Fanny, for her part, did not enjoy Latin or Greek. "Her chief difficulty," Peabody wrote, "is that she learns her lessons with so much facility that they do not do the service of disciplining her mind or of occupying her mind—thus leaving her mind to the invasion of every evil." Peabody was not specific—particularly the "every evil" it was she might have meant—but it could not have been too serious, given that nothing overly drastic was in the offing. Instead, Peabody proposed a "plan" that would provide Fanny with more personal instruction four times a week. "I shall give her long lessons, that will occupy the morning hours and I think you will perceive immediate improvement." Fanny seemed to enjoy the school, though it involved something of a trek to get there from her home, about a half mile on a straight line if she walked through the Common just above Frog Pond, or a tad longer if she went up Beacon and down Park to Winter. Fanny wrote her brother Tom at the Round Hill School in Northampton about her daily routine. "I now go to Miss Peabody's school, and I like her very well, though I have to walk in the cold, a great way, as it is in Franklin Place."

In her second letter, Peabody offered a more pointed evaluation. Though undated, the content makes clear she was responding to a query from Nathan Appleton regarding "my intentions respecting Fanny's studies this winter"—the second winter, she stated, that the child had been under her tutelage. Peabody's testy tone can be attributed partly to the fact that she was in the midst of relocating her school a few blocks away to Colonnade Row, a range of twenty-four brick houses on Tremont Street between West and Mason, part of Charles Bulfinch's development of Boston during the Federal period. "You will excuse my delaying this answer and writing it so hastily," she wrote in her final sentence, "for I am *moving* today."

The letter nonetheless outlined, detail by detail, Fanny's strengths and weaknesses, while expressing in general the rigorous curriculum Peabody had developed for the intellectual growth of girls. She complemented Fanny for "gaining a very pretty style of penmanship," but was still not at all pleased by her performance in Latin. "Fanny did not learn the Latin grammar thoroughly at first, and after she had studied some months last winter I was sorry I had not put her to studying it over again." Her general working concept, she then explained at some length—and rather pretentiously, it is fair to say—was that the children "might learn to think in the Latin arrangement of words," and "then inflect the nouns—and adjectives—and verbs." From there, Peabody "allowed" the girls "to throw the sentence into good English," encouraged them to ask questions, and then discuss how "to illustrate the comparative syntax of the two languages." She then reported that Fanny had been "exceedingly careless and rather indolent" in that department, but not severely enough to have "fallen out of the class."

The crux of Peabody's evaluation was that Fanny excelled in the things she liked, and lagged behind in those she found dull. "In all that required quick perception and judgment I found her quite on a par with the best in the school—but in application she is indifferent." Her progress in mathematics was spotty as well. "Fanny is very averse to this study—and fell behind her class from inattention at the time when I examined them in arithmetic, which I do every day, by requiring them to sit round in a class and tell me how they do the sums." Fanny liked geography, took "great interest" in history, and excelled in her French studies. "In general what taxes her memory without attracting her taste passes away from her mind as rapidly as it goes into it—and she learns lessons very quick. By dint of repetition I hope this will be impressed on her mind—and when she has more time I wish her to draw maps."

The letter continued on, outlining the structure of what Peabody emphasized, with two bold underlines, was "*my*" plan. She then put to Nathan Appleton the choice of what came next. "You must decide whether Fanny receives advantage from the plan. She has natural talent in abundance. She reads the best in her class—is quick in discriminating synonyms—and in all exercises which require ingenuity—and *beautiful* in whatever requires *taste*. But she dislikes hard study—is too willing to be assisted, and often when *we* would throw her upon her resources, she obtains assistance from her schoolfellows."

Peabody concluded by making what had to be a difficult recommendation to the doting father of—dare we suggest?—a somewhat spoiled and pampered ten-year-old: "We have but one punishment in our school which is that when there is neglect and carelessness in schoolhouse—there should be study at home an extra lesson. This serves as a stimulus to attention and industry. But Fanny has the privilege from home—of never studying at home. I cannot therefore enforce this rule upon *her* and being out of its reach, she has no mechanical stimulus to industry.

If you could think it consistent with the health of her body—for me to apply this rule to her—it would prove much to the health of her mind."

Whether or not that course of action—more homework—was adopted is not recorded, though in the same letter Peabody mentioned that Fanny's instruction in reading, composition, spelling, and defining words was being done "under the care" of William Russell, a noted elocutionist and lecturer at Harvard who served as the founding editor of the *American Journal of Education*, and who for a short time was a partner with Elizabeth and Mary Tyler Peabody in the Franklin Place school. Fanny and her sister, Mary, received instruction from yet another distinguished Boston teacher, George Barrell Emerson, a cousin of Ralph Waldo Emerson's and, like Peabody, a specialist in the education of young women. Among the Appleton family documents are several workbooks Fanny prepared under his tutelage, including an undated French exercise book with "Mademoiselle Frances E. Appleton, Chez Monsieur Emerson, Rue de Chestnut" written in her hand on the inside cover. Fanny's writing fills every page, with faint traces, in pencil, of a teacher's corrections, with the number of errors noted. There is also a letter in the Craigie House archives from Emerson to Fanny giving her permission to hold on to some books she had borrowed until classes resumed in the fall.

For guidance in artistic technique, Fanny was tutored by Francis Graeter, a German painter skilled in figure, landscape, and architectural art, and instructor at several progressive New England schools, including Round Hill, where Fanny's brother Tom was one of his students, and, beginning in 1830, at the program for girls in Boston directed by Elizabeth Peabody, who would describe him as "a gentleman who probably possesses the spirit of Art more completely than any instructor who has ever taught in this country." In addition to this, the Appleton girls learned ballroom etiquette from Lorenzo Papanti, an Italian expatriate who is credited with introducing the waltz to American society, and who with his son operated Papanti's Hall, a famous ballroom and theater at 23 Tremont Street.

Further refinement was provided by Frances Erskine Inglis, a Scottish woman with impeccable bloodlines who for a period in the 1830s operated an exclusive finishing school for the daughters of prominent families, notably those of Nathan and Maria Theresa Appleton. The Inglis school promoted instruction "in every branch of learning, intellectual and ornamental." Among the latter were dance-floor protocols, but front and center was the study of music, as Fanny recalled years later, when her former teacher was then known as the Marquesa Calderón de la Barca, having married a Spanish nobleman and lived for a period quite gracefully in Mexico. "Fanny Calderón was here for a day and I had a long chat with her at the Prescotts," she informed Emmeline Austin. "She has grown fatter but otherwise wholly unchanged, the same entertaining, careless spoken person as of yore. No foreign ways, no ambassadress dignity acquired from her Mexican life but just as frank and good humoured as when she guided my unwilling fingers over the piano-keys."

What Fanny had received from an early age, in short, was an individually crafted, highly sophisticated liberal arts education, with a premium placed on logic, initiative, discernment, and critical thinking. Complementing her structured studies was the influence over many years of Francis Lieber (1800–72), a German philosopher and legal scholar who emigrated to the United States in 1827, and became her tutor and confidant on many matters of heart and mind. Lieber had earned a doctorate in mathematics from the University of Jena, but was blackballed from teaching in Germany because of his liberal political views. Lying about his age, he enlisted in the French army, fought in the Napoleonic Wars, was wounded and imprisoned twice, and, like Lord Byron, volunteered in the cause of Greek independence. Finding sanctuary in England, he wrote scholarly articles and made a modest living instructing the children of well-heeled families, one of whom—Matilda (Mathilda) Oppenheimer—became his wife. In Rome, he tutored the son of the historian Barthold Georg Niebuhr.

With Niebuhr's help, Lieber emigrated to Boston, intending to introduce gymnastics and other recreational sports to American educational curricula, a German concept now accepted everywhere, but a tough sell then. In a much more successful venture, he compiled the *Encyclopaedia Americana*, a work in thirteen volumes that eventually sold more than one hundred thousand sets, with copies to be found in numerous libraries, including the one in Craigie House. In 1835, Lieber became a professor at the University of South Carolina, where he would remain for twenty-two years. As tensions between North and South began to mount, he left to teach in New York at what is now Columbia University. During the Civil War, two of his sons fought bravely for the Union Army, one of them losing an arm in battle, while a third died serving the Confederacy. While living in Boston, Lieber had lectured at the Boston Athenæum where Nathan Appleton was a benefactor. Appleton hired the dashing expatriate to tutor his daughters. For Fanny, it was a stimulating friendship nourished by a sustained correspondence and, after her marriage, by his occasional visits to Craigie House; "Dr. Lieber," as Fanny addressed him, even tagged along for a few days on her honeymoon trip.

THE APPLETONS CELEBRATED their safe arrival in Havre-de-Grâce—modern day Le Havre—with a dinner of fried sole and omelette soufflé, a treat Fanny admitted having enjoyed "to a most unfeminine extent," leaving them all "in danger of becoming veritable gourmands." The bread served warm from the oven with fresh creamery butter had her brother Tom murmuring "la belle France" with each bite. They set off the next morning for Paris—"we rumble at a very easy rapid rate"—paying their respects to history at every opportunity. Nathan occasionally broke away to "explore some manufactories," while Fanny and Mary went "lionizing," as they called visiting the top attractions they were determined to see, inspecting cathedrals, architectural ruins, and natural wonders as they turned up along their route. "Stood in the spot Jeanne d'Arc perished," she wrote in Rouen, " 'the heroine of the world!' "

Fanny was mesmerized by the French countryside; everything she saw—"houses, men, women, children, carts, horses, dogs—and donkeys, above all, with their ponies, and some with even ladies on their backs"—was "picturesque" to her eye. "There is *nothing* here one is not tempted to sketch." And the best was yet to come. "Tomorrow," she wrote on December 14, "we reach Paris—*Quelle idée!*" Arriving in the rain, they took rooms at Le Meurice, a luxurious hotel on Rue de Rivoli near the Tuileries Garden and the Louvre. Relieved finally to exchange the "lullabies of creaking masts and dashing waves" of the *Francis Depau* for a plush bed in a quiet room, Fanny described the lavish apartments as "mirrored and curtained *à la Française* and warmed and carpeted *à l'Anglaise*."

Over the next six weeks, the Appleton sisters were immersed in the life of the city, outfitting themselves in the latest fashions, meeting interesting people at a succession of fancy dinners; they attended concerts and plays at Salle Le Peletier, the Opéra-Comique, the Théâtre des Variétés, the Cirque Olympique de Franconi, and the Comédie-Française. Performances by the famed Italian soprano Giulia Grisi in Bellini's *Norma* and Rossini's *Semiramide*—the latter on New Years Eve—left Fanny spellbound. "I cannot attempt to describe the effect of that voice." She spent a morning at the Louvre marveling at "the atmosphere of poetry that the Italian School sheds along the walls, as from a thousand founts," and noticed "a great many copyists at work" throughout the vast treasure house, including "several females," leading her to muse: "Was I not envious?"

Toward the end of their stay in the City of Light, Fanny and Mary called on the Left Bank studio of Jean-Baptiste Isabey (1767–1855), renowned for having painted numerous heads of state and members of royalty, including a commission for the coronation of Napoleon Bonaparte and Empress Josephine. He agreed to do a watercolor portrait of the sisters seated side by side, a sublime miniature of the two which was exhibited at the Paris Salon of 1837 before being turned over to the Appletons, and now resides in the Craigie House dining room. "He is a charming old man with the gracious manners of a former age," Fanny wrote after her first meeting with the artist. "It will truly be an honor to be painted by him." The sisters sat for two hours every day for a week, "a tedious operation," but "enlivened by his anecdotes and droll remarks." Fanny was in awe of his technique. "Nothing can exceed the exquisiteness of his finish and the spirituality he throws into the eyes." Declaring their likenesses at last to be "satisfactory and excellent," Fanny and Mary took their leave, allowing Isabey to make the final touches on his own. "I sent him locks of our hair to copy." Their dresses and jewelry would be left to his discretion as well: "we hardly know what they will be, but trust everything to his preeminent taste."

Nathan Appleton had hired two coaches for his party's exclusive use

Miniature watercolor of
Mary Appleton, left, and
Fanny Appleton, 1835,
painted in Paris by
Jean-Baptiste Isabey,
Craigie House
dining room

throughout their European journey. "The largest is a sort of man-of-war on wheels," Fanny wrote, "green as the sea without, and within deep, roomy and comfortable, with charming accommodations for books before and behind and in packets at the side." Nathan had also hired a maid, Adèle, to tend to the needs of his daughters, and a valet, François, for the men. "Adèle rides in solitary dignity on a sort of rumble seat behind the big carriage where she is no small adornment for the establishment." Thus appointed and equipped, the Appletons resumed their travels on January 22, 1836, a dismal Friday, but otherwise a good day to be getting on their way. Fanny took note of their departure with what is arguably her best piece of writing thus far—supple, lyrical, fluidly paced, with a hint of anticipation that circles back deftly to where it began two months earlier:

> We left Paris in a drizzle. Rumbled down the Rue Rivoli, dashed thro' the Place du Carousel and along the quay, looked our last of the old Pont Neuf, Notre Dame and our daily rendezvous the Institut where perhaps good 'ol Isabey was sitting in his cunning little

boudoir adding a new grace to the pictured forms of the wanderers, and Paris—with all its life and its gaiety, its splendor and its meanness, its comfort and its mud, faded in the distance and we were once more fairly "wandering on the face of the earth."

An aspect worth noting at this point is the physical elements of Fanny's travel journal itself, what the French literary theorist Gérard Genette called the paratextual properties of a book. Fanny paid attention to what she had to say in these pages, and how it appeared—not only as a piece of writing, but as what I contend is an improvised form of self-publication intended, ultimately, for the eyes of others—and in that respect not unlike the hand-stitched fascicles that would serve the reclusive Emily Dickinson so well a generation later. This volume—one of six Fanny filled during her European tour—was bound in red Moroccan leather, with the initials *F.E.A.* embossed in gold on the spine. Set down on leaves of high-quality laid paper, the writing is uniformly neat and clean—what bibliographers call a "fair copy" likely prepared from an earlier draft, which does not survive. Her spiritual journal, by contrast, is replete with strikeouts, ink-outs, slice-outs, and tear-outs—another form of self-editing begun in her earlier years that also, in its own way, anticipates unknown readers.

There is no record of what kind of future Fanny Appleton may have fashioned for herself at such an early age, nothing in her letters or journals to suggest that she was keen on finding a worthy beau and settling down to a life of genteel domesticity, following the example of so many of her contemporaries. Perhaps she envisioned the life of an artist. Or perhaps she considered becoming a novelist and social critic like her "dear aunt Kitty," Catharine Maria Sedgwick, whom she regarded as a role model in the years before her marriage. She suggested off-handedly during this trip to Europe a passing interest in writing travel guides, and after her marriage, children's books.

Reading perceptively, and sharing what she read with others, was essential to her life, and language in general, with all its textures, tones, and nuances, fascinated her. "You know how I love to coin words," she reminded Robert Apthorp from Paris. "Coining words is next to coining ideas," she reiterated three years later. In the absence of any outright declaration of intent on her part, we cannot say either way. But as these early observations persuasively testify—and as would become even more apparent in the years ahead—Fanny cared deeply about the craft of writing, cared equally about art, and approached both with thought, discipline, and a practiced style.

5

Moving On

Thus closes another year—everyway the most important year of my life. I pause to look back, like one awakening from a sorrowful dream. How strangely it moves before me—and how dark. Far back stands the peaceful home I have left—and the friends I love are there—and there is a painful parting, and leave-taking of those that are never to meet again on earth—and from that far distance my father's face still looks toward me sorrowfully and beseechingly. Thus the year began in sadness. It has closed in utter sorrow.

—Henry Wadsworth Longfellow's journal, December 31, 1835

After arranging for the transfer of Mary's remains to the United States, Henry wasted little time departing Holland for Germany—the sooner the better, as far as he was concerned. "A beautiful morning, spring-like," he had written in his journal five days before his young wife died, still convinced that she would recover and be able to continue with their travels. "The ships on the river, with loose-hanging sails, are goodly and fair to see. O that we could start upon the Rhine today." Henry and Clara left Rotterdam on December 2, making their way up the river by steamer to Cologne, and by *diligence*—the French word for "stagecoach"—the rest of the way to Heidelberg. "Clara is still with me and in her society I find many a soothing influence," he recorded on the day of departure. "She has known much of sorrow and sadness in her short life, and can sympathize with those who mourn."

In Düsseldorf, they "strolled" into a Catholic church "just at the moment of the elevation of the host," and observed with interest the various rituals that followed. "The soft, subduing hymn that was chanted to the sounds of an organ, both soothed and cheered me. There is much in the Catholic worship which I like." In Bonn, Henry was awestruck by the sight of ninety thousand books shelved under one roof in the university library; a greatly anticipated audience with the poet, critic, and translator August Wilhelm von Schlegel immediately afterwards, however, was a decided dud. "I could not get him upon any topic of interest to myself," the encounter so boringly "discursive"—he "rather lectured than conversed"—that Henry "declined to record" anything the aging scholar said in his journal. "Still, I was much gratified to see the translator of Shakespeare. He is very much a gentleman—and takes snuff from an ornamented box of tortoise shell."

They arrived in Heidelberg on December 11, renting separate rooms in the heart of the old city near the famed Karlstor Arch, Henry in the home of one Frau Himmelhahn, a woman he would caricature in *Hyperion* as a town gossip and mischief-maker so "ignorant of everything" that she had once asked "whether Christ was a Catholic or a Protestant." Henry's well-established fancy for fashionable attire did not go unnoticed by the woman, which may well have persuaded him to lampoon her so testily later. "She says you have a rakish look, because you carry a cane, and your hair curls," Henry's alter ego, the fictional character Paul Flemming, is told by his friend the Baron of Hohenfels, in a Heidelberg chapter he called "Owl-Towers" for the top-floor "nest" the landlady commands on the Hauptstrasse—a perch where she can observe, through "round-eyed spectacles," everyone else's business on the street below. "Your gloves, also, are a shade too light for a strictly virtuous man," the Baron needles further, and "the women already call you Wilhelm Meister," a not-so-flattering reference to the title character of Goethe's influential coming-of-age novel, *Wilhelm Meister's Apprenticeship*, which Henry dismissed as being "decidedly bad" and "not good" at one point. "Do you know she has nearly ruined your character in town?"

Henry nonetheless lived under Frau Himmelhahn's roof for close to six months, through the winter and into the late spring of 1836. "They are the best in town," he conceded of the rooms, which had a splendid view of the famed Heidelberg Castle, a spectacular fortress dating to the thirteenth century moored atop a facing hill, a place of quiet refuge he often trekked to in late afternoons or early evenings, and where he would seek solace in the weeks leading up to his departure for Switzerland the following June. "Excepting the Alhambra of Granada," he would write his father, "I have seen nothing to compare with this ruin." His days, for the most part, were spent at Heidelberg University, networking periodically with key people he was constantly meeting, all the while seeking out interesting titles for the Harvard collections in the secondhand stalls and auction marts. In *Hyperion,* Paul Flemming—a young scholar like himself who has recently suffered a dreadful personal loss—assuages his grief by having "buried himself in books, in old, dusty books."

Henry spent most evenings in the boardinghouse where Clara was staying, playing whist, participating in musicales, and mixing with other artistically inclined tenants, a number of them students at the university. Particularly stimulating were the long literary discussions Henry had with Julie Happ, the erudite daughter of Clara's landlady, forging a friendship that extended beyond his stay at Heidelberg. Julie worked closely with Clara, who was determined to master the native language. "I will read and write German every day," she affirmed, committing herself in "sober earnest" to "not dally with it any longer." A singular accomplishment would be her translation of thirty-seven German songs with full musical accompaniments, a task that the noted philologist and linguist James Taft Hatfield declared in his 1933 monograph to have been rendered with "no mean mastery" of the language.

These distractions were helpful to Henry, but Mary was never far from his thoughts. Alone in his room one night, he was deeply disconsolate, and unable to sleep. "The clock is even now striking ten," he jotted in his journal, "and I am alone, yet not alone, for the spirit of her, who loved me, and who I trust still loves me—is with me. Not many days before her death she said to me: 'We shall be so happy in Heidelberg!' I feel so assured of her presence—and am happy in knowing that she is so. O my beloved Mary—teach me to be good, and kind, and gentle as thou wert when here on earth." A few days later, Henry learned that George Washington Pierce, one of his closest Bowdoin classmates and husband of his twenty-three-year-old sister, Anne, had died on November 15 of typhus fever, the news only reaching him now.

Late in January Henry advised his father that while "the sense of my bereavement is deep and unutterable," he was doing all he could to soldier on with his work. "You can well imagine that it required a great effort for me to discipline my thoughts to regular study." By good fortune he had met up with William Cullen Bryant, who was staying in Heidelberg with his family for the winter, a convenient circumstance in that Clara became friendly with the wife and two daughters of the famed American poet, journalist, and long-time editor of the *New-York Evening Post*, in its time one of the most influential newspapers in the United States. "It has been fortunate for Clara that they were here on our arrival," Henry told his father. "She finds their society very pleasant," a sentiment Clara expressed repeatedly in her journal. "I like them all very much and feel as much acquainted with them as if I had always known them," she wrote shortly after making their acquaintance. "Their little Julia is a sweet little affectionate creature," she said of Bryant's younger daughter, then six. "I wish I had her with me all the time."

Being able to be with people she liked was most welcome to Clara, since Henry was not in the habit of straying too far from the protective bubble he had built around himself. "I feel far happier and less alone than I have since I left America for I am not without sympathy," she wrote candidly of her new circumstances. "Mr. Longfellow is not associated with me in any of my pursuits nor do I participate in any of his. Therefore we do not contribute at all to the happiness of each other and my situation would be the same if he were not here." Henry felt it fortunate, too, to have met the man who a decade earlier had praised several of his poems without having the foggiest notion at the time of who he was. "Called on Bryant, who seemed well pleased enough to see a countryman," Henry wrote tentatively of their introduction. "He was pleasant and talkative, though he has little animation. He has a good face—calm and thoughtful—with a mild, light-blue eye, that is very expressive." An afternoon walk a few days later up to the ruins occasioned this further assessment: "I like him exceedingly."

George Ticknor had learned the "dreadful news" of Mary's death while he also was traveling in Germany, still grieving the loss of his five-year-old son. Henry informed Ticknor by letter a week after he arrived in Heidelberg that Mary "expired with perfect calmness and resignation," adding that "the feebleness of my wife's health" had precluded any thoughts of spending the winter in Berlin as originally planned. Responding immediately from Dresden on Christmas Day to "Monsieur le Professeur Longfellow," Ticknor urged his young colleague to "pray give yourself to constant and interesting intellectual labor," a form of inner healing, he stressed, "that will go further than any other remedy, at least such is my experience."

Of the twenty-four surviving letters Henry received from Ticknor between 1830 and 1868, five were written during this critical period, each of them newsy, informed, and laden with moral support for the talented young man he had anointed to succeed him at Harvard. When they became Boston-Cambridge neighbors who saw each other often, Ticknor's letters, with a few notable exceptions, were rarely more than perfunctory thank-you notes or formal invitations to dinner, the latter typically to start at five-thirty or six on a Friday or Saturday evening. These lengthy missives came when Henry's spirits were fragile, and fortified his dedication to what he would call "life's endless toil and endeavor" in the 1845 poem "The Day Is Done." Even at these lowest of times, he tried to remain focused, unlike his time on the Continent a decade earlier, which one critic of the travelogue *Outre-Mer* would call "a journey of sentiment, if not a sentimental journey, made in the blithesome spirit of a troubadour." His wife Mary had described a routine in which she and her companions kept themselves busy while her husband was absorbed in learning new languages. "Henry has become quite learned in the Swedish, and can already translate the Danish," she informed her father-in-law from Copenhagen, a considerable achievement in that they were only there for thirteen days before moving on to Holland. "He is studying Icelandic also, as I presume he has told you."

Henry's journal reflects similar satisfaction with his progress, evident in his summary of a session with Professor Mellin in which they took up the study of Finnish. "We compared it this morning with the English and the Swedish, taking three lines of each." The Finnish—and he provided a few examples—"seems to have as many vowels as consonants.

Double consonants seldom occur. The diphthongs are very numerous. This language has no resemblance to the Russian nor to the Swedish, nor to the Lappish language which are spoken all around it. It is a sister of the Hungarian." Danish, he wrote elsewhere, had "an unpleasant sound in my ear. For softness and beauty it cannot be compared with the beautiful Swedish."

Just as impressive is the extent of his reading in these languages, much of it also logged in his journal, together with a lengthy section of commentary he called "literary criticism." Even the three weeks Mary was bedridden in Amsterdam did not deter him. Once medical assistance was arranged and a nurse hired to attend her needs, Henry took lessons in Dutch, which he very quickly mastered. He also finished reading Esaias Tegnér's Swedish translation of *Frithiof's Saga,* and absorbed himself in the Low German epic *Reynke de Vos,* which he called a book that "keeps me late from my bed." Toward the end of January, William Cullen Bryant received word from the United States that his partner at the *Evening Post* was seriously ill, requiring him to return home earlier than expected, though his wife and daughters would stay on through the summer. This was disappointing news for Henry, but a relief in that Clara, at least, would continue to have people around for company.

This was a matter of no small concern, as Henry was still acting as her chaperone, with a responsibility to ensure her continued well-being. Clara, for one, was not at all excited about the prospect of going home, either, a suggestion she found "rather unkind and unnatural, considering the season and the unpleasant circumstances which have ever surrounded me the whole time so far that I have been here. Even the Rhine, which is the only part of Europe that I have seen yet that was worth seeing, we saw at an unfavorable season in December!" The very idea that she return to America in the dead of winter—"and then to be set down in the strange city of New York by myself with no friend in the world ready to hasten to me and welcome me and take me home"—left her "bitterly" bemoaning "the utter desolation of my situation." Not stated, but as Henry's account book documents—to the penny and in local currencies—was that Clara paid her own way on this trip, and had a voice, however cowed it may have been, in the conversation.

So for the short run they would all remain in Heidelberg, at least through the winter. By the time February rolled around, Henry was working on an ambitious endeavor that he described in a letter to Greene as a literary history of the Middle Ages, a speculative project that was commanding a great deal of his attention. "I have a blank book which I divide into centuries. Under each century I write down the names of the authors who then flourished, when they wrote, where their work, or extracts from them, may be found, and what editions are best. This is done in as few words as possible, prose and poetry being separated." He explained how the structure he had formulated "saves the process of writing and rewriting as you go along," with the result that he had "already accumulated six centuries of German literature."

Although this material was never published—written in a very neat and legible form, it is preserved as a bound manuscript among the Longfellow literary archives at Harvard—it nonetheless kept him occupied. His book acquisitions for the courses he would be teaching at Harvard flourished as well—the two-thousand-dollar stipend he had been given for this purpose was being spent productively. At one point Henry expressed concern to Ticknor that he had heard nothing about a shipment he sent to Cambridge several months earlier, anxious for some validation of the judgment he was showing in his choice of titles and hopeful of securing more funds for additional materials.

"I am sorry you feel disappointed at hearing nothing about your purchase of books for the college," Ticknor replied, "but, if you were as much used to the management of things there as I am, you would not even be surprised. The truth is, the sum that was given to you was considered as given to your discretion entirely; and nobody will undertake to pronounce a judgement upon the result of your purchases. Indeed, who knows whether you have chosen well in Swedish, Danish, in Dutch, but yourself, or who else knows whether it be worthwhile to have Schiller or not? But of one thing, you may, I think, be sure;—I mean a kind reception when you get home and a confiding trust that what you shall do, will be right."

As a diversion, Henry had begun to write an article on the origin of the modern drama, though his heart was not entirely in it. "The part relevant to the German Drama I shall write now, the remainder after I return home," though the essay was never completed and submitted for publication. Two days after he finished compiling his notes for the project—and a day after he "nearly froze myself to death in the University Library" reading classic German texts—his resolve began to weaken. "The winter," he groused, "has no end. I cannot go out into the fields and woods—but am shut up within these four walls—till I am ready to die of sadness." But his greatest need was for companionship. "Now that I most need a friend—and am lonely and distressed, and look around in vain for consolation—alas! No one who can be with me by day and by night and keep my thoughts from preying upon themselves."

A few weeks later, almost miraculously, just such an individual appeared in the person of one Samuel Ward Jr., a cousin of George Washington Greene's who for the previous two years had been enjoying the good life in Europe as an itinerant scholar and well-connected man of many interests, establishing a friendship that would thrive for the next half century. Seven years younger than Henry, Ward was the son of a wealthy Manhattan banker who had indulged his happy-go-lucky son's insistent desire to study abroad before joining the family investment firm, Prime, Ward & King. Henry recorded having met Ward on March 6 while attending a dinner party in honor of Mrs. Bryant, returning with him afterwards to his hotel, where they talked until four o'clock in the morning. There was a style and swagger to Ward that appealed to Henry. Impeccably dressed, cultivated, at ease in every social setting, the New Yorker's easy brashness and winning charm had a palliative effect on the otherwise straitlaced New Englander.

"He knows many of my Cambridge friends," Henry enthused. "Topics of conversation were not wanting. Ward seems to have many fine qualities—quickness and acuteness of intellect and a generous open-hearted disposition." They continued their "desultory tatter of men and things" over dinner the next day, with Ward sharing stories of his recent meetings in Dresden with Professor Ticknor, yet another mutual acquaintance. Ward struck Henry as a person who tries "to impose upon strangers a high idea of his own scholarship and talents," judging him also to be a "great talker," albeit one who is "himself too often the subject of his own discourse."

Their friendship was marked by a correspondence that Andrew Hilen calculated at more than three hundred and fifty exchanges. Ward's younger sister Julia, best known today as the author of "The Battle Hymn of the Republic," would become a close friend as well, thought even by people who knew both to be a worthy match for Henry during his years as a brooding widower, most vocally Harvard colleague Cornelius Conway Felton, who called her "the most remarkable person I ever knew." Julia married another Longfellow acquaintance, Samuel Gridley Howe, yet remained a lifelong friend, giving Henry the affectionate nickname "Longo," by which she and other members of the Ward and Howe families often addressed him.

Two months after Henry's death in 1882, Sam Ward wrote an appreciative essay of their friendship, recalling how pleased he had been to meet the poet in Heidelberg, having heard so much about him from his cousin. "Longfellow had led a secluded life since the death of his young wife, in Holland," he wrote. "My budget of rattling talk was, therefore, a cheering and interesting peep into the social world from which his mourning had so long excluded him; and I also had glimpses to unfold of literary men and the artists and scientists of Paris, where I had spent two winters and a summer. The day following I visited him at his rooms, which were strewn with books, in a house in the main street embracing a view of the castle."

Their conversations covered a full gamut of interests. "We had discussed German poetry and philosophy," Ward wrote, noting with special pleasure how Henry's "eyes sparkled" when he described his visit to the cemetery in Weimar where Goethe and Schiller lie side by side in a mausoleum. Ward corroborated Henry's account of the marathon get-together in his hotel—and that he did pretty much all of the talking—adding how "never a word" of Henry's creative aspirations had "passed his lips." It was only when he read "The Psalm of Life" in *The Knicker-bocker* two years later "that I realized how I had entertained an angel unawares." Ward treasured his memory of that first meeting. "With me it was a case of a love at first sight, which has burned with the steady light of a Jewish tabernacle ever since."

The forming of a new friendship—in that time and in that place—buoyed Henry's sprits, if only momentarily, but once Ward had left Heidelberg—and Henry accompanied him on horseback to make his stagecoach connection in a nearby town—he was alone once again with his grief. Clara wrote one night after Henry had helped her with her lessons how he confessed to taking "no interest in anything and that all his energy is gone." There was a brief respite in early April when they were joined by Mrs. Bryant, Julie Hepp, and a fellow boarder in the house of Frau Himmelhahn, a young Russian nobleman named Baron Jacques von Ramm—the model for the Baron in *Hyperion*—on a five-day excursion to Frankfurt.

An interesting side note to that trip was the purchase in Frankfurt of a plaster cast statuette of Goethe, which Henry used in *Hyperion* as the focal point of a conversation between Paul Flemming and the Baron, whom he described in the romance as "a miscellaneous youth, rather a universal genius," who "pursued all things with eagerness, but for a short time only"—a friendly description, perhaps, of his newly acquired real-life friend, Sam Ward. After visiting Goethe's birthplace, Flemming and the Baron pause outside the window of a downtown shop, taking note of the statuette inside, all the while discussing the recently deceased writer's many virtues and flaws. "It is strange how soon, when a great man dies, his place is filled; and so completely, that he seems no longer wanted," Flemming muses distantly, sounding a familiar Longfellow concern—the ephemeral nature of critical acclaim and celebrity. "But let us step in here," he says next. "I wish to buy that cast."

The first illustrated edition of *Hyperion* appeared in 1853 with one hundred wood engravings by the British artist Myles Birket Foster, who in an artist's note emphasized his commitment to achieving a "perfectly faithful representation" of everything he drew for the book, traveling, by his reckoning, "between two and three thousand miles" in pursuit of that goal. That Paul Flemming's plaster cast and Henry's plaster cast are one and the same is strikingly evident by comparing Foster's drawing with the actual object that stands atop Henry's Craigie House writing desk, positioned directly in front of him every time he stood to write, there for inspiration or nostalgia, or merely decoration—who can say? In all likelihood, it was a mix of all three.

Once he returned to Heidelberg, Henry's spirits floundered once again. "The clock is just striking three in the morning," he wrote on Saturday, June 4. "I have not closed my eyes all night; and have at length got up in despair of sleep, and having lighted two wax candles, am patiently waiting for day which just begins to dawn. The birds are singing—and even and anon the cock crows." A few days later, Henry and Clara set off on a somewhat longer trip down the Rhine to Koblenz, returning overland through Bad Ems, Bad Schwalbach, Wiesbaden, Frankfurt, and Schlangenbad, taking in the natural baths at various stops along the way. They were accompanied this time by Mrs. Bryant and her older daughter, Fanny Bryant. "At table," Clara wrote of one dinner they shared together on the road, "a gentleman began to talk with Mr. Longfellow and praised his German, as all foreigners do when we speak." For Clara, the brief journey had delivered a satisfying taste of what she had been hoping for all along. "It is certainly the most beautiful country I have ever seen," she wrote when they returned. "We had delightful weather all the time and I can truly say it is the pleasantest journey I ever made. Now if we can accomplish the journey to Munich and Switzerland I shall be quite happy."

But that trip—the one they had been talking about from the very beginning of their European adventure—would prove to be the most elusive of them all. Part of Henry's plan—and Clara very definitely figured into it—was to include a side trip to Milan and a reunion there with George Washington Greene, who had married an Italian woman, Maria Carlotta Sforzosi and was living in Florence. "I have a proposition to make," Henry wrote Greene on June 5, explaining that he was on "the eve" of leaving in a few weeks for Munich, hoping to travel from there across the Alps into Italy. "Now," he asked, "will you and Maria meet us in Milan, and travel in Switzerland with us? I say *us,* because Miss Crowninshield goes with me."

Henry had informed Ticknor a few weeks earlier that Clara would be accompanying him to Munich, the single condition being then "if we can find suitable companions," a matter of no small delicacy in these prudent years of what was about to become known as the Victorian age. Appearances—the "optics," as we might say today, of a single woman of twenty-three traveling alone abroad with a twenty-eight-year-old widower—was a matter of no small concern for the prim-and-proper Henry. A letter he wrote to Sam Ward at this time goes a long way to understanding the sense of propriety he always applied to personal matters. Ward had sent Henry a piece of short fiction he had written, seeking some feedback. "I think you must be crazy," Henry replied. "The phantoms of your brain are beautiful, but they are not holy, and in the silence of the night they visit ladies' chambers. There is a wild beauty in your episode of the Creole girl, but I must tell you as I have told you before: these matters belong to the great volume of unwritten sensations which ought to remain unwritten. Let me speak candidly. Your imagination needs baptism in cool pure water."

Henry and Clara returned from their eight-day trip with the Bryant women on June 19. "So once more in Heidelberg," he wrote in his journal the next day, languor again evident in his tone. Four letters that had arrived in his absence were waiting, including personal ones from Greene, Sam Ward, and George Ticknor, but the pleasure of their words was fleeting. "Torpor steals over me again," he decided, "and the monotonous every day life begins anew. My mind has lost its sensibility and does not feel the spirit. I cannot study: and therefore think I better go home." In the next sentence, he cast that thought aside with yet another idea. "Perhaps the air of the Fatherland will do me good."

Four days later, he chose the second option. "The day is bright and warm and I feel within me a strong desire to start on a journey." Mrs. Bryant had decided that she did not want to spend too much time away from her daughters, and declined to go along. A provisional commitment from Baron von Ramm, the Russian nobleman who had come along on the earlier excursion to Frankfurt, to join Henry and Clara with his sisters on this trip, did not pan out, either. "I think," Henry wrote finally, "I shall leave Clara here with Mrs. Bryant and start for Nuremberg and Munich." Once the decision was made, he wasted no time. "It is now nearly midnight and I start tomorrow morning at five for Stuttgart on my way to Munich." Clara recorded nothing of the change in plans, but it had to have been devastating to be left behind.

Sam Longfellow made no direct mention of Clara in the reverential biography he wrote of his brother, and her name was carefully excised from the excerpts that he used from Henry's journals and letters. He gave her two cameo mentions of no importance, in each case changing her identity from "Clara" to "C," with no context or explanation of who that might be, or even the gender. In the paragraph where Henry and Clara travel together from Amsterdam to Heidelberg—the one leg of their eighteen months abroad where they were not in company with someone else—Sam made fleeting reference simply to a "companion," who could have been anyone.

A few Longfellow scholars have wondered over the years if there was ever any intimacy between these two, the question fair enough given the time they were together in such close quarters, but the answer is always inconclusive. Fueling such speculation is a letter Clara wrote Henry in March 1837—a year after they had returned to the United States—that suggests a disagreement they may have had—over what, exactly, is lost in the mists of time. Written in German—a confident expression, it is fair to say, of what she had mastered while abroad—it was translated into English by Andrew Hilen in his 1956 edition of Clara's diary. "You always say that you are misunderstood, but I say you have misunderstood me," she wrote. "I make only one reproach to you, and you are not to blame for it either, only your disposition. You lack constancy." A few puzzling sentences later, there is this: "This indifference of yours will not cause me any *eternal* sorrow. But whenever I see you or write to you I must think of it and feel it too. Otherwise I have had no complaints. That I am right about this you will have to admit."

Nobody spent more time studying these materials than Hilen—close to half a century—and he admitted having no clue what Clara might have been alluding to in that letter. "What this paragraph means," he concluded, "written as it was in a moment of confidence, must unfortunately remain a matter for speculation." Only a few other letters between the two are extant, from which Hilen postulated only that their friendship had probably "progressed toward intimacy as well as informality," and in the absence of any corroborative evidence, quite correctly, in my view, left it there. In March 1838—a year after receiving that enigmatic letter—Henry paid a visit to Clara in Salem, arriving at six in the evening. "Went to find my good, gentle Clara; and took a long walk with her. She is a remarkable child;—and has most admirable traits of character: and an abundance of talent. Only too mean an opinion of herself."

Whatever the nature of their relationship, had Clara accompanied Henry on his journey to Switzerland, as both intended up to the last minute, the arc of this narrative would be following another trajectory entirely. As circumstances played out, Henry made his way alone to

Ownership signature in Longfellow's travel journal for 1835,
in Houghton Library

Munich and then to Innsbruck in Austria, where he arranged to travel
across the Alps to Milan, still hoping to meet up with Greene. Sam
Longfellow's explanation for what happened there is as good as any,
understated as it may be. "But a trifle," he wrote, "may often change
one's plans, and sometimes with important results." The trifle, in this
instance, was an irregularity with Henry's documents—he later called it
"some informality in my passport." Whatever it was, the border police
did not issue him a visa to enter Italy, requiring a change in plans that
diverted him to the lakes region of Switzerland.

The tenor of Henry's journal during these solitary weeks on the road
reflects a growing sense of literary awareness—a feeling that he was doing
something measurably more than recording each day's events. Key-word
titles appear at the top of each page, and where there is dialogue, it is
arranged to support the ongoing narrative. The overall structure follows
a coherent theme, with majestic surroundings providing a balm to bouts
of melancholy and soul searching. That so much of this material would
be repurposed in a quasi-fictional work should come as no surprise—
Henry had told his father he coveted eminence in a "literary way" above
everything else, and the sobering experiences of these recent months had
only fortified that aspiration.

As a written document, the journal for this period is clean throughout. The inclusive dates are May 21, 1835, to July 17, 1836, beginning on arrival in England and ending on the eve of departure for Switzerland. Pressed between the two front pages are a pair of green leaves, with no notation of where they are from, though on the next page is an excerpt from the medieval ballad *Reynard the Foxe*, with a phrase that evokes a scene among "trees clad with levys and blossoms, and the ground with herbes and flowers sweete smelling." Above that is a note, written in pencil: "A private journal, not to be printed in whole or part, on any consideration," clear-cut evidence of an authorial sensibility at work, and an awareness of its possible interest down the road to scholars. Henry had thrown himself into the study of languages and foreign literatures on this trip—the Scandinavian tongues he learned were add-ons he had pursued on his own—and he would commit himself to teaching them when he took up his post at Harvard in the fall. But at this critical juncture in his life, he was simply moving on. And in the summer of 1836, all roads led to Interlaken.

6

Bellissima Italia

I sat down upon the upper range, over which the horizon barely peeps, and imagined myself a Roman dame, whose upturned thumb could give forth the fiat of mercy to a suffering gladiator in the arena below. How many murders must these worthy nations have had upon their consciences, and with what coolness must they have regarded death, when they suffered life to hang upon the turning of a finger. Rather different "stuff" from modern dames, who shudder at a *coup de pistolet* in a mock Tragedy.

— Fanny Appleton's journal, recording a visit to the Arena of Nîmes, February 2, 1836

$\mathcal{F}$anny Appleton began the second volume of her European travel journal on February 1, 1836, in the South of France, having just paid her respects in Vaucluse to Francesco Petrarca, the fourteenth-century humanist poet commonly known as Petrarch. Visiting the remote village where the quintessential sonneteer lived periodically for fifteen contented years—and where he first laid eyes on Laura, the unattainable love of his life—she plucked a leaf from an ancient laurel tree in a "pretty little garden" said to have been planted there by the poet "as a shrine to receive his sighs and tears." Fanny affixed it to the first page of the journal, housed in a bright red leather binding, and remarkably well preserved to this day.

Vaucluse was a side trip well off the beaten path, made "thro' a road cut in the rock by the Romans," their goal "to enjoy a puff of the sentimental." They found the site "shut in a lovely little valley" crossed by the Sorgue River, home to the largest natural spring in France, "a stream exquisite enough to flow in Fairy-land," leading Fanny to speculate how often "the Magician whose enchanted wand made the rocks speak, and the woods bow low their mighty tops," had wandered there, absorbing "inspiration from its crystal eddies." The travelers stayed for two hours, "delightfully sketching and scrambling about," and enjoyed a basket lunch of cold chicken and Burgundy wine. In a letter to Robert Apthorp posted a few days later, Fanny would call Vaucluse "a little Eden," a place to remember forever.

Returning to Avignon, they next visited the gravesite of Laura de Noves, the presumed object of Petrarch's idealized obsession in the *Canzoniere* sequence of sonnets, where Fanny cut a sprig of juniper and pressed it, too, inside her album. From there, the group headed for Italy, pausing at points of interest along the way, notably in Nîmes, home to a Roman amphitheater where Fanny sat in the top row, fancying herself a "Roman dame" from antiquity passing judgment on gladiators battling for their lives in the arena below. Her thoughts—quoted above—shed some insight into her evolving sense of what it meant to be an independent woman in the early decades of the nineteenth century, and on her growing embracement of pacifism.

Viewing the Mediterranean for the first time, she beheld a sparkling sea of deep blue, the tint "so rich and heavenly that the sky looked pale beside it." One panoramic outlook reminded her of scenes painted by the French landscape artist Claude-Joseph Vernet. Arriving in Marseilles, she declared the busy port city to be "a forest of masts." The ride to Toulon traveled along sheer mountain roads that twisted "as if lightning had zigzagged itself a path thro' the solid rock." Abruptly, they came upon "gardens of orange trees," their "golden apples" glittering beneath dark green leaves. "It was like Aladdin's descent, through the vault, into the magic garden, where the trees were precious stones." Cannes and Antibes on the Côte d'Azur followed, with time allowed for a brief stop near the border for a scene that seemed "made to sketch."

Bidding adieu at last to *"la belle France,"* the entourage crossed the Val River into Italy—*"Bellissima Italia,"* Fanny proclaimed boldly in her

First page of Fanny's Italian journal, with cutting from Petrarch laurel tree

journal—and proceeded by way of Nice and San Remo on to Genoa. She deemed the city *"superba"* both in her journal and to Emmeline Austin, judging it an enchanted place where "marble and velvet seem to hang upon the air" in profusion. Checking into a restored palazzo on the quay with her family, Fanny was inspired sufficiently by "a setting sun streaming in thro' high and open windows on curtains and frescos" to imagine herself "a high-born maiden" gazing into mirrors thirty feet high, able on a whim to lean over marble balustrades and listen to fountains gushing below, inhale the enticing aroma of "orange-laden" breezes, "and have perchance—a Romeo!" This was not entirely a momentary fancy, as Fanny elaborated in a letter to a female friend in Boston, using an archaic noun as a euphemism to describe appealing young men: "You express great desire to hear about the agreeables I may come across—as we go now so little in society I have no chance to fall in with heroes—but when I do assuredly will I send a sketch for your divertissement. But a young lady is treated here as a nonentity (or a speculation) so I am afraid I shall captivate no Romeos this side the water."

A local attraction she judged of special notice was the Cathedral of San Lorenzo, empty when the Appletons visited, allowing for an unhurried examination. "It is of most singular architecture, looking more Gothic than Grecian, and more Saracenic than either;—is striped throughout in the same Zebra fashion as the exterior. There is a beautiful altar with angels by one of Canova's pupils, a curious group in bronze by John of Bologna wonderfully buoyant; and a magnificent chapel to John the Baptist into which females are not allowed to enter because one of the race caused his death!" The men were permitted to go inside, leaving the sisters outside as they waited. "While the gents explored it, Mary and I leaned on the marble balustrade and talked with a handsome young priest." A visit to Pisa entertained the young traveler not so much for the Leaning Tower, which "looked like an old friend" from her reading, but for the colorful gendarmerie that was out in force. "There are a great many soldiers about the streets, and I like this genteel-looking uniform of the Sardinian troops much better than the red pants and the shapeless great-coat of the French. These are very fine looking men and the officers' dark blue dress and scarlet-bordered coats are very becoming. We have not seen all the Palaces but have chosen the best. I feel sorry to part with Genoa."

Entering the town of Spezia, they encountered a "procession of beautiful peasant girls" who had just come "laughing along from church, quite like 'a scene on the stage.'" Fanny described their "costume du pays"—a distinctive regional attire of black velvet and scarlet bodices accented by "gay ribbons, and flowers in their hair"—while observing their complexions to be clear and fresh, their eyes blue, not uncommon physical characteristics for northern Italy. Each girl was wearing a "droll little straw hat" that covered "only the top of the head but looks picturesque." She drew a sketch in the margin of her journal depicting just such a girl. Later that day, an expansive view at sunset of the Gulf of Spezia led Fanny to consider the sad end of Percy Bysshe Shelley, who thirteen years earlier had "met his fate in this very bay which looks so treacherously placid," giving her pause to reflect: "How this atmosphere is like his poetry! he imbibed the very tinge which makes the mountains so purple, the skies so pearly, the water so blue;—the hues of a sea-shell, the countries of our dreams."

Resuming their journey the following morning, the entourage made yet another side trip, this one for barely an hour to Carrara, legendary since Roman times for the flawless white marble quarried from its nearby hills, and favored across the centuries by countless builders and sculptors, foremost among them the Florentine maestro Michelangelo Buonarroti, whose *David, Pietà,* and *Moses* endure as singular examples of his oeuvre in stone. Fanny was diverted by the "chisels and hammers resounding in every street," the relentless din being produced by teams of industrious artisans who "breathed life" into the "snowy blocks" brought down to them from the hills. A "most loquacious" guide took them to half a dozen workshops where "mountains of inexhaustible treasures"—clever copies, mostly, of timeless masterpieces originally meant to "enchant the world"—were everywhere available for purchase. "The dazzling whiteness of this marble is unequalled," she declared, adding wryly upon departure that "more gods and goddesses" were likely to have been carved into existence at Carrara "than old Jupiter ever reckoned in his Court."

Their unhurried travels continued through the end of the month, bringing them ever southward. "Can I believe that tonight I shall be in the Eternal City? My mind cannot grasp the bare idea," Fanny wrote on March 1, on the outskirts of Rome. At Baccano, they left their coaches and "ascended" a hill that gave them a commanding view of the Apennines on one side, a sprawling river valley crossed by the Tiber on another, with the cupola of St. Peter's barely visible on the distant horizon. "I thanked God in my heart that I had lived for this," Fanny wrote, deeply moved by the majestic prospect that lay before her, feeling that "we can now die in peace—it is the only earthly goal, which man truly yearns to accomplish here—below."

Once arrived in Rome, the Appletons took up quarters in the Piazza di Spagna at the bottom of the Spanish Steps, site of the Fontana della Barcaccia, sculpted at the beginning of the Baroque period by Pietro Bernini. Nearby, at 26 Piazza di Spagna, is the house where John Keats spent the final three months of his life, dying of tuberculosis at the age of twenty-five in 1821, and the site today of the Keats-Shelley Museum. Waiting for them when they checked in was a passel of letters from the United States, including one for Fanny from Catharine Maria Sedgwick. "What rapture!" Fanny exclaimed, "after starving so long for news" from home, to be so treated. Everything that she had seen on her trip thus far, however stimulating, "could give us nothing," she declared joyfully, compared to "a kind word from Aunt Kitty!"

Resting up for a day, the group embarked on a whirlwind of cultural immersion, Fanny and Mary ticking one "lion" after another off their list of must sights to see. "Hardly knew what to do or where to go first," Fanny wrote on March 3. "Was afraid we should stumble upon the Colosseum which I am determined to see first by moonlight." Saving that special treat for another time, they busied themselves with excursions to the Pantheon, the Circus Maximus, and the Pontifical Palace, each one taking history and tradition into account. "I am unworthy of Rome and feel ashamed to come so unprepared on all its wonders," she confessed, feeling a bit overwhelmed. A walk "by the light of a tallow candle" through the "grim passages" and "ghostly-looking cavities" of the Catacombs led Fanny to cite the first-century historian Valerius, who wrote how early Christians sought refuge from persecution in these underground tunnels. "This was enough for one morning," she decided, "and the rush of new ideas was quite bewildering—but here one's mind has to live fast."

Sketch of the Colosseum in Rome, viewed from the Palace of the Caesars, dated March 11, 1836, in Fanny Appleton's sketchbook

The next day the group accepted an invitation from a fellow traveler, a Mrs. Sidney Brooks, to join her on an evening visit she had organized to see the Colosseum by the light of a full moon—exactly what Fanny had been wanting, though her ardor cooled when she learned that three carriages filled with boisterous tourists were to be their companions. "I saw it would be absurd to muster up any sentiment or romance on the occasion with such a cortege and resigned myself to a commonplace 'lion' hunting!" Still, the trot by the Forum and the triumphal arches was pleasant enough, the moonlight creating a "vision of mighty spectres" that "seemed the wreck of a world: temples and noble columns and shattered pediments all scattered about every spot hallowed by recollections; and the whole ground one sepulchre of fragile glory. How sad is this wandering amongst the tombs."

Once inside the Colosseum, Fanny's early anxiety proved well founded, the rude, boorish, obtuse behavior of the others giving her "no chance to give way to the awe which that vast desolation breathes upon me." There were about fifty people wandering through the ancient landmark that night, many of them Americans, she was embarrassed to point out, all of them, it seemed, "laughing and chattering thro' the galleries" and making crude jokes as they plodded along, showing little respect for where they were. "To me it was desecration," she fumed. "I did not undertake to feel where I was, or to enjoy anything I saw. I was all wearied and disgusted and what might have been an inexhaustible delight became a heavy nightmare." She "never passed a more wretched hour" in her life, an especially egregious circumstance given the majesty of what she did manage to take in. "I can never forget glimpses of wild beauty as the torches flashed along the huge arches—like the glare of fiends beside the pale, celestial flooding of the clear moonlight."

Fanny did not leave the matter there, continuing with a fulmination that went on for several pages of her journal, forcing us to remind ourselves that she was eighteen years old at the time, and still feeling her way into an adult world, though instructive for what it suggests of her uncompromising passion for timeless works of art, and equally revealing of her character. At one point she asked a few rhetorical questions: "What is there creditable in insulting and mocking the most solemn sermon ever preached to men? Why are people ashamed of feeling strongly and deeply?" Summing up—and speaking strictly for herself—she gave thanks to the Almighty that "I can peep thro' the clay at times," expressing "gratitude that I am endowed with the 'folly of feeling.' "

It is at this point, too, that Fanny's journal increases in tempo, particularly as it involves the masterworks she discusses critically, and with remarkable acumen. In the Palazzo Barberini, she declared "a small collection of pictures in one room" to be "all I coveted" in the world, foremost among them the *Beatrice Cenci* by Guido Reni, a portrait "so lovely, so gently paled suffering but such a deep, deep sorrow in the parted lips and long last gaze of the sweet eyes." Examining the painting up close—it had already inspired a five-act play by Shelley and would be used to great effect by Nathaniel Hawthorne in *The Marble Faun* and Herman Melville in *Pierre*—Fanny dismissed copies she had seen as "too plain," and lacking the glow "which just tinges the cheek with red and relieves the simple white drapery with the rich gleam of golden hair escaping from the fatal turban. It is like the last strain of sad delicious music—those eyes—so imploring—haunt me."

Of Guido's *Aurora*, she saw "more poetry" in the large ceiling fresco he painted in 1614 "than almost any picture I know," finding the "majestic tread along the clouds" all "so lovely and different—the noble dappled steeds—Apollo and the magnificent Aurora so buoyantly borne along by the triumphant airs—the blue of the Sea—so full of poetry and so truly the Mediterranean! Oh! How fine it is." The Galleria Borghese revealed more wonders, Domenichino's *Diana and Her Nymphs*, Titian's *Sacred and Profane Love,* Raphael's *Cesare Borgia.* From there it was off to "the lovely little Temple of Vesta" for an appreciation of Leonardo da Vinci and Caravaggio. "I now know the different masters and find such a deep delight in reading their different tones, and imagining their different characters as their pencil treads firmly or meekly, mildly or gently."

At the Musei Capitolini, Fanny turned her attention to sculpture—a "rush and whirlpool of new objects"—noting "plenty of fine statues" and "interesting busts of all the emperors and philosophers" mingled among "heaps of curious things which I was too wearied to enjoy," yet considered "enervating to mind and body" all the same. Of everything she inspected on this trek to the top of Capitoline Hill, "the *Dying Gladiator* alone stood forth," never to be forgotten. "I like it better than all except it be the *Apollo*, who is, like a god, 'alone.'" She was reminded of Lord Byron's lines in *Childe Harold's Pilgrimage* upon seeing this very statue:

> I see before me the Gladiator lie:
> He leans upon his hand—his manly brow
> Consents to death, but conquers agony,
> And his droop'd head sinks gradually low—

Byron's description, which she excerpted from memory in her journal, "is so wonderfully true and a fair rival to the statue," she declared. "It ought to be written on the pedestal."At the Palace of the Caesars, she passed "a lovely morning most enchanting" enjoying the flowers and the ambiance of ancient relics. "I had not been here before and was fascinated with the picturesqueness of the ruins and the views in every direction." She sat on the terrace and sketched "till I was nearly sun-struck," producing one of the prettiest pictures she would make while in Italy. Another strenuous day of sketching antiquities at the Villa Albani occasioned a similar expression of unity with nature. "There was something indescribably melancholy in the atmosphere of today and peculiar to Italy": the blue of the sky was "unshadowed by a cloud," the nearby hills "exquisitely purpled with the faint haze which seldom deserts them, and no June day was milder, balmier, more delicious," but there was "languor on every living thing," she felt "a dead silence as if the whole world was falling into a fatal lethargy."

Mortality was on Fanny's mind yet again when she paused at the grave of John Keats in the Protestant Cemetery, a "lovely spot" that recalled for her a famous line from *Adonais,* Shelley's elegy for his friend: "It might make one in love with death, to think that one should be buried in so sweet a place." She then sought out the site, a few hundred yards away, where Shelley's ashes had been deposited, but was unable to find it. A ritual Fanny witnessed of a young "damsel" about to "take the veil" and become a nun left her taken by the novice's "thrilling intensity of expression," and the quiet fervor for a life of self-denial and piety she embodied, "her cheeks flushed, her lips murmuring praise, and her sweet profile beautifully shaded by her black, heavy drapery." Fanny admitted, even, to wishing she could somehow "have had her feelings"—but only, she added quickly, "for one half an hour."

Two weeks into her Roman interlude, Fanny visited the Vatican Library, which she would see several times before leaving the city. During her first walk through the galleries—this, also, was an evening tour by torchlight, but with a smaller, far more agreeable group of well-mannered people—she found the artworks about her so absorbing she wished she could "sit, and study, and dream myself into them!" Returning the next day, she marveled at how the torches casting light on "a long row of snowy silent statues" created "a most curious and ghostly effect." In the darkness, "they looked like an army" of apparitions, reminding her of a scene in the Giacomo Meyerbeer opera *Robert le Diable,* which she had seen in Paris, "where the tombs yield their dead."

The days were so busy that Fanny found little time to keep up with her correspondence, taking a break finally on March 22 to write a long letter to Emmeline Austin in Boston. "Sweetest Emmelina," she began, with a cheery Italian lilt, "I have not forgotten my promise to send thee a line from the Eternal City and to think that three weeks have been bounded along and I have found no chance I might by some wondrous luck." A rare opportunity of finding herself at last "solus" for an evening had been "just now threatened with a stupid invitation from two American youths who bolted into our apartment, sans announcement, to be introduced without our consent being demanded by one of our fellow passengers, another gauche Yankee, all the polish he ought to have gained on his travels being concentrated into the *growing* of a terrific pair of moustaches." That impertinence dispensed with—and Fanny Appleton was not one to suffer fools gladly—she brought Emmeline up to date on what she was doing. "These few weeks have been one whirl of delight. I can see nothing behind me but a chaos where churches, palaces, ruins, statues, pictures, obelisks and fountains are crowding upon each other in mad confusion." Pandemonium aside, she allowed it to be "a glorious thing to have such a world in your control—to say today we will stroll in the Forum or the Vatican or St. Peters; to have a dozen galleries enticing you with Raphaels, Titians," and other iconic masterpieces, "and study innumerable while I want to buy everything."

The two clueless American suitors were not an aberration. "There are about a dozen youths fresh from counting-houses and Yankee notions prowling about who claim the privileges of pouring in on us at all times of the day," she reported. "We have many nice parties together: we went one night to see the Vatican by Torchlight and an Italian acquaintance, a Mr. Visconti, a famous antiquarian, spouted forth before every statue." Of the many "Adonises" casting about for her attention, Fanny had nice things to say about "Mr. Jones," a "genteelish well-looking youth" from New York "with whom I sometimes flirt when I have nothing else to do." Now a full four months into the trip, she had a bit of perspective to share. "The mind has to live so fast and imbibe such a world of reminiscence and reality," she opined, noting the greatest difficulty was in trying to overcome the "sentimentality" that develops with such sensory overload, and to see things with clear vision. "I find I look daily with much less awe on the broken columns and brick vaults and can now feel little but the *picturesqueness* of the ruins."

Holy Week followed with a rush of formal events, including a packed Easter Mass in St. Peter's Basilica officiated by the pope, which Fanny thought "impressive" for its theatricality. Their time in Rome coming to an end, they began to pack and prepare to move on. For Fanny, the process involved visiting a few favorite places one last time—the Colosseum, St. Peter's, the Vatican Library, another viewing of the *Beatrice Cenci* painting in particular—and taking in a few other highlights she had missed. It had rained steadily during these final days, the sun finally emerging on their morning of departure, the "graceful aqueducts" the "last to bid us adieu" on the road to Albano. "Many a Niobe glance did I cast back as we galloped over the Campagna," she wrote, her reference to a tragic figure from Greek mythology forced to weep for eternity over the horrifying loss of her children. "If I leave Rome, Rome leaves not me; no longer are these names of ruins and pictures blank words, which I have ever echoed with longing, from a vague instinct, they are breathing truths never to desert me and whatever snug corner of the Earth receives me I will yet walk about old Rome, 'ay and smell it too!'"

But there was also the looming prospect of so much more of Italy yet to savor. In Terracina, Fanny sat on the rocks overlooking the Tyrrhenian Sea, a stretch of magnificent coastline known as Odysseus's Riviera for its presumed place in the *Odyssey* as home to the beguiling siren Circe. Fanny compared the waves "dashing" ashore to the rocky coastline of Nahant, an exclusive seaside community near Boston popular as a summer retreat among Beacon Hill royalty and Harvard notables throughout the nineteenth century. She sketched a tower on a promontory in the distance and declared the vista so beautifully enticing that "if a Circe" had lived there, "it would not amaze us."

A lovely seaside drawing Fanny made in Naples of the Castel dell'Ovo, seen from the balcony of what we can safely assume is an elegant hotel suite, includes, in the lower right, the figure of a slender young woman with corkscrew ringlets intently studying the landmark before her, sketch pad and pencil at the ready—undoubtedly a self-portrait. While in Naples, a "pilgrimage" to the tomb of the poet Virgil was worked in, along with a look at some papyrus scrolls recovered from the nearby ruins of Pompeii and Herculaneum. "They are black strips seldom larger than one's hand, as thin and fragile as gossamer, hardly a line with every word untorn," she wrote. "It takes six months to unroll one scroll!" At the excavated cities themselves, she was struck by the skillful design of everyday tools and appliances that had been unearthed. "The wall candelabras, lamps, and every variety of kitchen utensil all made in the most exquisite shapes and designs, ever to be imitated, never to be approached. Their poetical imaginations could not breathe ugliness even into a sauce-pan." The snuffing-out of the two cities eighteen hundred years earlier in a volcanic eruption of Mount Vesuvius got her to thinking once again about the uncertainties of life. "The awe of the Past never came so strongly upon me as here, frail matter doomed to revisit the glimpses of the moon, where all that breathed an interest within it had escaped beyond the search of prying modern eyes. Matter can be embalmed but the free soul was not cased in by even the bondage of a million years."

Further south along the coast at Paestum in Magna Graecia, home to three of the best-preserved Greek temples from the sixth century BC to be found anywhere, Fanny had what Shelley might have called an Ozymandias moment. "At a first glance they seem entire and nothing can be more impressive: so solitary and mysterious,—sole relics of a vanished city buried in the long grass; of all ruins the most beautiful and most unsolved," comparable in beauty, she felt, only to the Colosseum in Rome. "The monstrous blocks of stone seem reared by a race of Titans, and the grand, simple, Doric columns, tell of patriarchal days, when the World was untainted by luxury. They look as if they would endure forever—why should they not?"

In Pozzuoli, Fanny sketched the ruins of Cicero's villa and took a floral cutting for her plant album. With their meanderings through southern Italy concluded, they boarded a steamship in Naples for Livorno, where they met up again with Mrs. Brooks, just returning with her husband from Florence. The couple informed Mary and Fanny that the "beaux" of the city were "in the 'tip toe of expectation'" to be making their acquaintance.

"Our situation is delightful, on the Arno, overlooking a gay bridge and picturesque towers," Fanny declared upon arrival in the fabled city of the Medici princes. She noted the surprising absence of fountains, whose "musical murmurings," she thought, "tune aright the jarring discords of a city," but declared Florence nonetheless to be "a labyrinth of splendor!" They went directly to the Palazzo Pitti museum, pausing at one great painting after another, works of Caravaggio, Murillo, Andrea del Sarto, Rubens, which she evaluated individually. "Have I forgotten to put down the finest portrait in the world?" she added, singling out for special mention Raphael's *Giulio II*—Pope Julius II—"which is quite as good as having an interview" with the painter. Titian's haunting *Penitent Magdalene* caused her to wish the subject could "open her mouth and tell how she was painted when the whole world of painters is dying for the secret."

Beginning the third volume of her European journal at this juncture—the first two totaled 102,000 words, this would add another 56,000—Fanny concentrated more intensively on her art commentaries, consulting periodically with her brother Tom, whose formal training in the technicalities exceeded hers and who, for a time, would toy with the idea of becoming a professional artist, though he would spend much of his life buying, appreciating, and donating paintings to museums instead of producing original works himself. That said, he had a connoisseur's eye for things of beauty, and Fanny hungrily benefited from his knowledge. This, like all of Fanny's most satisfying relationships, had at its core a melding of inquisitive minds, a characteristic that would never change. Her journals and letters portray a woman who savored intellectual engagement above all else, and had little patience with banality. After a satisfying day of sightseeing and shopping ("bought gloves of a pretty French woman whose nice accent and smart establishment made me think me in Paris"), she had an evening visit from a Mr. Hare, and "a discussion about pictures" that she deemed "unsatisfactory as usual with those who only see with their eyes." She was far more satisfied, she wrote, by having come across the spot in the Piazza del Duomo where, Dante confessed in *La Vita Nuova,* he had sat for hours on end thinking about the ever-elusive Beatrice; that, at least, she could empathize with.

Upon visiting the Pitti museum the next day, Fanny told of having run into "beaux as usual," and made no attempt to disguise her coolness in the next sequence of sentences. "Dreadfully tired. How differently pictures affect us in wrong moods! The magic lies dead when our soul sleeps." She was more emphatic a few days later after a similar experience at the Uffizi. "Made a short visit to the Gallery—met beaux coming out as usual. They seem to track us by magic."

In yet another encounter, a trio of suitors found Fanny in her rooms

Fanny's sketch of the Castel dell'Ovo from the balcony of her seaside hotel in Naples includes a self-portrait of the young artist, pad and pencil at the ready.

on an evening when she dearly wanted to be alone, the rest of the family having gone off to the opera, leaving her to enjoy "a quiet I always covet, seldom find." She lit four candles and settled in snugly for the night, expressing one silent wish: "I hope to mercy no visitors are coming to disturb my repose." At that point the bell rang, and her French valet announced that three gentlemen had come to pay a visit, her brother Tom having carelessly informed them she was home by herself. Her dispirited response: "*Eh bien!—faites les entrer!*"—Fine—let them in. Not long after that, the young man she had flirted with when otherwise bored—Mr. Jones—came by after having formally bidden farewell, announcing he would be staying on in Florence after all. Fanny mused that "after such a well performed parting" the day before, "it was bad policy to remain," then added how the young suitor had "cut off his moustache from my mischievous hint the other day."

If these entries prove anything, it is that Fanny resented wasting precious time on trite distractions. We can take her at her word, then, when she claims to having had no interest whatsoever in commissioning the renowned Florentine sculptor Lorenzo Bartolini (1777–1850) to execute her likeness while in the city, the two-hour sittings such an enterprise required each day being too much of a drain on time she could otherwise spend prowling the art galleries. The suggestion came up during an outing with her siblings. "Driving along Mary and Tom besieged me so desperately to have my bust taken that as a matter of disinterestedness I yielded." Taken directly to the master's studio before she could change her mind, they "clinched the matter in a moment," to commence the next morning. "I have no wish for a marble immortalization," she insisted. "I sigh to spare from Florence."

But "spare from Florence" she did, and the daily "séances," as Fanny came to call her sessions with Bartolini, proved illuminating, especially with respect to process, which fascinated her. "I sit in a high chair of state while he punched in eyes, nose and mouth from a clay globe," she wrote of the first day. "He gets very much excited, shrugs his shoulders, rubs the clay up in his fingers and quite forgets his work but I like his frankness," a few days later. She judged the fifty-nine-year-old artist to be "a nice old man, short and broad with an intelligent good natured face and a smile that is full of drollery." Bartolini turned out to be quite

Sculpture of Fanny done by
Lorenzo Bartolini in 1836,
in the Mary Washington Parlor,
Longfellow House

the storyteller, too, regaling her with anecdotes of his famous clients.
His greatest patron had been Napoleon, for whom he sculpted numerous likenesses, including a colossal bust which is today in the Metropoli-
tan Museum of Art in New York. He had wonderful things to say about
the late emperor, which Fanny shared in her journal. "He was the most
peace-loving man on the Earth," the sculptor insisted, a leader "who
wished to regenerate mankind and give all equal advantages," waging
war with others only because "he was pushed to it." Bartolini had warm
recollections of Lord Byron and Madame de Staël, the famous French
woman of letters, but had no praise for Leopold II, Grand Duke of
Tuscany, whom Fanny would meet at a formal ball one evening where
she danced waltzes and quadrilles until well after midnight. Bartolini
despaired over the commission he had just received to do the duke's
bust. "It is hard," he sighed, "to flatter such ugliness."

By the time the maestro added his "last touch" to her likeness, Fanny
was sorry "to look my last on the old red chair" where she had remained
seated for hours on end over a ten-day stretch, generally satisfied with
the experience after all, even if he "makes me look solemn in clay." When

the Appletons said their final goodbyes, the sculptor bid them "a wave of a white hat"—which she sketched in the margin of her journal—and executed "a profound bow" as they trotted away in their carriage. The family celebrated that evening at the Teatro Alfieri opera house, seeing for a second time a bravura performance of *Marino Faliero,* a recently premiered *tragedia lirica* in three acts by Gaetano Donizetti.

With their time in Florence now at an end, Fanny again called on favorite places for one more look. At the Uffizi and Pitti galleries, she "ran thro' each dearly-loved nook," lingering in the octagonal room of the Uffizi known as the Tribuna to offer a benediction of gratitude: "Blessed be ye for the deep joy your sweet company has breathed within me." Should she never "gaze" on them again, it would nonetheless be "a joy for me when far away to know you are still beaming with light and beauty on your damask walls, still ready to receive the homage that my heart, if not my eyes, shall ever yield in how many pilgrimages to this one little room!"

Losing her mother and a brother so recently to the ravages of consumption made Fanny acutely alert to William's condition, particularly now, as the days became warmer and the humidity rose. Her cousin had been well enough to attend an opera a few nights earlier, but a deep, persistent cough convinced Nathan Appleton it was time to move along. Departing Florence on June 3, they headed directly for Bologna by way of the Apennines, the higher elevations during the passage providing some temporary relief. Word of a cholera epidemic in Venice persuaded them to proceed directly to Modena, where Fanny visited the Biblioteca Estense, at one time the library of the dukes of Este, with holdings dating to the fourteenth century. She admired a copy of the first printed edition of Dante's *Divine Comedy,* from 1472, and some "very curious manuscripts," including a book of hours illuminated with "exquisitely finished miniature landscapes," finding the physical adornments of the latter especially interesting. "I should so like to have all my favorite poesies printed in this way—in this clear old text—rich paintings and bordered cover—perhaps shall do it for myself some day."

At Parma, they visited the Teatro Farnese, a baroque-style theater built in 1618 by Giovanni Battista Aleotti that had fallen into disrepair, but retained the bare bones of its splendor. "It must have been an immense and magnificent affair," Fanny felt, though it had become a "sad wreck" of a place, a "poor mummy" from another age. "Tom jumped on the deserted stage and began spouting Hamlet to prove how readily the lowest whisper could be heard so perfect the construction." The next day, in Mantua, Fanny had "a long chat with Adèle," the French maid who had joined the entourage in Paris, judging her to be "most eloquent" in many subjects, with an intelligence that was "pas mediocre"—not mediocre. When they reached Switzerland, she had similar praise for the valet, François, who was gentle and attentive to Willy.

Arriving in Verona, the legendary home of the Montague and Capulet families, Fanny occupied herself at every turn with musings of Shakespeare's star-crossed lovers. "Seated ourselves near the blaze of a café and devoured ices by the light of the stars in a square where I could but fancy Mercutio fought and fell!" Later, she sat at her window "à la Juliet, my cheek upon my hand, a glorious moon, worthy of Romeo's oaths, showing its silver rays upon the silent piazza, all the curious carvings of the church betrayed by Caravaggesque light and shadow." At the garden of the Franciscan convent, "we tried to believe we plucked a flower" from the site of Juliet's supposed grave. She regretted leaving such a magical place so hastily. "Had the greatest desire to pass several days at Verona," but it was time to move along. "Dined as well as such heat would allow us and left in the P.M. to my infinite sorrow."

Bypassing Venice had been a "terrible disappointment" for Fanny, though Milan proved a worthy substitute, with the Biblioteca Ambrosiana and La Scala, the famed opera house, among the highlights. At the Santa Maria delle Grazie convent, she found Leonardo da Vinci's *Last Supper* "more perfect than I supposed considering its treatment." Once again, she wrote with a sharp critical eye about everything she saw, be it paintings, sculpture, architecture, scenery, library treasures, ballet, opera, or theater. She pursued, too, her hunt for literary landmarks, the home of Petrarch during his years in Milan and a fresco admired by Lord Byron at the top of her list. She found an Italian play with "tolerable acting" mildly entertaining, but "difficult to be understood with the Milan dialect which consists in pronouncing two syllables only in a word; a most lazy style of speech." She would, a few pages later in her journal, call it a "barbarous dialect."

A climb to the top of the Duomo di Milano—Milan's cathedral—provided yet another perspective. The structure took six centuries to complete, a singular achievement of Gothic splendor that left Fanny in awe. Despite the pounding heat, she "mounted to the roof" to make a "close inspection," with music from the organ "rolling its invisible waves thro' the dim arches" as she made her way upward. The golden statue of the Virgin Mary atop the main spire was "a glorious conception of the court of heaven," the overall effect of the majestic panorama "a hymn" in praise of "the most gossamer architecture that was ever moulded from marble," a tour de force of human achievement.

"Addio bello Milano," Fanny murmured as the family caravan made its way toward Lake Como, the party deciding to stay in the foothills of the Alps for a few days, the refreshing lake breezes proving most agreeable. "There was a magic in the twilight tonight that I never saw equalled even in my dreams," Fanny wrote after a stroll on a beach, a "triumph of the Italian atmosphere" that "glazed" the "beautiful scenery of lake and mountain down to a tone of mellow purple harmony." A day trip on a "small steamer" made for an agreeable diversion, a lunch of freshly caught trout at a charming lakeside inn the perfect midday repast. Even Willy "enjoyed this day of a thousand," and "longed to linger longer about these lovely shores." The village of Bellagio, set on a promontory jutting out into Lake Como, offered more scenic walks, one with "poor William sadly lagging behind." Another stroll "in the afternoon shadows to a quarry" left Fanny feeling sentimental. "Wept myself to sleep," she wrote the next morning, humbly grateful for "this visit of the angels."

After enjoying a "farewell row on the sweet lake," they were "riding on the Earth's back-bone" along twisting mountain roads once again, "gloriously skirting awful precipices"—all in all a "beautiful day to hail us o'er the border." Brother Tom, a great fan of hiking, parted with the main group to do a little "pedestrianism" on his own, promising to meet up with the others in Geneva. At Simplon Pass, Fanny looked furtively over her shoulder at the "luxuriant valley" receding in the background, recalling later that night to having feelings "very like what I fancy Eve's were when losing sight of her Eden." For the young traveler from Boston, it was a bittersweet welcome to Switzerland.

7

Switzerland

Perhaps the best cure for the fear of death is to reflect that life has a beginning as well as an end.

—William Hazlitt, "On the Fear of Death," 1822

$\mathcal{F}$anny's busy travel journal for July 20, 1836, records the Appleton party's cautious passage along breathtaking Alpine trails from Bern to Thun, a picturesque Swiss village where they settled in for a few days, surrounded by "noble mountains of purest snow." They took rooms in a "dashing new hotel" that looked out on a landscape of green fields that were "finely broken with trees thro' which glistens the lordly Aar" River where it joins Lake Thun—altogether a "fairyland" so "wondrously beautiful" that Fanny had trouble choosing which among the "tempting variety" of natural landmarks around her to sketch first. A "fascinating walk" that afternoon with Tom revealed other spectacles, most striking a twelfth-century castle with "sky-piercing spires" and a chateau "reflected in the clear water" that Fanny declared to be "quaint in form" and "rich in tint." Though reluctant to leave such a vista— "long to stay here," Fanny wrote of the scene—they returned in time to join the others for dinner.

"Prof. Longfellow sends up his card to Father," she entered next, noting offhandedly what to her was an extraneous afterthought on an otherwise exhausting day: an American scholar passing through the town where she and her family were staying had expressed an interest in making their acquaintance. What she wrote after that puts her feelings in even sharper perspective: "Hope the venerable gentleman won't pop in on us tho' I did like his *Outre-Mer*." Fanny, it is safe to surmise from this, knew nothing whatsoever about Henry Wadsworth Longfellow at the time, other than that he was a college instructor, and that he wrote a book she had read. That she used the word "venerable" literally— that she believed him to be a mature academic of some years—became evident when the two finally did meet, on the other side of Lake Thun in Interlaken, where the Appletons had checked into other lodgings, declaring him then "a young man after all or else the son of the poet."

Fanny's accounts of their interactions over the following days are concise and unadorned to the point of being almost reportorial, though what does come through in a fragmentary way is a growing respect for someone she came to regard as an intellectual equal. Henry astutely picked up on this penchant of hers, carrying on at length in areas he perceived were of mutual interest. But to be invited, as he later was, to join the Appletons on a portion of their travels, he also had to have been deemed worthy by Nathan Appleton, who was chaperoning two highly sophisticated young women on this trip, both of whom were bright, attractive, unattached, socially polished, and impeccably educated, a responsibility we can be sure he oversaw with attention and care.

"At the Hotel Bellevue I met Mr. Appleton, of Boston, going with his family to Interlaken," Henry remarked of the day he had sent his "card up" to the family's rooms. "How unlucky I am in not having met them there! I had but a few moments' conversation with him," and was off for Bern. But what Henry confirmed—that they did, in fact, meet face-to-face in Thun—has some bearing on everything else that followed. Though Henry was not descended from "old Yankee" wealth— neither, for that matter, was Appleton—he came from a respected New England family, and he was a Harvard professor, which in the absence of a minted pedigree or independent wealth, carried a cachet of its own in these circles. Henry, moreover, was a published author, and presumably made—as he usually did—a solid first impression.

Taking a room in Lausanne, Henry hired a cicerone—a guide—"to see things expeditiously," including the villa where Edward Gibbon had written the final volumes of his monumental *History of the Decline and Fall of the Roman Empire*. In Ferney, he visited the onetime residence of Voltaire, but left uninspired. "As I have neither love nor veneration for this arch-scoffer, the visit has not afforded me much gratification." In Geneva, he stayed in the Hôtel des Bergues; in the village of Chamonix, he chose the Hôtel de l'Union, with a spectacular view of Mont Blanc. His decision to linger there for two days proved propitious when he received a "pleasant" call from Thomas Motley of Boston, a Beacon Hill neighbor of the Appletons, "who is here with his family." Deciding to travel together, they shared a carriage to Thun and took a steamboat to Interlaken, where they "found the Appletons still stationary, as if there were a charm about the place."

Finding the top hotels fully booked, they took rooms where they could find them, Henry "secluded in a convent, or what was once a convent" for the night. "I hope for an adventure," he wrote before turning in, passing the night "in quiet sleep." Another room was found for him the next day at the pension where the Appletons were staying, and he joined the group there. "After breakfast we went off in a body to stroll in the woods as far as the ruins of an old castle, which some of the ladies sketched, while the rest of us sat under the trees. And thus the time slipped pleasantly away." A walk on the banks of the Aar after a late-afternoon dinner was followed by a concert in the evening. "Since I have joined these two families from America the time passes pleasantly," he decided the next day. "I now for the first time enjoy Switzerland."

Whatever direct interactions Henry was having with Fanny at this point are not recorded in either of their journals, though his entries suggest he was having a restful time. On August 3, they all left by steamer for a return trip to Thun, "a large party of us, the Appletons and the Motleys. We shall be some days together, a week or more probably. Nothing could be more pleasant." Henry wasted little time taking on the role of raconteur during their extended carriage rides, he usually joining Fanny, Mary, and cousin William. "A day of true and quiet enjoyment, travelling from Thun to Entelbuch on our way to Lucerne," he wrote. "The time glided too swiftly away. We read the 'Genevieve' of Coleridge, and the *Christabel,* and many scraps of song, and little German ballads of Uhland, simple and strange. At noon we stopped at Langnau, and walked into the fields, and sat down by a stream of pure water that turned a mill; and a little girl came out of the mill and brought us cherries; and the shadow of the trees was pleasant, and my soul was filled with peace and gladness."

Fanny recalled these same events with similar clarity, but from a somewhat different angle. She reported how "Mr L" was "talking to me all the while, about poetry," rhapsodizing about one of her favorites—Shelley—but also quoting at length "some poetical conceits" of Nathaniel Parker Willis, a now forgotten New England writer and editor who, it appears clear from her comments, was well known to both. What stands out is the utter disdain she openly expressed for the man and his work. She allowed that while Willis probably "has many such" expressions of occasional talent, the question for her was whether they were "inborn flashes" or—more likely in her view, and she coined a new word for the occasion—"well-polished prettinesses." She answered her own question: "If one could separate the man's personal character, so false, so flimsy, from his poetry, I might admire much more—his best thoughts now seem but affectations, mimicries of other people's best garnished out his own way." When Henry declared his newfound passion for this remarkable young woman some months later, one of his first compliments would be awe of her "genius"—her clearness of thought, her ability to cut to the core, her determination to hold back nothing of importance.

Fanny's take on the late-afternoon walk "to the old bridge" where she was pleased to "sketch the cloister spires from a wall, then on the other side of the river, a dark picturesque cottage," is otherwise comparable to Henry's. "A nice talk—delicious twilight," she wrote. "Replied to the courteous *guten abend* of the little children we met; my first German phrase." A "quiet evening" indoors led her to reflect on the general surroundings. "My heart clings to this dear valley—shall I ever see it again? When and with what eyes?"

She recorded how "Mr L gave us a lesson in German," choosing to read some "pretty ballads" of the Romantic poet Johann Ludwig Uhland, which she called "simple and touching." Toward nightfall, Fanny, Mary, and Henry "took a stroll along the river-side under the trees," viewing the "most poetical sunset I think I have seen in Europe," to her a "glorious 'illuminated' leaf of Nature's holy volume!" At a vista near Thun, they "wandered in dim twilight," pausing in a grove of trees, with "bats wheeling over our head, silence around and the huge masses of poplars like dim black cathedrals reflected in the clear water with stars as altar-tapers. Walked slowly home filled with calm and happy thoughts. Father quite alarmed at our absence."

Her description of the long carriage ride to Lucerne also confirms the basic points outlined by Henry, with a few added touches. "Mr L, William and moi together—read German, Coleridge, etc, all the morning so saw no scenery. A rush of chubby, pretty little girls, so droll in their black lace caps, as we alight to dine. Mary and I and Mr L sit down on logs over a crystal clear brooklet near a mill and sentimentalize over grass bent, whether it will or no, by the gliding stream; the 'miller's daughter' bringing us sour cherries." The next day brought more of the same: "Mr. L's journal and poetry, read aloud as before."

Once arrived in Lucerne, William's weakened condition left Fanny "wilted and weary" and "oppressed with sad thoughts." Henry may even have been getting on her nerves at this point. "Mr L. very inquisitive," she wrote edgily before retiring for the night. But his offer the next morning to stay with Willy while the others went on a sightseeing trip to Mount Righi was greatly appreciated. "He is a most gentle spirit," Henry wrote of the young man, "resigned and uncomplaining, as one who has already commenced 'his conversation in heaven.'" Continuing on to their hotel in Zurich, Fanny and Mary were delighted to find Tom "waiting at the door, with a slouched hat and a merry heart." Henry and Tom took to each other on the spot, both, in a way, possessing qualities the other coveted, which became more apparent in the years ahead. "I like brother Tom very much," Henry decided. "He is lively, clever and witty"—and also wealthy, free-spirited, and contentedly independent. Tom, for his part, respected artistic ability above everything else—and never wavered in his respect for Henry's talents and accomplishments.

During a row on Lake Zurich, the two men jumped off the boat "in the deep part of the lake," diving "down, down, down 'into those depths so calm and cool,'" Henry wrote, quoting two lines from *Outre-Mer* that recalled a similar experience frolicking with the Persiani family in Italy ten summers earlier. Tom, he added approvingly, "is a mighty swimmer, and my element is cold water." Evocative as the outing on the lake may have been for Henry, it did little to ease Fanny's mounting anxiety. At one point she plunged her hand in the water, hoping the chilly jolt would "mingle with my exhausted spirit—strengthen and cleanse it," but all she felt was more worry for William. "How can I think of myself while he is growing so feeble daily, so patiently relinquishing the active habits he delights in and breaking our hearts with his self-forgetting thoughtfulness of all about him?"

For diversion, Fanny took a "dip into Mr L's very graphic descriptions of little things" in his journal. A physician brought in to examine Willy reported grimly that any thought of his surviving a voyage home was "impossible"; even a journey to Paris "would be too much" for him. "Oh God—but how will the poor child bear this terrible disappointment! He seems calm tho' it is his death-knell, but he cannot get up stairs without aid. Dined in a thunderstorm: mingled tears with my soup." An evening walk with Henry "up a small hill in the town under a grove of huge, gloomy linden trees" left her contemplating the "dead, blank winter" to come, "but what is that to the pall the mind can weave for itself now."

During a lengthy carriage drive around Lake Zurich, Henry and Fanny translated into English "Das Schloss am Meere" (The Castle by the Sea), another ballad by Uhland. Finding her muse "very coy or drugged with poppies," Fanny nonetheless was pleased with her performance, and Henry heartily agreed, crediting her with translating "some of the best lines," even used her version later in *Hyperion*. Fanny would write out several holographic copies of the ballad, one in a bound volume she kept in the years before her marriage for poems of her own composition, called "Appletoniana," the other kept separately, and now in the Houghton Library. In a fine calligraphic hand, on what she unmistakably intended to serve as a "title page" for the latter, she wrote the name of the poem, the author, followed by the translators—"Fanny E. Appleton" and "Henry W. Longfellow." She had given herself top billing.

As the traveling party prepared to leave Zurich, there was general agreement that the roadhouse where they had just spent the night—the Hôtel du Corbeau, French for "raven"—was subpar, deemed even more disagreeable when a "most exorbitant" bill was presented for payment.

Henry jotted some "beautiful lines" of doggerel in the guest book, which Fanny copied out in her own journal, declaring it a "true and jocose admonition to future victims of this vile inn." Henry recorded the words in his journal as well, and reprised them later in *Hyperion*:

> Beware of the Raven of Zurich!
> 'Tis a bird of omen ill,
> A noisy & unclean bird,
> With a very, *very* long *bill.*

In the carriage ride that followed, Henry read two "soul-thrilling" sermons of the Unitarian minister Orville Dewey to William, which Fanny thought to have "pleased him much," particularly "that touching one on the 'Voices of the Dead.'" The three talked about religion and mortality during the "rainy and muggy ride," with William affirming "it much better to die of consumption than of a fever or accident," regarding such an exit to be "more natural, gliding from one state of existence to another." He regretted not being able to have done "something good in this world—but perhaps it is better to die young," and not having a memorial picture made for his mother. "Poor William is very feeble," Henry wrote. "We were fearful he would not reach Schaffhausen," and he persuaded them to stop near Bülach, where William could sleep for a few hours, and they could have a bite to eat. "I sat by him and bathed his forehead in cologne," Fanny wrote, leaving William's side only at his "earnest" insistence that she join the others in a grove of linden trees outside, shaded from the hot sun, all the while feeling "so out of this world" by the morning's gloomy conversation.

With Willy "refreshed by his rest," they continued on, Fanny reading aloud William Hazlitt's 1822 essay "On the Fear of Death." During a stop to feed the horses, she and Henry took a walk, the conversation turning idly to "talk about clouds and how so little can supply pleasure when in the mood." Both described separately the panorama laid out before them, using lovely variations on the same metaphor, Henry giving credit to Fanny for the central image. Here is what she wrote: "Everything had a Sunday look—a silence as if the trees were asleep in their pews. Steeped in sunshine quietness. Old man in the fields stalking about in cocked hat, breeches and red waistcoat like a revolutionary scarecrow." And Henry's take: "The scene was perfectly quiet; a breathless stillness as if all Nature were at prayer; and, as F. said, the trees looked as if they were standing up in their pews to sing. The waters of the Rhine were of a most lovely green. Nothing in the colors of human art could equal their beauty."

In Schaffhausen, Fanny and Henry walked into town "to hunt up some books to amuse the poor invalid," then sat in a park for a "long talk" about Boston, the people they both knew, and other "such dull topics." When they returned to the hotel, Willy was organizing "all the little presents he has collected for his family," and talked "with the utmost cheerfulness about the disposal of them," knowing "they can never be given by his own hand and will when received be sad legacies" of his passing. "Gave Mary and myself a Geneva brooch as a memento—precious indeed!" Henry was greatly impressed by William's courage. "It seems impossible that he should live many days. He is himself conscious of this, and is making his little gifts to friends with a calmness which is beautiful. How heavenly it is to die thus."

During dinner that evening, one of the people whose name we can be comfortably certain came up when Fanny and Henry were chatting in the town park about mutual acquaintances—George Ticknor—strode into the inn, unannounced. Ticknor stopped by, according to Fanny, because he had heard "a young American was ill in the house and thus stumbled upon us." The Ticknors and the Appletons were Boston neighbors, and frequent guests in each other's homes. Ticknor's wife, Anna Eliot Ticknor, was "all kindness and sympathy," and "very much shocked" to find William so ill. Henry was similarly surprised to see his colleague. "While we were at dinner this afternoon, who should come into our parlor but Mr. Ticknor! He has just arrived with his family from Constance. His winter in Germany has given him a most portly look."

During the few days of their stay, the Ticknors became constant companions—a special treat for Fanny, who left William in the care of François, the valet, for a day trip to nearby Rhine Falls, the largest waterfall in Europe. The welcome respite allowed her to observe a mechanical device she knew something about but had never seen in action. "Saw a pretty camera lucida reflecting the whole fall on a sheet, a miniature mov-

Fanny's copy of the poem she and Henry translated together from the German into English "by the margin of fair Zurich's waters," with her name appearing first

ing picture," she marveled of the curious instrument, which reflects rays of light through a prism onto a flat surface, ideal for sketching. Fanny was captivated by the depiction of movement on a stationary plane—the development of motion-picture technology was still decades away. "Spray wreathing sun sparking in the water—shadows changing—truly magical effect, having what pictures of falls always need—the motion. The spectral vanishing as day-light is let in was exquisite."

Back at the hotel, the Ticknors' young daughter, Eliza, paid William a visit, cheering everyone's spirits. "Tis a real delight to see a child—a bit of sunshine and her voice so tinkling and joyous," Fanny wrote. "Such a blessed state of hopefulness and trust—fresh from Heaven—not yet undermined by earthly experience. Shall we ever, ever regain this birthright?" On Sunday, Mrs. Ticknor brought William some flowers; Fanny spent the morning reading aloud a few psalms, and an afternoon walk "under shady trees" was followed by a "quiet night" in the hotel. William fell asleep early, the others "sat up talking" until one in the morning, the conversation covering a range of interests. Henry and Ticknor spoke at length about "education and German Universities," a conversation Fanny found "quite interesting," elevating, it is fair to propose, Henry's stature even further in her eyes. He had already proven himself an authority on literature, a talented linguist, an attentive conversationalist, a person of compassion, a poet. Now he was holding his own with a Beacon Hill power figure Fanny knew well, the same person who had chosen Henry to succeed him at Harvard.

Two days later, a passel of letters forwarded from Strasbourg arrived, including one that brought Henry's Swiss holiday to an abrupt end. "Received a letter just before dinner which rendered it absolutely necessary for me to start for Heidelberg without delay," he wrote on August 17, offering no further elaboration. Commenting on the letters just received, it is Fanny who fills in the blanks. "Mr. L gets one from Miss Clara C. which decides him to leave us immediately as she is out of patience awaiting an escort to America. Quite sorry to have him go." Henry moved swiftly, and responsibly. "Engaged a carriage at once, and at six in the evening took leave, and started on my way through the Black Forest." Reunited with Clara in Heidelberg, he described a "gloomy" ride from Baden to Strasbourg in which they "whiled away the time with whist; for the sky all tears, and the landscape with drenched garments, had no charms for us poor people, whose spirits were sufficiently sad, and whose voices had a muffled and mournful sound."

The day after Henry's departure, Fanny and Mary took a long walk up to "that lovely promenade," where she reflected on "the happy state of childhood, innocence and ignorance before the down is rubbed off and the skeleton in all things is revealed and that fiend Doubt become our fire-side companion." Her thoughts turned to her cousin who was "very, very weak today—has spoken little and dozed much." The next day, Fanny walked with her father "through vineyards high above the Rhine," admired an old fort with "mighty massive walls" and arches that reminded her of romances. "Refreshing to see strength in any shape." Exchanging pleasantries in German with some villagers occasioned thoughts of Henry, departed just two days earlier: "Miss Mr L. considerably." The cool temperatures had "invigorated" William, but not Fanny's general mood. "The first dry leaves make those of my soul rustle within me!"

August 21, a Sunday, dawned rainy and cold. William had passed the night fitfully, the "ravages of his disease" taking their toll. "He gets no sleep tho appears to doze—shuts his eyes from weakness." The morning was filled with a cluster of mundanities—a few letters from brother Tom and the Motleys had been delivered, and "some new Americans" had arrived. The hotel food was not to Fanny's taste, and there was no music to soothe her spirits other than "the falling leaves." An encounter on the town mall with two strutting peacocks got her thinking about "genteel" women dressed up in their gaudy finery—all appearance, little substance being the gist of her comments, none of them fully articulated, her pre-occupation being with other thoughts—and there she stops. The final two pages of the volume are blank, with no indication whatsoever that William Sullivan Appleton had died early on August 24, two months shy of his twenty-first birthday.

Henry learned of Willy's death from Tom Appleton, who wrote him with the sad news, sent to his forwarding address in Paris. "He desired me to remember him to all his friends and for me to thank those who had been kind in service to him in his illness, among whom he felt that you were warmly included." The bare particulars of William's passing were set down in a concise memoir Nathan Appleton wrote toward the end of his life, published posthumously by the Massachusetts Historical Society. He described William as a "sweet youth, who, for some time, had been suffering from a disease of the lungs," dying finally after having "lingered on for some weeks." A small church service was followed by "a procession to the burying-ground, where I obtained a lot in perpetuity, and afterward sent a monumental stone from Paris."

Departing from Schaffhausen, the Appletons visited Fribourg, Strasbourg, Baden-Baden, and Heidelberg. In Mainz, it is Nathan Appleton who tells us that "both my daughters were attacked with what the physician called a 'gastric fever,' by which we were detained six weeks." On the first anniversary of her departure for Europe, Fanny admitted to Robert Apthorp that "never did I love or appreciate home so much as now." Of the previous twelve months, she joked that she just might "gain a living" as an "authoress" of tourist guides. "But over all this magic, anxiety, decay and death have thrown a tinge of sadness and there is a green corner by the blue Rhine where many aching hearts have bound the circle of their thoughts. I meant to write much to you about my sweet cousin William for the unsullied purity of his character and gentle sweetness of his disposition so ennobled his decay, shed such an atmosphere of heavenly hope and cheerful resignation around his last moments."

She admitted to some uneasy "presentiments" when she left home, but had no idea that what she feared then would involve anyone other than herself. "I mention this only because it is the sole bit of superstition I ever indulged in. And I was again called to breathe comfort and hope to a gentle spirit hovering between two worlds." In the end, she found William's acceptance of his fate nothing less than inspirational. "From first to last he saw and felt his danger and met it with a Christian fortitude which was truly astonishing."

8

Pent-Up Fire

Look not mournfully into the Past. It comes not back again. Wisely improve the Present. It is thine. Go forth to meet the shadowy Future, without fear, and with a manly heart.

—motto of *Hyperion,* 1839, title page

The setting of a great hope is like the setting of the sun. The brightness of our life is gone. Shadows of evening fall around us, and the world seems but a dim reflection,—itself a broader shadow. We look forward into the coming, lonely night. The soul withdraws into itself. Then stars arise, and the night is holy.

—*Hyperion,* book I, chapter 1

By the time Henry reached his thirtieth birthday, on February 27, 1837, he had traveled extensively abroad, mastered numerous foreign languages, held a full professorship at one prestigious college and become a department chair at another. He had published poetry, scholarly essays, specialized texts, translations, and a well-received collection of travel sketches, all the while building a reputation that extended well beyond the comfortable world of academia. In his personal life, he had been blissfully married to a lovely young woman who died in the aftermath of a miscarriage, and then, in the unlikeliest of places, had been captivated by a Beacon Hill heiress he would describe in the weeks and months ahead as "the stately Dark Lady." Still, he made no mention at all of the chronological milestone he had just passed in his journal, which remained blank during these first months back from Europe, though he did write some deeply considered letters that offer keen insight into what was going on in his life.

The most significant gap in Henry's journal at this crucial interval spans nine months, from October 6, 1836, when he and Clara Crowninshield and the Bryant women sailed from France for New York, to July 22, 1837. He resumed the chronicle on that day to describe a thrilling ride on a steam-powered train that he enthused had "roared through the green meadows of Medford" north of Boston to Lowell, a trip of twenty-five miles. He marveled at how the cars had leaped forward "like a steed, when he feels the spur," declaring the experience to have "exhilarated" him "like wine." The Boston and Lowell Railroad opened in 1835 to carry raw cotton and finished textiles between the mills on the Merrimack River and the Boston wharves, but was popular also for introducing the latest wonder of the steam age to paying passengers.

Henry did not say why he went up to Lowell, though he must have known by then that Nathan Appleton had been one of the founders of the planned industrial community there fifteen years earlier, and that it was the cornerstone of the family's great wealth. Henry spent a night in a hotel he judged adequate, his stay otherwise recalled for the sight of "factory girls walking two and two, with calico gowns and downcast eyes" during an evening walk downtown. The journal ends abruptly once again nine days later, and is quiet for another nine months, resuming on February 27, 1838, Henry's thirty-first birthday, which he observed guardedly: "How much I have lived through this last year! It has been rich in experiences."

One of these experiences, we can fairly assume, was the "reunion," if we can presume to call it that, with Fanny Appleton, who had returned from Europe five months earlier. Henry had been living in an apartment building just off Harvard Yard on the corner of Kirkland and Oxford Streets owned by a professor in the law school. "That large, square, three-story house afforded several suites of pleasant rooms, and has probably been the home for a time of more men whose names are well known in the annals of the College and the Commonwealth than any other in Cambridge," Charles Eliot Norton recalled in a 1905 reflection of his own childhood growing up in the leafy neighborhood known then as Professors' Row.

"My earliest recollections of Mr. Longfellow are of the time when he was living there, and nothing but my later recollections of him could be pleasanter than those which I have of his kindness,—he a man of thirty to a boy of eight or ten years old. I still preserve among my treasures gifts he made me in those days for the enrichment of my little museum,— precious objects which he had brought home from Europe, the most interesting of all of them, perhaps, being a seventeenth century medal of the three kings of Cologne, whose legend and names are familiar to the readers of his Golden Legend."

Henry's first order of business was to structure a curriculum for his classes. "I am now occupied in preparing a course of Lectures on German Literature, to be delivered next summer," he reported to George Washington Greene. "I do not write them out; but make notes and translations. I think this the best way—most decidedly. In this course something of the Danish and Swedish (the new feathers in my cap) is to be mingled." As the academic year drew to a close, he began looking for new accommodations. "To go down to breakfast in a warm parlor is Christian," he decided, wanting no more "solitary meals, then, with 'Silence' written over the door, as in Monkish Refectory."

One summerlike day in May, he called on an acquaintance from the college who had been renting rooms at 105 Brattle Street, a sparsely settled country road known in Colonial times as Tory Row for the royalist sympathies of its affluent residents. The striking Georgian mansion had been built in 1759 by Major John Vassall, a loyal British subject whose family fortune came from slave-labor sugar plantations in Jamaica. Abandoned on the eve of revolution and confiscated by the provincial government, the property had briefly housed the Marblehead Regiment, a corps of volunteers comprised of North Shore fishermen later credited with rowing General Washington and his troops across the Delaware River in advance of the Battle of Trenton. Set back on a slope overlooking the Charles River, the yellow and white-trimmed house cast a striking profile to passersby, among them George Washington when he arrived to take command of the Continental Army on July 2, 1775. Vacated and spruced up, it became the general's official residence for nine months during the Siege of Boston. By the time Henry came calling, it was called Craigie House for Andrew Craigie, a former owner whose widow, Elizabeth, was the resident landlord.

In an informal journal of reminiscences relating to Craigie House and its history, Henry recalled being impressed by the beautiful view and cooling coastal breeze that swept up from the river. Learning that the law student was soon moving out, he asked about taking the quarters for himself. Mrs. Craigie curtly responded—presumably because of his youthful appearance—that she no longer rented rooms to students, but changed her mind after Henry identified himself as a professor, and the author also of *Outre-Mer*. Mrs. Craigie, it happened, was familiar with the book—even had a copy lying on a nearby side table.

"I have found two large and beautiful rooms in the Craigie house, and thither I go at the end of this term," he informed his father. "I shall be entirely my own master, and have my meals by myself and at my own hours." Once settled in, he advised George Ticknor, who was still in Germany, that he was living "delightfully" in his new quarters, "somewhat aloof, as it were; and around me are faces and voices, which constantly remind me of you." He was more expansive with Anne Longfellow Pierce, who after the death of her husband had moved back into

Craigie House, from *Homes of American Authors*, 1853

the family homestead on Congress Street in Portland, where she would remain for the rest of her life, dying in 1901 at the age of ninety. "In my new abode I dwell like an Italian prince in his villa. You enter, and the first thing that meets your admiring gaze is the author of *Outre-Mer* reclining on a sofa, in a striped calamanco morning gown:—slippers, red."

The mention of colorful garb led Henry to ask his sister to do some alterations on a "frilled shirt" he was adding to his already extensive wardrobe; helping outfit him with clothes, it emerges from their correspondence, was a domestic responsibility the young widow happily assumed for her adored older brother, even if it had to be coordinated from a distance. "*Dickeys* wanted" as well, "and likewise white linen handkerchiefs." Before departing France a few months earlier, Henry admitted to having purchased "an abundant supply of clothing," which, as he explained in a breakdown of traveling expenses for his father, accounted for his "drawing so much in Paris" from his funds. Among the earliest likenesses of Henry from these years is a paper silhouette executed in 1841 by the French portrait artist Auguste Edouart picturing the young professor decked out in a flared three-quarter-length great-coat and top hat, with a walking stick held casually in one hand. His taste for style and color was not lost on Harvard students, including those in the Hasty Pudding Club theatrical society, who composed a ditty about him:

> Just twig the Professor dressed out in his best,
> Yellow kids and buff gaiters, green breeches, blue vest;
> With hat on one whisker and an air that says 'go it!'
> Look here! the great North American poet.

One former member of the Hasty Pudding Club, Phillips Brooks, class of 1855, was able to recall the tune in its entirety more than thirty years after his graduation. The dapper professor, he remembered, was "extremely neat, precise, and fashionable in his attire, and was wont to wear English low splatterdashes, or gaiters, as we called them, and a gay silk necktie." In offering his amusing recollection, Brooks—remembered best today for writing the lyrics to the Christmas hymn "O Little Town of Bethlehem"—allowed that he "would not now be thus irreverent" to Henry's memory "were it not that it was well understood at the time that the poet had heard the verses and had a hearty laugh over them."

Another undergraduate already enrolled when Henry arrived in Cambridge was his younger brother, Sam, whose closest friend at the time was Edward Everett Hale. "Samuel Longfellow and I walked together, studied together, recited together, wrote verses together, and thus, naturally, when his brother Henry came to be Professor, I came to know him." Hale credited Henry with invigorating the otherwise "older company" of Harvard faculty with a "sort of breezy" life. "This handsome young Smith Professor undeceived them. He was fresh from Europe. He could talk in French with Frenchmen, Italian with Italians, and German with Germans. The very clothes on his back had been made by Parisian tailors, the very tie of his neckcloth was a revelation to the sedateness of little Cambridge." Despite his flashy appearance, the "friendly young professor" was "dead in earnest in his business," and "pushed all traditions aside" in his approach, which Hale and Sam observed firsthand. "He had his own views about teaching German, and when they told him there was no recitation-room for him, he said he would meet his class" in the parlor of University Hall. "You could take your constitutional walk with Longfellow, you could play a game of whist in the evening with Longfellow, you could talk with him with perfect freedom on any subject, high or low, and he liked to have you. I think myself that with his arrival a new life began for the little college in that very important business of the freedom of association between the teachers and the undergraduates."

ONCE HE HAD DISPENSED with itemizing his sartorial needs, Henry had another tidbit of information to share with Annie, expressed in four pithy words: "The Appletons have returned," offering no further elaboration. He was much more expansive with George Washington Greene: "To Boston I go frequently—and generally on foot," the route "into town" always the same, across the Charles River by way of the West Boston Bridge, a wooden tollway dating to 1792 that he would memorialize in an 1845 poem, "The Bridge." Henry's destination usually was

Elizabeth Craigie as a young woman, copy in oil of a watercolor commissioned by Longfellow, c. 1870, to honor the memory of his former landlady

the sloping walkway on the northern flank of the Boston Common, an elm-lined promenade in the heart of the city's cultural milieu where he could stroll up Beacon Street among the fashionable elite, dressed in his best European finery. "It is a pleasant walk," he told Greene, especially if "one has an object in view."

Once situated in Cambridge, Henry had reached out to the Appleton family, calling on the home of Nathan's older brother and next-door neighbor on upper Beacon Street, Samuel Appleton. He made a strong impression on Samuel's wife, Mary Lekain Gore Appleton, known to the family as "Aunt Sam," who wrote approvingly of the new suitor to Fanny—that Longfellow charm working its magic yet again. "The professor called to inquire after your health, and what a bright spirit he is, lively as a bird," she enthused, holding nothing back. "He is my *beau idéal* for a husband! Sensible, learned, industrious—and rather handsome."

Aunt Sam took sardonic note of "the attention and flattery" she understood Fanny had been receiving from "titled characters" calling on her in Europe, "but I can tell you one thing, ma petite, you will not scorn the society of Professors and such like when you return to

Boston." It may well be true, she granted, that "we have no Dukes or Counts" in the United States, "but we have a *Longfellow*." Two months later, the "Professor" came calling once again, and Aunt Sam found him "as soft and gentle as ever," adding that he was regarded in town to be "remarkably youthful and quite handsome—and could marry any of our belles—but he prefers the society of my ladyship! He looks so clean and smells so sweet I could kiss him."

Apparently relishing the role of matchmaker, Aunt Sam—who had no children of her own and doted on her nieces and nephews—had previously invited Henry to join her in extending greetings to Mary and Fanny at their hotel in Paris; he penned notes to both on January 8, 1837. Brief and gracefully written, the letter to "My dear Fanny" began as a reminder of the time the two had spent "by the margins of fair Zurich's waters" translating the Uhland ballad. "I remembered, also, the delight you always felt in reading whatever was beautiful in poems," and thus included his translation of an elegy by Friedrich von Matthisson, "a writer celebrated for the elegance of his style, and the pleasing melancholy of his thoughts." Henry was forwarding it—perhaps a bit too boldly at this point—"as a kind of Valentine; with my warmest wishes of a Happy New Year to all of you. It will serve likewise as a German lesson, during the master's absence. He hopes to resume hereafter his instructions in the *musical tongue*."

In a chatty letter to Fanny's brother Tom Appleton, Henry had a personal request to make. "And now the favor I have to ask; which is, that you would buy me at *Privat's*, Rue de la Paix, near the Boulevard, one dozen light-colored kid gloves (a little larger than your own) and one dozen small ladies' gloves *black*. I bought for every one else, save myself, and forgot that my sister was in mourning." An entry in the account book that Nathan Appleton kept for miscellaneous transactions records the purchase of "2 doz. gloves for Professor Longfellow."

WHATEVER MAY HAVE TRANSPIRED between Henry and Fanny is dimly expressed by Henry in his writings, and not at all by Fanny in hers. Whether or not there was an outright proposal of marriage, or whether Fanny simply said she was not interested in a serious relationship, is unclear. What is certain is that Henry found himself soundly rebuffed, not in any overtly hostile way, but decisively, and unable to let it go, the urgings of his closest friends notwithstanding.

In late 1837, he sent Fanny a pair of articles he thought she might enjoy, each with a perfunctory cover note. One of these—addressed to "Madonna Francesca"—took "the liberty" to tell her "what a delightful day I passed with you on Monday; and to say how much I wish these scraps of antiquated song may please you." Two months later, he sent her a set of castanets—he called them "castañuelas"—for use at a fête she and Mary would be attending. "Hoping you will all enjoy your-selves," he closed, concluding with an improvised quotation from the Acts of the Apostles—" 'sorrowing most of all that I shall not see your face' at the ball"—and then signed his full name, Henry W. Longfellow. With that brief, two-sentence note, their correspondence ceased—not to be resumed for close to four and a half years.

The first hint something was amiss comes in a letter Henry wrote Mary three months after the family had returned from Europe. Henry's relationship with Fanny's older sister had blossomed into a satisfying intellectual friendship, with Mary assuming the additional role of being what James Taft Hatfield called Henry's "trusty friend-at-court," the evidence for that more than a hundred chatty letters he received from her over the next forty-five years. One topic of mutual interest was Mary's love of German. The stated purpose of Henry's letter in this instance—opened with the greeting "Mein liebes Fräulein"—was to return a volume of *Reisebilder*, Heinrich Heine's four-volume collection of prose and poetry, with the request that "at some future day, you will lend me all the volumes; as I want to read them again, and am tempted to write a Review of the whole," something he ultimately did do, five years later, for *Graham's Magazine*. "Verily he is a beautiful writer," Henry remarked of Heine: "He is a Lord Byron in Prose; with all the fire, wit, feeling of the English poet, and more pathos."

Three lengthy paragraphs of literary musing followed, covering a number of European masters, with seminal works of Goethe, Jean-Paul Richter, better known as "Jean-Paul," and Dante central among them. "Truly I have a pretty medley on my brain this week," he explained, being in the midst of preparing lectures on diverse subjects, which led him, abruptly, to ask Mary this: "And what have you been doing in the front parlor? Shall I sit there no more with you, and read in pleasant books! Are those bright autumnal mornings gone forever?" The next paragraph, written entirely in German, was first published by James Taft Hatfield in his 1933 monograph, *New Light on Longfellow,* which focused primarily on Henry's contributions to German studies and scholarship; the passage was later translated into English by Andrew Hilen:

> Ah! You beautiful soul! It makes me quite sad in spirit when I think about it and see how the lovely dream there is ended,—how the clouds dissolve, and melt into tears, and everything becomes empty around me, and in my soul a gloomy night—a gloomy, starless night! And this I have had to say to you in German, because a foreign voice is a kind of twilight and moonlight, wherein one may say all sorts of things to women,—and so heartfully sincere! Even now I greet affectionately my dear, dear Fanny, whom I shall always love as my own soul. Ah! That little bit of judgment that one may have comes hardly into consideration when passion rages. How full becomes my heart! The last time we were together we left one another without understanding one another: for "in this world no one understands another easily." And that is very sad.

That said, he was of no mind to give up hope; eleven days later—during winter recess from Harvard and while visiting with his family in Portland—he asked George Hillard to pass "without delay" an enclosed letter on to "Madonna Francesca," the document itself since lost. "I tell you, I shall succeed in this, O thou of little faith," he wrote, a tacit acknowledgment that his inner circle was trying its best to dissuade him from the quest. But Hillard was a loyal friend, as his jaunty response attests:

> The precious lining was in the hands of the "dark ladye" within one hour after I took it out of the post office, which was this morning at 12. I saw the back of her bonnet (and there was expression even in that) at church today. So she is alive and well. I called there a day or two ago to lend Mary a book and was chatting away very

agreeably (I mean to myself) when Il Padre came in, and gave me a rather freezing reception, not knowing, I suppose, that I was a married man, and above the troubled atmosphere of hope and fear, in which you lovers beat your wings. I felt a numbness stealing over my tongue and soon took my leave. What an atmosphere of beauty and grace and tasteful luxury is diffused over the house. If you are ever its lord, I expect that poetry will ooze out of the pores of your skin. I delight to see you keeping up so stout a heart for the resolve to conquer is half the battle in love as well as war.

Whatever it was that Hillard had passed on to Fanny, it fell on deaf ears. Two weeks later, Henry wrote a letter to Greene that got directly to what was causing him unending anxiety, making him fearful, even, of maintaining his sanity. "A leaden melancholy hangs over me, and from this I pass at times into feverish excitement, bordering on madness; which confines me to my chamber for weeks." His emotional distress, he explained, had been triggered by a "nature" that "craves the love of some good being"—a "sympathy" to him as necessary "as the air I breathe," which brought him to the heart of his dilemma.

"To tell you the whole truth—I saw in Switzerland and traveled with a fair lady—whom I now love passionately (strange will this sound to your ears) and have loved ever since I knew her. A glorious and beautiful being—young—and a woman *not* of talent but of *genius!*—indeed a most rare, sweet woman whose name is Fanny Appleton." Along with her vibrant mind—which, notably, was paramount in Henry's description—was the young woman's physical appeal. "Tall, with a pale face. Well, that pale face is my Fate. Horrible fate it is, too; for she lends no favorable ear to my passion and for my love gives me only friendship. Good friends we are—but she says she loves me not; and I have vowed to win her affection."

SAMUEL LONGFELLOW MADE no mention whatsoever of this anguished letter to Greene in his 1888 biography, which for many years was the definitive treatment of his brother's life and work. Henry's highly uncharacteristic baring of the soul was so disarmingly candid in this instance, in fact, that it remained suppressed well into the twentieth century, kept under wraps by a de facto embargo of highly sensitive materials, most egregiously evident in *Young Longfellow,* the 1938 monograph by Lawrance Thompson, who vented his frustration in an endnote: "This closely written four-page quarto letter is one of the most self-revealing and therefore important autobiographical documents which Longfellow wrote," he declared of the stripped-down summary he was allowed to publish in a single paragraph. "I deeply regret that the Longfellow family refused me permission to quote it." Thompson's other endnotes list, in instance after instance, additional roadblocks, the rationale never fully clarified for him, but explicit enough to suggest that he was veering into personal areas the family had found uncomfortable. Point man for the family during these often contentious discussions was Henry Wadsworth Longfellow Dana—"Harry" Dana—resident curator at Craigie House throughout the years of Thompson's research on the book.

Dana could not prevent Thompson from publishing *Young Longfellow,* but he could restrict use of materials under his control. That he did so is evident not only in Thompson's endnotes, but in correspondence I was permitted to examine by the National Park Service, which has been custodian of the Longfellow Family Trust Archives since 1972. In one instance, Thompson asked permission to reproduce the Eastman Johnson portraits that Henry had commissioned of his friends and himself, all displayed prominently in his study. Dana refused, his explanation betraying an intention to use them in a history of Craigie House he was then proposing to publishers in New York and Boston, none of whom was showing any interest. Dana never disguised that he detested *Young Longfellow*; the archives show he maligned it in letter after letter, and undoubtedly pooh-poohed it in casual conversation with anyone who would listen. The biggest insinuation he made was that Thompson was young and inexperienced—implying that he was unprofessional, and unable, in his view, to focus on what was centrally important, and not be sidetracked by irrelevant distractions.

Thompson (1906–73) was fresh out of college and conducting research for a doctorate from Columbia University when he began looking into the early life of Longfellow. In later years, he was awarded a Fulbright Fellowship, served as director of special collections at Princeton

Samuel Longfellow (1819–92),
Henry's younger brother and
first biographer, from his
Memoir and Letters (Houghton
Mifflin, 1894)

University, edited the *Princeton Gazette,* wrote respected monographs
on Herman Melville and William Faulkner, and won a Pulitzer Prize
in 1971 for the second volume of a three-volume biography of Robert
Frost; he was anything but a lightweight scholar. The Longfellow Trust
files on this episode are substantial; the general thrust is that Thompson
had signed an agreement that a more seasoned writer would never have
entertained, that he submit his manuscript to the Longfellow family for
review in return for access to materials under their control.

Dana used this clause repeatedly to deny direct quotation of materials he felt were out of the scope of Thompson's original premise, and
insisted also that he revise his introduction no fewer than three times—
copies of the drafts are also in the files. One of Dana's primary concerns
was that Thompson was being too tough on Samuel Longfellow's air-
brushing of Henry's personal life, and that he had tiptoed entirely around
his brother's state of mind in the aftermath of Mary's death and during
his anguished pursuit of Fanny Appleton. Dana's principal concern, it
appears, was with anything that suggested Henry's distress, possibly,
even—as Andrew Hilen asserted outright in his collected letters—that

Fanny's ongoing rejection had culminated in his "emotional and physical collapse."

HENRY'S JOURNAL IS replete with mentions of him running into Fanny "by chance," so many of them following a familiar script. "Met Lady Fanny," he wrote on May 19, 1838. "She was as cool as an East wind. Left her at her father's door being obliged to decline her invitation to tea which to tell the truth seemed to me to be given reluctantly." His closest friends were deeply concerned about him. Even Clara Crowninshield inquired delicately as to his well-being. "I hear you have grown *pale* and *low spirited*. Is it so?" Henry's grumpy reply took exception to the characterization. "*Pale and low spirited*. If they had said *lank and silver-haired*, it would have been nearer to the truth; though not exactly true. One's spirits rise and fall, more or less, you know; but I am most of the time cheerful; and should be *ashamed* to be unhappy; as every man ought not to be." On a "prodigiously hot" Sunday in June, he found himself restless. "Lay upon the sofa, reading Goethe's *Hermann und Dorothea*,—a very simple, singular, and beautiful poem." The next paragraph changes gears entirely before ending abruptly in midsentence, closing with an undecipherable word that was later crossed out: "Strange! Day after day only one thought occupies my mind where ever I am whatever I am doing—that thought—that—"

"That"—and then silence—followed by a lapse of two weeks, picking up with a sequence of indifferent commentary indicating nothing out of the ordinary. There were more walks into Boston, several Fanny sightings, a short trip to New York, a few relaxing days in the Berkshires, business taken care of at the college, which included the difficult task of dismissing one instructor and replacing him with someone else. If Henry had a plan on how he might win the affections of the elusive "dark ladie," he never said so outright. But it was around this time, as fall was in the air, that he made what can be argued was one of the worst decisions of his life, second only, in my view, to his insistence on taking his first wife, Mary, with him to Europe in 1835.

Henry had always intended to write about his second trip to Europe, if not along the "sketchbook" lines of *Outre-Mer,* then something, at least, that would introduce American readers to German Romantic literature, and provide signposts to the many places he had visited. Now, another approach took hold, one that included those elements, but folded them into a thinly disguised work of fiction inspired stylistically by some of the German writers he had been studying—Jean-Paul and Goethe in particular—with an enchanting female character worked in who strongly resembled Fanny Appleton; he called this structure a "romance." What was likely driving all this is revealed in a lengthy letter to George Washington Greene that he reckoned to have spent three hours writing. He got directly to the point:

> And first of the "*Dark Ladie,*" who holds my reason captive. As yet no sign of yielding. As stately and sublime, and beautiful as ever! While I likewise sail with the flag nailed to the mast, to sink or conquer. She has been in the country all Summer, and has at length returned to town. But we seldom meet; never except by accident. I have given up society *entirely*: and live alone here, grim as Death, with only that one great thought in my mind. Meanwhile crowds are about her; and flatterers enough; and all the splendor of fashion, and suitors manifold. My hope and faith are firm planted in my righteous cause. If there be any difference between me and those about her—if our souls can understand each other—she will sooner or later find it so. If not—then I take this disappointment likewise by the hand; I bide my own time. But my passion is mighty; *gigantic;*—or it would not have survived this. Meanwhile I labor and work right on with what heart and courage I may, and despise all sympathy; and am quite reasonably cool for a mad-man.

Further on, Henry hinted at what was in the works, but otherwise kept his cards close to the vest. "As soon as I can bring my mind to bear upon a single point, with any effect, I mean to write something, that you shall hear of in distant Italy:—(if in no other way, by letter from me!)." In fact, Henry's journal shows that he was already embarked on such a project, and making very good progress. Two days earlier, he logged having written "a chapter in *Hyperion* which occupied all the morning."

An even earlier mention was made the previous month at a time when Henry was feeling mounting irritation with his academic responsibilities, echoing the frustration he had often felt at Bowdoin. "Perhaps the worst thing in a college life is this having your mind constantly a playmate for boys, constantly adapting itself to them, instead of stretching out and grappling with men's minds." Two days later, it was more of the same. "Lecturing is all well enough, and in my history is an evident advance upon the past. But now one of my French teachers is gone; and this dragooning of school-boys in lessons is like going backward. I do not like it, yet it makes the weeks whirl by at an incredible rate." And then, the next day, was this: "Looked over my notes and papers for *Hyperion.* Long for leisure to begin once more."

Similar entries appear in the weeks that follow, his principal complaint a lack of time for what had become a major work-in-progress. "I have so many interruptions," he complained on October 23. "No matter,—onward. If it be one chapter a week it would complete the book within a year." Six days later, he reported going directly to his study after leaving a faculty meeting, "and wrote half of chapter eight, Book II; namely, the last night at Heidelberg Castle." By the first week of November, multitasking seemed to be energizing his progress. "I feel better these college work-days, when I can let my electricity off among my pupils," he declared one Monday. "Activity,—constant, ceaseless activity,—this is what I need. My heart breaks when I sit alone here so much! A rainy day, and now a rainy night,—for a chapter in *Hyperion*! Let me see what I can do at a dash! Come out of thy drawer, thou thin, marbled portfolio. Open thy lips, and speak of Heidelberg and the Baron!"

Yet what emerged from that "flourish" was nothing but revision and meditation. "And as I sat and meditated deep into the night, I resolved to suppress one entire book; namely, *St. Clair's Day-Book,*" a reference to an early name of the narrator, St. Clair, before finally becoming Paul Flemming. Henry's very next sentence in the journal—his reason to "suppress," as he had put it, "one entire book"—was omitted by Sam Longfellow in his biography, and denied entirely to Lawrance Thompson: "For therein I had laid bare my soul too brave and open to the world." The discarded text for *St. Clair's Day-Book* does not survive among his literary manuscripts.

"A rainy day," he recorded three days later. "Passed the greater part of it at work upon *Hyperion*, retouching and writing. Wrote a new chapter one to Book III; namely, the short chapter on Spring. I am almost crazed today, away, away dark shadows. Leave me forevermore." The entry for November 13 finds him reorganizing material and working on an outline for what remained. The journal then becomes quiet, resuming with "a beautiful idea of introduction" three weeks later. "Then it shall stand— a thing by itself and yet in its theme chiming with the whole. Oh, if I can only perfect it as it stands in my imagination."

On December 15, 1838, Henry reported that another muse had begun to beguile him, marking what can be said was a turning point in his development as a professional writer—the realization that he could work on prose and poetry simultaneously. "A beautiful holy morning within me," he exulted in a passage that reads like an epiphany. "I was softly excited. I knew not why; and wrote with peace in my heart and not without tears in my eyes, 'The Reaper and the Flowers, a Psalm of Death.' I have had an idea of this kind in my mind for a long time, without finding any expression for it in words. This morning it seemed to crystallize at once, without any effort of my own. It would seem as if thoughts, like children, have their periods of gestation, and then are born whether we will or not." He wrote out a fair copy and sent it off to Lewis Gaylord Clark at *The Knickerbocker* in New York, who published it the following month.

"The Reaper and the Flowers" came second in a sequence of special poems that Henry had been tinkering with at this time, a grouping that he called "psalms." Unlike *Hyperion*, which would include a response in prose to his failed pursuit of Fanny, the psalms represented a coming-to-terms with the death of Mary. Henry's first effort in this sequence—"A Psalm of Life"—had taken shape six months earlier, before work on *Hyperion* had even started, and right after he had completed a scholarly article on Anglo-Saxon literature. Eager to take on "something new," he had a "long talk" with Cornelius Conway Felton, his Harvard colleague and a lifelong enthusiast of his work, one Saturday night. It was "one of the pleasantest evenings I have had for a long time," the conversation taking in "matters which lie near one's soul, and how to bear one's self doughtily in life's battle, and make the best of things." The mode of

Anne Longfellow Pierce,
Henry's sister, by Eastman
Johnson, in Longfellow
House dining room

creative expression that followed would be a poem, which Henry sent off immediately to Clark. "Has it not some spirit in it? If, however, you dislike it, into the *fire* with it."

Instead, Clark devoted a full page to "A Psalm of Life" in the October 1838 issue of *The Knickerbocker*, identifying the author simply as "L." Picked up and reprinted by other publications, it reached a national audience, resonating with lines that show up in common discourse to this day—"Life is but an empty dream," "things are not what they seem," "Let the dead Past bury its dead," "Footprints on the sands of time," "Learn to labor and to wait." It would prove, in the long run, to be what people in modern publishing might call Henry's "breakout" work, introducing his poetry to thousands of new readers, and establishing him as a vibrant voice in American letters.

While critics have always been divided on its literary merits, "A Psalm of Life" never lost its currency with the general public. In 1923, Henry Ford told *The New York Times* that the reason he had just bought and restored a three-hundred-year-old tavern in Sudbury, Massachusetts, renowned for having inspired the writing of Longfellow's 1863 collection, *Tales of a Wayside Inn,* was to express gratitude for lessons learned. "It's a small payment to Longfellow for four stanzas he wrote in 'A Psalm of

Life,' the first, second, sixth and ninth verses," he said. "I probably have got more out of that poem than any other poem. A great man, Longfellow." Three years later, the industrialist bought a blacksmith shop in the town of Uxbridge, Massachusetts, for similar reasons, this time for its having given Longfellow the idea for "The Village Blacksmith."

"A Psalm of Life" would be published in many languages throughout the world, including Sanskrit and Hebrew, even Chinese. In 1865, a delicately handcrafted ceremonial fan adorned on the panels with verses from the poem in Mandarin Chinese, painted by the imperial court calligrapher Dong Xun, was presented to Henry by Anson Burlingame, the American minister to China, during a dinner party at Craigie House. Henry identified the source and occasion of the gift in pencil on one of the bamboo handles of the fan, and kept it upstairs, in his living quarters, where it was discovered years later on the floor of a linen closet during a routine inventory in the early 1990s.

Far more significant is the renewed impulse Henry had now fully embraced for poetic composition. "It is raining, raining with a soft and pleasant sound," he mused not long after his night of intense discussion with Felton. "I cannot read, I cannot write,—but dream only. The visits of many pleasant thoughts, the coming and going of strange and foreign fantasies, have left my mind ajar, and it swings to and fro in the wind of various opinions. I have been looking at the old Northern Sagas, and thinking of a series of ballads or a romantic poem on the deeds of the first bold Viking who crossed to this western world, with storm-spirits and devil-machinery under water. New England ballads I have long thought of. This seems to be an introduction. I will dream more of this."

Dream more he would—and the Northern Sagas would have their influence in due course, too, and ballads would soon flow from his pen—but the first order of business was to complete *Hyperion*. Henry's journal for November is mostly quiet, resuming on December 4 with "a beautiful idea" for an introduction. "Then it shall stand—a thing by itself and yet in its theme chiming with the whole. Oh, if I can only perfect it as it stands in my imagination!" On December 10, the first part was "ready for the press." The following night, he made his "first appearance at a party this season" at the home of "Aunt Sam" Appleton. "A very bright, beautiful affair. My lovely Fanny there. Tried to speak unconcernedly and made poor work of it, no matter." But his unease carried over to the next day nonetheless: "Could not work this morning after the unusual occurrences of last evening. Wrote a page in *Hyperion* and could go no further."

Henry had given a few of his closest friends a vague heads-up on what was in the works, allowing only that he was writing a romance. His letter to Charles Sumner, who had been traveling then in England, is lost, but Sumner's reply expresses the "wish" that he had sent "some sketch of your Romance. I should rejoice to do something for you here, if I could, but you have given me no *data*." Henry was similarly evasive with Sam Ward. "I wanted to tell you what I was busy about," he said of an intention to write earlier, "then I thought I had better keep my secret, as I have not told it to any friend here. I hate to say what I am doing. With some authors, as with money diggers, when a work is spoken, the charm is broken, and the treasure sinks. I hope it will not be so in this case; though it has often happened to me before."

He admitted also to having resumed writing poetry after a long hiatus, "the Muse being to me a chaste wife, not a Messalina, to be debauched in the public street." But at the moment, he was still focused on *Hyperion,* and his entries over the next few months show him working "like a hero" to get it finished. A manuscript, finally, was "in the printer's hands" on June 8, and three days later proof sheets arrived. "It will look well," he declared, "and Felton says it reads well."

As publication day approached, his anxiety swelled. "I cannot move an inch till *Hyperion* is out of press," he wrote Sam Ward. "You will like it; because you will understand it with the *heart* as well as with the *brain*. I hope others will likewise; for if the book does not succeed will not the author,—as an *author,* be *dished?*" Ten days later, he informed Greene that *Hyperion* was "a *reality*; not a shadow or a ghostly semblance of a book," one in which he had "put my feelings, my hopes and sufferings for the last three years." The past few months in particular, he allowed with uncommon candor, had been a period when "I have been *very* near madness, and even death." Now, he looked to the future: "I have great faith in one's writing himself clear from a passion—giving vent to the pent-up fire."

9

Mutual Admiration Society

It is of great importance for a man to know how he stands with his friends; at least, I think so. Through good report and through evil report, the voice of a friend has a wonder working power; and from the very hour we hear it, "the fever leaves us."

—Henry Wadsworth Longfellow letter to
George Washington Greene, June 5, 1836

I called it *Hyperion,* because it moves on high among clouds and stars, and expresses the various aspirations of the soul of man. It is all modelled on this idea, style and all. It contains my cherished thoughts for three years.

—Henry Wadsworth Longfellow letter to
George Washington Greene, January 2, 1840

The first copies of *Hyperion* came off the presses in August 1839, an event of no small import as far as Henry was concerned, if only for the fact that it was done, finally, and out in the world. "This book is a reality; not a shadow, or a ghostly semblance of a book," he informed Greene. "My heart has been put into the printing-press and stamped on the pages. Whatever the public may think of it, it will always be valuable to me, and to my friends because it is a part of me." The finished product was an amalgamation of literary forms intended to accomplish several goals, the original ones—an introduction for American readers to the German Romantic writers Henry had discovered during his second trip to Europe, and a scenic tour of the many fabulous sights—were combined with a plot twist based on his failed quest for the affections of Fanny Appleton, presented in the guise of a fictional character he called Mary Ashburton.

The first mention in Henry's journal of a published review came on October 1; unsigned, the piece had appeared in the *Evening Mercantile Journal*, a Boston newspaper, the gist of it an unflattering assertion that the author had written a "mongrel mixture of description and criticism, travels and bibliography, common-places clad in purple, and follies 'with not a rag to cover them.'" Henry never responded publicly to negative criticism, and remained characteristically stolid in this instance. "Some one has made a savage onslaught upon *Hyperion*," he wrote bemusedly in his journal, taking it all in stride. "What care I? Not one straw. He has pulled so hard that he has snapped the bow-string. He seems to be very angry. What an unhappy disposition he must have, to be so much annoyed!"

Hard on the heels of that notice came an unsigned review in *Burton's Gentleman's Magazine*, a Philadelphia periodical edited by Edgar Allan Poe, who had chosen the moment to initiate a disparagement of Henry's work he would come to call his own "Little Longfellow War." His off-the-rails assault would continue well into the 1840s and include unfounded charges of plagiarism. There were other writers Poe disliked, but for reasons still unclear, he trained his heaviest artillery on Henry, whose stature and material success were steadily on the rise. Henry never denied that a good deal of what he did was "derivative" of European genres and meters he used as models, but the inference that he lifted texts outright was patently absurd, and has never been supported by any credible evidence. In 1846, Henry recorded having discovered that the image of a fallen star in his poem "Excelsior" was similar to one in "The Mocking-Bird" by the poet John Brainard, an unwitting circumstance, he maintained, but similar all the same. "Of a truth," he added, "we cannot strike a spade into the soil of Parnassus, without disturbing the bones of some dead poet."

Poe offered no specifics to support his trashing of *Hyperion*, though he was adamant that Henry's days of public favor would be short-lived.

"We have no design of commenting, at any length, upon what Professor Longfellow has written," he declared. "We are indignant that he too has been recreant to the good cause. We, therefore, dismiss his *Hyperion* in brief. We grant him high qualities, but deny him the Future. In the present instance, without design, without shape, without beginning, middle, or end, what earthly object has the book accomplished?—what definite impression has it left?" Henry's reputation ultimately did suffer, the most egregious victim of the modernist movement's wholesale dismissal of traditional literary forms, a reality not lost on Poe's apologists, who cite it as proof of his prescience in such matters, though the reality is more complex than that, having more to do with cultural politics and less with literary merit.

What Poe trumpeted publicly was not necessarily reinforced by what he advanced privately, either, especially evident in two letters he wrote to Henry a year and a half after his attack on *Hyperion*. Poe had just been named editor of *Graham's,* successor to *Burton's Gentleman's Magazine*, with a national circulation then approaching forty thousand copies a month, and was eager to recruit Henry as a contributor. "I should be overjoyed," he wrote, "if we could get from you an article each month—either poetry or prose—length and subject a discretion. In respect to terms we would gladly offer you carte blanche—and the periods of payment should also be made to suit yourself." Poe expressed his "highest respect" for Henry's work with words that can be read as hypocritical at best, obsequious at worst: "I cannot refrain from availing myself of this, the only opportunity I may ever have, to assure the author of the 'Hymn to the Night,' of the 'Beleaguered City' and of the 'Skeleton in Armor' of the fervent admiration with which his genius has inspired me."

In declining the offer—"I am so much occupied at present that I could not do it with any satisfaction either to you or to myself"—Henry extended a palm leaf of sorts to Poe's fawning confession that he had "no reason to think myself favorably known to you." His reply: "You are mistaken in supposing that you are not 'favorably known' to me. On the contrary, all that I have read, from your pen, has inspired me with a high idea of your power; and I think you are destined to stand among the first romance-writers of the country, if such be your aim." Poe's follow-up attempted another tack—perhaps Henry might consider writing for another magazine his employer, George R. Graham, was then considering, but never launched? "The amplest funds will be embarked in the undertaking. The work will be an octavo of 96 pages. The paper will be of excellent quality—possibly finer than that upon which your *Hyperion* was printed." Henry opened negotiations directly with George Graham the following year, after Poe left the magazine. They worked productively together on numerous projects, including *The Spanish Student,* a dramatic work in verse inspired by a Cervantes tale, and published in three consecutive issues of *Graham's Magazine.*

Poe, meanwhile, intensified his attack, which Henry ignored with a silence that had to have been infuriating. He made no mention of him at all in his journal for three and a half years, and then only offhandedly, at a time when he was wondering what to call the heroine of a long narrative poem he had just started to write. "Shall it be 'Gabrielle,'" he mused on December 7, 1845, "or 'Celestine,' or 'Evangeline'?" Two days later he mentioned having just read "a very abusive article upon my poems" by William Gilmore Simms, a Southern author and a great favorite of Poe's, who shared his views. "I consider this the most original and inventive of all his fictions." The next day, he praised a "superb poem" by his friend James Russell Lowell that he had just read in *Graham's Magazine.* "If he goes on in this vein," he offered, "Poe will soon begin to pound him."

A review in the *New-York Daily Tribune* on December 20 by Margaret Fuller, who never warmed to his work, either, drew what for Henry amounted to an annoyed response but, given the tenor of her scorn, is remarkable for its restraint. The "furious onslaught," as Henry called the lengthy notice, had avowed him to be a poet of "moderate powers" with "no style of his own," declaring further that little of what he wrote emerged from personal experience or observation. "Nature with him, whether human or external, is always seen through the window of literature. There are in his poems sweet and tender passages descriptive of his personal feelings, but very few showing him as an observer, at first hand, of the passions within, or the landscape without." Henry had a single response: "It is what might be called 'a bilious attack.' She is a dreary woman." Not one to hold a grudge, his attitude toward Fuller softened appreciably four years later when news spread that she had become a mother—and taken a husband ten years her junior—in that order. "We hear that Margaret Fuller is married in Italy, to a revolutionary marquis, secretly married a year ago, and has a baby! It will do her a prodigious deal of good."

Henry usually preferred another kind of response to his critics. Two weeks after Fuller's excoriation of his work had been published, he learned that "The Belfry of Bruges" was "succeeding famously well" in the marketplace, and that the poems "To a Child" and "The Old Clock on the Stairs" were popular with his admirers. "This," he declared, "is the best answer to my assailants," and left the matter there. The general public had also responded favorably to *Hyperion*. Over time it became a go-to handbook for travelers to the Rhineland, and an essential reference to German Romantic literature.

Numerous illustrated editions would appear in the years ahead, including one published in 1865 with twenty-four albumen prints of castles, villages, mountain glaciers, and literary sites across Germany, Switzerland, and Austria taken by the landscape photographer Francis Frith, qualifying it as the first printed book to feature photographic images. In 1918, the literary scholar W. A. Chamberlain called Henry the "foremost interpreter to the American public of German life for his generation," and credited *Hyperion* for much of that success. James Taft Hatfield cited twenty-five German authors and poets whose works were introduced to American readers in *Hyperion*, including Goethe and Schiller.

Very rarely did the early critics discuss in any depth the autobiographical elements that deal with the Mary Ashburton character. Those that did, such as his good friend Cornelius Conway Felton in the sixteen-page review he wrote for *The North American Review,* did not connect the episode directly to the author. Paul Flemming is introduced in the early pages of the book as a grief-stricken American traveling through Europe, having recently lost the "friend of his youth," the precise relationship vaguely stated, but the suggestion clear enough that it was spousal. "He could no longer live alone, where he had lived with her," was the rationale for the trip abroad, a great distance from home necessary so that "the sea might be between him and the grave."

As *Hyperion* opens, Flemming is "pursuing his way along the Rhine, to the south of Germany," a region he remembered well from a previous journey. "He knew the beauteous river all by heart;—every rock and ruin, every echo, every legend. The ancient castles, grim and hoar, that had taken root as it were on the cliffs,—they were all his; for his thoughts dwelt in them, and the wind told him tales." Significantly, it is the sound of Mary Ashburton's voice, not her appearance, that first captures Flemming's attention. He is aware of a "female figure, clothed in black" who enters a public gathering space in a Swiss inn where he is waiting to be assigned a room, and listens as she joins in a conversation with other guests, her words "spoken in a voice so musical and full of soul" that he calls it "a whisper from heaven." Because it is twilight and the surroundings dark, he does not have an opportunity to match the sound with the face before he is called out by the landlord and directed to his assigned quarters.

Flemming later asks a friend he has made on the journey who the young lady "with the soft voice" was, and is told her name: Mary Ashburton. "Is she beautiful?" he asks, eliciting an answer that could not have pleased Miss Appleton one bit when she read it. "Not in the least," he is told, "but very intellectual. A woman of genius, I should say." Flemming swiftly backtracks on this crude assessment, pointing the finger elsewhere. "They did her wrong, who said she was not beautiful," he insists, noting that Ashburton's face has "a wonderful fascination in it," a "calm, quiet face, with the light of the rising soul shining so peacefully" through it. "And O, those eyes,—those deep unutterable eyes."

Fanny Appleton, we know from her passport, was five feet ten inches tall when she sailed for Europe—two inches taller than Henry—and carried herself with confidence. So endowed, too, was Mary Ashburton. "The lady's figure was striking. Every step, every attitude was graceful, and yet lofty, as if inspired by the soul within. Angels in the old poetic philosophy have such forms; it was the soul itself imprinted on the air. And what a soul was hers! A temple dedicated to Heaven, and, like the Pantheon at Rome, lighted only from above." Flemming thereupon spends a fortnight with Ashburton and her widowed mother, seizing every opportunity to be near the young woman, who, we are told, is "in her twentieth" year. "He conversed with her; and with her alone; and knew not when to go. All others were to him as if they were not there. He saw their forms, but saw them as the forms of inanimate things."

Together, they translate into English a ballad by Uhland—"The Castle by the Sea," the same poem rendered by Henry and Fanny, with the same result: the lady's version being the better of the two. When the moment calls for a folk tale, Flemming invents one out of whole cloth. Ashburton matches Flemming insight for insight on topics of weight and significance, and enthralls him with her ability to draw evocative scenes in her sketchbook with assured ease. During one stop, Flemming is "reclining on the flowery turf, at the lady's feet, looking up with dreamy eyes into her sweet face, and then into the leaves of the linden-trees overhead."

We can only speculate on how mutual acquaintances in Boston and Cambridge responded to Henry's public confession that his alter ego was "haunted" at all times of the day by thoughts of the young woman. "He walked as in a dream; and was hardly conscious of the presence of those around him. A sweet face looked at him from every page of every book he read; and it was the face of Mary Ashburton! A sweet voice spake to him in every sound he heard; and it was the voice of Mary Ashburton! Day and night succeeded each other, with pleasant interchange of light and darkness; but to him the passing of time was only as a dream. When he arose in the morning, he thought only of her, and wondered if she were yet awake; and when he lay down at night he thought only of her." In the end, his intensity proves to be too much for Mary Ashburton. Flemming is sensibly advised to accept the harsh reality of failure and move along—the same advice Henry had received from his own support group. "I love this woman with a deep, and lasting affection," Flemming counters in response. "I shall never cease to love her. This may be madness in me; but so it is."

On Beacon Hill, the general reaction to *Hyperion* was silence, but in private, everyone knew who was who among the players. Writing to Fanny Calderón de la Barca in the summer of 1840, the historian William Hickling Prescott told how Fanny Appleton's "bright eyes were filled with sadness" at a party he had recently attended in Newport, the absence of her sister Mary causing continued distress. "That separation has cost her a heartache—the only one I suspect she has ever known, for she walks 'in maiden meditation, fancy free,' and free in fact, I suspect, in spite of all poor Longfellow's prose and poetry."

Three years later, when there was a rapprochement, the tongues were wagging overtime. Inviting an acquaintance in New York to visit him in Massachusetts that summer, Charles Sumner noted that he would likely "find Longfellow a married man" when he arrived, "for he is now engaged to Miss Fanny Appleton,—the Mary Ashburton of *Hyperion*,—a lady of the greatest sweetness, imagination, and elevation of character, with the most striking personal charms." Julia Ward Howe recalled after Henry's death how well-known it had been years earlier that Fanny was "the supposed prototype of Mary Ashburton," and that "conjectures were not wanting as to the possible progress and denouement of the real romance which seemed to underlie the graceful fiction. This romance indeed existed, and its hopes and aspirations were crowned in due time by a marriage which led to years of noble and serene companionship."

That said, it would be a mistake to suggest that Henry was spending all his time pouting about his private life to the exclusion of everything else. Within the space of a single year, three works—*Hyperion,* his prose romance; *Voices of the Night,* his widely admired first collection of poetry; and *The Spanish Student,* his play in three parts—had appeared in print. Significant, too, as these three efforts indicate, is that he was working concurrently with different literary forms—an unacknowledged bow in the direction of Goethe, maybe, whose proficiency in multiple disciplines was an inspiration to him, the figurine of the German writer kept front and center on his writing desk a validation of that.

If there was solace to be found in the short run, it came from a group of professional people who provided support to Henry in many ways, including favorable notices several of them wrote of *Hyperion* for influential publications. On more than one occasion, this group would be anointed the Mutual Admiration Society, a description they all embraced. The friendships Henry firmed up at this time endured for the remainder of his life, most of them with men, but a few with women as well, most notably Julia Ward Howe, the brilliant sister of his friend Sam Ward; Catherine Eliot Norton, the wife of Andrews Norton; Annie Adams Fields, the wife of his longtime editor James T. Fields; and his landlady, Elizabeth Craigie, for whom he developed a special affection in the short time he knew her. If likability is innate, he had it in abundance, apparent from the briefest of encounters to the most cherished relationships. "Once your friend, Longfellow was always your friend; he would not think evil of you, and if he knew evil of you, he would be the last of all that knew it to judge you for it," William Dean Howells wrote a few years after Henry's death.

People extolled his knack for paying attention to what they had to say, and for never uttering anything he might one day regret having said. "A part of Mr. Longfellow's charm was his way of listening; another charm was his beauty, which was remarkable," the Boston socialite Mary E. W. Sherwood (1826–1903) wrote in an entertaining memoir of her many encounters with well-placed literary, social, and political figures of the nineteenth century. The portrait artist Wyatt Eaton (1849–96) recalled being "struck by the great intentness, almost a stare," Henry had cast during the course of several sittings. "His eyes were so brilliant that he really seemed to be looking one through. It was this gaze that I tried to get in my portrait."

The writer William Winter (1836–1917) regarded Henry as a mentor, so much in awe of him, according to Ernest Longfellow, that he was "too timid to refuse" his father's offer of a cigar every time he came, "which invariably made him sick, so that he would have to retire to the garden." Winter recalled a conversation he had with Henry about Edgar Allan Poe, by then long since deceased. "I was sitting with him, at his fireside, and when I chanced to observe a volume of Poe's poems on his library table, I inquired whether he had ever met Poe and was assured that he had not. Longfellow opened the book and read aloud a few stanzas of the poem 'For Annie,' remarking that one of them, containing the line 'And the fever called living is over at last,' would be an appropriate epitaph for its writer. There was not a shade of resentment in either his manner or voice. 'My works,' he said, 'seemed to give Mr. Poe much trouble; but I am alive and still writing.'" Henry then offered Winter some counsel. "You are at the beginning of your career, and I advise you never to answer the attacks that will be made on you," the example of his own approach to Poe obviously implied. "I did not then know, but subsequently learned, he naturally attracted to himself all persons intrinsically noble. His gentleness was elemental. His tact was inerrant. His patience never failed. As I recall him, I am conscious of a beautiful spirit; a lovely life; a perfect image of continence, wisdom, dignity, sweetness, and grace."

Winter was not aware—or if he was, he never let on in print—that there had been an extraordinary gesture of kindness on Henry's part with respect to Poe, evident only by examination of his incoming correspondence and personal account books. In 1850, Henry received a letter from Maria Poe Clemm (1790–1871), both aunt and mother-in-law to Poe, since her "dear Eddy" had married his first cousin, Virginia, the daughter of this woman, who was the daughter of his paternal grandfather. Poe had died the previous year. "Muddy," as Poe called her, was then living in Lowell, and wrote Henry, a total stranger, asking for help—a tactic she used with other writers, including Charles Dickens, who—like Henry—sent her small sums. Her letters to Henry, fifteen of them in the Houghton collections, are worth reading if only for the boldness she brought to bear, asking him to send, in addition to money, signed first editions of his books and autographs she could sell. That Henry did so—without commenting on it to anyone—is further evidence of his compassion and goodwill.

Given the number of best-selling books he had on the Ticknor and Fields front list in the days following the Civil War, Henry was a special client of the firm, according to Edwin D. Mead (1849–1937), who went to work for the publisher in 1866 as a low-level office assistant. It was not uncommon for Ralph Waldo Emerson, Harriet Beecher Stowe, John Greenleaf Whittier, Oliver Wendell Holmes, William Dean Howells, or Longfellow himself to visit their offices, by then relocated from the Old Corner Bookstore on Washington and School Streets to larger accommodations on Tremont. Henry was already an international celebrity when Mead came aboard, and whatever "concerned Longfellow concerned every boy at 124 Tremont Street." Henry "knew us every one, every time," he wrote. "His smile as he opened the door said: 'Here we go again!' and his entrance was always a benediction. As I now look back, his seems to me to be the noblest face and presence that I ever knew."

Henry became acquainted with the classicist Cornelius Conway Felton (1808–1862) while still teaching at Bowdoin and arranging to get his textual translations published in Boston and Cambridge. Fluent in many languages, Felton taught at Harvard for more than thirty years. "As a Greek scholar," a eulogist for the Smithsonian Institution wrote

Cornelius Conway Felton, by Eastman
Johnson, 1846, in the first-floor study
of Longfellow House

following his death, "he was not surpassed for breadth and accuracy by
any other in the land." Felton was named professor of Greek at Harvard
in 1832, four years before Henry joined the faculty, and became Harvard's president in 1860. He was a champion of Henry's writing, even
worked with him on his anthology of world poetry, and is thought by
some, myself included, to have been the person who in 1845, under the
pen name Outis (from the Greek word οὖτις, for "nobody"), wrote a
brilliantly erudite defense against Poe's spiteful charges of plagiarism,
resulting, ultimately, in Poe's retraction.

It was Felton, too, who introduced Henry to Charles Sumner, a high-
energy Boston lawyer who moonlighted for a time as a law instructor at
Harvard and became, in time, Henry's closest friend. Along with Sumner's law partner, George Hillard, and Henry R. Cleveland, an aspiring
writer, the men formed an informal social association they dubbed the
Five of Clubs, and met regularly for dinner and conversation, usually
at the Tremont House, leading one "ironical lady," in the words of Julia
Ward Howe, to dub them the Mutual Admiration Society, a nickname
that found its way into the newspapers, and stuck.

Cleveland's principal contribution was to ensure a proper ambiance
for club gatherings, his largesse made possible by the happy circumstance of having married a wealthy socialite. In a posthumous tribute—

he died in 1843 at the age of thirty-four—George Hillard described his "sweet" spirit as being driven by a "wide and generous hospitality" and an "almost maternal fondness and tenderness of feeling." A staple of their Saturday soirees was freshly shucked oysters served with champagne, a tradition Henry continued several decades later when hosting meetings in his home of the Dante Club. Cleveland's death opened the way for Samuel Gridley Howe to join their ranks. A practicing physician, abolitionist, and reformer, Howe achieved widespread fame for his work at the Perkins School for the Blind with Laura Bridgman, sightless and deaf from scarlet fever when she began instruction under his direction in 1837 at the age of seven. It was during a field trip to see Bridgman with Henry and Sumner that Julia Ward was introduced to her future husband.

George Washington Greene, recipient of close to six hundred letters from Henry over the four decades of their friendship, held a special place in the poet's pantheon of intimates. Henry did not love him for his intellect, which was decent but by no means staggering, or his sage advice, since he typically was the one griping the most about the vicissitudes of life, and the one who needed the most assistance through the many years of their acquaintance. Henry loved Greene, it seems, simply because he was Greene, a fellow New Englander he had met in Marseilles when he was nineteen, the man who introduced him to Italy, the man who like himself had a grandfather who had fought honorably in the Revolution.

It was at this time, too, that Nathaniel Hawthorne reached out to his old college classmate, reminding him of their days a decade earlier as Bowdoin undergraduates. The two had never been close, but with just thirty-eight students in the class of 1825, they had crossed paths from time to time, even delivered honors orations once on the same program. Hawthorne would tell Annie Adams Fields many years later that "no two young men could have been more unlike" at Bowdoin; Henry, he told her, was a "tremendous student, and always carefully dressed, while he himself was extremely careless of his appearance, no student at all, and entirely incapable of appreciating Longfellow." Impressed by the success of *Outre-Mer,* Hawthorne sent Henry a copy of *Twice-Told Tales,* his newly published book. "We were not, it is true, so well acquainted at college that I can plead an absolute right to inflict my 'twice-told'

Nathaniel Hawthorne, 1846,
by Eastman Johnson, in Henry's
study at Longfellow House

tediousness upon you," he wrote frankly, "but I have often regretted we were not better known to each other, and have been glad of your success in literature and in more important matters."

Henry responded in the best way possible—proclaiming the arrival of a major new talent in an effusive notice for *The North American Review.* "When a star rises in the heavens, people gaze after it for a season with the naked eye, and with such telescopes as they may find," he wrote, using imagery likely inspired by talk of Harvard erecting a powerful observatory on property adjoining Craigie House. "In the stream of thought, which flows so peacefully deep and clear through this book, we see the bright reflection of a spiritual star, after which men will be prone to gaze 'with the naked eye and with the spy-glasses of criticism.'" The immediate result was a friendship that held firm to the day Hawthorne died at the age of fifty-nine in 1864. Henry mourned "dear Nat's" passing in his "Elegy for Hawthorne," a nine-stanza poem that concluded with sadness for works left undone:

> There in seclusion and remote from men
>   The wizard hand lies cold,
> Which at its topmost speed let fall the pen,
>   And left the tale half told.

> Ah! who shall lift that wand of magic power,
> And the lost clew regain?
> The unfinished windows in Aladdin's tower
> Unfinished must remain!

AS 1841 BECAME 1842, Henry was deeply depressed, suffering a case of the blues so severe that he had decided to take a "water-cure" in Germany to relieve his various ailments. Those plans were put on hold when word arrived from England that the celebrated author of *Pickwick Papers, Oliver Twist, Nicholas Nickleby,* and *The Old Curiosity Shop*—Charles Dickens—was coming to the United States for a series of public appearances, with the first stop of the tour being Boston. It was a testament to Henry's growing stature as a literary lion in his own right that he was asked, along with Oliver Wendell Holmes, to coordinate a proper reception for the esteemed visitor, an opportunity they both embraced.

Dickens described to his close friend and future biographer, the critic John Forster, the frenzy that greeted his arrival in Boston. "How can I give you the faintest notion of my reception here; of the crowds that pour in and out the whole day; of the people that line the streets when I go out; of the cheering when I went to the theatre; of the copies of verses, letters of congratulation, welcomes of all kinds, balls, dinners, assemblies without end? There is to be a public dinner to me here in Boston, next Tuesday, and great dissatisfaction has been given to the many by the high price (three pounds sterling each) of the tickets." Henry made an afternoon call on Dickens at the Tremont House, bringing with him Harvard colleagues Felton and Jared Sparks. Later that night, in letters to Sam Ward in New York and his father in Maine, Henry deemed the day to have been "glorious." To his father, he added how Dickens was "engaged three deep for the remainder of his stay, in the way of dinners and parties." He described him as "a gay, free and easy character" with blue eyes, long black hair, and a "fine bright face."

Dickens readily accepted Henry's invitation for a Sunday walking tour of the city, their route to parallel many of the spots along the harbor that now dot the heavily trod Freedom Trail historic district, including the wharf where the Boston Tea Party was staged by the Sons of Liberty in 1773; Charles Sumner accompanied them on the promenade. At the Seamen's Bethel Church in the North End, they attended a sermon delivered by the fiery Methodist minister Edward Thompson Taylor, an outspoken advocate of the temperance movement, and renowned for his work on behalf of itinerant sailors. Leaving the chapel, they passed by Paul Revere's house and the Old North Church, then proceeded into Charlestown and the Navy Yard, home port of the USS *Constitution*, immortalized by Holmes twelve years earlier as "Old Ironsides" in a poem that saved the frigate from the scrapyard.

At Copp's Hill Burying Ground, they looked at the tombstone inscriptions of Revolutionary War dead; at Bunker Hill they admired the towering stone obelisk just being completed to memorialize the battle fought there in June 1775. What they discussed we can only surmise, but Henry may well have mentioned that two months before that momentous battle took place, General Washington had commandeered a house in Cambridge to serve as his headquarters and residence during the Siege of Boston, the very building where he was then living. Dickens, in any case, accepted Henry's invitation to join him there the following Friday for breakfast.

Henry by then had three spacious rooms on the second floor, one ideal for receiving visitors. His invitation to Sam Ward brimmed with ebullience. "When shall you be here? Dickens breakfasts with me on Friday. Will you come? Let me know beforehand, every place at table is precious." Ward could not make the "bright little breakfast," as Sam Longfellow described it, but half a dozen Harvard bigwigs did break bread with the man of the hour. Dickens took a coach to Cambridge, and walked the half mile from Harvard Square—known then simply as the Market Place—to Craigie House. On the way over, he passed the "spreading chestnut tree" on Brattle Street made famous in "The Village Blacksmith," which had appeared in *The Knickerbocker* a year earlier and was just being published in Henry's second collection of verse, *Ballads and Other Poems*. They concluded the morning with a stroll over to Gore Hall, home then of the Harvard College library, where other admirers alerted in advance of the visit were waiting.

Informed of Henry's evolving travel plans, Dickens minced no words about what stops he expected would be included on his itinerary: "My dear Longfellow," he wrote from New York. "You are coming to England, you know. When you return to London, I shall be there, please God. Write to me from the continent, and tell me when to expect you. We live quietly—not uncomfortably—and among people whom I am sure you would like to know; as much as they would like to know you. Have no home but mine—see nothing in town on your way towards Germany— and let me be your London host and cicerone. Is this a bargain?"

TORMENTED THROUGHOUT his life by a variety of chronic ailments, Henry was forever seeking relief. Mentions of headaches, neuralgia, blurry eyesight, toothaches, dyspepsia, dizziness, colds, and insomnia turn up often in his journals and letters, though rarely to the point of forcing him to abandon his work ethic. An exception came on January 24, 1842, when he asked the Harvard Corporation for a six-month leave of absence to take a therapeutic "water-cure" and dietary program then being offered at a former Benedictine convent at Marienberg overlook- ing the town of Boppard on the Rhine. "In this time," he wrote, "I propose to visit Germany, to try the effect of certain baths, by means of which, as well as by the relaxation and sea-voyage, I hope to re-establish my health." School officials were not overly pleased by this, but granted the request; he got his six months, to begin in May. He would write just one piece of poetry that summer, a sonnet scrawled out on a sheet of scrap paper he called "Mezzo Cammin," drawing his title from the opening line of Dante's *Inferno* ("Nel mezzo del cammin di nostra vita"), which translates into English as "Half Journey." The poem reflected harshly on what Henry felt he had accomplished in his first thirty-five years, and remained unpublished during his lifetime:

> Half of my life is gone, and I have let
>   The years slip from me and have not fulfilled
>   The aspiration of my youth, to build
>   Some tower of song with lofty parapet.

Not indolence, nor pleasure, nor the fret
  Of restless passions that would not be stilled,
  But sorrow, and a care that almost killed,
  Kept me from what I may accomplish yet;
Though, half-way up the hill, I see the Past
  Lying beneath me with its sounds and sights,—
  A city in the twilight dim and vast,
With smoking roofs, soft bells, and gleaming lights,—
  And hear above me on the autumnal blast
  The cataract of Death far thundering from the heights.

Henry did find sufficient time to go book hunting, advising Sumner that he had "dispatched" to Rotterdam "a large box of books to go by first ship" to Boston. "I know not how it is, but during a voyage I collect books as a ship does barnacles. These books are German, Flemish, and French." Another bright spot was meeting the poet Ferdinand Freiligrath, who would translate many of Henry's poems into German in the years to come. Freiligrath's radical political views also influenced Henry to contribute, however mildly, to the cause of abolition back home. "Oh, I long for those verses on slavery," Sumner had written from Boston. "Write some stirring words that shall move the whole land. Send them home and we'll publish them. Let us know how you occupy yourself with that heavenly gift of invention."

Henry's response, jotted down during a break from his therapy, was noncommittal. "There is no inspiration in dressing and undressing," he wrote of his daily routine. "Hunger and thirst figure too largely here, to leave room for poetical figures." His mood brightened when he heard from Dickens: "Your bed is waiting to be slept in, the door is gaping hospitably to receive you, I am ready to spring towards it with open arms at the first indication of a Longfellow knock or ring; and the door, the bed, I, and everybody else who is in the secret, have been expecting you for the last month." Once he had arrived in London, Henry was accommodated in grand style. Overnight, the lows of "Mezzo Cammin" soared to intoxicating highs. "I write this from Dickens' study, the focus from which so many luminous things have radiated," he informed Sumner. "The raven croaks from the garden; and the ceaseless roar of London fills my ears. Of course, I have no time for a letter, as I must run up in a few minutes to dress for dinner."

It was nonstop for two weeks, elegant dinners, concerts, plays, "Shakespeare on the stage as never he was seen before." There were drinks with the book illustrator George Cruikshank and the portrait painter Daniel Maclise, and an après-play get-together with the actor William Macready at Drury Lane following his performance in *As You Like It*. Dickens graciously presented copies of *Ballads and Other Poems* to his friends; and just as Henry had shown him the Boston waterfront, Dickens worked in a few side trips of his own, one to see "the tramps and thieves" of the London slums, "the worst haunts of the most dangerous classes."

Henry's mornings were not passed idly, either, not with the Savile Row fashion district nearby, and the opportunity to be fitted for some stylish English clothes and shoes. "McDowall, the boot maker, Beale the Hosier, Laffin the Trousers Maker, and Blackmore the Coat Cutter, have all been at the point of death, but have slowly recovered," Dickens teased in a letter posted a few weeks after Henry's departure. "The medical gentlemen agreed that it was exhaustion, occasioned by early rising—to wait upon you, at those unholy hours." In the little down time he did have, Henry read *American Notes,* which Dickens had given him on arrival. "I have read Dickens' book," he informed Sumner of the new release. "It is jovial and good natured," though at times "very severe," a subtle alert to what would be received by many in the United States as a rebuke of the dark underbelly of American culture. "You will read it with delight and, for the most part, approbation. He has a grand chapter on Slavery."

During a turbulent voyage home, Henry responded to the pleas of his friends. "The great waves struck and broke with voices of thunder," he wrote Freiligrath after his return. "In the next room to mine, a man died. I was afraid they might throw me overboard instead of him in the night; but they did not. Well, thus 'cribbed, cabined and confined,' I passed fifteen days. During this time I wrote seven poems on Slavery. I meditated upon them in the stormy, sleepless nights, and wrote them down with a pencil in the morning. A small window in the side of the vessel admitted light into my berth; and there I lay on my back, and soothed my soul with songs."

Issued by the Cambridge publisher John Owen, *Poems on Slavery* did not attack slave owners directly, focusing instead on the lives of African Americans, portraying them with broad, sentimental strokes. Nowhere did he minimize the humiliations they endured, nor did he downplay in any way the immorality of human bondage. In "The Slave in the Dismal Swamp," a "hunted Negro" on the run, "infirm and lame" from repeated beatings, lies "crouched in the rank and tangled grass" like "a wild beast in his lair," the sound of a "horse's tramp" in pursuit and a "bloodhound's distant bay" filling the air. A central image in "The Slave's Dream" is the "driver's whip" that maintains order among the oppressed; taking the form of a ballad, "The Quadroon Girl" tells of a beautiful young woman on an island paradise, presumably in the Caribbean, who is sold for "glittering gold" as chattel to a passing ship captain, her fate to be his "slave and paramour in a strange and distant land." The most poignant of the seven poems, "The Witnesses," describes a sunken ship "half buried in the sands" in which "lie skeletons in chains," with "shackled feet and hands":

> These are bones of Slaves;
> They gleam from the abyss;
> They cry, from yawning waves,
> "We are the Witnesses!"

Because the poems avoided expressing outright condemnation and outrage, they were judged too tame in some quarters. Margaret Fuller called them "the thinnest of all Mr. Longfellow's thin poems; spirited and polished like its forerunners; but the topic would warrant a deeper tone." Henry himself would describe the verses as being "so mild that even a Slaveholder might read them without losing his appetite for breakfast." They were deemed provocative enough, however, that the Philadelphia publisher Carey & Hart excluded them from an edition of Henry's collected works. Nathaniel Hawthorne, for his part, was stunned. "I was never more surprised than at your writing poems about slavery," he allowed. "You have never poetized a practical project hitherto." John Greenleaf Whittier was sufficiently impressed that he urged Henry to run for Congress under the aegis of the Liberty Party, an abolitionist group he had helped found. "Though a strong anti-Slavery man, I am not a member of any society, and fight under no single banner," Henry replied, unequivocal in his determination to remain out of the crossfire. "Partisan warfare becomes too violent, too vindictive for my taste, and I should be found but a weak and unworthy champion in public debate."

And he never wavered. "I am glad I am not a politician, nor filled with the rancor that politics engenders," he wrote in his diary. Asked by a New York activist in 1852 for a few lines of commentary for the cause, he declined again: "I think no one who cares about the matter will be at any loss to discover my opinion on that subject." Many years later, Henry's son Ernest would write that his father "hated excess or extremes" of all sorts, and "believed in the *juste milieu*"—the happy medium—in everything. "He was not a rushing river, boiling and tumbling over rocks, but the placid stream flowing through quiet meadows. He hated war, he hated violence in any form, and though nothing roused his indignation like injustice, he was for peaceful measures if possible."

HENRY'S JOURNAL IS quiet during the early weeks of 1843, suggesting a sense of calm that is reinforced by his letters, which show at long last acceptance of Fanny Appleton's aloofness. "My Etna *is* burnt out," he conceded to Sam Ward of his expired hopes, "my Boundary Line is settled. Impassible Highlands divide the waters running North and South. 'Let the dead Past bury its dead' and excuse me for quoting myself"—but quote "A Psalm of Life" he did, and that, it would appear, was that. Then, in early April, he was invited by the Nortons to a party for Tom Appleton, who was departing yet again for Europe. A few years earlier, Fanny's sister, Mary, had married Robert Mackintosh, the son of an English diplomat, and moved to London; her father, meanwhile, had taken a second wife, Harriot Coffin Sumner, who in quick succession bore him three children—William Sumner Appleton (1840–1903), Harriet Sumner Appleton (1841–1923), and Nathan Appleton Jr.

(1843–1906)—and assumed all domestic responsibilities at 39 Beacon Street. Now, Tom was off for the other side of the Atlantic.

How Henry and Fanny found themselves alone in a quiet alcove for a little tête-à-tête—it was the doing, in all likelihood, of their mutual friend Catherine Eliot Norton—is anyone's guess. But speak they did, openly and candidly, for the first time in years, including some discussion of *Hyperion*, apparently to Fanny's satisfaction, given what came next. "You must come and comfort me, Mr. Longfellow," she said, allowing how lonely she was going to be in the weeks ahead. Henry might just as likely have been struck by a meteorite. He would write on April 13, 1844—the first anniversary of their rapprochement—that "the day and evening shall be kept as a holiday and be blessed for evermore." Quoting Dante, he declared it the miraculous arrival of a Vita Nuova— a new life—of happiness, which he would repeat again and again on that date in the years that followed.

10

Castles in Spain

Must I say that I felt almost *sadder* at parting with the *mountains* than with the kind hearts that have made such sunshine around us. Nature has been the *one* friend I have vainly sought elsewhere—and here where it is grander and lovelier than many mortal spirits, I have basked in its every shadow with a visionary's fervor.

—Fanny Appleton, journal, August 31, 1835

I would fain do some good before I die that my heart may not sink within me, hereafter, when compelled to answer "what has thou done in thy mortal life?" As the poor ballet dancer could only reply that she had danced thro' it, so I fear I may be able to say, only—"I have mused and sighed"—pirouetted from hope to despondency, from aspiration to contrition—but rarely to action. I do pray, however—so God may yet vouchsafe me a useful career—the power to accomplish half the good I plan.

—Fanny Appleton, letter to Emmeline Austin, 1838

I pity you in dull Boston; here we are as merry as crickets—and as full of occupation as ants.

—Fanny Appleton, letter to her brother Tom,
July 5, 1839, from Stockbridge, Massachusetts

*F*anny had always found the Berkshire Hills of her mother's childhood enchanting, not only for the purity of the air she could breathe, but for the company she kept, and the glorious surroundings that spurred her creative spirit. A two-month retreat to the region in 1835 had been a revelation, allowing her to feel "delightfully un-cityfied" the entire time, free to go "rambling" through the fields whenever the spirit moved, able to pick flowers by the banks of the Housatonic River and spend hours on end "sketching the ruralities." If there was a eureka moment during that summer stay—mounted ostensibly for the benefit of her ailing brother Charley—it came on the afternoon she witnessed an unforgettable panorama "along the edge of the horizon," the "most intense and dazzling refulgence" she had ever seen.

It was, to her trained artistic eye, "a pure, white light, as if the sun had been drawn out over the whole expanse," against which "the leaves of the trees, and the buildings stood out like bits of bronze." Added to that, amber clouds "canopied the whole sky as with a golden curtain," while slivers of blue "pierced through like turquoise set in gold." Crowning it all was a "very brilliant and perfect rainbow in the east round which the lightning sported, trying to shame its beauty, with its superior glare." Fanny had never viewed "such a smile upon the heavens before." It was as if "the fierce lightning has rent away the veil of the temple and we were allowed a glance into the overwhelming glory of the 'Holy of Holies!'"

In succeeding summers, Fanny and Mary spent much of their time among a group of well-bred and talented people who opened a thrilling world of intellectual engagement for them. Long recognized as a seasonal gathering place for artists, writers, musicians, actors, and educators, the Berkshires would be anointed by the nineteenth-century activist minister Henry Ward Beecher as America's version of England's Lake District, so beloved by the British Romantics. At a "little red cottage" in Lenox, Nathaniel Hawthorne wrote *The House of the Seven Gables* and *Tanglewood Tales*; seven miles away in Pittsfield, Herman Melville produced *Moby-Dick* and *Pierre,* which he dedicated to "The Most Excellent Purple Majesty of Greylock"—Mount Greylock—visible from the house he

A Fanny Appleton sketch of the "ruralities" in the Berkshires, dated August 3, 1835

called Arrowhead. Another Pittsfield neighbor, Oliver Wendell Holmes, composed some of his finest odes at Canoe Meadows, site now of an Audubon Wildlife Sanctuary; and twenty miles away, in Cummington, stood the homestead of William Cullen Bryant.

The Berkshires have been equally attractive to gifted women, and thus no surprise that Mount Holyoke College (1837) and Smith College (1871), two of the fabled "Seven Sisters" of higher education, found welcoming homes for their all-female institutions in the region, and continue to rank among the best liberal-arts schools in the United States. In the early years of the twentieth century, Edith Wharton found comfort on a 113-acre estate in Lenox she called the Mount, today a National Historic Landmark and museum open to the public.

WHEN FANNY WAS sixteen years old, she began making entries in a marbled notebook with a red leather binding maintained separately from her other writings, a sequence of deeply personal reflections kept intermittently through 1852 and known to scholars as her "Spiritual Journal." It begins on May 13, 1834, a year and a half after the death of her mother, with two rather extraordinary paragraphs that give some indication, however fragmentary, of what she was hoping to accomplish with her life:

> Let me write,—write,—write,—let me write *out* myself: let me spread out my heart, as a map, whereon I may gaze—not a quicksand, rock, or dangerous harbour shall escape my keen observation.—I hardly know, yet, what wrong and foolish feelings are lurking there;—I have not *dared* to look.—Now, nothing shall be concealed; it may be appalling to see your very innermost, deeply hidden sentiments dragged into daylight, in all their nakedness and deformity, and exposed to the wond'ring gaze, even of yourself; it seems very like peeping behind the sacred veil; but it must benefit—and *may* cure me, of *much*.
>
> I will write as I *feel*, and will not shrink from seeing myself as I am; as I am seen, by a higher Power.—If I ever live to be old (which I never feel to be probable) perhaps I may laugh heartily at the nonsense this book will contain; at the foolish, girlish fancies here displayed—and so I will write it, because, it is a pity any one should lose a really hearty laugh.

One lengthy passage, written two and a half years later in Mayence, France (now Mainz, Germany), was addressed directly to "My Mother! Oh my Mother!" at a time when Fanny was grieving the loss of her cousin Willy a few weeks earlier. Taking the form of a "prayer" to a departed soul, the entry is framed plaintively around a compound question: "Does thy sainted Spirit never hover over thy deserted Child, never breathe around her its atmosphere of love, to soothe her sorrow and fortify her weakness, never come to her in the weary night when she lies awake weeping for thee, as now, never smooth her pillow, which no other hand but thine has ever smoothed; never smile upon her prayers and sorrow over her sins?"

A running subtext expresses hunger for a guiding spirit to fill the gaping void. "I feel so alone without thee! In sickness, when did I ever support, before, my own aching head, smooth my own disturbed pillow? I shut my eyes and think I hear that soft step, that foot I have so often kissed, near my bed, as in spite of illness or weariness it nightly came, I think I feel that kind hand perform its never failing ministry of maternal love around my head to keep me safe and warm, that cheek bent over mine, whose delicate texture was, from my earliest childhood, a wonder and a loveliness that I have teased to touch as a child, fearful of soiling, rests its timid fingers on the leaf of a rose, while that gentle voice, more musical than the sleeping sea at twilight, breathes in my ear its nightly benison: 'Good night, my child; forget not your prayers.'—Oh that I could dream thus forever! What a making of loneliness and misery!"

In an attempt to find just a such a guide, Fanny had reached out to the Massachusetts author Catharine Maria Sedgwick, a first cousin once removed of her mother who lived much of the year in Stockbridge, a picture-postcard community on the Housatonic River well known today for a variety of cultural attractions, notably the Norman Rockwell Museum and, in tandem with the nearby town of Lenox, Tanglewood, the summer home of the Boston Symphony Orchestra. Unmarried throughout her life, Sedgwick was beloved by numerous nieces and nephews, one of whom, Katharine Sedgwick Minot, cared for her in the final years of her life. Fanny's first letter to "Dearest Aunt Kitty" is dated June 15, 1835. "I am getting so jealous of your correspondence with my sister Mary," she began, "and so unwilling to be utterly forgotten by one whom I have looked up to with the most extreme reverence and affection from my earliest years, that I boldly come to entreat for a share of your love and interest. Will you grant it me my own Aunt Kitty? You have known me only as the wild, romping girl, who used to scour Berkshire hills,—or, for the love of fun assist in beating eggs, or mopping the piazza according to my ever varying moods of order or disorder." What Fanny sought was some equal time with her sister. "We are truly now so alone in the world (since she who made our world has left us) that we cling with more real fondness to those few loved ones we have known the longest. Are you not one of these, my dear Aunt Kitty, and will you not be a dear, kind friend to us poor damsels, to counsel us and direct us as your warm heart will ever prompt you? I know you will."

With that, Fanny had another declaration to express, "that I love you dearly, want you to love me half as well," and a single appeal to make: that "you write me a few lines, someday, if I dared to make so many requests at one stretch." Sedgwick's speedy answer set in motion a correspondence in which Fanny periodically sought motherly advice over the next eight years. "Most gladly would I be to you—as far as in me lies—the friend you ask of me," Sedgwick replied eleven days later. "I have certainly years enough for a mentor, but alas, with years, wisdom does not always come," but she was happy to offer her best. "So dear Fanny, take me, and if I cannot counsel you, I can *feel* with you, and that is sometimes quite as well."

Catharine Maria Sedgwick was a woman of consequence in antebellum America, a highly successful author of numerous stories and sketches, along with a dozen books that reached a wide audience, including editions in French, German, Italian, Swedish, Danish, and Dutch. Her first novel, *A New-England Tale; or Sketches of New-England Character and Manners* (1822), was inspired by her recent conversion to Unitarianism and the teachings of William Ellery Channing. She was one of fifteen authors to be profiled in *Homes of American Authors* (1853), and the only woman included. She was described in the accompanying essay as being "one of the first Americans of her sex" to be "distinguished in the republic of letters, and in the generous rivalry of women of genius which marks the present age."

Twenty of the letters "Aunt Kitty" wrote to Fanny before her marriage survive, but only two of the ones sent to her by Fanny—including that most revealing first one—have been preserved, though the content makes clear that Sedgwick was usually addressing various concerns Fanny had raised. In one response to an unrecovered letter, Sedgwick wrote how much the correspondence meant to her. "Thank you for your letter, for every word," she began. "I cherish this spiritual communion with you." One reason these exchanges have gone unexamined until now is likely because they are not kept among Fanny's papers in Cambridge, but at the Massachusetts Historical Society in Boston, repository of a mammoth archive of materials documenting two hundred and fifty years of the Sedgwick family of western Massachusetts and New York, particularly those of Theodore Sedgwick (1746–1813), Catharine Maria's father. A delegate to the Continental Congress and a signer of the Declaration of Independence, Theodore Sedgwick served as the fourth Speaker of the House of Representatives in Washington, later

Catharine Maria Sedgwick,
engraving after W. Croome,
from the book *Female
Prose Writers of America* by
John Seely Hart (1852)

as a United States senator, and, for the final eleven years of his life, as a
member of the Massachusetts Supreme Judicial Court.

As a young lawyer in 1781, Theodore Sedgwick secured the freedom
of a black woman named Elizabeth Freeman under provisions of the
recently enacted constitution of the Commonwealth of Massachusetts,
effectively ending the practice of slavery in the state. The woman, known
as Mumbet, moved in with the Sedgwick family as a domestic helper
and childhood nurse to Catharine Maria, who would tell her story in an
1853 essay for *Bentley's Miscellany*, "Slavery in New England." Mumbet
and Catharine Maria are buried side by side in a Stockbridge Cemetery
family plot known as the "Sedgwick Pie" for the arrangement of the
headstones in concentric circles around Theodore and Pamela Dwight
Sedgwick at the center.

Catharine Maria traveled widely, and was welcomed lavishly throughout Europe. Intellectually, she was enriched by a circle of accomplished
women, including the internationally renowned Shakespearean actress
Fanny Kemble, who bought a country home in nearby Lenox. After a
trip to Stockbridge, the Irish-born writer Anna Brownell Murphy Jameson would describe "Miss Sedgwick" as "by far the most gifted and love-

able person I have met on this side of the Atlantic." Her influence on Fanny was considerable, the evidence for that expressed by Fanny herself in her journal and correspondence. "My head swelled at seeing Aunt Kitty, and I was dumb," she noted a week after arriving in Stockbridge in July 1835. "How I had yearned for this moment,—how I longed to throw myself on her neck and pour out in a flood the pent up fountains of many sorrows! And there she was, and others were by, and I could not speak."

Fanny described the bond she soon established with Sedgwick in a lengthy letter written to Isaac Appleton Jewett in the summer of 1838. She and Mary were then "passing a week" at a country inn just six miles from Stockbridge with a group of women that included Fanny Kemble. She compared the Berkshires to the artistic masterpieces she and her cousin had so recently savored in Europe. "To me such Nature as I now enjoy is an equivalent and teaches true content, especially the nature of refined minds and noble hearts such as beat six miles from me now and under the same roof a few nights since." Miss Sedgwick, she declared, "is now my Rome, my Raphael, my Italy—her mind is a better gallery than the Louvre—her heart—a purer fountain than the Trevi—a more abiding sunlight than haunts Pausilippo! Her character in its winning simplicity—spiritualized-perfection and St John-like love for all humanity—is a world in itself and worth all this rhapsody." In another letter, to Emmeline, there was more of the same. "I am enjoying myself excessively—for it is a rare good fortune to be in the constant influence of such rich minds and noble hearts as our friends here are gifted withal."

It was around this time that Fanny loaned one of her travel chronicles to Sedgwick, who was about to embark on a trip of her own to Europe. "Thank you, again and again, for sending me so much of one volume of your personal journal," Sedgwick wrote. "I don't know whether the expectation of going over the same scenes quickens my imagination, or whether it is that *merely* the power of your vivid writing but I feel as if I were with you, and enter with you, as complete sympathy as if I were into all your enchantments and annoyances—one thing I am resolved on that is if I ever see the Colosseum by moonlight it shall not be with a party of tourists any one of whom shall carry his pattern-card to verify his goods!—The journal is *beautifully* written, dear Fanny, and is so much better than those got up by the tourists or the fireside talk of a dear friend."

Sedgwick held on to the volume well into 1839, making good use of Fanny's insights in preparing her itinerary. "Once more my thanks, dear Fanny, for the loan of your journal—which has been out of your possession an unreasonable time," she wrote a few months before her departure. "If ever I see the scenes you so well describe I shall look on them with *your* eye. Do not misunderstand me my dear. I do not mean those beautiful Persian orbs that roll in your head, but that eye of sympathy you have opened in my mind—or set there—as you please." Sedgwick spent October 1839 to May 1840 in Italy, recounting her journey in *Letters from Abroad to Kindred at Home,* including visits to the landmarks discussed by Fanny. The precious chronicle was back in Fanny's hands by the end of 1839; once it had been returned, she informed Jewett how she had "been reading over my journal in Rome today; tis like rubbing Aladdin's lamp."

THE DESCRIPTION OF Catharine Maria Sedgwick's "stylish neighborhood" in *Homes of American Authors* emphasized that "several of the best houses" there were "tenanted by women," the larger point being that economic independence was not the exclusive province of men in this progressive corner of the country. Though unsigned, the essay was written by George William Curtis, an active supporter of women's suffrage in the years ahead whose close friendship with the Longfellows is the focus of a later chapter in this book. "The prosperity and beauty about them," he wrote of the women's residences overlooking the Housatonic, "is a formidable argument in favor of the capacity of the sex to be the managers of their own property! These are the kind of arguments which can be most potently and most gracefully used by those who contend for the 'rights of women,' and against which, even those that are confuted by them may be willing *not* to 'argue still.'"

It was in this very neighborhood where Fanny had hoped to establish a summer place of her own—a "castle in Spain," as she often called her dearest, usually unreachable, dreams, at other times a "chateau en Espagne"—each a reference to the medieval French love poem *Roman de la Rose,* in which the image is used precisely for that purpose. In Fanny's scenario, she and Mary would retreat there in glorious independence, welcoming guests for afternoon teas and hosting gatherings of the sort they enjoyed with Aunt Kitty and her entourage. For their visit in 1838, the sisters stayed with various friends and relatives. "We are whiling away August under my Grandmamas roof," she advised Jewett, "driving in a broken backed carriage and steed somewhat the worse for wear—through these lovely valleys, which are very like Wales—or Baden Baden." The daily routine was agreeable, leading her to share an ambitious plan then in the works.

"Having no old castles to explore I build glorious Spanish ones— more habitable and less melancholy," but all that was about to change. "Father at my especial boon is about to purchase some ground for a summer villa—in Stockbridge valley—one particular site there having struck my fancy, combining an exquisite view—the verdure-fringed Housatonic winding below the lawn and a noble grove behind—fine mountain outlines—and at a mile distance—the best society—the Sedgwicks." Railroad service with Boston was in the works, too, Fanny added, linking them "conveniently with town and yet at a safe distance from afternoon bores." The next sentence, though clearly tongue-in-cheek, says as much about her idealized goals as anything else: "Mary hints we shall represent the romantic spinsters of Llangollen!" Largely unknown today, the "Ladies of Llangollen," as they were called in the late eighteenth and early nineteenth centuries, were two aristocratic Irishwomen who in 1778 "eloped" to a cottage in North Wales, indulging their passion for reading, gardening, and entertaining, and becoming, in the words of the visiting German prince Hermann Ludwig Heinrich von Pückler-Muskau, "the two most celebrated virgins in Europe."

The Stockbridge site Fanny had chosen was currently occupied by an old farmhouse, giving her free rein to visualize the design as she saw fit. "Italian villas, English cottages and so on float thro' my brain night and day and the busy prospect of realizing such Chateaux en Espagne gives a spring to my mind it was lacking somewhat," Fanny told Emmeline. "How often I see it all built and you, carina, enjoying with me those noble groves." Fanny implored her father to close the deal quickly: "It combines everything and I am more anxious than ever to have it decisively purchased." The Sedgwicks, she added, "think the price not too extravagant," and deemed it "the gem of Stockbridge." Early the following year, Nathan Appleton paid $2,800 for the two adjoining lots his daughter had requested, totaling thirty-five acres. When construction might begin, however, was another matter entirely. For their five-month stay in 1839, the sisters rented a cottage overlooking a dramatic bend in the Housatonic known as an "oxbow," naming their little hideaway Yale Manor, after their landlords there, Allen and Alma Yale.

"We are independent young ladies at present and as well known to every man, woman and child in Stockbridge," she informed Emmeline, asking her to not "insult our spinster independence by writing us under anybody's *care*. I am happy to inform you that we are most satisfactorily established here at last—keeping *open house* (exclusive of country freedom of open doors and windows morning and night) and have already been favored with nearly all the male visitors the place affords." Further on, she reported that her sister was "deeply studying" Mary Wollstonecraft's *Vindication of the Rights of Woman,* "and I trust is now satisfactorily assured what they are."

For company, there were about twenty "damsels" the sisters met with frequently, a good number of them students in an exclusive school oper-

The Sedgwick mansion on the Housatonic River in Stockbridge, Massachusetts, from *Homes of American Authors* (1853). Fanny's dream of a "castle in Spain" would have been built on thirty-five acres of nearby land.

The British actress Fanny
Kemble, Berkshire neighbor
of Catharine Maria
Sedgwick, by Richard James
Lane (1829), lithograph,
National Library of Wales

ated in Lenox by Elizabeth Dwight Sedgwick, the wife of Aunt Kitty's
brother Charles. Fanny Kemble and Sedgwick led periodic discussions
there, Kemble often giving impromptu recitations of Shakespeare and
singing songs. Known as Mrs. Sedgwick's School for Young Ladies—less
formally as "the Hive" and "the Culture Factory"—the program operated from 1828 to 1864. Alumnae included the stage actress Charlotte
Cushman; Ellen Emerson, daughter of Ralph Waldo Emerson; Jennie Jerome, the daughter of a New York financier and the mother of
Winston Churchill; and Harriet Hosmer, the first American woman to
achieve distinction as a professional sculptor.

TOWARD THE END of a long letter to Emmeline in early July of
1839—headed at the top "Stockbridgiana"—Fanny asked two concise
questions: "Have you seen the Prof's novel? What is it like?" When
Hyperion finally came off the press a few weeks later, a copy was sent to
her courtesy of the author by way of Isaac Appleton Jewett, whom Henry

had encountered at an event in New York. It is telling of something—petulance, anxiety?—that he did not send her a copy directly, nor did he inscribe the one he sent. He certainly knew where she was, and how to contact her, had he been so disposed. "She is now absent in the country," he informed George Washington Greene on July 29, "gone with her sister, to pass the Summer. She thinks perhaps that during the long vacation I shall stroll that way. She is mistaken. Such are not my tactics. I move not a step toward that city. But next week I shall fire off a rocket, which I trust will make a commotion in that citadel."

Fanny's immediate response to *Hyperion* is to be found in a letter penned eleven days later, once again to Emmeline. "There are really some exquisite things in this book," she began evenly, "tho' it is desultory, objectless, a thing of shreds and patches like the Author's mind. The type and *cool cover* are fascinating; then the style is infinitely polished and sparkling with many beautiful poetical 'concetti'—for his scholastic lore and vivid imagination create infinite comparisons, very just and well carried out."

Paul Flemming, the "hero," she continued, "is evidently himself, and he sticks ludicrously to certain particulars which will proclaim it sufficiently to annoy him—I should think. The heroine is wooed (like some persons I know have been) by the reading of German ballads in her unwilling ears and the result is equally natural in both cases! The adventures have not the same zest of novelty to us as to other people—as we have had the misfortune to have been behind the scenes—and seen the decorations without the advantages of foot-lights."

Fanny surmised that many of Henry's "old ideas" and "old lectures" had "been fused into these graceful chapters," an observation that James Taft Hatfield would confirm a century later in his 1933 monograph on Henry's German writings. "A pity," Fanny continued, "they should achieve their destiny solely by enlightening the dull brains of college-boys or scornful maidens! An author should only not bestow gratis his bright coinings upon his friends. The title is cousin German to the book, but certainly has no natural relationship. For there are more shadows than sunshine therein—probably given as some of our towns are christened, from the necessity of some name."

Fanny's opinion of Henry's writing did not soften over the next year and a half, either; writing to Emmeline on Christmas Eve 1841, she had a stinging observation to make of *Ballads and Other Poems*. "The Professor has a creamy new volume of verses out," she wrote, "the cream of thought being somewhat thinner than that of the binding." Of far greater concern at this time was the status of her longed-for chateau overlooking the Housatonic, a prospect that quite unexpectedly was in great jeopardy. Fanny had brought Jewett up to date on December 29, 1839, describing the recent weeks as "a bitter-sweet time which unlocks as much sadness as joy," the Stockbridge project being just one of several developments she had to report.

Topping the list was news that after a two-month courtship, her sister had married Robert Mackintosh, the son of a prominent British government official she had met in the Berkshires. Mary's sudden absence was already causing "desolation" almost "more than I can bear," she allowed, so much that "I feel a dead weight crushing all thoughts of the future. I half believe it all a dream on which some gracious dawn will arise. This is a shamefully selfish feeling for I have as much trust, as any mortal can have in the destinies of another, that she has every chance of gaining by this change a fuller more satisfactory happiness than she ever enjoyed in the feverish state of spinsterhood."

Her plans now on hold, Fanny traveled the following month to Washington, where her newly remarried father was once again lobbying on behalf of Northern manufacturing interests, and where they would dine at the White House as guests of President Martin Van Buren. She described for Emmeline several balls she attended on Embassy Row, and men she had met. "I have left myself no room to tell you that tho' I am occasionally envious of the supreme content of Mary and Mackintosh"—her reference was to her brother-in-law's privileged social circle—she had decided to "eschew all diplomats" as possible suitors; her antipathy for empty artifice, presumably, had remained unchanged by the glitter of the capital city.

Catching up with Jewett a few weeks later, Fanny confirmed that her dream of an oxbow villa was ended. Mary's marriage had effectively "blown that fair castle in the air quite away," casting upon her a "gloom heavy as those mountain shadows," with "one lonely spinsterhood no longer the independence two could claim." She nonetheless planned "to

A portrait of Longfellow by
Samuel Laurence (1854) that
Fanny said was her favorite
likeness of Henry

be with my dear friend Miss Sedgwick" that summer, and had no plans
to sell her property.

Once they were a couple, Henry would share his wife's enthusiasm
for the Berkshires, even buy a piece of land adjoining hers, doubling its
size to seventy acres. On July 22, 1848—a week after observing their fifth
wedding anniversary—they visited Stockbridge to take in the full sweep
of their property. "Passed an hour at the Ox-bow," Henry wrote in his
journal. "What a lovely place! On three sides shut in by willow and alder
hedges and the flowing wall of the river; groves clear of all underbrush;
rocky knolls, and breezy bowers of chestnut; and under the soil, marble
enough to build a palace." He then jotted down an image that we can
safely assume was suggested to him by Fanny—the same one she had
shared for years with her closest confidants: "I build many castles in the
air, and in fancy many on the earth; and one of these is on the uplands
of the ox-bow, looking eastward down the valley, across this silver Dian's
bow of the Housatonic." Three decades later, Henry wrote a poem that
reflected on youthful dreams and unrealized aspirations, choosing for
his central metaphor a magical place where he had once dared to dream
of a bright future. It was published in the May 1876 issue of *The Atlantic*

Monthly, and appeared two years later in *Keramos and Other Poems.* Here
is how it begins:

> How much of my young heart, O Spain,
>   Went out to thee in days of yore!
> What dreams romantic filled my brain,
> And summoned back to life again
> The Paladins of Charlemagne,
>   The Cid Campeador!

And here, fourteen searching stanzas later, is how it concludes:

> How like a ruin overgrown
>   With flowers that hide the rents of time,
> Stands now the Past that I have known;
> Castles in Spain, not built of stone
> But of white summer clouds, and blown
>   Into this little mist of rhyme!

Henry was not someone to squander a good idea, however many decades
it took him to absorb and transform it into limpid verse; "Castles in
Spain," of course, is the title.

HER DREAMS OF BUILDING a "chateau en Espagne" dashed, Fanny
returned to Boston and began making plans for an extended stay in
England with Mary. On May 2, she attended a gala at the home of
George and Anna Ticknor, which she described in a long letter to Jewett as being "very agreeable," beginning with "sewing and chat before
dinner" in an "elegant drawing-room heaped with the spoils of foreign
travel," and then a "true, literary bonne bouche" of readings and learned
discussions. A sumptuous dinner by twilight was followed by an interlude of classical music, topped off by a visit to Ticknor's library, "richer
in taste and literary wealth than any other in the country. I feasted my
eyes on many rare volumes—gave a school-girl pause over Byron with
the author's name and presentation of it to Mr. T in the beginning, the

most satisfactory kind of autograph, and got overwhelmed in a Dante as venerable as printing."

Not once in Fanny's letter—and it fills eight quarto pages—is there any mention that one of the guests at 9 Park Street that night was "the Professor" from Cambridge. We know Henry was there because he described the festivities in his journal before retiring for the evening:

> Once more the sheltering night has come. Like an ass! I went to town to-day and dined tête-à-tête with Hillard. Then walked up and down the Common. Then the devil put his hoof into it and put it into my head to call on the Ticknors. I plunged into a room full of ladies. Among them sat Fanny—stately as a statue to whom Hillard was passing assiduous court. He worships rising stars, it is his weakness. I came away soon. My blood was changing to gall and became poisonous like that of a baited bull. Came back to Cambridge and went to Mr. Norton's. There I beheld what perfect happiness may exist on this earth, and felt how I stood alone in life, cut off for a while from those dearest sympathies for which I long.

Henry expressed the apparent finality of it all four months later in a discursive cluster of letters written over a three-day period to George Washington Greene, begun ostensibly to review and critique a manuscript his friend had written on the Italian poet and novelist Alessandro Manzoni, which would appear the following month in *The North American Review*; he judged it "beyond comparison the finest thing I have seen from your pen." He moved on, inevitably, to the status of his most pressing concern—"the lady, whom I *loved*"—whose given name he had no need otherwise of stating:

> We are now wholly in separate orbs, and hardly see each others faces in one year. The passion is dead; and can revive no more. Though on this account I lead a maimed life; yet it is better thus, than merely to have gained her consent—her cold consent—even if it could have been done. So of this no more—no more—for evermore! For though I feel deeply what it is *not* to have gained the love of such a woman,—I have ceased to think of it;—and remember it only, when

I see that my elasticity is nigh gone, and my temples are as white as snow. Three of the best years of my life were melted down in that fiery crucible. Yet I like to feel deep emotions. The next best thing to *complete success* is *complete failure*. Misery lies half way between. But you have thrown me into a deep reverie, with your *query,* and I can write no more tonight. I shall smoke, and then to bed. I must contrive to send you *Hyperion* which is the *Apology* for my madness.

Fanny would reference *Hyperion* that November in another letter to Jewett, who by this time had been teasing her for having become something of a cause célèbre in New Orleans and Cincinnati, cities where he had been spending time in pursuit of a law career. "I am much amused at your account of my *fame* in Cincinnati and shall take care never to go there, t'would be such a pity to disenchant it. My vanity is *not* flattered because it is all for the heroine of H. who is as unlike me as most creations of the fancy transcend flesh and blood. Don't feel bound now to flatter me, 'cause it's no use, and I prefer to be entertained with any thing else. Your letters are too gallant already; don't think because you are writing to a woman she must be dosed with sugarplums. I hate sweet things—that is, too many of 'em." On another matter relating to a certain "Mr. Hudson" they both knew—one "who you thought would prove such a dangerous attaché"—she reported that "we see very rarely, and I especially, as he has a horreur of all petticoats unyoked to male attire, alias single women."

This little aside is typical of the comments we find Fanny making on the matter of possible suitors—the overall impression being one of bemused indifference for men she finds wanting. A name that turns up periodically in her letters and journals—albeit without much comment one way or another—is that of Alleyne Otis (1807–73), a well-bred Bostonian who grew up at 45 Beacon Street, a few doors away from the Appleton residence. Alleyne was the son of Harrison Gray Otis (1765–1848), whose many attainments included stints as a congressman, a United States senator, the mayor of Boston, and by virtue of some crafty deals involving the most desirable pieces of real estate in the city—18.5 prime acres on the south slope of Beacon Hill acquired from the artist John Singleton Copley being his most spectacular coup—one of the wealthiest men in America. Both families holidayed in Newport and Nahant; both attended the same balls and functions; both knew, worked, and socialized with the same people.

Among many mentions of various Otis family members in Fanny's letters, Alleyne's name shows up half a dozen times over a seventeen-year period, nothing to suggest in any way his having been a prospective beau. He rates inclusion here by virtue of a single page of typescript that has been in a folder of miscellaneous Fanny Appleton materials at Long-fellow House for close to a century; Lawrance Thompson records having come across it in the early 1930s, but mentioned it only in passing. It is a partial transcription of a letter Alleyne wrote on March 20, 1840, to Joshua Francis Fisher of Philadelphia, a Harvard classmate with whom he maintained a long correspondence, now preserved in the Historical Society of Pennsylvania.

In this letter—given to Harry Dana by a granddaughter of Fisher's—Alleyne reported that he would be going to a "little party" that evening

VIEW OF BEACON STREET, BOSTON.

A view of upper Beacon Street facing Boston Common, c. 1843, wood engraving by John Andrew, published in *Gleason's Pictorial Drawing-Room Companion*

at the Appleton residence, leading him to expound on the young women of the house, whom he knew from when they were little girls. Since her marriage to Mackintosh, Otis wrote, Mary had "lost that nervous, embarrassed, and almost peevish manner which did her often so much injustice," and now seemed "tranquil, amiable and happy." Alleyne found Fanny, on the other hand, to be "neither more nor less charming than before her trip to Washington—when I see her come into a room in the ev'g in full dress I am on the point of falling in love with her—at any rate with her distinguished air and fine eyes—but the d[am]n of it is I never can get any farther—but on the contrary find the effect too soon evaporates. To be serious, if I were ever so desirous of marrying, I be d[amne]d if I think I ever could fall in love with a Boston woman. They are, and always were, wet blankets to me."

Personally, I detect a smoke screen here; my considered belief is that Alleyne made a run at Fanny and was soundly rebuffed, if only for what others had to say about his character, which if even remotely accurate would have made him a nonstarter in her estimation. Samuel Eliot Morison, the two-time Pulitzer Prize–winning biographer and historian whose many works include a life of Harrison Gray Otis, had little to say about Alleyne beyond noting that after considering a career in law, he had "decided that work was not for him, and lived to a ripe old age without doing another day's labor." Charles Francis Adams—son of one American president and grandson of another, minister to Great Britain during the Civil War, and another Harvard classmate of Otis's— referred to Alleyne in his diary as an "ass" who was "mean" and "stupid." The sculptor William Wetmore Story remembered Alleyne as someone who "*did* nothing, he only *was*: which, in the antediluvian America, was always a note of character."

These biting assessments tell us all we need to know about whatever hopes Alleyne Otis might have had with Fanny Appleton, arguably the prize catch of Boston society at the time, if that was his intention. A man who was "mean," "stupid," "did nothing," and merely "was"—a man who coveted appearance above content—was not someone who would have passed muster with a woman who thrived above all else on authenticity and intellectual honesty. Fanny never called Otis a bore in any of her letters, though she came fairly close on July 6, 1840, just four months after he had disparaged her as a "wet blanket" to his pal in Philadelphia. Writing to Emmeline from Newport, where the Otis and Appleton families were vacationing, she confessed she would rather be in Boston "listening to tortured flutes and French horns" with her dearest friend instead of "'making night hideous' with the blasé atmosphere of Alleyne breathing about." Her literary reference, in quotes, of "making night hideous" is to the scene in *Hamlet* where the prince of Denmark confronts his father's ghost, and is beckoned to follow "beyond the reaches of our soul." It is rushed and elliptical, but makes the point with a plucky élan that is so typical of Frances Elizabeth Appleton. Her disdain for status without substance was expressed more forcefully during her tour of Europe after meeting, at her father's insistence, some prominent visitors from home she found personally obnoxious. "I can't help turning up my nose un peu at such people," she wrote in her journal, adding how she could "never be a radical republican—must have refinement and intelligence and can never get up the least species of reverence for mere wealth."

"I *FEEL* YOUR TRIAL in parting with Mary," Catharine Maria Sedgwick wrote Fanny from Italy on May 11, 1840. "I have perhaps too vivid a realization of the uncertainties of life. And I am sure that whatever new ties come to you and Mary nothing will ever take the place of that most beautiful affection." That said, Aunt Kitty moved ever so delicately on to other matters. "Oh dear Fanny. I have a world to say to you and I feel how little satisfactory such communications can be on one sheet of paper!" But as to what was foremost in her thoughts: "I must think and speculate about your destiny." She then confessed to having "almost a mother's feeling about it, and yet I am in ignorance" almost "as if we were strangers"—which led to the central thrust of the letter:

> I have had a suspicion that you were interested in some one—I think that you once hinted this—and there is but one person of all your train on whom I could get this sentiment—yet I am puzzled for knowing very well his devotion to you. I do not see what but some perverse bias of your affections can have kept the affair in abeyance so long. Now you will not think I am trying to look into your

heart any further than you would voluntarily open it to me—No—I am perfectly content to which I have no answer to what I am now writing—but only I find it most natural to say to you that which is so much in my thoughts. It is well that this great affair is decided for us; for so I think it is. The waters swell till their force bursts open the gates which surely we should never of ourselves open.

Who might Aunt Kitty have been asking about? She does not say directly, though it seems reasonable to propose, through a bit of triangulation, that the "some one" was Henry Wadsworth Longfellow. Her letter to Fanny, written from Rome, is dated May 11, 1840. Six days earlier, George Washington Greene—still the American consul there—wrote a chatty letter to his friend in Cambridge that told how the noted author Catharine Maria Sedgwick had just "passed several weeks" in the city, and that "I have seen as much of her as I could." Of immediate interest to Henry, he continued, was that this "delightful woman" was also "the intimate friend of Miss A., and of her own accord, told me that she was every day expecting to hear of your success. She talked a great deal about this and I am the more confident in my belief that you cannot fail—tho' some cause or other has thus far been acting against you."

Three months later, Sedgwick took the matter up again when responding to a letter from Fanny, which has since been lost. "Fanny, my dear child, how can you talk of intrusion—it is the first strange word I ever have read in one of your letters: are you not my own dear child?" She expressed hope that the two would see each other in the Berkshires that summer, even though it would be without Mary. "I am sure dear Fanny it will be much like a poor bird coming home to the haunts without its mate." Sedgwick then segued once again into delicate territory: "I suppose you may guess what rumors have greeted me" since returning from Europe, added to the talk she had heard "on the other side of the water" of an "aspirant" for her affections. Once again, Aunt Kitty did not name an individual; but hope, certainly, could spring eternal. "You will dutifully let me be informed on this subject as soon as you are fairly in daylight yourself!"

In May of 1841, Fanny and Tom sailed from Boston on the steam packet *Columbia* to spend some time in England with Mary, who had recently given birth to a son. Fanny kept a journal of the passage, far less exuberant than the first, though still perceptive as ever, her impressions on this voyage kept compactly in a miniature notebook no larger than a deck of cards. The sight of porpoises and whales and a mammoth iceberg were of interest, and a congenial friendship was established, once again, with the ship's captain. Three days after arriving in London, she was introduced to Thomas Carlyle, and enjoyed several visits to the theater. She was "wonderfully impressed" by a performance given by the actress Rachel Félix, known professionally as Rachel, in a "tiresome formal drama only redeemed by her genius." She returned home that October, and settled into a routine that portended little change in her immediate future.

Of all the sound advice Aunt Kitty had to share with Fanny, nothing could have been more consequential than a letter of six paragraphs, written so hastily it is undated, though the context suggests late 1842 or early 1843, after Fanny's return from England. There is no indication of where it was written, and the envelope was not saved. The content is concise and to the point: "I saw Prof—L. for the first time last Eve'g. Why Fanny, how charming he is! What beau idéal are you cherishing in your holiest of holies that nothing invented in mere mortal mould will satisfy you! A curious phantom his fine manly figure and beaming face has dispelled and I c[oul]d not help half wishing even on this short acquaintance that you might follow Mary in the role of Beatrice!"

Whether or not Aunt Kitty's enthusiastic approval helped tip the scale is conjectural, yet we can be sure her advice was taken seriously—it always was. Henry's journal does not indicate when or where he was introduced to Sedgwick, but for two New England writers who moved in parallel planes, it could have been Boston, New York, western Massachusetts, or perhaps Shady Hill, the home of Andrews and Catherine Eliot Norton on Professor's Row in Cambridge, which Sedgwick once called the "temple of Boston aristocracy." Given the mutual interest Henry and Sedgwick had in Fanny Appleton, it is a fair bet they sought each other out, wherever it was they happened to be, when they did meet. Affable, urbane, articulate, and smartly attired as ever, Henry made a solid impression, which Sedgwick was moved to share with her "dear child" the very next day.

II

Magic Circle

Oh come to me my dearest Henry I cannot live until Saturday without seeing thee. I could not help hoping for thee today altho' I forbade it, trembling at the weakness of my heart.

I cannot write—oh come and let me tell thee how wholly I am thine. Let no eye ready thy joy before mine—

—Fanny's acceptance of Henry's marriage proposal, May 10, 1843

The Tenth of May! Day to be recorded with sunbeams! Day of light and love! The day of our engagement; when in the bright morning—one year ago—I received Fanny's note, and walked to town, amid the blossoms and sunshine and song of birds, with my heart full of gladness and my eyes full of tears! I walked with the speed of an arrow—too restless to sit in a carriage—too impatient and fearful of encountering anyone! O Day forever blessed; that ushered in this *Vita Nuova* of happiness! How full the year has been!

—Henry Wadsworth Longfellow's journal, May 10, 1844

A beautiful rain. Fanny sitting up to her breakfast in the darkened chamber, lovely as June itself. Dear Fanny—you grow more beautiful— more precious every hour.

—Henry Wadsworth Longfellow's journal, June 22, 1844

What a year this day completed! What a golden chain of months and days, and with this diamond clasp—born a month ago! I wonder if these old walls ever looked upon happier faces or thro' them down into happier hearts.

—Fanny Longfellow's journal, July 13, 1844

*W*hatever Henry said to Fanny in that corner alcove of the Norton house, it calmed the resentment she had harbored since the publication of *Hyperion* four years earlier. One of the few letters she sent to him known to survive—only nine, by my count, the obvious reason being that once together, they pretty much remained together—was written six days later, on April 19, 1843. "Dear friend," she began—not "Henry" or "Professor," but definitely a start in the right direction— "I have just received your note and I cannot forbear telling you that it has comforted me greatly. I trust with all my heart that it is—and will be as you say—that a better dawn has exorcised the phantoms for aye, that its cheering, healthy beams will rest there as in a perpetual home within those once-haunted walls you speak of."

The "note" from Henry she mentioned has been lost, but the thrust of what it had to say can be deduced from her next paragraph. "I could not well disguise, I own, how much some of your words troubled me. I should never have ventured to speak so frankly to you had I not believed the dead Past *had* buried its dead, and that we might safely walk over their graves, thanking God at last that we could live to give each other only happy thoughts. I rejoiced to see how calmly you met me, until Saturday when I trembled a little, as we are apt to do for a long treasured hope. But I will put aside all anxiety and fear, trusting upon your promise." She closed by remarking on the passing of a "sulky April shower" outside, "but how the grass is brightening under it."

For many decades, and well into the twentieth century, what Fanny said, exactly, in her note of May 10—quoted in its entirety above—has been characterized vaguely by Henry's other biographers as an acceptance of his proposal, with no further elaboration. Edward Wagenknecht's judicious selection of Fanny's letters and journals, published in 1956, ignored it entirely. In his landmark edition of Henry's correspondence, Andrew Hilen wrote simply that Fanny had "surrendered unconditionally" to him in accepting his proposal. But Hilen did not downplay its overriding significance: "The date is a most important one, for with his engagement Longfellow began the long career of material comfort and spiritual placidity that the public has generally associated with his name."

Lawrance Thompson wanted dearly to reproduce what Fanny had written in the April 19 and May 10 letters in *Young Longfellow*, but was soundly rebuffed by the Longfellow family in both instances. Correspondence I examined in the Longfellow House Trust archives leaves no ambiguity over why they were suppressed, a latent expression of Victorian reticence to acknowledge physical attraction of any kind being at the core, even if no impropriety whatsoever was being suggested. In denying Thompson's request, Harry Dana wrote that the family was "reluctant to give permission to print letters that were never intended to be made public. Mr. Longfellow himself, by not merely tearing out pages from the diary, but by blacking out many other passages, evidently intended that curious eyes should not in future peer into these matters. If a few passages escaped his attempts at obliteration and a few notes have by chance survived, it seems almost unfair to try to reconstruct the narrative on these slender threads."

The one problem with that logic is that Henry appears to have mindfully held on to the letter, not destroyed it as he had done with his first wife's, Mary's, journal and courtship correspondence, materials that had brought him unendurable pain. This letter, by contrast, "ushered

Winter view of the State House from Boston Common, by Thomas E. Marr, 1898

in" Henry's "*Vita Nuova* of happiness." Even more telling, Henry kept the precious note in its original envelope, addressed in Fanny's hand to "Professor Longfellow" in Cambridge, postmarked in Boston "May 10 MS." It was further endorsed—and indisputably in his hand—with the full date, "May 10, 1843," rendering the idea that a tsunamic declaration of commitment such as this survived "by chance" highly unlikely.

Lawrance Thompson tried to make that point in a futile plea that the family reconsider Dana's refusal. "It isn't likely that these two letters would shock anyone, or be considered indelicate," he argued. "One is purely a letter in which two estranged people settle an old quarrel and end by discussing the weather. That could hardly be called a love letter. The second, so short, is like a lightning flash that clears the atmosphere—and it does, I confess, make such a perfect climax to my study that I should be greatly disappointed to leave it out." But Dana required Thompson to leave it out, along with a "staggering" number of other materials deemed "too personal" as well.

Anything that suggested intimacy was out of bounds, "passion" being a word Victorians avoided when characterizing their relationships; yet it certainly applies here. Once Henry and Fanny were a couple, they were rarely apart, as Henry himself made clear when asked once if he might be traveling to England any time soon, and if so, would he be bringing his wife? "It is part of our theory of life," he replied, "never to be separated." Not only were they happily married, all available evidence suggests they were contentedly married. Fanny's heated reaction to a rumor about the nature of their love life coming out of Northampton is a telling case in point. James Russell Lowell, she confided to Emmeline, had heard that "Henry and I were among the unhappy slaves of the matrimonial oar!! It is frightful to me that anybody could ever conceive, or fabricate, such an impossibility, and when I heard it it gave me a fit of misanthropy to think what calumnies and lies may be circulating about us while we fancy ourselves living peaceably secure from the wagging of a malicious tongue."

Henry never tired of expressing his gratitude at having once again attained marital bliss, however restrained his comments may have been. But he did let his guard down a tad on December 21, 1845, an otherwise "dull, dark and dismal day following snow in the night, sending a chill through every door and bore" of the house. Fanny was just then emerging from confinement following the birth four weeks earlier of Ernest, their second child, whom they called Erny. "Crept about the house like an octogenarian," he logged of the previous night's assignation, exultant in having enjoyed a "delicious"—the next word is indecipherable, but the suggestion is "interlude"—"with Fanny in her chamber where we dined like a law student and a grisette in their *mansarde*."

Henry's sly use here of *grisette*—synonymous in nineteenth-century France with pretty working-class women who frequented the bohemian arts scene, often posing seductively as models—and *mansarde*—an attic or garret—is a clear reference, according to the Longfellow scholar Christoph Irmscher, "to George Sand's provocative novel *Horace* (1842), which describes an affair between a young man from the provinces and a Parisian working-class girl," the young man of the story being a law student. Given Henry's numerous mentions of George Sand in his journal—at least twenty of them by my count—along with no fewer than eight appreciative references to her work in Fanny's correspondence, that is an entirely plausible theory. There are, moreover, ten books by Sand in the Craigie House collections. So her work was known to both. As for the reference to a law student, it is possible that Henry may have been thinking of just such a person who had occupied the rooms when he visited Craigie House for the first time eight years earlier—"Mr. McLane, a law-student, who occupied the south-eastern chamber."

A MONTH AFTER clearing the air to each other's satisfaction, Henry and Fanny were engaged, a turn of events that intimates in both their circles found extraordinary. "This news will astonish you doubtless as it is just beginning to many others," Fanny wrote her aunt Martha "Matty" Gold in Pittsfield a few days after accepting Henry's proposal. "How it was gradually brought about you shall hear by and bye, or rather what is there to tell but the old tale that true love is very apt to win its reward. My heart has always been of tenderer stuff than any body believed and it needed not many propitious circumstances to set it visibly flowing."

They were married on a Thursday evening in a simple ceremony with no groomsmen or bridesmaids, exchanging vows by candlelight in

Nathan Appleton's majestic 39 Beacon Street town house. Some fifty friends and family members were there to toast their happiness. With the grand spiral Bulfinch staircase serving as a backdrop, Fanny made her entrance dramatically to the front parlor, where the groom awaited. "Fanny was in all respects the perfection of all brides," Henry's sister Anne Longfellow Pierce wrote, and her "darling brother never looked one half so handsome in all his life." Fanny wore a "simple white muslin dress," her veil and adornments "of natural orange blossoms." A storage box containing "natural history specimens" once treasured and preserved by Fanny includes a fragile object identified as the "garland worn by Miss Appleton on her wedding day." As a wedding present—and I regard this as one of the most telling material objects preserved in Longfellow House—Fanny gave Henry the elegantly bound volume of sketches she had executed in Switzerland when they first met seven years earlier. On the front pastedown opposite the first sketch, she wrote the date, July 13, 1843, and this inscription: "Mary Ashburton to Paul Flemming," her reference to *Hyperion*'s principal fictional characters a clever variant of the line in "A Psalm of Life" that she had quoted in her note to him of April 19—that the dead past had buried its dead.

HENRY AND FANNY SPENT their first few months as Mr. and Mrs. Longfellow in motion, a fortnight in Cambridge, brief stays in Portland and Nahant getting to know each other's in-laws, then off on an eleven-day wedding excursion to the Berkshires and Catskills, with Charles Sumner, Francis Lieber, and Emmeline Austin tagging along for portions of the trip. Returning to Cambridge, they rented rooms at 105 Brattle from the lexicographer Joseph Emerson Worcester, who had leased the property from Mrs. Craigie's estate, although the arrangement was unambiguously short-term.

Nathan Appleton would have preferred seeing his adored younger daughter take up residence on Beacon Hill, where she had been born, raised, and introduced to proper society, and not across the river in an aging house that needed serious work, regardless of the impressive provenance it may have had as the onetime residence of General Washington. But with Harvard faculty still expected to live in Cambridge—and since subleasing rooms from Worcester was not a long-term solution—another course of action took shape, as Fanny informed her brother Tom. "I wish you could see how freshly, richly green our meadows are looking, frequent rains have put a June varnish upon all the country, and our river expands at full tide into a lake. We have decided to let Father purchase this grand old mansion if he will." Nathan Appleton was still giving the idea some thought a week later, as Fanny implied in a letter to Matilda Lieber, Francis's wife. "We have got to love so much this old house with its fine views and associations (Washington slept where I am now writing) that I think Father will buy it for us to abide in always."

Come September, Nathan Appleton was still at his summer retreat in Lynn on the North Shore, and still making up his mind—to which Fanny added another thought for consideration. "If you decide to purchase this would it not be important to secure the land in front, for the view would be ruined by a block of houses?" Once back in Boston, Appleton wasted no time, and bought the property from the Craigie estate for $10,000. For another $2,000, he added the stretch of land in front down to Mount Auburn Street facing the Charles River, today the site of Longfellow Park, an open space with a memorial to the poet in bronze and marble executed in 1913 by Daniel Chester French. And he signed off on an additional $3,000 for household necessities, all of them fully itemized—carpeting, wallpaper, a piano, mirrors, china, even a marble-topped mahogany commode for the master bedroom. "It is a fine thing," Zilpah Longfellow deadpanned in a letter to her son Sam, "to have a noble heart with a noble fortune."

With that detail settled, the couple left for a six-week stay in New York City to deal with Henry's eyes, which were causing him tremendous discomfort. His overall vision was fine—he never wore glasses—but unspecified pain made it difficult for him to read and write (he suspected too much work by candlelight to be the culprit). They arranged for treatment with Dr. Samuel MacKenzie Elliott, a prominent oculist whose patient list included John Jacob Astor and Horace Greeley, and took rooms at the Astor House on the corner of Broadway and Vesey Street in lower Manhattan, a bustling neighborhood that proved a little too fast and loose for Fanny's taste. She described New York City for Charles Sumner as a "maelstrom" that "does not improve on acquain-

tance," finding herself "more and more wearied with its feverish devo-
tion to perishable things." For amusement, she and Henry had met
socially with a number of well-placed people. "We were greatly struck
with the want of beauty in the women and of culture in the faces of the
men—after Boston," she had decided. "The houses too seem as ignorant
of books—one stumbles upon everything else that money can buy, but
nothing like a Library have I seen."

On the plus side, they had gotten together with Fanny Kemble,
who was performing in the city, and dined several times with the writer
Nathaniel Parker Willis, whom Fanny had ridiculed in Switzerland seven
years earlier. "Willis I half like in spite of myself," she now decided,
admitting that his "manners are greatly changed since he went abroad,
they are more natural and gentlemanly." Willis had become a columnist of some local repute, a man about town with many contacts. "It is
amusing to read his gossip in the Mirror as we got it au natural first,"
she joked to Emmeline. "We have a stately sullen looking bride here he
thinks very elegant and high bred and beautiful to which his wife says,
'I always qualify Willis' very beautifuls.' "

Henry's eye treatments finally concluded, the couple took up permanent residence in Craigie House in late October. "We have but just
returned to our home and are enraptured with its quiet and comfort
after that Pandemonium, New York," Fanny duly informed Sam Longfellow, who was rapidly becoming one of her regular correspondents. "It
has now, too, the sentiment of the Future as well as the Past to render it
dearer than ever, for since we left it has become our own, and we are full
of plans and projects, with no desire, however to change a feature of the
old countenance which Washington has rendered sacred."

THE NEWLYWEDS SPENT their first New Year's Eve together quietly
at home with Emmeline Austin as their houseguest. In the afternoon,
they called on a few acquaintances to exchange seasonal greetings, then
returned for a quiet dinner by candlelight. Afterwards they took a night-
time drive "in a broken backed sleigh" around Mount Auburn Cemetery, just a half mile west of Craigie House off Brattle Street. Fanny
found "the landscape ghostly with skeleton trees upon hills of frozen

The journal Fanny kept on her honeymoon, 1843

snow" that night, "gleaming like marble sepulchers." The pristine sky had been "all roses," the evening star "as pure and full of love as the eye of an angel," the moon's "winter shadows" strikingly beautiful and "delicately penciled in snow," suggesting to her finely tuned artistic sensibility "the shadow of a shade." Before retiring for the night, she read a commentary in *The North American Review* of Rufus Griswold's *The Poets and Poetry of America* by the up-and-coming Boston essayist Edwin P. Whipple, which she judged to be a "brilliant and a remarkable production" for a young man of just twenty-two, "but too many youthful arabesques if one must be critical."

Fanny's sharp eye for detail was not lost on her husband, who had been putting her to work on a mammoth anthology of more than four hundred poems he was translating into English with her enthusiastic assistance. *The Poets and Poetry of Europe*—the first effort of its kind in the United States—would be published the following year by Carey & Hart of Philadelphia in two volumes, some nine hundred pages containing material selected from ten European literary traditions. Fanny was contributing on a number of fronts, most immediately by reading aloud pertinent passages for her husband, but helping on the translations as well. "How much time I wasted over Latin Grammar and Caesar's Commentaries which should have been given to English grammar and English history," she complained at one point, "but I do not repent the aid Latin has been to me in other languages and in my own." In a detailed update to George Washington Greene, Fanny reports how she and Henry "get on bravely with our book of Translations, and are now upon the German having printed the Anglo-Saxon, Icelandic, Danish, and Swedish." The original manuscript in the Houghton Library shows numerous textual notations in her hand. She also contributed some commentary: "Wrote a little in Swedish preface," she stated proudly one morning; another entry boldly described the ongoing effort as "*our book.*"

After spending one morning on Danish poetry, the couple went into Boston for an early dinner at 39 Beacon Street, returning in time to meet with Francis Bowen, the editor of *The North American Review.* Fanny wrote of having "read him into" a "better appreciation" of the "heart and talent" of James Russell Lowell, a former student of Henry's and a promising poet who would stop by several weeks later for tea. Fanny described "Young Lowell" that afternoon as "looking very picturesque with his shapely beard" and eager to discuss "the great reforms this country is to display," prefiguring the stance he would take as an opponent of slavery in the years ahead; in time, Lowell would succeed Henry as Smith Professor at Harvard.

For a change of pace from a full day devoted to Icelandic literature, they relaxed in the evening with *Les Mystères de Paris,* a serial novel by the French writer Eugène Sue that had appeared in ninety parts in *Journal des débats* over the previous eighteen months. Fanny confessed being "sickened at heart with its horrors," shocked that "such hells of infamy exist in the souls God has made." They were also making good progress with *History of the Conquest of Mexico,* the newly released best seller written by Fanny's former Beacon Hill neighbor William Hickling Prescott, which Henry advised his brother Sam was "making a great noise in the literary world."

One Friday, Fanny did double duty, reading some "Danish ballads to Henry," then correcting "proofs all morning," of what she did not specify, but presumably the translations, or possibly some of the other editions of Henry's earlier work they were preparing for the press. Six days later, she paused to admire her husband's painstaking work habits. "H. is so careful to be right that we get on slowly, but surely. I have fairly entered into a league with the devil (printer's) whose red locks appear daily at our threshold. Walked with my beloved to the Printing Office and inspected woodcuts in the metal." She listened carefully, too, to the lectures Henry prepared for his students, complaining at one point that she could not attend because women were not allowed in the classrooms. "I have proposed, à la Portia," she told her sister-in-law, making reference to a famous scene in Shakespeare's *Merchant of Venice*, "disguising myself in male attire to hear them, but have now resigned myself to getting a rehearsal only."

To fill herself in on Henry's earlier life, she had also been reading his journal. "How I wish I had the record of every hour of his dear life. I am thankful to glean any part of it that was lost to me, how much thro' my own strange blindness. It is intensely, painfully interesting to me to see how his great heart rode over the billows of every cruel experience, as over the sunny sea which I trust it will now never lose. I regain my birth-right in him, as it were, by reading these faithful pages." What would now become a hallmark of their partnership—an energetic union that was mutually rewarding—is readily apparent: "Enjoy with all my heart Henry's dictations; never weary with quaffing the flowing waters fresh from the spring of his rich mind."

The evening readings had become precious for Henry, whose vision problems had not improved, as he confirmed in a letter to his brother Sam, then on the island of Fayal in the Azores serving as a tutor to the children of the American consul. "Since last summer I have not been able to read nor write, from having strained my eyes by carelessly using them in twilight." Sam had lived in Craigie House with Henry while studying at Harvard Divinity School, and had himself taken dictation for many of his brother's letters. What Henry did not mention—but which would have been immediately apparent to his brother's practiced eye—was that other than Henry's closing signature, the full body of the text was in Fanny's hand, including a cheery postscript of personal greeting of her own at the bottom.

Another letter Henry dictated to Fanny asked the English scholar and lexicographer Joseph Bosworth if he had yet seen "the shilling edition" of *Voices of the Night,* which had just been published in England by Clarke & Co. It is an interesting aside for the light it sheds on Henry's growing savvy in the world of book making. "It is very pretty, though, I am sorry to see, rather carelessly printed," yet he was "glad" nonetheless "to see it in this form, being an advocate of cheap editions, which, like light and well trimmed vessels, run far inland up the scarcely navigable streams, where heavier ships of the line cannot follow them." At that point, Henry picked up the pen and scratched out a paragraph in his own hand. "I believe I have written you about the bad state of my eyes. Since midsummer I have not been able to use them for reading or writing. Within a week or two, however, I have so far recovered my sight as to add a few lines to a friendly letter, now and then. This enables me to tell you how truly happy I am in the affection of my beautiful wife, and to praise her for many endowments of mind, and heart and person."

In January, Fanny was making plans to attend a forthcoming ball in Boston being organized by Harriot Coffin Sumner Appleton, her father's second wife, and trying to decide what she should wear. "Such things seem to me now upon another planet—so out of the whirl of city life are we; within a magic circle of repose I care not to break," she remarked, quite an admission for a woman who just a year earlier was one of the most talked-about socialites of them all. "Our fire-side evening readings are delicious," she declared of her new regimen, "and any interruption is a grievous jar in the harmony that encircles our happy hearts and hours."

Not long after the Longfellows took title to Craigie House, the *Boston Evening Transcript* published an article under the headline "Washington's Headquarters at Cambridge," which reported this: "It is understood that the apartments in the house, which were occupied by Washington have undergone no alteration since that time, and the Professor will suffer no changes in their architecture to make them conform to fashion. It is also said that he intends to enrich one room, at least, with furniture that has been in the possession of Washington." The idea that the house would become a museum was news to Henry. "Some of the Boston papers say we are going to have one room filled with old furniture, once belonging to General Washington; but we know nothing of this."

Henry's sketch of Fanny relaxing after an evening of reading,
dated January 31, 1847

Though determined to retain the character of the house, Henry and
Fanny had no interest whatsoever in creating a shrine or museum dedicated to General Washington, their fundamental responsibility, as they
saw it, to ensure the integrity of the building. "[George M.] Dexter, the
architect, comes out to look upon the field of battle and contemplate the
pulling down of old barns and general changes of house and grounds,"
Henry reported during the early stages of restoration. "In the repairs I
shall have as little done as possible. The Craigie house is decidedly conservative and will remain as much in its old state as comfort permits."

Upgrades they did authorize enabled Henry to appreciate the crafts-
manship that had gone into the original construction. "On taking off
the old shingles we found on the roof 5045 pounds of lead. This would
have been worth knowing in Washington's day, when they melted the
pipes of the church organ for bullets and here over his head were nearly
three tons of lead, concealed under the shingles." The old mansion was
not precisely what it was in Washington's time, either. The original footprint had been retained, but the Craigies had put on an extension—an
ell, as it is known—and added the two porches on either side they called
piazzas.

What records we have of the fare served at their table indicate that it was always first-class, "champagne and cold oysters" being a favorite for Henry's closest friends. Fanny wrote in one entry of being disappointed Emmeline Austin had been unable to come over as planned. "Expected dearest Em to dinner but she did not appear, so my chowder, and ducks and olives came to a poor market." Venison appears periodically in her notes as an entrée, reported, in one instance when served at her father's town house, as being "rather tough despite Papa's exulting, à la Cratchit"—a reference to Bob Cratchit in Dickens's *A Christmas Carol*, which they had recently read—"that there never was *such* a haunch."

Henry, in his journal, mentioned an afternoon call on Emmeline "in town" being highlighted by "tea and strawberries." An afternoon visit in March from some friends featured pleasant conversation and chicken salad. On an "oppressively warm" day in April—so uncomfortable "we arrayed ourselves in white and read Job as a bracer"—Sumner "walked out to dinner a-blaze with the heat—cooled him with a cold dinner and salad." A meal with two proper Bostonians from prominent families, Edward "Ned" Newton Perkins and Harry Lee—"the former certainly very handsome and elegant," Fanny remarked approvingly, "the latter overflowing with Parisian delights and full of French vivacity"—was highlighted by an evocative discussion of Europe, "until visions of Venice began to disturb my American content. I am now glad I have not seen it, for if I ever can see it, how glorious to share its marvels with the poetic heart which keeps pace with every throb of my own."

There is a cookbook in Fanny's hand in the archives that contains recipes for such dishes as "celery sauce," "salad dressing," "oysters and macaroni," and "hunting pudding," though nothing to suggest she ever did any cooking of her own. Those chores were handled by a domestic staff that during the years of her marriage varied from four to six people, including a cook, a maid, a nurse for the children, a gardener, and, while Tom Appleton was traveling, occasional use of his coachman. In the aftermath of the financial Panic of 1857—what Fanny called "the evil times" to her sister—"a little money just now is very welcome, for our household expenses seem to absorb everything, tho' we live simply enough, and never indulge in parties." She had even given up her seamstress—"and yet the four servants are [still] a great expense."

SOMETHING FANNY WAS not discussing at great length in the early weeks of 1844, at least in her journal or letters, was that she was then expecting her first child. She mentioned a "fever flush" on January 24, and that "the ague has returned today with double power," but she was hazy about the cause. She did offer one decidedly vague assessment of her condition, however: "Poor mortal bodies how can ye stand so well these screwings up and lettings down." The first direct statement from Fanny that she was with child appears on February 21 in the context of her changing appearance, and the practical matter of what she would wear at her stepmother's ball.

Clothing designed specifically for maternity wear did not exist yet as a fashion concept—that was entirely a development of the twentieth century—and women of a certain station who chose to be seen in public during the later stages of pregnancy usually did so by wearing improvised garments that obscured their expectant status as much as possible. Fanny was no exception to this, as her notation makes clear. "I have out grown my wedding dress and it will no longer cover one beating heart only."

As the gala approached, she had a seamstress modify the gown in an expandable manner that softened her appearance—and wore it that night to 39 Beacon Street. Fanny would describe the evening as a "very magnifique affair," the "whole house thrown open and the display of flowers unsurpassable." Many "lovely girls" were in attendance, all "very well dressed." She admitted to being "amused after my seclusion by seeing so many familiar faces," but felt "no inclination for more balls," at least in the foreseeable future. "Beautiful as this was it seemed prose after the poetry of my every day life. The pleasing flutter of such things is gone, but 'beauty is a joy forever' and these human and vegetable flowers delighted my eyes."

Fanny's declaration of impending parenthood expressed a week earlier had also sparked a spiritual reflection on the path she had chosen for herself. "Oh Father let the child but be as happy, and far better, than the mother and I pray for no other boon. Feel sometimes an awe and fear of myself,—a fear that my heart is not pure and holy enough to give its life-blood, perhaps its nature to another. What an awful responsibility already is upon me! God alone knows how much my thoughts and temper may mould the future spirit. Let me strive to be all truth, and gentleness and heavenly mindedness,—to be already the guardian-angel of my child."

FOLLOWING A "VERY AGREEABLE" February dinner for "The Club" in which the talk was "more literary than merry," Fanny and Sumner lobbied Henry to strengthen a poem they had been urging him to write since their visit to the Springfield Armory in western Massachusetts the previous July during the couple's honeymoon. They were struck during that visit by the surreal sight of many thousands of firearms—notably the Springfield rifle later of Civil War fame—racked vertically in open tiers, the muzzles pointed upward, suggesting to the young bride the image of organ pipes. To Fanny's amusement, Sumner had mistaken another guest in the arsenal for the tour guide, "and tried to enlighten him upon the folly and wickedness of collecting guns instead of books." Having herself felt "very warlike against war" by the sight of so much firepower gathered in one place, Fanny thereupon "pleased Henry" with her comment that the weapons reminded her of "organ pipes for that fearful musician Death to play upon." The image led her to ponder further "upon the noble uses the money wasted upon these murderous purposes might be put," leading her to "spur" Henry into writing "a peace poem" that would use the stacked muskets for a central metaphor.

Seven months after putting the bug for such a premise in her husband's ear, she enthused that the poem "has already a spirit-stirring sound which must unseal men's eyes, as the song of the angels at Bethlehem." Sumner had joined Fanny in insisting upon "a more ferocious verse." She suggested "Cain's curse as a good ending," stressing, however, that Henry would make the final call. "We could throw in raw metal to the furnace—but he alone could fashion it into a useful, graceful weapon." Three weeks later, she was pleased to record that the "peace-poem is fully cast and comes forth perfect," and that she had "found" for her husband "a good motto" for him to use in the writings of the Christian Fathers.

"The Arsenal at Springfield"—a full, fair-copy of the text in Fanny's hand is kept among her personal papers—consists of twelve quatrains that reflect on the unspeakable horrors of warfare, and foresees a time in which universal peace eliminates the need for weapons. For the central image, Henry used precisely what his wife had proposed, a huge cluster of burnished gun barrels that rise from floor to ceiling in a cavernous armory not unlike the pipes of a church organ. For a climactic sequence at the end, he summoned forth the biblical references Fanny suggested, along with the argument that she had also proposed—the idea of committing national resources to the production of good works instead of armaments:

> Were half the power, that fills the world with terror,
>   Were half the wealth bestowed on camps and courts,
> Given to redeem the human mind from error,
>   There were no need of arsenals or forts:
> The warrior's name would be a name abhorred!
>   And every nation, that should lift again
> Its hand against a brother, on its forehead
>   Would wear forevermore the curse of Cain!

A MONTH BEFORE her due date, Fanny allowed herself to wish for a girl. "Lined a basket with pink cambric for an expected guest," she wrote hopefully, then turned more serious. "The house entirely ours tonight: ran, like a child, thro' the rooms to enjoy the feeling of possession, but felt the desolation likewise. Cannot resist planning for the future with a confidence in life and happiness I never knew before, and yet I am so near what is thought a dangerous crisis! Be moderate in hopes, oh heart."

As the big day approached, Fanny's stepmother and a few of her Beacon Hill friends paid a visit, bringing along some "diverse Lilliputian garments" sent from Europe by her brother Tom. When they left, Fanny took a seat at the elegant writing desk that had come with her to Cambridge from Boston, and took up her pen. "Henry took his sunset row on the river," she began. "Sat at window and followed the flashing of his oars with my eyes and heart. He rowed around one bend of the river, then another, now under the shadow of the woods and now in the golden sun-light. Longed to be with him and grew impatient for wings he looked so far away. How completely my life is bound up in this love—how broken and incomplete when he is absent a moment; what infinite peace and fullness when he is present. And he loves me to the utter most desire of my heart. Can any child excite as strong a passion as this we feel for each other?"

Charles Appleton Longfellow—"Charley" to one and all—was welcomed into the world on June 9, 1844. Fanny reported on July 13 of having "joyfully" celebrated her first wedding anniversary with a carriage ride through the neighborhood, her first outing with the new baby. A festive dinner—"our first in the dining room"—was highlighted by the surprise serving of "some of our wedding-cake" from the previous year. It was on this occasion, too, that she ended the practice of keeping a daily journal, the demands of motherhood more compelling. She would continue to write long, thoughtful letters and record the goings-on of her "chicks" in several notebooks she charmingly titled "Chronicle of the Children of Craigie Castle," but she now had other responsibilities. "With this day my Journal ends," she wrote with a flourish, "for I have now a living one to keep faithfully, more faithfully than this."

"THE ARSENAL AT SPRINGFIELD" appeared in *Graham's Magazine* in May 1845, and was reprinted seven months later in *The Belfry of Bruges and Other Poems*. Its appearance coincided with the entry into public affairs of Charles Sumner, whose reformist agenda opposed the use of armed combat to resolve national differences. In a controversial Independence Day oration he delivered in Boston's Tremont Temple on July 4, 1845, called "The True Grandeur of Nations," he decried the wisdom of spending $200,000 each year to warehouse 175,118 muskets at the Springfield Armory, a stockpile that had cost taxpayers $3 million to acquire, "but whose highest value will ever be, in the judgment of all lovers of truth, that it inspired a poem, which, in its influence, shall be mightier than a battle, and shall endure when arsenals and fortifications have crumbled to the earth."

Three days after Henry completed writing "The Arsenal at Springfield," he put the finishing touches on "Nuremberg," which Fanny described as being "perfect of its kind, so rich and flowing and with a good soul in its Gothic frame." It, too, was published in *The Belfry of Bruges*. Included in another section set aside for "songs" was "The Old Clock on the Stairs," inspired by an "ancient timepiece" in the childhood home of Fanny's late mother in Lenox. And in a small grouping of "sonnets"—a form Henry had used sparingly to this point in his career—there appeared "The Evening Star," a fourteen-line tribute to his "beloved, sweet Hesperus"—in Greek mythology, the personification of the planet Venus as viewed in the evening. This would be the only love poem Henry ever personally saw through the press:

> Lo! in the painted oriel of the West,
>> Whose panes the sunken sun incarnadines,
>> Like a fair lady at her casement, shines
>> The evening star, the star of love and rest!
> And then anon she doth herself divest
>> Of all her radiant garments, and reclines
>> Behind the sombre screen of yonder pines,
>> With slumber and soft dreams of love oppressed.
> O my beloved, my sweet Hesperus!
>> My morning and my evening star of love!
>> My best and gentlest lady! even thus,
> As that fair planet in the sky above,
>> Dost thou retire unto thy rest at night,
>> And from thy darkened window fades the light.

The Belfry of Bruges appeared in print two days before Christmas, by which time there was another new member of the family, Ernest, who had arrived on November 23, 1845. "Got my last proof from the printer; so that my second boy and my fourth volume of poems come into the world about the same time," Henry wrote. Sumner joined the Longfellows for Thanksgiving that Thursday, "with such a rain as I have seldom seen at any season," and together they "drank the baby's health." Over dinner, Sumner and Fanny discussed with Henry his next project, a long narrative poem he was calling "my idyll in hexameters," which he began the following morning, tentatively titled Gabrielle for the heroine, an

Acadian woman he would later name Evangeline. "I do not mean to let a day go by without adding something to it, if it be but a single line. Fanny and Sumner are both doubtful of the measure. To me it seems the only one for such a poem."

It was good talk in the dining room a few years earlier that inspired Henry to write *Evangeline: A Tale of Acadie* in the first place. Nathaniel Hawthorne had come over one night from Salem, bringing with him a local minister, the Reverend Horace Lorenzo Conolly. After the table had been cleared, Henry asked Hawthorne what he was working on to keep himself busy. "I have nothing to write about," Hawthorne replied, whereupon Conolly reminded him of an idea he had suggested just a few months earlier; what was wrong with that? he wondered. "It is not in my vein," Hawthorne said blithely, rousing Henry's curiosity. "What is the story? Do tell it. Perhaps it will be in *my* vein."

As passed on to Conolly by a parishioner, the story—possibly apocryphal, possibly not—told of a bride and groom in British-ruled Nova Scotia separated on their wedding day by a notorious episode of forced deportation imposed during the French and Indian War known as the Expulsion of the Acadians. Having no idea where her husband had been sent, the distraught bride wandered "all her lifetime" in a futile search, finding him finally on his deathbed. "The shock was so great," Hawthorne had written in a notebook he kept for ideas and suggestions, "that it killed her likewise."

Henry confirmed years later that he had been surprised "this legend did not strike the fancy of Hawthorne," and stressed that he had sought reassurance from his friend before proceeding. "If you have really made up your mind not to use it for a story, will you give it to me for a poem?" Hawthorne readily "assented," according to Henry, and "moreover promised not to treat the subject in prose" until he saw what "I could do with it in verse." In his telling, the fictional Evangeline Bellefontaine crisscrosses the eastern United States, finding her husband, Gabriel Lajeunesse, at long last, in a Philadelphia almshouse. Not long after the poem appeared in print to widespread acclaim, Hawthorne extended his congratulations, and Henry replied in gratitude. "I owe entirely to you, for being willing to forgo the pleasure of writing a prose tale, which many people would have taken for poetry, that I might write a poem which many people take for prose."Among those to applaud Henry's use of hexameters was the English novelist Anthony Trollope, whose fulsome praise for *Evangeline* came thirty-five years after its publication, the benefit of hindsight informing his judgment. "A friend consulted before the writing would have cautioned him of difficulties, and would have told him that their rhythm better suits the Greek or Latin language, with its closely defined prosody, than the English, which depends chiefly upon its verbal attractions, or rhymes and cadences. He would have warned the poet against the monotony of this measure when applied to English, and would have proved to him by reading a passage aloud that it falls into a sing-song melody. But, had the friend waited till the total result had been accomplished, he would not have repelled the attempt."

12

Camelot on the Charles

Once, ah, once, within these walls,
One whom memory oft recalls,
The Father of his Country, dwelt.
And yonder meadows broad and damp
The fires of the besieging camp
Encircled with a burning belt.
Up and down these echoing stairs,
Heavy with the weight of cares,
Sounded his majestic tread;
Yes, within this very room
Sat he in those hours of gloom,
Weary both in heart and head.

—from "To a Child," 1845

Fanny gave her first party in Cambridge; and a charming one it was. The house is beautiful and when lighted looks like an enchanted palace. Among the notabilities present were the Spanish Minister Calderón, a very cordial, hearty gentleman; and English Minister Parkingham, a silent, dull John Bull; though the ladies say he is delightful.

—Henry Wadsworth Longfellow's journal,
October 16, 1846

Any misgivings Henry's closest friends might have had about his using dactylic hexameters for *Evangeline* were dispelled by the robust sales the poem began to record, and the enthusiastic response it generated from readers around the world. "The third thousand of *Evangeline*," he wrote two weeks after publication, and by December 6, 1847, two more printings had been ordered, a pattern that would continue, edition after edition, in the weeks thereafter, reaching thirty thousand copies in print within two years of its release. A decision Henry made the previous summer to part ways with the Boston publisher John Owen had proven to be astute. After looking over his "accounts with printers and publishers," he had concluded that "between eleven and twelve thousand copies of the *Voices of the Night* have been sold"—yet he was seeing no proceeds. "Determined to take my books from Owen, but he has gone quite to pieces, and cannot get his affairs in order, so as to go on with publishing for a year to come. He is deeply in my debt, and I must find some other publisher."

That very afternoon—July 7, 1846—Henry met with the leading Boston publisher of the day, William D. Ticknor (1810–64), a cousin of George Ticknor's, in his offices at the Old Corner Bookstore. They struck a deal on the spot, "namely, that he shall have the books, paying me twenty cents per copy" for the rights to print pages from the stereotype plates of his works, which Henry, quite astutely, had shrewdly insisted on owning. This unusual arrangement with a publisher provided income above and beyond the standard royalties he received on sales, all the while enabling him to control every facet of what today would be called his intellectual property. "His own method not only brought him author's pay," the book historian William Charvat explained in a meticulous breakdown of Henry's income from his writing during these years, "but made him a publisher's partner who shared in some of the profits of book manufacture." An additional advantage was that "he could choose his own printer and thus control more effectively the typography of his books."

Henry remained with William D. Ticknor and Company—to be known more famously in a few years as Ticknor and Fields—for the remainder of his life, becoming close to James T. Fields (1817–81), the sagacious junior partner who would serve as his trusted editor. He also established a warm friendship with Fields's vivacious wife, Annie Adams Fields (1834–1915), whose literary salons in their home on Charles

Street at the base of Beacon Hill became legendary, and whose reflections on the many writers she knew are invaluable.

Henry was exceedingly proud of *Evangeline*, and equally generous in dispensing presentation copies. Nathaniel Hawthorne and Charles Sumner received theirs on November 1, 1847, the official publication date, but they were not the first so favored; that honor was reserved for Fanny, whose copy, now in the Houghton Library, is dated two days earlier, October 30. Also receiving copies that day were five other women who had come to Craigie House for the christening of the couple's third child, a girl, named Fanny for her mother. Henry's sister Mary Longfellow Greenleaf and her mother-in-law got copies, along with the wives of two Harvard Divinity School professors who had officiated the ceremonies, Anna Eliot Norton being one of them; another went to the baby's resident nurse.

Born on April 7, the child had made medical history by being, in her father's words, the first baby to be delivered "in this part of the world"—namely, North America—with the assistance of ether as an obstetric anesthetic. It was an achievement of no small magnitude, and highly controversial, so much so that no physician could be found who would administer it to Fanny, not even Henry's friend at the Harvard Medical School, Dr. Oliver Wendell Holmes, who in time would be credited with coining the word "anesthesia." "No physician has tried it in cases of accouchement," Henry wrote in his journal, using an archaic word for the process of giving birth, "nor seem very much disposed to try it."

The use of the vapor was limited at that time to general surgery and dentistry, having gained limited acceptance following a pair of procedures at the Massachusetts General Hospital in Boston five months earlier. The fear in cases of childbirth was that ether could possibly threaten the health of the mother or be unsafe for the baby. That perception began to change on January 19, 1847, when ether was administered to a Scottish woman with a severely deformed pelvis, the physician's opinion being that the extreme pain of labor likely in her case, along with the added danger of an impacted baby, warranted its application; a healthy child was born, and the mother reported no ill effects.

Opposition to its use was expressed most forcefully by Dr. James Pickford of Brighton, England, who wrote in the *Edinburgh Medical and Surgical Journal* that pain was actually "desirable" in the "majority" of medical cases, its absence, in his view, for the "most part" hazardous to the patient. "In the lying-in chamber nothing is more true than this; pain is the mother's safety, its absence her destruction." There were those, too, who believed the agony of childbirth was divinely ordained punishment for Eve's errant behavior in the Garden of Eden.

Having learned of the Scottish success with the anesthetic, Fanny asked Henry to investigate. A month before her due date, he attended an informal meeting of the American Academy of Arts and Sciences in Nathan Appleton's town house, lured there by a "long discussion about the great discovery of the age,—the Nepenthe,—sulphuric ether." On April 1, he went into Boston again, this time to meet with Dr. Nathan Cooley Keep, founding dean of the Harvard Dental School and a pioneer in the use of ether in tooth extractions. With time growing short, they got together again five days later "to hold further parley" on a strategy they were formulating. They agreed that the dentist would administer the vapor to Fanny, while a midwife monitored the delivery. The following morning, Dr. Keep was summoned to 105 Brattle Street, where everything went smoothly. Henry broke with another protocol and remained by Fanny's side the entire time. "This morning was born (at twenty minutes past ten) in the Craigie House a girl, to the great joy of all," he proclaimed in his journal, Fanny having "heroically inhaled the vapor" of the ether, "and all the pains of labor ceased, though the labor itself went on and seemed accelerated. This is the first trial of ether at such a time in the country. It has been completely successful. While under the influence of the vapor, there was no loss of consciousness, but no pain. All ended happily."

A year after baby Fanny's birth, Dr. Walter Channing, a Harvard Medical School physician and younger brother of the Unitarian minister William Ellery Channing, published with Ticknor and Company *A Treatise on Etherization in Childbirth*, a pioneering evaluation of 581 cases submitted to him by forty-five physicians in the aftermath of Fanny's painless delivery. He reported no instances of death among mothers or infants from its use; occupying an appendix of its own was the full clinical report of Dr. Nathan Cooley Keep, which the dentist had written on April 10, 1847, and first published in *The Boston Medical and Surgical Journal*, under the title "The Letheon Administered in a Case of Labor."

Henry was sufficiently impressed that he called on Dr. Keep the following day and had "a double tooth extracted under the ethereal vapor." On inhaling it, he "burst into fits of laughter" while his "brain whirled round, and I seemed to soar like a lark spirally into the air. I was conscious when he took the tooth out and cried out, as if from infinitely deep caverns, 'Stop;' but I could not control my muscles or make any resistance, and out came the tooth without pain." Henry stayed in Boston that afternoon to have dinner "at No. 39"—the Appletons'—who to a person "think us very bold to have been the first in such an experiment but as it is successful and Fanny is better than she has ever been before or after confinement, it is well, and everybody seems glad it was done." There was resistance, in other words, in the Appleton household to Fanny using the anesthetic, which was expressed just as vocally on Henry's side of the family, as Fanny recognized in a letter to her sister-in-law Anne Pierce. "I am very sorry you all thought me so rash and naughty in trying the ether," she wrote, noting that "Henry's faith gave me courage," and making clear that the initiative had been hers alone, not her husband's. "I had heard such a thing had succeeded abroad where the surgeons extend this great blessing much more boldly and universally than our timid doctors."

And she took satisfaction in what her action heralded for the future. "Two other ladies I know have since followed my example successfully and I feel proud to be the pioneer to less suffering for poor weak womankind. This is certainly the greatest blessing of this age and I am glad to have lived at the time of its coming and in the country which gives it to the world, but it is sad that one's gratitude cannot be bestowed on worthier men than the first discoverers, that is men above quarreling over such a gift of god." Henry could not have been prouder of his wife. "Women have so much to suffer! I told her she could congratulate herself upon having it in her power to show her country-women how some of this agony might be safely avoided."

———

AMONG THE HUNDREDS of domestic objects preserved in the Craigie House storage compartments are numerous playthings and items of
children's apparel, the most affecting to my eyes a tiny pair of scuffed
leather shoes formerly worn by Little Fanny, who died seven months shy
of her second birthday on September 11, 1848, after a short illness. We
know very little about the girl other than that she was sweet-tempered
and a joy to her parents and brothers.

"My courage is almost broken," Fanny wrote in "Chronicle of the
Children of Craigie Castle" ten days into a sudden illness the family
doctor vaguely described as "congestion on the brain." Watching her
daughter slowly "sinking, sinking, away from us" was a period of "agony
unutterable." At length she held Little Fanny's hand, "heard the breathing shorten, then cease without a flutter." Fanny "cut a few locks from
her holy head"—there is one in the Craigie House storage vault—and
had the child placed in the library "with unopened roses about her, one
in her hand, that little hand which always grasped them so lovingly."
Following services in the home, she was buried in the family plot at
Mount Auburn Cemetery. Fanny confessed to having a "terrible hunger of the heart" to hold her namesake once again. "Every room, every
object recalls her—and the house is desolation."

Henry described his daughter's funeral with equal poignancy: "Our
little child was buried to-day. From her nursery, down the front stairs,
through my study and into the library, she was borne in the arms of her
old nurse, and thence, after prayers, through the long halls to her coffin
and her grave, henceforth and forever to me a *Via Dolorosa*! For a long
time, I sat by her alone in the darkened library. The twilight fell softly
on her placid face and the white flowers she held in her little hands. In
the deep silence, the bird sang from the hall, a sad strain, a melancholy
requiem. It touched and soothed me."

Fanny would give birth to three more children, all girls—Alice Mary
arriving in 1850, Edith in 1853, Anne Allegra in 1855—and each would
live a full, productive life, even capture the public's fancy in "The Children's Hour," a ten-stanza poem of domestic fulfillment published in
The Atlantic Monthly seven months before the first shots were fired on

Longfellow House dining room, with the Thomas Buchanan Read portrait of Alice, Edith, and Annie Allegra, and George Peter Alexander Healy's painting of Fanny, at the left

Fort Sumter, a pleasant corrective, editor James Fields had astutely predicted, to the prevailing sense of gloom and impending disunion for the "parental public." With several phrases that endure in daily discourse, the origin unknown to the overwhelming majority of those who use them—notably "the patter of little feet," "voices soft and sweet"—the poem was universally embraced, the appealing notion of three little girls and their nightly romp down a grand stairway into Papa's welcoming lap striking a soothing tone:

> From my study I see in the lamplight,
>   Descending the broad hall stair,
> Grave Alice, and laughing Allegra,
>   And Edith with golden hair.

To illustrate the poem, Fields had commissioned an engraved reproduction of a large portrait of the three girls painted by Thomas Buchanan Read that occupies a central place in the Craigie House dining room. It appeared in magazines and newspapers and on thousands of *cartes de visite,* one of which was mounted in a makeshift tin frame and worn as a locket by a combatant in the Civil War found lying among the dead after the Battle of Gettysburg in 1863. His identity, and whether he was fighting for the Union or the Confederacy, were never determined; but the sentiment of homespun yearning expressed by the image—and the poem it illustrated—is entirely devoid of factional politics. The pendant made its way to Craigie House, and was presented in the 1930s by the Longfellow family to the Maine Historical Society, its place made appropriate there by the pivotal role played in the battle by the Twentieth Maine Volunteer Infantry Regiment, and the extraordinary leadership at Little Round Top of Medal of Honor recipient Joshua Chamberlain, later governor of the state, and for twelve years president of Bowdoin College.

HENRY'S BOND WITH Charles Sumner was uncommonly special, made even closer now by the addition of Fanny to their inner circle. It helped, too, that Fanny and Sumner were already well acquainted. A cousin of Nathan Appleton's second wife, Harriot Coffin Sumner Appleton, Charles had been a frequent guest at 39 Beacon Street, and when he was recovering from an illness in 1844, it was Nathan and Harriot Appleton who welcomed him to their summer retreat in the Berkshires for an extended stay. Fanny and Charles also shared a mutual friendship with the political theorist Francis Lieber; and it was Fanny, not Henry, who had invited Sumner to join them on a leg of their honeymoon trip. "I am sure you cannot resist the combined temptations of this prospect and will agree to become a deserter from Court Street for a week at least," she wrote him from Nahant.

In a lengthy letter to Matilda Lieber written shortly after taking title to Craigie House, Fanny wrote how "proud and happy" she would be to "show you my 'poet's corner,' sacred to the burned woes of Bachelordom." Henry's friends in the Five of Clubs "have greeted me like brothers," she was pleased to report, "and in all of them is there much to value and admire." Sumner, she added, "is perhaps nearer our hearts than any—what a noble nature and how true a soul belong to him." She expressed her added conviction that he "richly deserves" and would greatly "appreciate the blessing of a happy home and I trust will soon find it." Sumner, in fact, was constantly complaining about the woes of being a bachelor, a situation that would be remedied finally in 1866 when, at the age of fifty-five, he married the widowed daughter-in-law of Massachusetts representative Samuel Hooper, but the marriage was painfully unfulfilling for both, and ended in divorce seven years later. The Harvard historian John Stauffer, whose work-in-progress when we met for a wide-ranging conversation was a fresh consideration of Charles Sumner, told me that what Sumner wanted above all else in a woman was a quality he could not readily find—a clone, in essence, of Fanny Longfellow.

"Sumner realized that so many of the society women he had interacted with—women like Fanny, but Julia Ward Howe is another example—were smarter than the men, and the reason is because women of a certain stature had been exquisitely instructed by private tutors. There were no secondary schools then for women, the only alternative was one-on-one education with these brilliant tutors, who were really great teachers. The two most reliable statistics in education, going back as far as they go, is the ratio of students to teacher, and the degree to which the teacher has autonomy to be creative. Like Longfellow, Sumner was drawn to upper-class women fundamentally because of their intelligence. What they wanted was an intellectual peer—an intellectual partner—because they were so passionate themselves about the life of the mind, and the arts, and all fields of human inquiry. No woman I know of exemplifies that more than Fanny Longfellow."

As 1843 came to a close, Sumner made a special gift to Fanny that verily took her breath away: the holographic manuscript copy of her husband's breakthrough poem, "A Psalm of Life," that had been entrusted to him by Henry. "Your New Year's gift is incomparably the most precious one I ever received; not only in itself but because its possession was not lightly appreciated by you," Fanny wrote in grateful acknowledgment. "How can I justly thank you for so generously resigning it to me? Only my wishes from the very bottom of my heart that the happiness, to which your friendship adds so much, may be but a 'second sight' or image of your own, and that this year may dissipate the gloom of the last.'"

Sumner was the eldest of nine children in a family of modest means, his liberal-minded father the sheriff of Suffolk County. They lived in a largely impoverished neighborhood known as the "North Slope" of Beacon Hill, home in the nineteenth century to 75 percent of the city's free African American population, an estimated two thousand people clustered along what the National Park Service today calls the Black Heritage Trail. The elegant homes of the rich and the powerful, in stark contrast, stood on the "South Slope" side of Pinckney Street, in the affluent enclave facing Boston Common.

Sumner excelled in the classics at Boston Latin School, and from there attended Harvard College and Harvard Law School, where his mentor was the United States Supreme Court justice Joseph Story. When introduced to Henry by Cornelius Felton in 1837, he was a struggling attorney who filled in for Story during the jurist's many absences, longing for a career of his own in education. With that long-term goal ostensibly in mind—and as a sort of "rounding out" exercise—he spent two and a half years in Europe immersing himself in the literature, culture, and arts of the Continent. With Henry's marriage, Sumner was the last bachelor remaining from the Five of Clubs, a circumstance he lamented candidly. "I am alone,—alone," he wrote Francis Lieber on the afternoon of Henry's wedding. "My friends fall away from me." In that same letter, he made clear his opinion of Henry's place in American literature, and his response to those who felt that he should be doing more in the way of political engagement. "I do not think it essential that the first poets of an age should write *war odes*," he declared. "Our period has a higher calling, and it is Longfellow's chief virtue to have apprehended it. His poetry does not rally to battle; but it affords succor and strength to bear the ills of life."

Henry, meanwhile, had heeded the urgings of his new bride and did write the "peace poem" she had suggested—not a "war ode" by any means, but a rousing expression of nonviolent alternatives to warfare that Sumner championed in the years ahead. With each public utterance Sumner now made, with each fiery article he wrote, the farther he moved from the practice of law to becoming a full-time reformer—and the more enemies he made. In 1846, he openly criticized Congressman Robert C. Winthrop, a pillar of the Boston establishment, for his support of the annexation of Texas and the Mexican War, both designed, he charged, to add slave territory to the Union. Calling out one of their own so brashly—Sumner declared that Winthrop had committed "gross disloyalty to Truth and Freedom" and was a modern-day Pontius Pilate with blood on his hands—did not sit well on Beacon Hill. Formal drawing rooms where Sumner had so recently been welcome—the parlors of Harrison Gray Otis, Abbott Lawrence, the Eliots, the Dwights, the Guilds—were suddenly closed to him. Even his friendships with Five of Clubs members Felton and Hillard, both of whom supported the states' rights position on abolition, were strained, resulting in fewer meetings of the group.

Most devastating, perhaps, was the rejection of George Ticknor, often cited as the "gatekeeper of Boston society," and decidedly conservative politically, who declared Sumner persona non grata at his 9 Park Street gatherings. "To be admitted to such a house as Mr. Ticknor's was a test of culture and good breeding; to be shut out from it was an exclusion from what was most coveted in a social way by scholars and gentlemen who combined the fruits of study and travel," the Sumner biographer Edward L. Pierce wrote of the ostracism. Ticknor's response to a guest who asked if Sumner would be at a dinner party one night was succinct and to the point: "He is outside the pale of society." Sumner's dream of securing a professorship at Harvard Law School had vanished as well, the pathway to a career of teaching and scholarship closed by the conservative hierarchy that still controlled the university.

Among those to challenge Sumner's charges directly was Nathan Appleton, whose Lowell mills relied on Southern plantations for raw materials, and who as a former member of Congress was known as a "Cotton Whig" for helping secure protective tariffs on foreign imports of textiles. Appleton rebutted Sumner's claim that nations had no need "to rely upon simple abstract justice without force to back it," and demanded clarification. Sumner's response was cordial and upbeat, but with a nonchalance that did nothing to ease tensions. "Have I not answered your queries? I shall enlist you as a raw recruit in my army. I will inscribe your name when I visit you," which he hoped would be soon, and at the Appleton cottage in the Berkshires later that summer. "I long for a breath of the mountains and a seat under your roof. When I can get away, and for how long, I know not." He closed with "my love to your wife." Years later, William Appleton, one of Nathan Appleton's sons with his second wife, Harriot, would write in a paper for the Massachusetts Historical Society that "Charles Sumner was, till 1846, a most welcome and beloved guest in my father's house."

When the Whigs nominated the Louisiana slave owner and Mexican War hero Zachary Taylor to be their nominee for president, Sumner joined five thousand "Conscience Whigs" in Worcester, Massachusetts, on June 28, 1848, to support the selection of former president Martin Van Buren as the Free Soil candidate. Sumner did not give the main address, but his were by far the most widely quoted remarks. He blamed Whigs and Democrats alike for empowering slavery to expand throughout the land, and claimed the selection of General Taylor had resulted from "an unhallowed union—conspiracy, let it be called—between two remote sections: between the politicians of the Southwest and the politicians of the Northeast—between the cotton planters and fleshmongers of Louisiana and Mississippi and the cotton-spinners and traffickers of New England,—between the lords of the lash and the lords of the loom."

Those provocative words—"the lords of the lash and the lords of the loom"—indelibly defined the speech. Unlike slave owners in the South, whose numbers were numerous, there were only so many "cotton-spinners" in New England who could be considered "lords of the loom." One was Abbott Lawrence, a textile manufacturer and philanthropist for whom the mill-town Lawrence, Massachusetts, sixteen miles downstream from Lowell on the Merrimack River, had been named—and until then also a friend and neighbor of Sumner's—and another was Nathan Appleton, who, needless to say, was aghast at the allegation, and demanded a retraction. When Sumner refused, Appleton formalized their parting with an economy of words: "I have regretted your course the last two years but more in sorrow than in anger. I have regretted to see talents so brilliant as yours and from which I had hoped so much for our country, take a course in which I consider them worse than thrown away. But I have been inclined to consider you as acting under impulses

Charles Sumner, Five of Clubs
portrait by Eastman Johnson,
1846, in Longfellow's study

which are a part of your nature rather than from selfish calculation." Sumner's response was to accept an invitation to run for Congress as the Free Soil candidate against Robert Winthrop.

Henry and Fanny found themselves in an awkward position, and chose to walk a fine line. Sumner was welcome at their table, and a bed was always available for his overnight stays, except, of course, when Nathan Appleton might be visiting, June 20, 1849, being an example. "Please do not come to dinner tomorrow Wednesday, as I expect some one whom you might not care to meet," Henry wrote in a guarded note of just two sentences. "Come on Thursday, when I shall have another one, whom you will care to meet—namely Hawthorne." At one point Fanny wrote Sumner a letter that does not survive, but the thrust of it was an attempt, according to an entry in Henry's journal, of "dissuading him from further persecution of the old Winthrop quarrel." Her concern was occasioned by a feisty comment of his published in the local press that caused discomfort in "certain quarters," leading Henry to mutter: "We wish this ugly wound might heal up forever."

The couple deeply lamented their friend's drift into rough-and-tumble politics. "Sumner passed the afternoon with us," Henry wrote one Sunday at the height of the race. "After tea, I walked half-way into town with him. He looks somewhat worn with 'free soil' campaigning. Nothing but politics now. Oh, where are those genial days when literature was the theme of our conversation? Are they forever gone?" Fanny's recollection of the day's events was similar: "Went to church. Sumner in afternoon. Working hard for Van Buren; to resign politics he says after the election. I trust it may be so. It consumes his life and leaves us no delightful literary conversations."

In October Henry attended a rally in Cambridge where Sumner's speech was met by a chorus of catcalls from a group of unsympathetic law students. He found it distasteful. "Ah me! It was like one of Beethoven's symphonies played in a saw-mill! Sumner spoke admirably well. But the shouts and the hisses and the vulgar interruptions were not pleasing. They grated on my ears. I was glad to get away; besides a pent-up room seems not the place for such things." To nobody's surprise, the Free Soil candidates failed at the ballot box, as third-party crusades usually do, though the initiative undertaken in Worcester would ultimately create the Republican Party, and in time secure the presidency in 1860 for Abraham Lincoln. Writing to Henry's brother Sam shortly after the 1848 election, Fanny expressed being "truly thankful there is peace at last," if only for the short run, "and until we know the worst the new administration will bring us, let us hope for the best." She bemoaned the "howling wilderness of politics, where men become as wild beasts and tear each other with ignoble fury,—even the best and wisest not being exempt from the insane rage which blinds them to all the virtues of an opponent."

They knew all along, she acknowledged, that Sumner had "little hopes of victory," yet he "gained so much" from the experience. "With his eyes open to the result, he has destroyed his social position in Boston, and, altho' he has gained hosts of friends elsewhere, he is there almost a Pariah. It is melancholy to see the incredulity of men without lofty aims in the pure fervor of those that have them. As they cannot elevate themselves to their height they place them lower than their own range of motives." This was quite the admission for Nathan Appleton's daughter to make. She was conflicted by the schism that had widened between her father and Charles, had allowed it, even, to enter the chronicle she kept of her children's daily activities. "Read Papa's and Sumner's correspondence," she scribbled one afternoon after church. "Neither can get the other's point of view." Two days later, Sumner came by after a lecture, eliciting another condensed comment: "Bread and potato salad and talk kept us up till midnight."

IN JULY OF 1849, Henry traveled to Portland to be with his ailing father, one of the few times he would ever be separated from Fanny for any length of time. "How I long to know all you have been suffering," Fanny wrote several days into his absence. "My thoughts have been momently trying to penetrate the curtain between us—so strange and oppressive to me. A long, long kiss just here—ever thy Fanny." As Stephen Longfellow's condition declined, Fanny joined Henry in Maine for what turned out to be his father's final days. Writing from Portland, she brought Sumner up to date on a novel she was reading, Jedediah Vincent Huntington's *Lady Alice, or, The New Una,* finding herself "thrilled by his plaintive melodies, so like those of an Eolian harp, but, also like those, they are depressing and enervating, and even his religious emotion is to me too much mere emotion—not a self-controlling power." But Fanny's purpose in writing was for another reason entirely. She had just reread the published text of Sumner's "True Grandeur of Nations" address from four years earlier—it was printed internationally in multiple editions—and was sending him what amounted to a fan letter, feeling, perhaps, that his spirits needed some propping up during what were for him exceedingly contentious times.

"I wanted to tell you," she wrote, "what joy and hope it has given me, what a sisterly pride I take in the author of words so strong in truth and wisdom. 'Truth is mighty'—this thought has been with me ever as I read, and also the feeling how feeble are bayonets and even serried ranks of men, armed with the strongest gifts of earth, and marshalled by human intelligence, beside this overwhelming force of well-arrayed, thoroughly disciplined truths—words I should say, which win every outpost by a coup de main and occupy the citadel before we have thought of resistance." She then finished with a flourish: "You, perhaps unconsciously, seem to have met your foe with his own weapons,—and to have conducted your whole discourse with the judgement and energy so often wasted on fields of blood. Hereafter we shall have fields of ink only glorious, for the 'pen is mightier than the sword.' "

Later that year, Sumner took on a new crusade, agreeing to argue a case before the Massachusetts Supreme Court's chief justice, Lemuel Shaw, on behalf of a free African American girl from his old neighborhood who was being denied admission to public schools then open only to whites. The action, *Sarah C. Roberts v. the City of Boston*, was entered initially in the Suffolk County Court of Common Pleas by Robert Morris, one of the first black attorneys licensed to practice law in the United States. After being denied relief there, Morris invited Sumner to come aboard as co-counsel. The facts of the case were straightforward enough. Five-year-old Sarah Roberts had tried unsuccessfully to enroll in five schools closer to her home than the ill-equipped segregated one set aside for black children located a half-mile farther away, leading her father to file suit, claiming that the Massachusetts state constitution had mandated equal access for every citizen. Judge Shaw ruled against Sarah's appeal in 1850, but Sumner's ringing argument, built on four resonant words—"equality before the law"—would be incorporated in state legislation enacted five years later mandating desegregated schools throughout the Commonwealth, and find their way into the Civil Rights Acts of 1964 and 1968.

AS SUMNER HAD correctly predicted, there were to be no "war odes," but Henry still managed to reflect on what was happening around him in ways that went far deeper than the day's headlines, "The Building of the Ship" being an example. There is no documentation to indicate what motivated him to write the poem, no eureka moment such as the one ten years earlier when press accounts of several schooners running aground in foul weather off the North Shore of Massachusetts, with "twenty bodies washed ashore near Gloucester, one lashed to a piece of the wreck," moved him to take pen to paper and write "The Wreck of the Hesperus."

"The Building of the Ship" began as little more than an "occupational" poem that uses the fundamentals of a certain craft as a vehicle to tell a story—in this instance the life cycle of a sailing vessel from the time of design and construction to the end of its days, with a master shipbuilder and his daughter the central characters. That Henry grew up in a seaport community where shipbuilding was a principal industry undoubtedly played a role in his choice of subject. More problematic is the substitution he made of five ringing lines near the end of the poem, written on the proof sheets after the copy had been submitted for publication and set in type. The last-minute change created a work that would prove so powerful it brought tears to the eyes of Abraham Lincoln during the darkest moments of the Civil War, so resonant that Franklin Roosevelt dispatched a handwritten copy to Winston Churchill as England stood alone against Nazi Germany in 1941. The relevant lines:

> Thou, too, sail on, O Ship of State!
> Sail on, O UNION, strong and great!
> Humanity with all its fears,
> With all the hopes of future years,
> Is hanging breathless on thy fate!

Henry's journal, in this instance, is helpful only with the chronology. On June 18, 1849, he recorded that he was writing a new poem, "The Building of the Ship," and mentioned it next three months later with a similar economy of words. Four days after that, he indicated simply that it was finished. For insight on what may have contributed to the genesis of the work, we must go back six years to October 1843, when Henry and Fanny were staying at the Astor House in New York. Fanny noted in one letter to Sumner how "Mackenzie and his wife have been in town and I had a glimpse of them just before they left. What a fine sweet face she has. I looked with great interest at those eyes which wept themselves dim on his account—tears came to them, still, when I spoke of the desire Boston has to welcome him warmly."

"Mackenzie"—the same Alexander Slidell Mackenzie Henry met in Spain during his first trip abroad—had called on the Longfellows, and brought with him his wife of eight years. Fanny's mention of him only by surname suggests a mutual familiarity with Sumner as to who he was, and why his wife might have "wept [herself] dim on his account." Navy Commander Slidell Mackenzie, it happened, had just recently been acquitted at a sensational military trial on charges of having unlawfully

Half-length portrait of Henry and Fanny with their
sons taken in Portland, Maine, in August 1849.
"Had a daguerreotype of Fanny and myself and the
children taken, the two latter very charming, the two
former not perfectly satisfactory," Henry wrote in his
diary.

ordered the execution at sea of three men off the coast of West Africa on
December 1, 1842, on charges of fomenting mutiny. The sailors under
his command had allegedly schemed to seize the heavily armed brig-
of-war, the USS *Somers*, kill the officers, and convert the ship into "a
piratical cruiser." Given a perfunctory hearing, the men were ordered
hanged from the main yardarm in full view of the assembled crew, their
bodies then buried at sea—an object lesson for everyone. A further com-
plication: Philip Spencer, the accused ringleader, was the son of John C.
Spencer, secretary of war for President John Tyler.

Midshipman Spencer had a history of causing trouble on two other
ships and admitted his complicity on the *Somers*. Though no overtly
hostile act had taken place, there were a number of suspicious incidents

that had raised the alarm. In his defense, Slidell Mackenzie claimed that the very nature of the ship's mission—the training of raw recruits and inexperienced midshipmen for regular duty at sea—had created among the few professionals aboard a dangerous situation in which "their own lives were in a state of momentary peril." The crew of the *Somers* "were almost all apprentices; many of them men in physical strength, but all of them boys in mind," Slidell Mackenzie argued. "Their youthful feelings were peculiarly open to sympathetic appeals; their undisciplined imaginations liable to be easily beguiled by seductive pictures of the freedom and pleasures of the rover's course. The season of youth, especially of untutored youth, is proverbially exposed to temptations." One immediate result of the *Somers* affair would be the establishment of the United States Naval Academy at Annapolis as a seagoing counterpart to the United States Military Academy at West Point.

The popular New York author James Fenimore Cooper, whose oeuvre included a three-volume history of the United States Navy, wrote a lengthy condemnation of Slidell Mackenzie's actions, taking dismissive note in particular of the defendant's other career as a writer. "This officer enjoyed probably a much higher literary reputation than he merited, and his literary associations gave him the advantage of possessing the support of many willing and ingenious pens." Among the unidentified but widely presumed "literary associations" in his corner was Henry Wadsworth Longfellow. "The voice of all upright men—the common consent of all the good—is with you," Henry assured Slidell Mackenzie after his acquittal. To that, Charles Sumner—perhaps at Henry's behest?—penned a fifty-page legal analysis of the affair for *The North American Review*, which concluded that the actions taken had been justified by the exigencies of the moment. "I have not yet read it," Henry informed Slidell Mackenzie, "but hear it spoken of by all as very able, and as putting your defence upon stronger and more unassailable grounds than even your legal advisers did. You will see more, and more my dear Mackenzie, how stronger you are supported in this quarter for maintaining the right at any sacrifice."

We hear next from Slidell Mackenzie three years later, when he "passed the night" at Craigie House, talking "of the old and the new." A "very good fellow," Henry declared, "with very sound sense and great love of literature." Fanny was less than enthusiastic this time around, not for want of their guest's charm or intelligence—"I like him in the main," she confided to Emmeline—"but it seemed to me like child's talk," specifically "his military exultation in our Mexican achievements." As a committed pacifist, she found it "strangely barbarous" that Slidell Mackenzie should "find any glory in that wholesale butchery and murder" so recently committed. "War is to me, now, like the fair Enchantresses of old—when once disenchanted of their false show, simply wicked and disgusting. A warrior is not so respectable a man to me as a butcher, and quite as unpleasantly associated."

Years later, Herman Melville, a first cousin to Lieutenant Guert Gansevoort, second-in-command on the *Somers,* drew on the affair for the novella *Billy Budd,* which centers on the hanging of a young crewman aboard a British warship for killing a petty officer who had falsely accused him of planning a mutiny. Henry never wrote anything about the episode for publication, though he did draw significantly on his friend's expertise for his poem on shipbuilding, the evidence for that to be found in three essays Slidell Mackenzie wrote on maritime matters for the Encyclopædia Americana, the brainchild of their mutual friend Francis Lieber. The most significant of these, "Ship," fills thirteen double-columned, oversized pages in the compendium for the letters *R* and *S,* and is one of the lengthier entries in the entire series. Its "object," stated outright by Slidell Mackenzie, was "to convey a plain yet palpable idea to those to whom it is yet a mystery" how, "in our day, a ship is built, masted, rigged, and, finally, manoeuvred"—exactly the sort of thing that is described in the poem. First published in 1831, the encyclopedia was reprinted often through the 1860s. Henry had a set of the 1844 edition; his signature appears on the title page of volume 11— the volume containing the "Ship" essay.

On September 18, 1849—at the very time he was working on the poem—Henry welcomed Francis Lieber to Craigie House for "a charming visit." Slidell Mackenzie had died quite suddenly the previous year from a heart attack while horseback riding, making it highly likely his name came up during Lieber's stay. "Lieber has a full mind, and discourses admirably well," Henry wrote after his guest's departure, leaving us in the dark yet again on the substance of their talk. But two days later, he recorded this: " 'The Building of the Ship' goes on. It will be rather long. Will it be good?" Published two months later in *The Fireside and the Seaside,* the poem was hailed for the patriotic sentiment expressed triumphantly in the final lines, and for its fidelity to detail, tradition, and the nuances of shipbuilding. Twenty years after its first appearance, an esteemed naval architect in England, Sir Edward James Reed, who had served as chief constructor of the Royal Navy from 1863 until 1870, declared Henry "the author of the finest poem on ship-building that ever was, or probably ever will be." Everything Henry needed to know about the nuts and bolts of the process had been covered fully by his late friend.

As to how he came, at the last minute, to replace one key segment with another—the "Sail on, O UNION, strong and great!" passage—we have Harry Dana to thank for comparing the holographic copy of the poem alongside the change made in pencil on the publisher's proofs. In the original version, the vessel has an uncertain end, a victim of decay and oblivion. With the new lines, the closing metaphor became a celebration of common purpose, with the name of the ship—*Union*—boldly proclaimed in capital letters. Underneath the edit, Henry wrote the date, November 11, 1849, the very day Charles Sumner had come calling to savor a ringing political speech he had given at Tremont Temple, and the day before a hotly contested primary election was being held to field a candidate for the district's empty congressional seat.

Both Henry and Sumner had backed the Reverend John G. Palfrey, the Free-Soil candidate and an ardent abolitionist, which was their principal topic of conversation. "Urged him to take ground against any coalitions, by which the anti-slavery principles of the Free-soil Party may be suppressed," Henry wrote of their talk that night. Since Henry showed pretty much everything he wrote to Sumner, it is no stretch to suppose they also took time to discuss his new poem, and that he was inspired to make a stirring statement in support of their shared convictions. What is certain is that first thing the following morning—Election Day—Henry dispatched his hastily made modification to Fields, with two questions: "What think you of the enclosed instead of the sad ending of 'The Ship'? Is it better?"

On February 4, 1850, Fanny Kemble announced she would include a reading of "The Building of the Ship" in a Shakespeare program she was

The journal Longfellow kept to record the income he earned from his books, opened to a section itemizing the first twenty-one editions of *The Song of Hiawatha,* at right, and translations, at left

giving in Boston the following week for the Mercantile Library Association. Henry and Fanny sat in the front row of Amory Hall for the performance, the attendance reported as three thousand people. Henry marveled as Kemble stood out "upon the platform, book in hand, trembling, palpitating, and weeping," giving "every word its true weight and emphasis"—a tour de force in every respect. "She prefaced the recital by a few words, to this effect; that when she first saw the poem, she desired to read it before a Boston audience; and she hoped she would be able to make every word audible to that great multitude." Fanny was similarly moved by Kemble's virtuoso presentation. "She stood forth without desk, and gave it off con amore with the greatest effect, the whole flow and meaning most beautifully rendered, and the part about the flag with great emotion, as also the close. It was listened to in breathless silence, and followed by warmest applause. It was a very nervous moment for me but a happy one. No voice but hers could so have rung its changes and given the rhythm so perfectly. She is a wonderful creature, one of those rare creations which come only once in a hundred years."

13

At the Summit

The Liebers took tea with us, and Sumner and I went to the Observatory with them. We saw the jagged silver edge of the moon; and two stars, one red and one blue. What a beautiful telescope, turning slowly and noiselessly its immense bulk at the touch of a finger, to any point of the sky! Ah, if one had a mind so well balanced, and swinging on such noiseless hinges, one might easily sweep all the heaven of thought.

—Henry Wadsworth Longfellow's journal, August 27, 1849

*F*rom the day the first foundation stones were set in place for the Harvard Observatory on what was once Craigie House property, Henry was thrilled by the prospect of getting closer to the stars. Unveiled amid considerable fanfare in 1847, the Great Refractor, as the apparatus soon became known, was hailed in the press as the "most powerful telescope in the world," a distinction it would hold for twenty years. For Henry, the massive optical instrument became a gateway to the heavens, a region of poetic inspiration that figured often in his creative imagination. Technological miracles in general fascinated him—the steam locomotive, anesthetics, giant engines that drove printing presses, all things of wonder, and rapidly becoming commonplace by the middle of the nineteenth century.

A year after taking his first magnified peek at the cosmos, Henry witnessed another miracle of engineering, this one observed from the front parlor of his father-in-law's Beacon Hill town house. More than one hundred thousand people had gathered in Boston Common to celebrate the "grand introduction" of running water into Boston from a sprawling reservoir in the western suburbs, the much-anticipated milestone made possible by an intricate network of pipes, pumps, gatehouses, and aqueducts. "I saw the endless procession for two hours from a corner window; a grand show. And best of all, the fountain—the fountain as it throbbed and rose higher, higher, through the leafless trees, in the rose twilight."

In 1850, a railroad spur linking Harvard Square in Cambridge to the North End of Boston began offering hourly service, a brisk ten-minute trip in each direction. "It is luxurious too," Fanny wrote her brother, "with purple velvet and rosewood, and far surpasses omnibus comfort except in not landing you at your door and carrying you to an undesirable part of Boston! I therefore have not yet tried it." Henry, on the other hand, had become a regular, taking his first round trip one morning for pure pleasure. "Bought one or two books, for my special edification and the work I have in hand. *Calumet Dictionary of the Bible* and Brand's *Popular Antiquities*."

On March 12, 1851, Henry learned the sad news of his mother's "sudden death" that morning by way of "a telegraphic dispatch from Portland." He boarded the next train to Maine, arriving by early evening. Years later, he would shake his head at progress of a different sort, the "curious sight" in South Boston of a newly launched ironclad warship, "with revolving turret, like the *Monitor*," named the *Nahant*: "How ingenious men are in the ways of destruction."

On a far less monumental scale, Craigie House was among the first residences in Cambridge to be fitted for gas lighting and central heating, to have a flush toilet, and to install a shower for bathing, the latter a primitive contraption still in place in the second-floor washroom near the master bedroom, and the source of a hilarious incident at the expense of Charles Sumner, a person not known for having a sense of humor, especially when the laughs were on him. When Henry was showing his friend the device, he explained how fresh water stored in a box above the ceiling was released by the pull of a lanyard; Sumner stepped inside the stall and absentmindedly did exactly that, releasing a soaking torrent that demonstrated, to the great amusement of everyone but him, its functionality.

Samuel Gridley Howe's renowned work with the deaf and visually impaired at the Perkins School for the Blind stirred Henry's imagination of what great deeds were possible through patience and ingenuity, made satisfying to him in 1852 with the receipt of a letter from Laura Bridgman, the star pupil of the program who had so enraptured Charles Dickens during his 1842 visit. In carefully blocked-out letters, Bridgman expressed to Henry how much her reading of *Evangeline*—it had actually been tapped out in code on her wrist—had transformed her life, and how she looked forward to meeting its heroine "with my soul in Heaven when I die on the earth," so real was the fictional character in her heart.

When researching material for *Evangeline,* Henry eagerly took in a local showing of the artist John Banvard's *Moving Diorama of the Mississippi,* a forerunner to Thomas Edison's Kinetoscope, and in its time a hugely popular form of public entertainment. A self-taught artist originally from New York, Banvard spent much of 1840 and 1841 in a small skiff on the Mississippi drawing hundreds of sketches. Over the next four years he painted a sequence of views on twelve-foot-high sheets of canvas that were stitched together and coiled on a giant spool, creating a panorama the *Boston Journal* described as a display of the river's many "bends and bayous, its turbid waters and its snags, and the towns and villages, and forests and swamps and plantations, indeed all the scenery on its banks for the distance of twelve hundred miles, extending from the mouth of the Missouri to the city of New Orleans." The mechanics were described as the turning of "upright revolving cylinders, which unfold the painting gradually."

The timing could not have been better. "I see a panorama of the Mississippi advertised," Henry remarked with special interest. "This comes very à propos. The river comes to me instead of my going to the river; and as it is to flow through the pages of the poem, I look upon this as a special benediction. I shall lose no time in seeing it." Henry's factual research in the Harvard Library and the Boston Athenæum had already been extensive, so much that he felt at one point he had too much information. "In materials for this there is superabundance. The difficulty is to select, and give unity to variety." To achieve "complete tone and expression," he needed to capture the atmosphere of a region that, for him, would always remain a distant hinterland. Henry never traveled farther west than upstate New York, and would never venture farther south than Alexandria, Virginia. He never visited the village of Grand-Pré in Nova Scotia, either, a point often raised by niggling critics who suggest that had he done so, he would have seen no "murmuring pines" or "hemlocks bearded with moss," the "forest primeval" that had so captured his fancy having vanished decades earlier to the relentless assaults of fire and deforestation.

In the absence of firsthand observation, he routinely turned to graphic illustrations published in the books, newspapers, periodicals, and ephemeral imprints of the day, the more exotic the better, as the numerous folders of pictorial materials and cuttings gathered by both Henry and Fanny over the years attest. Independent of those collections are the ten thousand photographic images they acquired, some of them daguerreotypes dating to the earliest years of the process. Other genres include ambrotypes, cyanotypes, calotypes, tintypes, heliotypes, platinum prints, albumen prints, glass plates, *cartes de visite*, and stereoscopic images, along with the mechanical devices necessary to view them. For the Banvard panorama, a day trip into Boston with Fanny was required, but it was well worth the effort. "Very good," he judged of the presentation. "One seems to be sailing down the great stream, and sees the boats and the sand-banks crested with cottonwood, and the bayous by moonlight. Three miles of canvas, and a great deal of merit." He expressed his approval more directly in a piece of writing that was next up on his to-do list. "*Evangeline* is ended," he confirmed on February 27, 1847. "I wrote the last lines this morning. And now for a little prose; a romance, which I have in my brain, *Kavanagh* by name."

Published in 1849—and it would be Henry's last work of prose fiction—*Kavanagh: A Tale* has a satiric subplot that involves a publisher named Hathaway and an occasional author named Churchill. Early in their dealings, the two have a galloping discussion about what kind of literary patrimony America should be striving to develop. Hathaway emphasizes his preference for "a national literature commensurate with our mountains and rivers; commensurate with Niagara, and the Alleghenies, and the great lakes," and paramount among his priorities—no big surprise here—the making of a "national epic that shall correspond to the size of the country; that shall be to all other epics what Banvard's

Panorama of the Mississippi is to all other paintings;—the largest in the world."

Hathaway's naïve suggestion that the sheer scale of Banvard's panorama equates with literary excellence leads Churchill to expound on the matter with a perspective that neatly fits Henry's own conviction about literary accomplishment, which is that it is not measured by size but by content. "Great has a very different meaning when applied to a river, and when applied to a literature," Churchill says. "Large and shallow may perhaps be applied to both. Literature is rather an image of the spiritual world than of the physical, is it not?—of the internal, rather than the external. Mountains, lakes, and rivers are, after all, only its scenery and decorations, not its substance and essence. A man will not necessarily be a great poet because he lives near a great mountain. Nor, being a poet, will he necessarily write better poems than another, because he lives nearer Niagara."

Henry's wider attitude on the matter of "literary nationalism" emerges in response to Hathaway's declaration that if literature is "not national it is nothing," leading Churchill to demur yet again. "Nationality is a good thing to a certain extent, but universality is better," he says. "All that is best in the great poets of all countries is not what is national in them, but what is universal. Their roots are in their native soil; but their branches wave in the unpatriotic air, that speaks the same language unto all men, and their leaves shine with the illimitable light that pervades all lands. Let us throw all the windows open; let us admit the light and air on all sides; that we may look towards the four corners of the heavens, and not always in the same direction."

Of the several arguments put forth in support of a Longfellow renaissance, front and center are his cosmopolitan views of life and literature, which considered now in retrospect are leagues ahead of their time. "If there is a reason to rediscover Longfellow today," Christoph Irmscher told me, "it is because of the multicultural version of America in which he so fervently believed. One could even make the case that his rich personal life—and the fact that both he and Fanny 'trained' for their amazing relationship during trips to Europe that opened their horizons in ways that remained inaccessible to their less brilliant contemporaries—is deeply connected to this alternative version of America that is so different from the nationalism that still pervades the works of Emerson or Melville."

WHEN THE OLD VASSALL MANSION was owned by the Cambridge real-estate wheeler-dealer Andrew Craigie (1754–1819), the property embraced more than one hundred and fifty adjoining acres of open land, much of it used for farming and the grazing of livestock. Craigie aptly called the higher elevation to the north Summerhouse Hill for a seasonal cottage he had built there to escape the stifling heat so common in July and August. A natural spring nearby delivered fresh water to the mansion through an aqueduct of hollowed-out logs. Ice harvested in the winter was stored in an insulated shed for use in the summer, and plants grown in a heated greenhouse—the first of its kind in Cambridge— provided produce and flowers in the winter. Just beyond a grove of trees to the immediate west, in the middle of a tiny island on a small pond, both long since filled in and replaced with residences, Craigie had erected large ornamental statues of classic figures. At the back of the residence he had a spacious stable for his horses, and several outbuildings for general maintenance and upkeep of his garden. To the original footprint of the house, he had added a large ell at the back, and at each side two symmetrical piazzas with exterior rows of white columns, giving the mansion the distinctive façade it retains to this day.

A veteran of the Battle of Bunker Hill, where he ably assisted in treating the wounded, Craigie served as apothecary general to General Washington during much of the Revolution, qualifying him as the nation's first pharmacist. After the war, he became a speculator in securities and the architect of various real-estate ventures that included construction of a toll bridge to Boston, known during its many years of operation as Craigie Bridge. In his authoritative 1877 history of Cambridge, Lucius R. Paige wrote that Craigie came to own "almost the whole of East Cambridge." The dinners and functions he hosted were legendary for their extravagance, and his young wife, Elizabeth Shaw Craigie (1772–1841), a great beauty in her youth, was celebrated for her irreverence for tradition, her quick wit, and a consuming passion for French culture. Henry recalled her fondly as being "eccentric to the last," and always attired wearing "a turban and a slate colored" gown. "In matters of religion she was a free thinker. Voltaire was one of her favorite authors. She used to say that she saw God in Nature, and wanted no mediator to come between him and her. She had a passion for flowers and cats and in general for all things living."

Andrew Craigie's schemes ultimately led to indebtedness, and he was able to ward off creditors only by remaining secluded inside his house on weekdays, emerging on Sundays when the state's strict blue laws prohibited the sheriff from serving him with papers. He died intestate and insolvent. To help pay off her husband's debts, Elizabeth began renting out rooms to Harvard faculty. Among tenants who lived there prior to Henry's arrival were Josiah Quincy (1772–1864), Edward Everett (1794–1865), and Jared Sparks (1789–1866), each destined to serve terms as president of Harvard College. While living at 105 Brattle Street, Sparks, then a rising young historian, edited the first three volumes of a twelve-volume compilation of correspondence, formal addresses, and notes of an even earlier occupant—George Washington.

By the time Henry moved in, most of the land had been parceled off and sold. Harvard acquired the six-acre site of Craigie's summer cottage and renamed it Observatory Hill in anticipation of the fifteen-inch equatorially mounted refractor telescope it had commissioned from Merz & Mahler of Munich. Site preparation began in 1842 with a twenty-six-foot base of poured cement and gravel. On top of that, five hundred tons of Quincy granite chiseled into precisely calibrated blocks were assembled to form a conical pedestal, known as the pier, upon which an eleven-ton tripod was set in place. With the installation of a copper-plated dome, the total elevation reached forty-three feet. Once it was operational, the new telescope had a focal length of twenty-two feet eight inches.

A few weeks after scanning the skies with the instrument, William Cranch Bond, astronomical observer to the university, invited Harvard president Everett to "rejoice" that "the great nebula in Orion has yielded to the powers of our incomparable telescope." A succession of discoveries—newly identified comets, astounding auroras, sunspots, meteor showers, the dusky ring of Saturn, and a previously unobserved moon of Saturn, Hyperion—captured the public's imagination. Among

Early copy of an 1848 lithograph of the Harvard telescope,
credited to B. F. Nutting and A. Sonrel, first used in
William Cranch Bond's *Description of the Observatory
at Cambridge* (vol. 4, 1849)

those lobbying for its establishment had been John Quincy Adams, the
sixth president of the United States and an ardent amateur astronomer, and Nathaniel Bowditch, the renowned Harvard mathematician
credited with introducing the principles of modern navigation at sea.
Though owned and maintained by Harvard, the project was fully funded
by public subscription. Retired long ago from active use, the telescope
nonetheless remains in situ and fully functional.

Henry logged a dozen visits there over a twenty-one-year period, and
probably made more than that. Living virtually in the shadow of the
dome, he had monitored progress from the beginning, walking up "over
the fields" behind his house one April afternoon in 1844 with Charles
Sumner "to the new observatory, not yet completed." On October 30,
1847, an entry in Bond's guest book noted that "Prof. Longfellow [and

his] Lady, his brother and Mrs. Wedgewood from England, [and] an English Gentleman, and also a poor fellow who had journeyed all the way from New Bedford expressly to look through the telescope" had come calling. "We obtained some of the most satisfactory views of Saturn that we have ever had."

One of Henry's companions that night was a visiting professor who had just lectured on the "immense and awful idea of space, which no man's brain can sound." Their other sightings included Orion and its nebula. "It is a curious effect of looking through the telescope to make one feel warm in a cold night; that is, to forget the body wholly." On another visit, he admired Neptune, "a weak, watery, distant planet; glorious belted Saturn, large as a moon; and Mars, blazing with light." A viewing of Saturn's rings was to him like seeing a "gash" across the planet's face. Four years later, he took three dinner guests to see "Jupiter and the outskirts of the moon." His last recorded visit was in 1871 with a British member of Parliament. "The soul," he declared of that night's communion with the heavens, "seems to assert its supremacy and to walk among the stars." During a visit to Philadelphia with his family in 1850, he remarked after an evening walk along "gas-lighted streets" how comfortable he felt that time of day. "I like to look at a new city by night. It has a strange, magical effect."

Images of stars, planets, constellations, and the evening sky are prevalent throughout Henry's body of work, so much so that the critic Newton Arvin declared him in 1961 to be "a poet of the Night," discerning in much of his poetry a state of "longing for unconsciousness, even oblivion" that "runs strangely counter to other reaches of his feeling." This is apparent in "Hymn to the Night," the first poem in *Voices of the Night,* and published at the same time plans for the observatory were being finalized. It opens with a remarkable impression of the Milky Way that engages all of the senses, beginning with what the narrator *hears*— and only then can see and feel:

> I heard the trailing garments of the Night
> Sweep through her marble halls!
> I saw her sable skirts all fringed with light
> From the celestial walls!

> I felt her presence, by its spell of might,
>   Stoop o'er me from above;
> The calm, majestic presence of the Night,
>   As of the one I love.

A notebook Henry prepared three years into his marriage at his wife's request—he inscribed "To Fanny the Beloved, October 6, 1846" on the first page—concisely summarizes how he came to compose the poems in that collection, before she was privy to everything he wrote; he called it "Manuscript Gleanings and Literary Scrap Book." He recalled composing "Hymn to the Night" in the summer of 1839 "while sitting at my chamber window late on one of the brightest nights of the year." Similarly, "The Light of Stars" was written "on a beautiful summer night," from the same vantage point. "The moon, a little strip of silver, was just setting behind the groves of Mount Auburn and the planet Mars blazing the south east. There was a singular light in the sky; and the air cool and still." That poem opens with these two stanzas:

> The night is come, but not too soon;
>   And sinking silently,
> All silently, the little moon
>   Drops down behind the sky.

> There is no light in earth or heaven
>   But the cold light of stars;
> And the first watch of night is given
>   To the red planet Mars.

As the observatory neared completion in 1845, another poem of the night, "The Occultation of Orion," appeared in *The Belfry of Bruges and Other Poems*. In a later printing, Henry appended a note that represented something of a disclaimer: "Astronomically speaking, this title is incorrect; as I apply to a constellation what can properly be applied to some of its stars only. But my observation is made from the hill of song, and not from that of science; and will, I trust, be found sufficiently accurate for the present purpose." One modern critic nonetheless deemed Hen-

Samuel W. Rowse
portrait of Fanny, 1859,
in the master bedroom,
which inspired the sonnet
"The Cross of Snow"

ry's application of an "occultation" to be technically correct. "The action in the poem involves two everlasting and irreconcilable principles; there is Orion and there is the moon—there is war and there is peace in the universe, and there is little promise that these eternal and autonomous opposites can be harmonized."

AMONG HENRY'S CAMBRIDGE NEIGHBORS WAS Dr. John White Webster (1793–1850), a chemistry professor in the Harvard Medical School with whom he maintained a cordial, though not overly close, relationship, as borne out by the handful of perfunctory letters they exchanged periodically on matters of passing mutual interest. Their wives were well acquainted, too, and occasionally they all got together in each other's home. Just a month before the doctor became the prime suspect in what would mushroom into the most sensational murder trial of the nineteenth century, Henry recorded having attended "a Matinée Musicale at Dr. Webster's" house on nearby Garden Street, a "brother and sister being the musicians," the woman a "very simple, naïve damsel, playing delightfully on the pianoforte and he very, very well on the violin, but not so delightfully, the damp weather having damaged his strings."

A quiet man of good breeding and solid achievement, Dr. Webster's dark side was a tendency to live well beyond his means, a weakness that led him to borrow money from Dr. George Parkman (1790–1849), like himself a trained physician from a distinguished family, whose income—aside from a considerable inheritance—came from property ownership and money lending. Parkman was something of an eccentric, a lanky, angular man whose high top hat made him appear even taller than he was when out collecting rents and calling on debtors. Fanny would call him "a good-natured Don Quixote" when word spread in November 1849 that he had failed to return home from his rounds the day after Thanksgiving. "It is feared," she confided to Emmeline, "he may be murdered."

Once it was determined that the two men had met at the Medical School on the day Parkman went missing, and that he had gone there to collect an overdue debt, suspicion focused on Webster. The Medical School building where he taught was located then on North Grove Street next to the Massachusetts General Hospital, near the Charles River. Thanks to the electric telegraph, which had gone online for much of the country over the previous five years, the case attracted intense attention, the shocking involvement of two highbrow Boston physicians with strong Harvard connections—the missing Dr. Parkman had provided the land for the location of the Medical School—made the story irresistible. Fanny gave Emmeline a thorough overview of the situation:

> You will see, by the papers what dark horror overshadows us like an eclipse, that all thoughts are soiled by suspicions of murder, but you cannot easily conceive how we feel here, how impossible it is for us to believe Dr Webster guilty, knowing him as we do. Not to speak of his character, which has been above all suspicion, he is a man of simple, child-like disposition, passionately fond of flowers, music, nervous, and I should think physically a coward. Therefore, if in a moment of passion, he had been tempted to strike a blow which proved fatal, we cannot imagine he could conceal it in his

countenance, nor be at ease in the presence of others, whereas he has been perfectly so for the last week, and the evening of the day the supposed murder was committed he passed at a neighbor's, with his family, with his usual cheerfulness.

Police dragged the Charles River and Boston Harbor in search of a body; twenty-eight thousand handbills seeking information were distributed; a three-thousand-dollar reward was offered—all to no avail. On Friday, November 30, a janitor discovered some body parts in a closed vault below the doctor's private privy.

"As we drove into town this morning," Henry wrote on December 1, a Saturday, "we heard to our great dismay that Dr. Webster had been arrested on suspicion of having murdered Dr. George Parkman, the missing man!" Later that day, a jawbone with false teeth was removed from a stove in Webster's office. Before long, a tea chest containing a headless, armless torso stowed beneath a collection of minerals was revealed. The defense would later argue that this was a medical-school laboratory, after all, and that corpses—many of them acquired on the black market, it was further disclosed—were dissected there all the time. "Nothing talked of but the murder," Henry grumbled. "We in Cambridge cannot believe Dr. Webster to be guilty, though the circumstantial evidence may, for the present, look very strong against him." December 3 dawned "rainy, cold, bleak, and cheerless"—Henry's words: "The frost covered boughs of the trees creak and lash the air that seems polluted by the cry of murder!"

Fanny wrote two long letters the next day, each arguing that despite the grisly discovery of a few generic body parts, the murder of a specific individual had yet to be established. "It seems to me a strange thing to arrest a man on suspicion of a deed not known to be done," she maintained to Emmeline, who was living then in upstate New York with her husband and two children: "It is the most awful tragedy that ever gloomed upon a Christian community." As an "act of kindness," she had called on Mrs. Webster, but the woman was seeing no visitors. "I have the liveliest sympathy for her,—she is such a gentle, sensitive, charming little woman, and her daughters are very amiable. What a blight on their whole lives, even the suspicion, for I cannot think any thing can be proved, black as the evidence looks. Heaven send a ray of light upon the truth, and relieve our minds of this horror and mystery!"

On a far less "painful subject, to which every one comes back as by a fatal proclivity," Fanny then reported having just read with Henry a new novel by an English author going by the name of Currer Bell, whose first book, *Jane Eyre*, had captivated them the previous year. The pseudonymous author was not yet identified as Charlotte Brontë, and the gender still presumed by most to be male, but Fanny was having none of it. "There is so much two women have to say to each other. I have felt this more keenly reading *Shirley*. It is admirable,—nature itself, and the style wonderfully vigorous and natural." There could, she then asserted, "no longer be any doubt" in her mind—and she was way out ahead of everyone else with her hunch—"but a woman's genius sounds those depths. How I wish I could read it with you."

With Fanny's next letter, to Mary Greenleaf, it was once again all about the "dark horror" of the murder case, and how the Harvard community was in great turmoil. "You cannot conceive the growing excitement since Dr Parkman's disappearance, and the state of things in the Medical College." Before long, Dr. Nathan Cooley Keep—the dentist who had assisted Fanny during the birth of her third child two and a half years earlier—identified the dentures as being a set he had made for the missing man; his testimony would mark the first time that dental records were introduced as evidence in an American trial. Other forensic findings would be just as path-breaking, as would the entire notion of "circumstantial evidence" so routinely applied in the criminal-justice system today, along with the instruction by Elizabeth Craigie's cousin Chief Justice Lemuel Shaw that the jury did not need "absolute certainty" to convict, only "guilt beyond a reasonable doubt." There were issues, too, with what constituted "murder," and how that differed from "manslaughter." Whether the crime was premeditated or committed on impulse came into play, too, all of it followed carefully by Henry, Fanny, and the entire Harvard community.

Henry could think of little else. "This horrid murder haunts the streets and the homes and will not go away! It darkens the evening lamps, it poisons every dish, it infects every breath of air! It repeals itself like an echo in the brain and murders the peace and tranquility of the village."

On December 12, he and Cornelius Felton called on Dr. Webster at the Leverett Street Jail, where he was being held in a "whitewashed cell" they found warm but not well lighted. "There sat the Doctor reading, nervous but not unnatural in his appearance. He talked freely about his case, but showed no particular emotion, save when I told him that the Musical Association Concerts had been given up in Cambridge out of a feeling of sympathy for him."

The trial began on March 19, 1850, with reporters from the major capitals of Europe in attendance. "God help him," Henry wrote. "I fear the general belief is against him." He soon would complain that the trial "drags on heavily and slowly," and wished for a merciful conclusion. "The papers are full of it and nothing else. It infects the air." Boston police estimated that sixty thousand people were admitted to the courtroom over the course of the proceedings, ushered in and out by groups at ten-minute intervals. On March 31, a Sunday, Charles Sumner came by with one of his brothers for dinner. "They brought the fatal news of Webster. Last night at eleven o'clock, the Jury brought in a verdict of 'Guilty.' The scene was horrible; so says Sumner and well I believe it." Appeals were filed and dismissed. After every avenue had been exhausted, Webster confessed to killing Dr. Parkman, but insisted he had acted in rage when pressed to either pay his debt or suffer public humiliation.

"We have survived the horrors of the Webster trial and its dreadful termination, but such a painful excitement will never fall again upon our community," Fanny informed her father, then on an extended holiday for his health. "The sentence was a great shock tho' not unexpected, particularly by those who watched closely the trial and saw the evidence drawing every day fatally round the criminal. In New York and Philadelphia the papers express great dissatisfaction with it, and petitions are talked of to the Governor. His wife and daughters, I see by tonight's paper, have been also to beg for a commutation of the punishment." Webster appeared "more rational since the verdict, and prays with his family very devoutly and talks of having made his peace with God," she added, "but I doubt if there is any real repentance as yet. It is fearful to see how easily he lost his foothold in men's regard—how very little respect all classes seem to have had for him—for years. He seemed a very genial, amiable man, but was utterly wanting in all principle or honesty."

In one respect, at least, Fanny would get a single wish fulfilled—that "this will be a death-blow to public executions." The hideous denouement to the case, witnessed by twenty thousand people, came on August 30, 1850. "Poor Dr. Webster was executed this morning! He bore his fate with great firmness," Henry deemed of what would turn out to be one of the last public hangings in the state, as well as the only instance in the long history of Harvard College in which a respected member of the faculty was executed for having committed a crime. "So ends this dismal tragedy, that like a pestilence has polluted the air for nearly a year. I hope this may be the last execution we shall ever have in Massachusetts! Cain, the first murderer, was not hanged! Let a mark be set on all murderers, and let them work forever in State's Prison."

QUITE APART FROM the trial of the century taking place in Boston was a proceeding of grave national concern unfolding in Washington, DC involving another local man named Webster—Daniel, in this instance, who represented Massachusetts in the United States Senate. Determined to stave off the breakup of the Union at any cost—and to the great consternation of Henry, Fanny, and their soul mate in these matters, Charles Sumner—the senator had taken a conciliatory position on the Compromise of 1850, a major section of which required that all runaway slaves who had found sanctuary in the North be returned to their masters in the South.

Faced with mounting unpopularity in Massachusetts, Webster resigned from the Senate to become secretary of state for Millard Fillmore, who had assumed the presidency upon the death of Zachary Taylor, creating an opportunity for Sumner to fill the newly vacated seat—but not before a process mandated by a quirk in the US Constitution played itself out first. Senators, at that time, were not yet elected by popular vote—that would be corrected in 1913 with ratification of the Seventeenth Amendment—but by a consensus of the state legislatures. Henry had felt all along that his friend was "too good, too noble, too free, too independent for the purposes of politicians," and half wished he had stayed out of the fray. As the slow process plodded on, Fanny reported that Sumner was "hanging still" six votes shy of victory, and that he remained "cheerful and unconcerned, not desiring the post, thinking he can be as useful in private life." After three tedious months of closed-door bickering, a compromise finally was reached, and Sumner's margin of victory—over Robert Winthrop, no less—was by a single vote.

"We have had quite exciting times in Boston since you left," Fanny wrote in a summary review of noteworthy events for her father, the Sumner election being just one of several she had to convey. Causing her particular alarm was a "trial without judge or jury" for an escaped slave named Thomas Sims, who had been "marched off with three hundred policemen as guard" to a ship in the harbor for his "return to slavery." Such strong-arm tactics were "thought, by many, a great indignity in Massachusetts, and the Court House was chained against an imaginary riot." Fanny did not mention an earlier incident involving an escaped slave from Virginia named Shadrach Minkins, who was liberated from federal custody by a mob and whisked off to Canada by way of the Underground Railroad. It was that fiasco that led to the show of force in the Sims case, which, in turn, "caused a great indignation throughout the State, where Northern freedom is thought as important a matter as Southern slavery."

Placing the incident in further perspective—and with remarkable openness, given the fissure that still remained between her "dearest Papa" and her husband's closest friend—was Fanny's added conviction that it "rather helped Sumner's election, which I fear will not give you much pleasure, but you can feel sure that whatever he does, as Senator, will be dictated by a sincere conviction and an earnest desire to do right, and a statesmanlike broad view. He did not wish it, and would gladly resign now if his party could choose a man of the same opinions in his place, for he has no political ambition whatever, and was more depressed at the moment of his success than during the long and doubtful contest." She was fearful, too, she acknowledged, for Sumner's safety. "I think all his enemies will do him violence some day, for they now singularly misunderstand him and we are in a position to judge him with peculiar impartiality."

Though recusing himself from the public outcry, Henry's sympathy for the plight of African Americans, and the less fortunate in general, found expression in other tangible ways, as repeated entries in his personal account books demonstrate, with entry after entry recording modest cash contributions under such headings as "colored school," "negro school," "South Carolina negro school," "negro preacher," "negro church," "soldier's widow," "children's home, North Street Mission," "house of refuge," "colored soldiers," "Tennessee refugees," "orphan asylum, Mobile," among many others.

Henry was inspired by the example of Ellen Craft, an escaped slave from Georgia who had found refuge in Boston by taking advantage of her light complexion. Disguising herself as a white gentleman traveling with a manservant—actually William Craft, her husband—she made her way north. In an 1860 memoir, William Craft wrote that they chose Boston because "public opinion in Massachusetts had become so much opposed to slavery and to kidnapping, that it was almost impossible for any one to take a fugitive slave out of that State." There was, as well, a free black community on the North Slope of Beacon Hill, where numerous escaped slaves had found sanctuary, and where the Crafts took up residence in 1848. Once passage of the Fugitive Slave Act made cooperation with slave catchers compulsory, the Crafts became a target. With the help of an abolitionist group known as the Vigilance Committee, they fled to England, got jobs, and raised a family. Henry had an opportunity to meet the couple in February 1850 while visiting with Fredrika Bremer (1801–1865), an eminent Swedish writer and ardent champion of women's rights who was then four months into a two-year tour of the United States.

Bremer would write about her experiences in *The Homes of the New World: Impressions of America*, a three-volume travelogue that focused on all aspects of American culture, including slavery; it appeared simultaneously in Swedish and English in 1853, the American edition going through five printings in a single month. During her travels, she became acquainted with Catharine Maria Sedgwick, Ralph Waldo Emerson, James Russell Lowell, Nathaniel Hawthorne, Washington Irving, and, of course, Longfellow, who was fluent in Swedish, and had read her books in the original. Visiting the library at Harvard, she was pleasantly "surprised to find one portion of the Swedish literature not badly represented," the reason for that "owing," she added, "to the poet Longfellow, who having himself traveled in Sweden, sent hither these books. He

Escaped slaves
William and Ellen Craft,
from William Still,
*The Underground Railroad:
A Record of Facts, Authentic
Narratives, Letters* (1872)

has also written about Sweden, and has translated several of Tegnér's poems."

She told of attending several dinner parties, "one very excellent at the house of Professor Longfellow and his handsome and agreeable wife." Among the guests were James Russell Lowell and his wife, Maria, and the Shakespearean actress Charlotte Cushman and her companion, Matilda Hayes, a translator of George Sand. The literary bent of the evening had Henry rejoicing how they had just entertained a "whole table full of authors and authoresses! We fed them upon canvasback ducks, quail, Roman punch, three kinds of American wines." It was altogether "very charming," an opinion shared by Bremer. "Longfellow is an agreeable host, and gave us American wines, sherry and Champagne. The latter I thought especially good; it is made from the Catawba grape at Cincinnati." She ranked Craigie House "among the most beautiful and the most artistic homes I have seen here."

One of Bremer's goals had been to interview and sketch slaves and slaveholders. She met, too, with Native Americans, women from every social level, including prostitutes, and became the first woman to observe the United States Congress in session from the public gallery. Henry visited her on February 12 at the Revere House, where she "made a sketch of me in her book." While there, Ellen Craft, "the slave woman who ran away disguised in man's clothes as a young master, her husband going as her slave," came in. "When Miss Bremer told me who it was, and spoke of man's clothes, Ellen hung her head and said she did not like to have it mentioned, 'some people thought it was so shocking.' Miss Bremer laughed at this prudery, as well she might; and we both urged her to be proud of the act." Bremer described the visit at greater length in her book, noting that it was William Lloyd Garrison who had brought Craft in to meet them.

Henry called on Bremer several times before she left Boston, in one instance taking the new train into town to fulfill a request of his wife's. "On Monday the Longfellows had a cast taken of my hand in plaster of Paris, for here, as elsewhere, it is a prevailing error that my hands are beautiful, whereas they are only delicate and small," she wrote in bemusement. Fanny nonetheless was overjoyed, as she explained to Matilda Lieber. "She has given me a cast of her hand which I begged for a souvenir," she wrote, delighting at its delicacy, and for being the appendage that had "written so many charming books." The cast is kept today in the basement storage vaults—a perfectly shaped woman's hand with an identification written by Henry in pencil on the wrist.

Bremer's book reached American shores at a time when Henry was thinking long and hard about writing full-time; her glowing words could only have buttressed his desire to make the move. "Longfellow, the author of *Evangeline*, is perhaps the best read and the most popular of the poets of America," she wrote, crediting him with possessing qualities distinctive to the "elder poets" of all countries. "Those sentiments, whether happy or sorrowful, which exist in the breast of every superior human being, are peculiarly his domain, and here he exercises his sway, and in particular in his delineation of the more delicate changes of feeling. In *Evangeline* alone has he dealt with an American subject, and described American scenery."

Bremer also expressed her admiration for Henry's work privately in a letter he requested to facilitate a meeting with Jenny Lind, the internationally renowned Swedish opera singer, who was giving several concerts in Boston in September 1850. Bremer happily obliged, "though I do not think the Poet Longfellow needs any introduction [other] than the mentioning of his name." Henry and Fanny were exhilarated by Lind's performances. "She is very feminine and lovely," he declared. "Her power is in her presence, which is magnetic, and takes her audience captive before she opens her lips. She sings like the morning star; clear, liquid, heavenly sounds." Despite a frenetic schedule, Lind met with Henry at the Revere House three days later after an afternoon concert. "Jenny came in and we had an hour's chat." They got together again several times the following year during another series of Boston concerts. One of those times was at Craigie House. "There is something very fascinating about her," Henry decided, "a kind of soft wildness of manner, and sudden pauses in her speaking, and floating shadows over her face. Her brow and eyes and hair are beautiful and childlike."

HENRY HAD NEVER MET Harriet Beecher Stowe before publication of *Uncle Tom's Cabin* made her an immediate sensation in 1852, though he knew her husband, the Reverend Calvin Ellis Stowe, having attended Bowdoin College with him three decades earlier. He reached out to her directly on January 29, 1853, with a fan letter and an invitation to dinner. "I congratulate you most cordially upon the immense success and influence of *Uncle Tom's Cabin*. It is one of the greatest triumphs recorded in literary history, to say nothing of the higher triumph of its moral effect." In accepting, Mrs. Stowe graciously added how fortunate it would be for them to meet, since she was leaving soon for Europe. "I hope that I shall be able to say in England that I have seen Longfellow!" Three weeks later, they dined in Craigie House. "How she is shaking the world," Henry exulted later that night. "At one step she has reached the top of the stair-case up which the rest of us climb on our knees year after year. Never was there such a literary coup-de-main as this. A million copies of a book within the first year of its publication!"

A year later, he finally made up his mind. "Henry, as you have doubtless heard, is weary after twenty-five years teaching, and has decided to resign his Professorship—to have time for other things and to feel free, but he will remain in the harness until the summer vacation," Fanny informed her brother-in-law Sam. Two months after that, on April 19, 1854, at 11 a.m., in a packed assembly room of University Hall, he gave his final lecture, "on the last Canto of Dante's *Inferno*," with a "brief account" of the *Purgatorio* and *Paradiso* thrown in for good measure.

14

Pericles and Aspasia

A delightful stroll with Fanny on the cliff, watching the sails in sunshine and in shadow, and our own shadows on far-off brown rocks. This is our last evening walk at Nahant, and it is gone like the sails and the shadows.

—Henry Wadsworth Longfellow's journal, August 28, 1850

The sea was glorious this morning; after a long tranquility it was all alive again and full of its noblest energy—renewing all my old passion for its vigorous freshness and beauty.

—Fanny Longfellow, letter to Emmeline Austin, July 28, 1851

You can not escape the ocean here. It is in your eye and in your ear forever. At Newport the ocean is a luxury. You live away from it and drive to it as you drive to the lake at Saratoga, and in the silence of midnight as you withdraw from the polking parlor, you hear it calling across the solitary fields, wailing over your life and wondering at it. At Nahant the sea is supreme. The place is so small that you can not build your house out of sight of the ocean, and to watch the splendid play of its life, is satisfaction and enjoyment enough. Many of the cottages are built directly on the rocks of the shore.

—George William Curtis, "Nahant," in *Lotus-Eating* (1852)

*F*or those who could afford the luxury of getting away, the arrival of summer around Boston and Cambridge usually meant packing the family up and heading off for cooler climes, the sea breezes of Nahant and Newport being traditional favorites, the crisp mountain air of the Berkshires another. Henry and Fanny found respite in each of these elite enclaves during the years of their marriage, often inviting selected friends to join them for varying periods of time. For their 1850 and 1851 holidays, they rented a "low, long house in the village" of Nahant, a craggy slip of a town on the northern rim of Massachusetts Bay, and for much of the nineteenth century the warm-weather retreat of choice for a mix of the city's movers and shakers and top educators from Harvard, who had established a cozy little coven there of their own; Fanny once described its clannish ambiance as "Boston in summer clothes." In a feature article for the *New-York Daily Tribune,* George William Curtis expanded on the favor it enjoyed: "No city has an ocean-gallery, so near, so convenient and rapid of access, so complete and satisfactory in characteristics of the sea, as Boston in Nahant."

When Curtis (1824–92) offered that homage to the tony seaside haven, he was on the fast track to becoming a writer of consequence, his polished manner and sunny disposition giving him entree to circles that mattered in mid-nineteenth-century America. Born in Rhode Island and privately tutored in Boston and Providence, Curtis moved to New York with his family as a teenager. Between 1844 and 1845, he spent eighteen months at Brook Farm, the experimental community in West Roxbury, Massachusetts, and after that on a communal farm in Concord, establishing meaningful relationships with George Ripley, Nathaniel Hawthorne, Charles Anderson Dana, Margaret Fuller, Theodore Parker, and Ralph Waldo Emerson.

In 1846, Curtis embarked on four years of foreign travel that took him through much of Europe, Egypt, and Syria, all the while keeping a journal and writing occasional dispatches for the *Morning Courier and New-York Enquirer.* A book drawn on those experiences, *Nile Notes of a Howadji,* appeared in 1851, followed the next year by *The Howadji in Syria,* giving him widespread recognition at an early age, and a catchy nickname. Derived from a Turkish word for "merchant," *howadji,* as Curtis applied it, was "the universal name for a traveler." In the years that followed, he worked as a critic and feature writer for the *New-York Daily Tribune,* an editor for *Putnam's Monthly Magazine,* and a columnist for *Harper's New Monthly Magazine* and *Harper's Weekly,* where he became editor in 1863. He also made a name for himself as an orator championing the causes of abolition and women's suffrage, and was a founder of the Republican Party. Over four decades of professional writing, he wrote newspaper articles on many topics, and several other books, including a novel. Not long after meeting Henry and Fanny, he produced a series of travel essays for the *Tribune,* including his take on Nahant, later published in *Lotus-Eating: A Summer Book.*

Henry's first mention of the Howadji appears on March 22, 1851, when he and Fanny gave a dinner for Charles Eliot Norton and a friend of his—George Curtis of New York—whom he had met in Paris. "They are just returned from Eastern travel, and their talk is of the Sphinx and the Pyramids. Mr. Curtis is the author of *Nile Notes of a Howadj;* a rhapsody on Egypt, I imagine by a few extracts I have seen. A very pleasant, amiable young man, of the Emerson school I should say." Two days after that, Henry and Fanny attended a "very nice supper" for Curtis hosted by Andrews Norton, the father of Charles, at his Shady Hill home. The cuisine was Italian, Henry noted approvingly, "the whole illuminated with a huge straw-covered flask of Chianti wine," and the conversation so congenial, "we sat till nearly one o'clock."

In his next visit to Craigie House, Curtis gave Fanny a copy of his *Nile Notes,* which "we begin to read with much delight," Henry recorded—"we" being code for their favorite pastime, *she* reading aloud each night to *him.* "It is the poetry of the Nile and a very remarkable book." Henry offhandedly mentioned in the next entry that he was putting the finishing touches on *The Golden Legend,* having just read the entire draft to Charles Sumner, which his friend had deemed "very learned and original!" Henry nonetheless decided to rewrite the first scene, "putting the blank verse into rhyme. It makes it less ponderous; for blank verse—at least my blank verse—seems to me very heavy and slow."

A week after receiving *Nile Notes,* Fanny informed Sam Longfellow how much she and Henry had enjoyed such "a very summery book," one so "full of glowing Tennysonian pictures." She identified the author as "an amiable youth named Curtis" they had recently met, and offered similar praise that same day to Tom Appleton, adding that the book's "soft Lydian airs" had "lulled" her and Henry into forgetting "the harshness of this land of storms and mental conflicts." Curtis achieved this, she added, by "deliciously" creating a "languid atmosphere" notable for its "many sly touches" of humor. "It is very soothing to the nerves so I recommend it as a gentle medicine—even tho' it be to you of poppies. He said to me 'It is a very young book'—but that is why I like it,—for I love that golden shore from which I feel sliding away, as I dare say you do today. But we are among those favored few who can always row back to it for an hour's stroll, when we like, however strong the current sets down stream."

A few months later, the Longfellows were on Nahant, with just 1.2 square miles of land area the tiniest municipality in all of New England. The name is derived from a Native American word meaning "almost an island," a perfect description for what in essence is a narrow peninsular projecting from the city of Lynn in Essex County southward into Massachusetts Bay, the two connected by a narrow causeway and forming the eastern flank of Lynn Harbor on the North Shore. Early in their stay, Fanny wrote her cousin Isaac Appleton Jewett, then in Europe, that they were still wanting for stimulating company. "We take long walks, and read quiet, meditative books, and see many tolerably pleasant people. But I confess I do hunger and thirst, occasionally, for more literary people, or rather thoughtful, earnest people—so many are shallow and occupied by trifles. There is so little real, rich cultivation here, good, deep soil, and again I envy you some of your English acquaintances." That ennui would soon be relieved by the arrival of Curtis, who spent a good deal of time in their company over the next several weeks.

For their 1852 vacation, they rented a "spacious" house in Newport, Rhode Island, "delightfully situated on the clover-scented cliffs with nothing but turf between us and the sea and a most extensive view of the latter from our windows," as Fanny described the "cottage" for her sister-in-law Anne in Maine. They found everything "in fresh order" when they arrived, and best of all, it was "filled with a few very agree-

Daguerreotype taken during summer sojourn in Newport, 1852. Henry stands at right with the top hat, next to Julia Ward Howe and Tom Appleton. Fanny is seated in the middle between two friends, John G. Cosler and Horatia Freeman.

able friends of ours." Not arrived yet, but expected presently, was "the Howadji Mr Curtis," leaving them still with "two rooms besides desiring occupants which complete our number." Before the summer was out, Samuel Gridley Howe and Julia Ward Howe would join the party—the seasonal rate was eighteen dollars per room per week—making for a "very merry" holiday retreat.

On their first day in Newport, before they had so much as settled into their quarters, "a singular damsel" had appeared unannounced, "shrouded in a white veil and saying, 'I am the Sybil,'" as Fanny would later relate the incident. Henry had no earthly idea who the woman was; the veiled figure thereupon identified herself as one Faustina Hasse Hodges, an organist and composer who had written several letters to Henry "on musical matters," six of which are in the Houghton collections. Fanny described her as "a romantic beauty" with a "decided talent, if not genius" as a composer, and a musician "who plays with wonderful brilliancy," her curious behavior notwithstanding. "Such strange damsels there are in this country," she concluded with characteristic aplomb, "and such odd things they do."

Bizarre as the incident may have been, it underscores the impact Henry's work was beginning to have throughout American culture, and how it was finding fruitful voice away from the printed page. Among the materials maintained in the Longfellow House archives are several hundred examples of original sheet music, many of them beautifully lithographed, a number inscribed to Henry by the composers, all adapting a poem or verse from Henry's oeuvre. I was able to document five of his poems that Hodges adapted for musical adaptation. Henry made no mention of the Newport encounter in his journal, concentrating instead on the good company of his wife and guests.

"We went and sat by the sea under the cliff," he wrote of one afternoon walk, "and watched the breakers and the sails, and thought the rocks looked like the Mediterranean shore, and that the Italian language would sound well. Here in truth, the sea speaks Italian; at Nahant it speaks Norse." During an unaccompanied stroll into town a few days after that, he paused by "a shady nook, at the corner of two dusty, frequented streets," his attention diverted by an "iron fence and a granite gateway" that led to an enclosed burial ground next to an inactive synagogue. Escorted inside by "a polite old gentleman who keeps the key," he came upon a cluster of old graves, nearly all of them "low tombstones of marble, with Hebrew inscriptions, and a few words added in English or Portuguese." Drawing on this unusual encounter with the past, he would later write "The Jewish Cemetery at Newport," a poem that commemorates the small community of Sephardic Jews that had moved fitfully from place to place after being forced out of Spain and Portugal in the fifteenth century by the Inquisition, finding sanctuary finally in 1658 in Rhode Island, which fourteen years earlier had granted freedom of worship to all religious sects.

Henry and Fanny did some sightseeing, too, visiting landmarks associated with the late William Ellery Channing, a native of Newport, and also Whitehall, the country farm where Bishop George Berkeley, the Anglo-Irish philosopher, wrote the book *Alciphron* in the early 1700s. But their most agreeable moments were spent with their companions, front and center among them Curtis, who by now had become friendly with the entire family. Ernest Longfellow, the couple's second-born child, would remember Curtis for his "great charm of manner," a "most musical voice," and a "sweet disposition," altogether "one of the most delightful of men" to ever visit their home. Alice Longfellow described him as one of their "most radiant and delightful" houseguests, "so handsome, and gracious, and kind" to the children. "He was much given to falling in love, though we did not know that, and thought he quite belonged to us."

Once returned to Craigie Castle that fall, Fanny savored "the acquaintanceships and friendships" that had deepened in Newport, hoping they would not be "as evanescent as the summer" weather they had all enjoyed so thoroughly. "I cherish an especial interest in the Howadji, and his beautiful and loveable disposition has won much upon both of us," she told Tom Appleton. "He deserves the best of fortunes and I trust will secure it, for few could resist such a combination of good looks, talent, and goodness of heart."

The aspiring Boston poet William Winter was introduced to Curtis at Craigie House when both were young men just embarking on their careers. Winter described Curtis as being "lithe, slender, faultlessly appareled, very handsome," rising at his approach, and "turning upon me a countenance that beamed with kindness, and a smile that was a welcome from the heart." Curtis had the manner "of a natural aristocrat—a manner that is born, not made; a manner that is never found except in persons who are self-centered without being selfish; who are intrinsically noble, simple, and true." Of his oratorical skills, Winter wrote that Curtis spoke in "a level tone," always "without a manuscript" in front of him; whether his speech was long or short, "he never missed a word nor made an error."

Curtis became friends with the Longfellows at a time when Henry was a dominant force in American letters, with many triumphs yet to come. His enthusiasm for Henry's work was unqualified, and as a trusted insider, he had direct access to the entire family. Of equal weight was the esteem Curtis had for Fanny, going so far as to suggest—in print—that she was a modern version of Aspasia of Miletus, a legendary intellectual from ancient times who drew praise from such figures as Socrates,

George William Curtis, 1854,
by Samuel Laurence

Anaxagoras, and Phidias, along with the undying love of Pericles, hailed by Thucydides during the Golden Age as the "first citizen of Athens." As towering female figures from antiquity go, Aspasia was not a queen, like Helen of Troy, Cleopatra of Egypt, or Zenobia of Palmyra; she was not even allowed Athenian citizenship by virtue of her Milesian bloodlines, and for that reason unable to marry Pericles. Instead, her stature and influence came through words—her expertise as a master rhetorician and philosopher, memorialized in the writings of Plato, Sophocles, Xenophon, Cicero, and Athenaeus; the best-known biographical treatment of her is to be found in Plutarch's *Lives of the Noble Greeks and Romans,* written around AD 100.

In her personal life, Aspasia bore Pericles a son, also named Pericles, and advised him on many matters. It was asserted by some that she composed the great funeral oration Pericles delivered during the Peloponnesian War. An academy she established in Athens for young women became a chic salon for influential men. "Socrates himself would sometimes go to visit her, and some of his acquaintances with him," Plutarch wrote, "and those who frequented her company would carry their wives with them to listen to her." In *Menexenus*, one of the Socratic dialogues, Plato has Socrates deliver a speech he claims to have learned from Aspasia. In his *Memorabilia*, Xenophon has Socrates quote Aspasia directly on a number of matters; Athenaeus suggested that it was Aspasia who taught Socrates rhetoric.

For Curtis to imply that Fanny was a kind of Aspasia to Henry's Pericles, then, is bold by any yardstick, leaving open, however slightly, the inference that she was more than muse to Henry: she was perhaps, at least in his eyes, an essential nutrient to his creative impulse. Based on a number of findings—praise be for paper trails—I can assert with confidence that for a period she was certainly all of that for Curtis. The first reference he made to Aspasia came in his 1851 *Tribune* essay about Nahant, which was reprinted the following year in *Lotus-Eating*, a collection of travel pieces in which he ranked northeastern summer resorts for people of a certain stature, or what William Dean Howells called "fashionable life at American watering-places." The hardcover edition featured illustrations by John Frederick Kensett, a talented artist of the Hudson River School, who would become an art instructor for Fanny and Henry's son Ernest. Here is the pertinent segment:

At Nahant you cannot fancy poverty or labor. Their appearance is elided from the landscape. Taking the tone of your reverie from the peaceful little Temple and glancing over the simple little houses, with the happy carelessness of order in their distribution, and the entire absence of smoke, dust, or din, you must needs dream that Pericles and Aspasia have withdrawn from the capitol, with a choice court of friends and lovers, to pass a month of Grecian gaiety upon the sea. The long day swims by nor disturbs that dream. If haply upon the cliffs at sunset, straying by "the loud sounding sea," you catch glimpses of a figure, whose lofty loveliness would have inspired a sweeter and statelier tone in that old verse, you feel only that you have seen Aspasia, and Aspasia as the imagination beholds her, and are not surprised; or a head wreathed with folds of black splendor varies that pure Greek rhythm with a Spanish strain,—or cordial Saxon smiles and ringing laughter dissolve your Grecian dream into a western reality.

A fair question to ask is whether there is any supporting evidence to show that Curtis was anointing Henry and Fanny the Pericles and Aspasia of their generation. The first confirmation that he was doing exactly that comes from Fanny herself in a letter to Emmeline. "Do you ever see the New York *Tribune*?" she asked. "In one paper of this month is a very nice account of Nahant by Howadji Curtis, and in a later one of Newport. There was also a very good one about Lake George discriminating very well the difference of our scenery and the European." She then added that "his Mot Notelpa," a character quoted in two instances, "is Tom," her brother, and that "I am complimented under the name of Aspasia (a dubious compliment!) in the Nahant one."

The "dubious" misgiving was undoubtedly made mindful of the many vicious attacks made on Aspasia's character by the political enemies of Pericles, including unfounded allegations that she was nothing more than a clever, conniving, opportunistic courtesan, perhaps a high-end prostitute. Aristophanes even claimed in *The Acharnians* (425 BC), his earliest surviving play, that she was responsible for instigating the Peloponnesian War. While obscure today, Aspasia was well-known in nineteenth-century literary circles, certainly by Henry and Fanny, who were both schooled in the classics. There is, in addition, a copy of Walter Savage Landor's popular epistolary novel of 1839, *Pericles and Aspasia*, in the Craigie House library, bearing Henry's personal bookplate. Present there as well are comprehensive histories of ancient Greece by Oliver Goldsmith, William Mitford, and William Smith, and if we know anything at all about the Longfellows, it is that they read their books.

Curtis gave many of his real-life characters fictitious nicknames. The one he used in *The Homes of American Authors* for Tom Appleton—Mot Notelpa—is an anagram of his name, with a single "p." He referred to Nathaniel Hawthorne as "Monsieur Aubépine," a play on the French word for the shrub hawthorn, and a sobriquet Hawthorne himself used for the mock preface to the story "Rappaccini's Daughter." The one he gave to Bronson Alcott—Plato Skimpole—was suggested to him by Fanny, and used in a way that leaves no doubt that she was his Aspasia. Confirmation comes in a letter Fanny wrote to Tom Appleton announcing that *Homes* had just appeared, "with capital sketches of the various mansions and beautifully written essays upon them and their owners by

various hands. The 'Howadji' has done ours and Emerson's and Hawthorne's with his usual grace and humor, wickedly fastening upon poor
Alcott the name I gave him of Plato Skimpole."

The phrase to be underscored here is "the name I gave him" for Bronson Alcott, a figure in the Emerson circle known for having established
the alternative Temple School in Boston (1834–41), and for dispensing
his philosophical maxims in "Orphic Sayings," a series of prosaic apho-
risms for *The Dial* magazine. Fanny had conveyed her negative opinion
of Alcott's pithy pronouncements to Emmeline a decade earlier when
discussing the general merits of the periodical, which for the four years
of its initial existence (1840–44) was an organ of the transcendentalist
movement. "There is much readable in the *Dial,*" she allowed, but felt
there was also plenty of "nonsense," too, and if her friend had by chance
"stumbled on" Alcott's "Orphic Sayings," she would have noticed a "shal-
lowness of absurdity this age must have lived to reach." Fanny was by
no means alone in her assessment; *The Knickerbocker* published a parody
called "Gastric Sayings," and *The Boston Post* compared the maxims to a
"train of fifteen railroad cars with one passenger."

In his essay, Curtis identified Alcott as the "Orphic Alcott—or Plato
Skimpole, as Aspasia called him," and repeated the derisive nickname
three more times. The key phrase there, needless to say, is "as Aspasia called him." The "Plato" part of the coinage was a sarcastic reference to Alcott's orphic deliberations; "Skimpole" likened him to Harold
Skimpole, a bumbling character in *Bleak House,* the Charles Dickens
novel then causing a minor sensation in the English-speaking world,
and widely assumed to be an unflattering caricature of the British critic
Leigh Hunt.

As a reference to Alcott, the sobriquet caught on, and appeared in
print occasionally in the years that followed, usually framed as "the name
George Curtis called Alcott." There is an amusing footnote to this, one
I would never have found without benefit of a shot-in-the-dark Google
search using "Plato Skimpole," "Alcott," and "Curtis" as my key words.
Among the items that turned up was a letter to *The New York Times
Saturday Review of Books* in 1898. The writer of the letter, identified only
by the initials E. L. C., called into question an assertion made in what
was then a newly published volume of Curtis's letters to the effect that

"Plato Skimpole was Margaret Fuller's name for Alcott." That was highly unlikely, the letter writer continued, since Margaret Fuller had drowned at sea off Fire Island in 1850, a full two years before *Bleak House* was published, meaning that she had been given credit "for someone else's witticism."

A week later, three other readers weighed in, filling most of an entire column in the newspaper. The first wrote to clarify a point— it was *not* Curtis who attributed "Plato Skimpole" to Margaret Fuller, it was the person who had edited the posthumously released letters. "I should doubt very much whether any one but Curtis was responsible for the nickname." The next letter writer went to the original source and referred directly to *Homes of American Authors,* and quoted Curtis verbatim, where "Aspasia" is identified as the source, leading to a single question in the headline: "Now Who Was This Aspasia?" With all the principals long since deceased, and nobody around to come forward and clear the air, the matter has remained unresolved for more than a century—until now.

In 1853, Curtis was named editor of *Putnam's Weekly.* The following year he spent a fortnight at Craigie House gathering information for his *Homes of American Authors* essay. Fanny had hoped to make Curtis "acquainted more with Boston" during that June stay, but inclement weather kept them anchored to Craigie House. She was able to arrange "a small musical party" for him, which featured the vocals of a lovely young woman from Boston, delivered in "the purest Italian style," her "magnificent voice" so "powerful and rich" that her performance "woke all the children, but they were luckily quiet." Curtis was so "enchanted" with the woman he went into Boston by himself the next day "bearing a fresh bouquet of roses from our garden. She is a very pretty girl besides, with much quiet self-possession."

The following Sunday, Henry took a carriage drive with his wife and their houseguest to nearby Waltham. "A feeling of the country, with fresh odors of fields and woods and the sight of great gray barns. After dinner drove Curtis into the Old Colony Railway, and so departed another friend whom we prize and love much. A very gentle, joyous spirit, with a sharp eye for the weakness of humanity and great pity and compassion for them likewise." Among Curtis's colleagues at *Putnam's* was one

Charles F. Briggs, with whom he corresponded often while away on writing assignments. During this extended stay at Craigie House, he drafted a letter to Briggs that begins with an extraordinary paragraph that speaks for itself in the context of this chapter: "I am staying now with the poet and his wife. What though it rains, or shines? It is quite the same to me. I sit and look over the melancholy meadows at the winding Charles, and quote my host, or, which is better, I contemplate my hostess, and thank God for the gracious and beautiful woman for whom, clearly, the woods, flowers, the stars, sun, and men were created."

Two months later, at the height of summer, Catharine Maria Sedgwick, Fanny's "dear Aunt Kitty" of previous years, sent a cordial letter of reference to Henry on behalf of a visitor, requesting "a kind reception" when he came calling. "I hope you and dear Fanny are enjoying these summer months as they pass," she continued, switching subjects deftly. "The season, even from the first of May, has verified all the poets have sung of it. Have you both forgotten the lovely hill-side by the Housatonic?" Sedgwick concluded by noting she had at that moment a mutual acquaintance in her house—there, we can presume, doing an interview for an essay, possibly the one about her in *Homes of American Authors*:

Drawing of the Longfellow cottage on Nahant, from the Longfellow print collection. The house was destroyed by fire in 1909; only the stone foundation remains on the site.

"Your friend and your wife's admirer (what conjugal strength when both can be united!) is at this moment singing mellifluously in our little parlor and I think the song's prosperity lies in the ears that listen to him." Sedgwick moved on to her closing goodbye, then added a postscript to identify the visitor: "I have omitted George Curtis' name. Perhaps you could have guessed it."

What Sedgwick meant by that comment—"what conjugal strength when both can be united!"—is open to interpretation. I believe "Aunt Kitty's" conversation with Curtis—who like her was a professional writer—had involved a bit of shoptalk, and what they agreed is possible when two people they both knew well pursue a common goal. Fanny, to be clear, was the first person to insist that Henry was the poet in the family, going back to the first weeks of their marriage, when she was urging him to write "The Arsenal at Springfield," and vision problems had occasioned a temporary slowdown in his writing. "Now that the vein is again opened," she informed George Washington Greene, "I hope much will flow from it and if his Pegasus needs a spur, I can answer for it being duly applied, as I feel guilty, in a measure, for his sluggish pace of late." She used a similar image with her mother-in-law: "I am a pretty active spur upon his Pegasus, and wish it were possible for a poet, in this age of the world, to surrender himself wholly to his vocation."

To her closest friends and relatives, Fanny mentioned works in progress with the authority of someone who was directly involved in the process, her "our book" collaboration being just one example. A few others from her correspondence illustrate the point.

"I suppose I can now tell you that he is correcting the proofs of a long poem called *Evangeline* written in hexameter," she informed Emmeline. "It is a very beautiful touching poem I think and the measure gains upon the ear wonderfully. It enables greater richness of expression than any other, and is sonorous like the sea which is ever sounding in Evangeline's ears." To Sam Longfellow, she previewed *The Song of Hiawatha*: "I hope you will like it. It is very fresh and fragrant of the woods and genuine Indian life, but its rhyme-less rhythm will puzzle the critics, and I suppose it will be abundantly abused." A self-effacing comment Fanny made to one of Henry's sisters in 1858 during composition of *The Courtship of Miles Standish* not only claimed direct involvement, but asserted further that they collaborated on a regular basis. "Henry has been writing a poem of some length, and we sit in the summer-house and correct proof and discuss this line and that these sunny days. I am ashamed to say that he always takes my suggestions, which may not improve the poem!"

If there is one overriding criticism that applies to Henry's journals, it is that he tells us very little about his creative process—which had he done so would go a long way to explain exactly how he worked with his wife. One entry, written when he was about to commit himself totally to the writing of poetry, offers some insight. "How brief this chronicle is, even on my outward life. And of my inner life, not a word. If one were only sure that one's journal would never be seen by anyone, and never get into print, how different the case would be! But death picks the locks of all portfolios, and throws the contents into the street for the public to scramble for."

Seventy letters Curtis wrote to Henry are in the Harvard collections, the first written around the time they met in 1852, the last in 1880, a year and a half before Henry died. They are uniformly respectful, cheery, and friendly, many written to coordinate visits, all of them while Fanny was alive extending "love," "affection," or "kindest regards" to Mrs. Longfellow and the children. There are no letters from Curtis to Fanny in the Houghton Library, but there are two in Longfellow House, one of them, dated November 5, 1854, announcing his engagement to Anna Shaw, the daughter of the Boston abolitionists Francis and Sarah Blake Shaw, and sister of Robert Gould Shaw, who would gain fame as commander of the Fifty-Fourth Massachusetts Regiment, the first all-black unit from the Northeast to see combat in the Civil War.

"My dear Mrs. Longfellow," Curtis began, "I don't know that you will be glad to hear of my engagement to Anna S. but I do know that you will be glad that I think myself happy." The next two pages assured Fanny that he was happy with his choice, judging Anna to be "inexpressibly lovely and dear" to him. "I have not forgotten some little things you said to me, and I have profited from them. Therefore you may believe how sure I am, that at last, when you know her, you will say as I say all the time in my heart, 'for she is as inimitable to all women as she is inaccessible to all men.' She is not to be easily known." Curtis closed with a single request: "It seems to me only too good. It makes me very humble and very proud to know how much she loves me. Good bye. Give my love to Mr. Longfellow—and give me your blessing." Curtis and Anna were married a year later, and took up residence on Staten Island. "A generous box of wedding-cake" announced the wedding, Fanny informed Tom, which took place the day before Thanksgiving. "I sent Curtis a bronze ink stand with an ibis on it to remind him of his Howadji days, while the sober metal recalls the graver duties of the present."

There is one more episode in the matter of George William Curtis and his friendship with the Longfellows to be discussed here. Once again, we must be mindful that so much of what is expressed on paper at this time is implied, not directly stated. The Harvard historian and chronicler of nineteenth-century American culture Lawrence Buell characterized this Victorian conceit for me as "the tacitness of the period," the tendency to communicate in a fashion that would be "understood without being openly expressed," a brief note Fanny wrote to Emmeline early in 1857 being a classic example. It was a cover letter, basically, for the gift of some pineapple jam from the Caribbean "which may possibly be agreeable to you," courtesy of her sister and her brother-in-law Robert Mackintosh, who between 1850 and 1855 had served as governor general of Antigua and viceroy of the British colony of the Leeward Islands. Included in the package was a copy of *Prue and I,* a book written by George William Curtis and published the previous fall, "which, if you have not read, may help off an invalid hour." It contains, she then added, "a subtle sweet fancy which I think you will like." Nowhere in Fanny's surviving correspondence do we find another mention of the book. The "subtle sweet fancy," as she coyly put it to her dearest friend, is to be found on the dedication page:

> TO MRS. HENRY W. LONGFELLOW,
> *In memory of the happy hours at our
> Castles in Spain.*

The inscribed copy Curtis presented to Fanny—in bibliographical parlance, the "dedication copy"—reads "Mrs. Longfellow from her aff., George Wm. Curtis," and is dated November 12, 1856, a year and a day *after* he had informed her of his engagement, and two weeks to the day *before* his marriage. His "Howadji days," as Fanny had put it in her letter to Tom Appleton, and as she had reminded Curtis with her wedding gift, were indeed in the past.

Not only did Curtis dedicate the book to Fanny, but a strong argument can also be made that he used her as a model for Prue, the character who inspires the unnamed narrator's passion for flights of fancy. Written as a series of light sketches and meditations, *Prue and I* is narrated by an aging bookkeeper who contemplates places he has visited only in his imagination. His wanderings reach full flower in a chapter called "My Chateaux," and—it should come as no big surprise—include stimulating visits to what they both call "castles in Spain."

"A man must have Italy and Greece in his heart and mind, if he would ever see them with his eyes," he explains in a prefatory note. "For my part, I do not believe that any man can see softer skies than I see in Prue's eyes; nor hear sweeter music than I hear in Prue's voice; nor find a more heaven-lighted temple than I know Prue's mind to be. And when I wish to please myself with a lovely image of peace and contentment, I do not think of the plain of Sharon, nor of the valley of Enna, nor of Arcadia, nor of Claude's pictures; but, feeling that the fairest fortune of my life is the right to be named with her, I whisper, gently, to myself, with a smile—for it seems as if my very heart smiled within me, when I think of her—'Prue and I.'" A "subtle sweet fancy," indeed, as Fanny described the book to her dearest friend.

15

Balance and Harmony

Much is said now-a-days of a national literature. Does it mean anything? Such a literature is the expression of national character. We have, or shall have, a composite one, embracing French, Spanish, Irish, English, Scotch, and German peculiarities. Whoever has within himself most of these is our truly national writer. In other words, whoever is most universal is also most national.

—Henry Wadsworth Longfellow's journal, January 6, 1847

I have at length hit upon a plan for a poem on the American Indians, which seems to me the right one, and only. It is to weave together their beautiful traditions into a whole. I have hit upon a measure, too, which I think the right and only one for such a theme. At present it delights me. Let us see how it will prosper.

—Henry Wadsworth Longfellow's journal, June 22, 1854

Between these two Saturdays *Miles Standish* has marched steadily on to success. Another five thousand are in press; this is very good for one week bringing in all, an army of twenty-five thousand. Fields tells me that in London ten thousand were sold the first day.

—Henry Wadsworth Longfellow's journal, October 23, 1858

A day after seeing George William Curtis off on the Old Colony Railroad at the Kneeland Square Depot in Boston, Henry got started on his next project. "I could not help this evening making a beginning of 'Manabozho,' or whatever the poem is to be called," he recorded, a title for the undertaking still up in the air, but the direction clear. "His adventures will form the theme, at all events." The next day, he was poring over the voluminous writings of the American ethnologist Henry R. Schoolcraft (1793–1864), best known for a series of in-the-field studies of Native American cultures, and for an 1832 expedition to the source of the Mississippi River. Henry concentrated on "three huge quartos" of historical material Schoolcraft had compiled, though he found it "ill-digested" for the most part and "without any index," but useful nonetheless for his immediate purposes. In a burst of energy that carried into the next day, he wrote "a few lines," giving himself a solid start: "Manabozho's first adventure and lamentation for his brother should follow."

By midweek, he had come up with another title. "I think I shall call it, *Hiawatha*," he had decided, "that being another name for the same Manito," an Ojibwa word for "spirit," though the two in fact were not the same, as Schoolcraft had erroneously indicated—not that it would have bothered Henry had he known, since "Hiawatha" had a far more pleasing lilt to it. "I chose it instead of Manabozho," he explained to Ferdinand Freiligrath, "for the sake of euphony." For the better part of 1855, the course held steady. "If I had one hundred hands, I could keep them all busy with *Hiawatha*," he exulted. "Nothing ever absorbed me more." Free finally from teaching, he found that the writing "occupies and delights me," despite the flow of letters from readers he felt obligated to answer, and periodic misgivings that he might be overstretching himself. "Then the theme seizes me and hurries me away, and they vanish."

It was around this time, during the embryonic stages of composition, that Henry received from Charles Sumner a gift, courtesy of his brother George Sumner, also a lawyer, who had returned from a business trip to the Midwest with a few images taken in the early 1850s by Alexander Hesler, a Chicago daguerreotypist who had been commissioned by

Harper & Brothers to photograph the Mississippi River from Saint Paul, Minnesota, to Galena, Illinois, for a series of books being planned under the general rubric of Harper's Traveler's Guides. The project never came to fruition, freeing Hesler to sell copies in his gallery, an option made possible by a new process that used collodion-on-glass negatives—also known as wet plates—to transfer daguerreotype images directly onto specially treated salted paper. George Sumner gave one of Minnehaha Falls to Henry. The picture of cascading water—like the word "Minnehaha" itself—became a central image in the poem, and the name for Hiawatha's ill-fated wife.

Shortly after *Hiawatha*'s official release in November 1855, Hesler received a first-edition copy in the mail. On the flyleaf—but with no

Daguerreotype of Minnehaha Falls by Alexander Hesler, 1855, copy given to Longfellow while he was writing *Hiawatha*

explanation attached as to what had occasioned such a gift from a perfect stranger, especially one so famous—was the inscription: "Mr. A. Hesler with compliments of the author." It was only when George Sumner returned to Chicago and filled Hesler in did the photographer realize that he had contributed to the making of an American classic, as he would tell the Minnesota Historical Society years later. Other than what George Sumner might have told him about the poem's genesis, Hesler knew nothing of how *Hiawatha* actually came to be, and thus mistakenly believed that his photograph inspired the writing itself, when in truth Henry had been toying for some time with the idea of an epic poem that would be decidedly American in both character and narrative, though not necessarily in form or structure, for which he relied heavily on European models.

Long after his literary reputation had been secured—but well before he began writing the work that became *The Song of Hiawatha*—Henry befriended a former Ojibwa chief, Kah-ge-ga-gah-bowh, who had converted to Christianity and become a Methodist minister, taking the name George Copway. During a lecture tour to Boston in 1849, Copway called on Henry to give him a copy of *The Life, History, and Travels of Kah-ge-ga-gah-bowh (George Copway)*, his autobiography, published two years earlier. Henry recorded six meetings with the chief over the next two years, once to view an exhibition at Amory Hall of Peter Stephenson's *The Wounded Indian,* a heroic sculpture in marble that Henry judged "very good" in "sentiment at least," and suggestive of the *Dying Gladiator* statue he had admired many years earlier in Italy. Together, they also took in a lecture given by the natural scientist Louis Agassiz, a Swiss zoologist and geologist who had become one of Henry's closest friends since taking a position in 1847 as head of the newly established Lawrence Scientific School at Harvard, and was founder there of the Museum of Comparative Zoology. Agassiz's remarks on this occasion—based as they were on strong antievolution views that, over time, would greatly diminish his professional standing and reputation—embarrassed the poet. "We went together to hear Agassiz lecture on the 'Races of Men,'" Henry recorded later that night, limiting his sarcasm to a single sentence: "He thinks there were several Adams and Eves and several gardens of Eden."

Henry was by no means the first poet to write a verse romance about the "red man's saga," with at least eleven appearing in print prior to his effort, according to the late Daniel Aaron, the founding president of the Library of America, and a distinguished historian of American literature at Harvard who was a champion of Longfellow's work until the day of his death in 2016 at the age of 103. Henry decided to write *Hiawatha*, Aaron wrote in the introduction to a 1992 edition of the poem, only after finding the "right and only measure" for the lines in the *Kalevala*, the national epic of Finland. The raw material came from the "loosely assembled fragments" of lore and legend that had been compiled by Schoolcraft, who later dedicated a book to Henry, recognizing him for having demonstrated in *Hiawatha* a "pleasing series of pictures of Indian life, sentiment, and invention."

Once out in the world, *Hiawatha* sold so quickly that Henry could hardly keep pace with the heady numbers being passed along to him by James Fields, four thousand copies on the first day alone, fifty thousand within the first two years in the United States, many thousands more abroad, and in many languages. There was a mix of critical response, including the appearance of numerous parodies, an exercise made tempting by the tom-tom tempo of the meter, unrhymed trochaic tetrameter, similar to that of the *Kalevala*. One of the first to appear—and arguably the most amusing—was *Hiawatha's Photographing*, by Lewis Carroll, whose title character is a photographer who attempts to make a family portrait, but fails because the subjects either move too soon or pose too strangely. An enthusiastic proponent of photography in its early years, the author in 1865 of *Alice's Adventures in Wonderland* found the particular rhythms of *Hiawatha* uncommonly attractive to imitate in a playfully zany poem. Here are the opening lines:

> From his shoulder Hiawatha
> Took the camera of rosewood,
> Made of sliding, folding rosewood;
> Neatly put it all together.
> In its case it lay compactly,
> Folded into nearly nothing;
> But he opened out the hinges,

Pushed and pulled the joints and hinges,
Till it looked all squares and oblongs,
Like a complicated figure
In the Second Book of Euclid.

Fanny had anticipated negative feedback, had even advised Henry
to be more forthcoming in explaining his reasons for employing such a
challenging cadence. "*Hiawatha*'s metre makes quite a talk in the Athenaeum, I see," she informed her sister, Mary, adding that Ferdinand
Freiligrath had also raised questions, "but it was a pity he could not
know that it was the similarity of Indian song with Finnish which suggested that metre, making it the true one to use. I always scold Henry
for not explaining more in his notes. He forgets people are not as wise
as he is, and might have saved himself much misinterpretation both in
regard to this, and *The Golden Legend*," which had been written in the
same measure.

To the one audience that mattered, though—the reading public—
the poem was an unqualified success. In the years to come it would
inspire a full range of creative works, notably, but by no means exclu-
sively, paintings by Albert Bierstadt, Eastman Johnson, Thomas Eakins,
William de Leftwich Dodge, Thomas Moran, and Robert S. Duncan-
son; sculptures by Augustus Saint-Gaudens and Edmonia Lewis; the
second movement of Antonín Dvořák's Symphony no. 9, *From the New
World*; a trilogy of cantatas by the composer Samuel Coleridge-Taylor;
and numerous choreographic adaptations. Artists commissioned to illustrate editions of the book have included Frederic Remington, Harrison
Fisher, N. C. Wyeth, and Armstrong Sperry. Currier & Ives published
seven Hiawatha prints between 1857 and 1867; three dramatizations
have been made for the screen, including a 1913 silent film directed by
Edgar Lewis, noteworthy for using a cast of Native Americans. In 1937,
Walt Disney weighed in with *Little Hiawatha,* an animated short in
the Silly Symphony series. Alexander Hesler's still image of the falls,
meanwhile, acquired its own following, while the site itself, now Minnehaha Park in Minneapolis, became an instant tourist attraction. An
idealized statue by the Norwegian sculptor Jacob Fjelde, erected there in
1912, depicts Hiawatha cradling in his arms the dying Minnehaha—her

Lithographic art for a box of Longfellow Cigars, with images from *Hiawatha*

name in the Dakota language translates as "rapid water" or "waterfall." Beyond artistic interpretation, *Hiawatha* penetrated all levels of American culture—giving its name to a National Forest in Upper Michigan; a park in Chicago; a paddleboat on the Mississippi; an eighty-six-mile train route operated by Amtrak on the western shore of Lake Michigan; dozens of schools and streets throughout North America; incorporated cities, even, in Kansas and Iowa—and created, along the way, a cottage industry for such themed items as Hiawatha chewing tobacco, playing cards, bicycles, games, toys, postcards, porcelain bowls, dishes, even Hiawatha soap (an eBay search of "collectibles" using "Hiawatha" as the key word brings forth hundreds of variations to the theme).

And all that is just for one poem. In "Longfellow in the Aftermath of Modernism," Dana Gioia pointed out how *Evangeline* "was adapted into an opera, a cantata, a tone poem, a song cycle, and even a touring musical burlesque show. Later, it became a movie three times—in 1929 starring Dolores del Rio, who sang two songs to celebrate Longfellow's arrival in talkies. 'The Village Blacksmith' became a film at least eight times, if one counts cartoons and parodies, including John Ford's 1922 adaptation, which updated the protagonist into an auto mechanic." The list, truly, goes on and on.

TO READ HENRY'S JOURNAL and correspondence at this time, what stands out is how deftly he was navigating his way through what had become heavily crowded waters; everything was in balance, regardless of the demands and distractions. In January 1855, he and Fanny attended three bravura performances in Boston by the Italian soprano Giulia Grisi: one of Vincenzo Bellini's *I Puritani*, another of his *Norma*, the third of Gaetano Donizetti's *Lucrezia Borgia*. "Grisi is grand, with her superb style and her tragic bursts of passion. A splendid woman," he raved. "Her voice has lost some of its power and freshness; but still she sings right royally and is Queen of the Lyric Drama."

The opera came as a welcome respite from the din of world events. "This music for a season drowns the cannon of Sebastopol, which for the last month has 'volleyed and thundered,' in our ears," Henry wrote of the nearly year-long siege of the Russian seaport on the Crimean Peninsula, a pivotal standoff among a cluster of warring nations that would result in the loss of 128,000 lives.

A few weeks later Henry and Fanny called on the widow of Charles Follen, a former colleague on the Harvard faculty. "She read us a passage from a letter she had just received from Lady Byron; a dying soldier on the field before Sebastopol was heard murmuring over and over 'footprints on the sands of time,'" one of the most frequently quoted lines from "A Psalm of Life."

While hardly the sort of compliment a writer is comforted to hear, it is an indicator nonetheless of the readership Henry's work was reaching worldwide. "Over here it is more of a reputation to *know* Longfellow than to have written various immortal works," James Russell Lowell wrote half in jest from Paris to the wife of William Wetmore Story. From India, Charles Eliot Norton thanked Henry for having written on his behalf to the poet laureate of Delhi, "which has brought me so many entertaining experiences that I am tempted to write to you of them, and to thank you again for the introduction."

Fanny learned through Charles Sumner that the lavish country estate of the Scottish man of letters, member of Parliament, and consummate bibliophile Sir William Stirling-Maxwell "is crammed with rare treasures

Daguerreotype of Fanny
reading to Charley and
Ernest, c. 1849

of art as his fields are with rare cattle," and that "he has a bull named Hiawatha and a cow Minnehaha." She shared a number of these anecdotes with Mary in England. "I tell you all this because it may amuse you, and I love to think Henry is so well appreciated among strangers. How much more would they think of him if they knew him personally, for the best of him is not in his books as it is with many poets. The overflowing goodness of his heart, his tenderness towards every human creature, in fact to everything having life, is but faintly hinted at in them."

February brought forth an interlude of calm and contemplation, and a succession of "quiet evenings at home, and readings by the fireside." First up on the to-read list was *History of the Conquest of Peru* by William Hickling Prescott. There were some provocative lectures to attend as well, a very "charming" one in particular given by James Russell Lowell, who had succeeded Henry as Smith Professor at Harvard, and there was no interruption in the teas and dinners they hosted.

Many years later, the poet's eldest daughter, Alice Longfellow, would recall the pleasure her father took in welcoming a diverse succession of people to their home. "Society and hospitality meant something quite real to Mr. Longfellow. I cannot remember that there were ever any formal or obligatory occasions of entertainment. All who came were made welcome without any special preparation, and without any thought of personal inconvenience. Mr. Longfellow's knowledge of foreign languages brought to him travelers from every country—not only literary men, but public men and women of every kind, and during the stormy days of European politics great numbers of foreign patriots exiled for their liberal opinions. As one English man pleasantly remarked, 'There are no ruins in your country to see, Mr. Longfellow, and so we thought we would come to see you.'"

Alice described a seamlessness in her father's routine. "There was really no line of demarcation between his life and his poetry. One blended into the other, and his daily life was poetry in its truest sense. The rhythmical quality showed itself in an exact order and method, running through every detail. This was not the precision of a martinet; but anything out of place distressed him as did a faulty rhyme, or defective metre." She credited her father's equanimity to a nature that was "thoroughly poetic and rhythmical, full of delicate fancies and thoughts. Even the ordinary details of existence were invested with charm and thoughtfulness."

Ernest Longfellow, in his memoir, described his father as being "very methodical and careful in his ways," someone who believed in "having a place for everything and everything in its place, and kept with the greatest care anything that could be useful. He always carefully folded up and put away, in a drawer devoted to the purpose, the wrapping paper that came on bundles, and untied, never cut, the string, and put that away in another drawer, thus having them both on hand when needed. The paper that he wrote his manuscripts on was of a certain kind called cartridge paper, and cut to a certain size and kept in large quantities for this use."

Among the many objects Henry preserved was a box of premium Havana cigars, still unopened, and tied by twine. Another box containing a miniature wedge of cast iron was opened in 1972, when the National Park Service assumed custody of the house; on the cover was a note in Henry's hand identifying the fragment as a "bit of an anvil one hundred years old" used by Dexter Pratt, the model for "The Village Blacksmith." He even saved the stubs of pencils he used to write some of his best-known works, all carefully identified on strips of paper coiled around each one. Fanny did a good deal of the same, keeping dozens of her children's drawings, their letters to Santa Claus, the journals and diaries they maintained, their playthings, articles of clothing, and swatches of fabric she had chosen for their fashions.

Henry also maintained a plentiful supply of fine wines racked in his cellar; a fulsome inventory of silver coasters and a variety of fine crystal glassware attest to how frequently the beverage was served at table. One occasional visitor to Craigie House, Ralph Waldo Emerson, found a bit of pretension apparent in all this, as expressed cattily in one of his journal entries. "If Socrates were here, we could go and talk with him, but Longfellow, we cannot go and talk with; there is a palace, and servants, and a row of bottles of different coloured wines, and wine glasses, and fine coats." But the ever-prudent Sage of Concord was nonetheless in the minority on this point. A week before Thanksgiving in 1848, Henry welcomed a number of literary figures from the area. "At dinner," he wrote, "Hawthorne, Thoreau, Channing," among others, including his younger brother Sam—"all philosophers." A Sunday without company was an exception to the norm. "For a wonder," he joked on just such an occasion, "no guests at dinner to-day."

OF THE THOUSANDS OF ITEMS amassed by the Longfellows, artifacts a researcher will not find in Craigie House are firearms acquired while Fanny was alive and managing the household, with one glaring exception, and it is quite remarkable that such a derelict piece was kept at all—a percussion musket disjointed in two pieces, with a shattered breach where the left hand of the "shooter" would have been positioned. Unlike so many other domestic objects Henry and Fanny took time to identify, this has no such legend attached to explain its presence. Yet it was retained, probably, according to James M. Shea, director emeritus of Longfellow House and the person who supervised the cataloguing of the building's contents during his twenty years at the helm, because Henry and Fanny were "the curators of their own lives," determined to document the unpleasant along with the pleasant.

Charley, the couple's firstborn child, was energetic from the time he

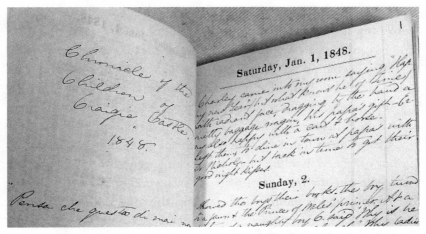

Opening page of Fanny's "Chronicle of the Children of Craigie Castle"

was born, assertive, often difficult to handle, yet much beloved by the family. Fanny described him variously as being "slow to acquire notions of obedience," "disobedient and self-willed," and "very active and eager in disposition." Once, "after an ebullition of temper," she found him "troubled in spirit," and there were times when she was openly exasperated with his behavior. "I know not how to control him," she allowed after one outburst. "I get very tired scolding and coaxing and wish I knew the best way to manage," after another. A few months later came this: "Charley struck me with a stick and the pain made me cry like a baby. He has grown very insolent, but a few words from his Papa softened him and he begged my pardon very penitently." Still, she admired his love of action, and in a letter to Henry's mother she judged him "a very good little boy on the whole."

An avowed pacifist, Fanny loathed weapons of any sort. Not long after the first shots had been fired on Fort Sumter, she expressed her conviction with utter clarity. "I abhor war wherever and whenever produced, and trust this will be a short one." But as Charley grew older, he would not be denied, and in the spring of 1856, Henry allowed him to have a musket meant to fire percussion caps—a toy, basically, albeit a functional one. Packing it with a full load of gunpowder one afternoon, Charley fired off a round, causing the breech to burst. "He was at Fresh Pond with a larger boy, who had the presence of mind to tie a cord tightly round his wrist," Henry wrote in his journal, and "walked homeward, a mile or more, with his dreadful wound"—the loss of a thumb—adding how he "does not feel what it is to be maimed for life."

Fanny's agitation was palpable. "He bought the gun with money he had saved up, but Henry had told him only to use percussion-caps with it, but the temptation was too great—he yielded and was severely punished," she explained to Henry's sister Mary Greenleaf. "It has been a sore trial to us, completely unnerving us for the time, the thought of our boy's maimed hand has been before our eyes and hearts through all the sleepless nights and anxious days." Seven years later, Charley's thirst for action would come to the fore again, this time with even greater consequence; but more immediate was yet another violent distraction to contend with, this one taking place just two weeks later on the floor of the United States Senate.

Charles Sumner's "conspicuous" effort to repeal the Fugitive Slave Act in 1854 had fallen short, but earned him, in Henry's estimation, "much honor." Fanny, typically, was more expansive. "We are all greatly excited about the dreadful Nebraska wickedness," she admitted to Sam Longfellow of a bill being sponsored in the Senate by Stephen A. Douglas of Illinois, which would invalidate the Missouri Compromise of 1820 and allow the territories of Kansas and Nebraska to choose whether they entered the Union as free states, or slave states. Fanny found a good deal of hypocrisy among Northern Whigs who "pretend indignation" at the advancing bill, known as the Kansas-Nebraska Act, and feared their words of protest would be "of the most luke-warm kind," a conviction that left her feeling even more helpless with what might come next. She drew on a line from John Milton to make her point. "War, Slavery, Pestilence, and Famine seem to threaten the poor weary Earth. I wish she had four as potent champions—but what do I say—'a million blessed angels lackey her,' and there is no fear she will long be surrendered to the power of her enemies." Passage of the act led directly to the formation of the Republican Party in 1854 by a coalition of breakaway Whigs and abolitionists that included Sumner and George William Curtis among its organizers, deepening the divide even further.

When Kansas finally did attempt to enter the Union as a slave state two years later, Sumner led the opposition, which he put forth in a five-hour oration delivered before a packed Senate gallery in two sessions on May 19 and 20, 1856, a speech he called "The Crime Against Kansas." Eschewing subtlety entirely, he called Senate colleague Stephen Douglas, the prime sponsor of the bill, and seated near him in the chamber, a "squat and nameless animal" unsuitable for service as an American senator, and branded Andrew Butler of South Carolina, who was not present, with keeping an "ugly" mistress—"the harlot Slavery," a creature "lovely to him" yet "polluted in the sight of the world." A flabbergasted Douglas was overheard murmuring at one point that "this damn fool is going to get himself shot by some other damn fool."

Two days later, after the Senate had adjourned for the afternoon, a distant cousin of Butler's, Congressman Preston S. Brooks of South Carolina, entered the chamber from a side door and confronted Sumner at his desk, where he was seated and franking copies of his speech for mailing. Using a gold-tipped gutta-percha walking stick for a weapon, Brooks began beating Sumner about the head, shoulders, and upper body. Unable at first to maneuver his long legs from beneath the bolted desk—he stood six feet four inches in height—Sumner finally struggled to his feet and attempted to flee. But the brutal attack continued, "thirty first rate stripes" in all, by the assailant's own boastful reckoning, end-

SOUTHERN CHIVALRY — ARGUMENT versus CLUB'S.

The caning of Charles Sumner on the floor of the US Senate by Congressman Preston Brooks of South Carolina, lithograph, John L. Magee, 1856

ing only with the shattering of his cane, whereupon Brooks left Sumner lying motionless on the chamber floor, bleeding profusely.

Widespread outrage in the North was matched by mocking jubilation in the South, polarizing the sectional divide even further. Events that followed—the Dred Scott case in 1857, John Brown's raid on Harpers Ferry and his subsequent hanging in 1859, the election of Abraham Lincoln in 1860 under the banner of an emergent Republican Party— pointed the country toward further confrontation. Sumner's recovery, meanwhile, was slow, his seat in the chamber left conspicuously empty during his absence. "Sumner's health does not seem to improve—even softening of the brain has been feared, but I cannot believe so pure a light is to be quenched in such a manner," Fanny noted with concern two months after the attack. A clergyman in South Carolina, she told her brother Tom in England, "had to leave his parish because he would not countenance the Brooks outrage. Is not that incredible fanaticism?"

Within weeks of the attack, Massachusetts congressman Anson Burlingame took to the floor of the House and from the podium declared Brooks to be the "vilest sort of coward," even questioned his "manhood" and sense of Southern "chivalry." Brooks—who was fined but never jailed for the assault—responded by challenging Burlingame to a duel, thereby ceding to him the choice of place and firearms and the right to take the first shot. Burlingame chose the Ontario side of Niagara Falls, and—expert marksman that he was—rifles as the weapons to be employed. As the agreed-upon day approached, Brooks offered the lame excuse that it would be too dangerous for him to travel through hostile Northern states, and prudently decided to be a no-show. "Burlingame has had a great fuss with Brooks about a duel, who has showed the white feather again, not venturing to Canada to fight him, which place was proposed as out of the jurisdiction of the country," Fanny told Tom. Sumner, she added, "still lingers in great debility. He has been to Cape May and is now in the mountains."

Reelected with minimal opposition in 1858, Sumner made an extended trip to Europe before resuming his duties in Washington, a strategy Fanny fully endorsed. "Perfect intellectual rest will be the best cure for him. He is softened and calmed by his long illness, all the gentler, sweeter parts of his nature are brought out, but he feels, with a sigh, that his reelection makes him a public man for life," she told Sam Longfellow. Responding seven months later to news that Preston Brooks had died from a respiratory infection, Fanny felt the sudden turn of events "should hush our selfish people into a shuddering pause." Sumner harbored "no personal feeling" against Brooks, Henry made clear. "He looked upon him as a mere tool of the Slaveholders, or, at all events, of the South Carolinians. It was their way of answering arguments."

WITH THE ORIGINAL FIVE of Clubs now a fraternity of the past, Henry became an active member of a newly formed social group known as the Saturday Club, the inspiration of Ralph Waldo Emerson, with a lot of new blood infused, including James Russell Lowell, Oliver Wendell Holmes, James T. Fields, Louis Agassiz, and the publisher Moses Dresser Phillips. As Tom Appleton began to spend more time in the United States, acquiring an elegant town house on Commonwealth Avenue near the Public Garden and filling it with splendid artworks, he, too, became a welcome participant, his sharp wit always in season. The men gathered at the Parker House on the last Saturday of each month for dinner, libations, and erudite conversation.

That the interests of these men went well beyond mundanities is evident by a meeting on May 5, 1857, when the idea for a new periodical to be called *The Atlantic Monthly Magazine*, shortened later to *The Atlantic Monthly*, and these days simply *The Atlantic*, was proposed by Oliver Wendell Holmes. An impressive nucleus of Boston-Cambridge-Concord heavyweights—Emerson, Thoreau, Louisa May Alcott, and of course Henry Wadsworth Longfellow—were eager to contribute. Henry had voiced his support of the initiative a week earlier when invited by Lowell, the first editor, to come aboard. "Lowell was here last evening to interest me in a new Magazine, to be started in Boston," he recorded. "Told him I would write for it if I wrote for any Magazine."

Henry's first effort on their behalf, "Santa Filomena," appeared prominently in the November 1857 premiere issue, the first of fifty pieces he would contribute to *The Atlantic Monthly* in the years ahead, and noteworthy in that it involved a living, readily identifiable person, something he typically avoided doing. The subject in this instance was

Florence Nightingale (1820–1910), the English nurse whose pioneering efforts on behalf of the sick and wounded during the Crimean War had become the stuff of legend. Sixteen years earlier, Henry had modeled the title character of "The Village Blacksmith" on Dexter Pratt, a hardworking but otherwise anonymous neighbor whose home and workshop were located a few houses away from his own at 54 Brattle Street, a building that still stands today, though the "spreading chestnut tree" of the opening line is long since gone, the victim in 1870 of a streetwidening project. The wood, at least, was used productively to craft a handsome armchair that was presented to Henry as a seventy-secondbirthday present from the schoolchildren of Cambridge in 1879.

Pratt was never named in "The Village Blacksmith," nor was Florence Nightingale in "Santa Filomena." But Henry's clever coinage of "Filomena" for the title—the Latin word for "nightingale" is *philomela,* and "Philomena" is the name of an actual saint—left little doubt about who he was celebrating, as Fanny emphasized in a letter alerting Mary to its imminent publication. The Mackintosh and Appleton families, it happened, were well acquainted with the Nightingales, a prominent English family, and it was probably on this account that Henry selected her for his subject. His brother-in-law Tom Appleton also had a close friendship with Florence, was even thought a few years earlier to have had romantic aspirations for her. "Tom had a beautiful note from Florence Nightingale by the last steamer—all about Henry's poems, but that did not alone make it beautiful in my eyes," Fanny wrote Emmeline in 1846. "I liked the freshness of her thoughts and the simple expression of them." She described another "remarkable letter" Tom received from Nightingale—and which he also shared with the family—as being "full of talent and a most beautiful nature."

Henry, for his part, did not know Nightingale personally, never mentioned her in his journal, and they never corresponded directly, though he did receive a gracious letter of appreciation from Parthenope Nightingale, Florence's sister, on behalf of the family, after publication of his poem. What motivated him, then, to do something professionally he rarely did, and on such a prominent stage, is open to speculation. The most likely incentive came from his wife and brother-in-law, though his dear friends Julia Ward Howe and Samuel Gridley Howe were close to the nurse as well; Julia even named a daughter Florence in Nightingale's honor, and wrote a poem of her own, "Florence Nightingale and Her Praisers," in tribute. To these personal testimonials from people close to him were press accounts that appeared during the Crimean War, giving Henry all the necessary background he needed to write something splashy and fast. One of the more influential pieces to appear had been published two years earlier in *The Times* of London, written from the front lines by a man who had worked closely with Nightingale in the Scutari hospitals, John Macdonald, whose lengthy dispatch included these observations:

> Wherever there is disease in its most dangerous form, and the hand of the spoiler distressingly nigh, there is this incomparable woman sure to be seen. Her benignant presence is an influence for good comfort even among the struggles of expiring nature. She is a "ministering angel" without any exaggeration in these hospitals, and as her slender form glides quietly along each corridor, every poor fellow's face softens with gratitude at the sight of her. When all the medical officers have retired for the night, and silence and darkness have settled down upon those miles of prostrate sick, she may be observed alone, with a little lamp in her hands, making her solitary rounds.

Henry saw an opportunity to write on a subject that was dear to Fanny's heart—a paean, in essence, to gallant women everywhere—and to do it, on deadline, for a new magazine he was eager to support. Here are his final three stanzas:

> On England's annals, through the long
> Hereafter of her speech and song,
>   That light its rays shall cast
>   From portals of the past.

> A Lady with a lamp shall stand.
> In the great history of the land,
>   A noble type of good,
>   Heroic Womanhood.

> Nor even shall be wanting here
> The palm, the lily, and the spear,
> The symbols that of yore
> Saint Filomena bore.

Though Nightingale was already well-known and widely admired when "Santa Filomena" appeared, these words from the most influential poet in the world raised her status to another dimension entirely, a circumstance not lost on her biographers. "Early in the war, Florence had been compared to Longfellow's most famous heroine, Evangeline, who becomes a Sister of Mercy and serves the sick," the British author Mark Bostridge pointed out in a recent treatment of her life. In "Santa Filomena," by extension, he continued, Longfellow "associates 'A Lady with a lamp'" who goes about "her nightly rounds 'through the glimmering gloom'" with the fictional Evangeline. By shining a spotlight on a living example of "Heroic Womanhood," the American poet had, as a consequence, ensured "Nightingale's rise to secular sainthood"—and helped create a "cultural icon."

I asked the Longfellow scholar Christoph Irmscher why he thought Henry, as a general rule, avoided writing about living people. "Longfellow was the poet of the backward look," he replied. "When he writes about Agassiz, he does so by evoking his childhood and youth; when he honors Florence Nightingale, it happens by way of what he has read, which conjures a vision for him. He's not the poet of immediacy, not comfortable with the form of direct address—not an occasional poet, in other words, the way Oliver Wendell Holmes certainly was."

HENRY WRESTLED OFTEN with finding the right title for a poem, be it *Gabrielle* or *Evangeline*, *Manabozho* or *Hiawatha*, *Sudbury Tales* or *Tales of a Wayside Inn*. As he moved ahead on a "kind of Puritan pastoral" about his *Mayflower* ancestors who had settled in Plymouth a quarter of a millennium earlier, he was torn between naming the poem for a key character—*Priscilla*, for Priscilla Mullins—or for the theme of the work itself: *The Courtship of Miles Standish*, which eventually won out. His journal entries during the composition of this, his last long-form narrative poem, are succinct and professional, offering very little insight on its composition. What emerges is a sense that he was doing his job, and doing it well, resulting in yet another international best seller.

With *Miles Standish* successfully through the press, Fanny was tempted by an invitation from Charles Eliot Norton and his wife to "pass the summer with them at Granada, as it touches Spain," which "but for the children," she allowed, "I would not hesitate, for I think Henry needs a change. This country is too dry and juiceless for a poet— he needs to have the fountain within inspired and refreshed by the dews of a different sky, now and then, or it stagnates in our emotionless life, emotionless except with quiet joys and sorrows, the smaller delights, like gentle breezes, which keep the waves alive, are so wanting." As she was preparing to decamp with the family for Nahant that summer, she wrote Sumner a letter much like the one fifteen years earlier after reading his "True Grandeur of Nations" oration. This time her praise was for his address "The Barbarism of Slavery," in which the senator had urged for the admission of Kansas as a free state, a debate that had remained unsettled since the days of the caning, and his first official remarks since resuming his duties.

"Allow me to congratulate you upon your great speech, the truest and most exhausting exposition of Slavery that was ever made, I imagine, since civilization was darkened and retarded by it. The power and calmness you combine with such severe truth, and willingness to grant all honorable exceptions, make it unanswerable. The beauty and feeling of the commencement, and the very delicate and Christian way in which you allude to your own experience of the barbarism you expose especially touched me." She added how it "must have been a great relief" for him to "pour forth in one Niagara, these long-accumulated convictions," and that he was able to do so "with such strength is a great matter of rejoicing to us. Now you know that your recovery is real and trustworthy." She closed by expressing the hope he might find some time "to get safely back to us, and that we shall enjoy a little free and pleasant talk before we desert Craigie Castle for our smaller castle on the Sea."

16

Hour of Darkness

First grand display of buttercups in the grass. How beautiful they are!
The purple buds of the lilacs tip the hedges; and the flowery tide of
spring sweeps on. Everywhere in the air the war like rumor of drums
mingles discordantly with the song of birds.

—Henry Wadsworth Longfellow's journal, May 20, 1861

As flies to wanton boys are we to th' gods.
They kill us for their sport.

—Shakespeare, *King Lear,* act 4, scene 1

The election of Abraham Lincoln on November 6, 1860, did nothing to ease tensions between North and South; it only heightened them. As the year drew to a close, the prospect of what was once unthinkable—fratricidal conflict on American soil—moved closer to certainty. Nerves were on edge, pessimism was rampant, even a "very pretty" ball a week before Christmas could not dampen the prevailing gloom. Fanny wore a "much admired" gown of "moire antique" silk with black flourishes that her brother Tom had just sent over from Paris, "prettily trimmed with lace and ruches," but frivolity was nowhere apparent that night in Papanti's Hall. "There has been little gaiety anywhere as you may suppose under these absorbing anxieties, and the newspapers are the only rich harvesters," she bemoaned to

Mary in England. "The news-boys' voices resound in the streets, in one unbroken chorus, like that of a Greek tragedy, full of ominous matter."

The opening gambit arrived on December 20, with the secession of South Carolina. On that same day, the January 1861 issue of *The Atlantic Monthly* came off the presses, featuring a tale in verse of heroism in pursuit of liberty that Henry had hoped would inspire his fellow citizens to preserve their precious patrimony. "Paul Revere's Ride" putatively recalled the American Revolution, but its more immediate purpose was hammered home in the six concluding lines, where the verbs shift from past to future tense:

> For, borne on the night-wind of the Past,
> Through all our history, to the last,
> In the hour of darkness and peril and need,
> The people will waken and listen to hear
> The hurrying hoof-beats of that steed,
> And the midnight message of Paul Revere.

Henry had begun writing the poem the previous April after making an "expedition" to the "old town" neighborhood in the North End of Boston with George Sumner, visiting many of the same historic sites he had shown Charles Dickens eighteen years earlier. "We go to the Copp's Hill burial-ground and see the tomb of Cotton Mather, his father and his son; then to the old North Church, which looks like a parish church in London. We climb the tower to the chime of bells, now the home of innumerable pigeons. From this tower were hung the lanterns as a signal that the British troops had left Boston for Concord." Whether or not this excursion inspired what came next is unstated, but his notation four days later suggests a clear linkage: "I wrote a few lines in 'Paul Revere's Ride,' this being the day of that achievement."

Critics of the poem relish nothing more than to nitpick its factual inaccuracies, entirely missing the point of what Henry had in mind. As much as anything else he ever wrote, this was a ballad in the traditional sense, an exercise in homegrown folklore composed with the quaint hope of eliciting an emotional response. Had Henry intended otherwise, he would surely have drawn on a narrative the historical Paul

"Paul Revere's Ride," prepared during World War II by the Office of
War Information, 1942–45, from National Archives series Pictures
of the Revolutionary War

Revere wrote in 1798, with which he was fully familiar. While Henry
was teaching at Bowdoin and moonlighting as a freelance writer, the
full text of Revere's personal recollections was included in a lengthy biographical essay that appeared in the October 1832 issue of *The New-
England Magazine*, illustrated with a full-page lithographic image of
the patriot. On the page preceding that image appears a sonnet, "Art
and Nature," identified as being "from the Spanish of Francisco de
Medrano," the translator not credited, but unquestionably Henry, since
the poem appears in the eleven-volume edition of his collected works
published in 1886 in an appendix for previously "unacknowledged and
uncollected translations."

Also included in that same issue of the magazine—and also "unacknowledged and unattributed"—was the fifth installment of an experimental novel Henry had been tinkering with called *The Schoolmaster*,

drawing heavily on his recent travels to Europe. Much of that material would find its way into *Outre-Mer,* which appeared in pamphlet form in 1834, and between hard covers the following year. Packrat that he was, he held on to his copies, especially those documenting his own work, and in this instance we do not have to guess. On April 27, 1877, a full forty-five years after the fact, he answered a reader's query with a one-sentence reply: "Dear Sir, In Buckingham's *New-England Magazine,* Vol. III, p. 310, you will find a letter of Paul Revere, giving a full account of his Lanterns and his ride. Yours truly, Henry W. Longfellow."

In commemorating the poem's one hundred and fiftieth anniversary in 2011, the Harvard historian Jill Lepore quoted from a letter Henry received in 1880 from a nine-year-old girl in Ohio, one of hundreds sent to him by admiring youngsters over the years. "I have learned some of your poems and love them very much," Berta Shaffer wrote, leading Lepore to observe dourly that "for a poet's literary reputation, to be read by children—and especially to be loved by children—is the sweet, sloppy kiss of death." Yet for all its issues, "Paul Revere's Ride" remains the most memorized poem in American history, its cadence mimicking the sound of a horse galloping through the countryside, the rider alerting the citizenry to redcoats on the march.

"THE DISSOLUTION OF THE UNION goes slowly on," Henry lamented in January, as six more Southern states seceded, with four more to follow. "Behind it all I hear the low murmur of the slaves, like the chorus in a Greek tragedy, prophesying, Woe, woe!" Fanny expressed fleeting hope that "after the 4th of March"—the inauguration of Lincoln—"a firmer hand will guide us to calmer waters." Formed on February 4, 1861, in Alabama, the Confederate States of America named Jefferson Davis, a onetime United States senator and Member of Congress from Mississippi, to be its president. Davis had served as secretary of state under Franklin Pierce, a Bowdoin alumnus, class of 1824, and a dear friend of Nathaniel Hawthorne's, who had written his campaign biography and served as consul to Liverpool during his administration. Henry kept discretely to himself whatever he felt about Pierce, remaining mum, even, when Hawthorne, in 1863, defiantly dedicated *Our Old Home,* a collection of English sketches, to the former president, then greatly out of favor, "as a slight memorial of a college friendship, prolonged through manhood, and retaining all its vitality in our autumnal years."

Henry learned of the attack on Fort Sumter within hours of the first salvos being fired in Charleston Harbor. "And so the War begins! Who can foresee the end?" In the early days of probing gamesmanship that followed, he found himself able to concentrate on little else. "When the times have such a gunpowder flavor as at present, all literature loses its taste. Newspapers are the only reading. They are at once the Record and the Romance of the day." Hoping to find some "contrast" to the dispiriting developments, he dipped into a volume of the seventeenth-century Spanish poet Pedro Calderón de la Barca's *Autos sacramentales,* a form of dramatic literature notable for offering solace in troubled times. "It has a far-off, dreamy sound, like the ringing of church bells in a little Spanish village."

On the last Sunday of the month, the Longfellows attended a service at Appleton Chapel in Harvard Yard, which had been built three years earlier with a bequest from Fanny's uncle Samuel Appleton. "I was glad the pulpit did not thunder a war-sermon to-day," Henry wrote. "We are given to too much talk and at present the North is warlike enough, and does not need arousing." Then came May Day, historically an occasion for hope and renewal—but not this year. "The word May is a perfumed word," Henry decided. "It means youth, love, song; and all that is beautiful in life. But what a May-day is this! Bleak and cheerless. And the little girls with bare necks, and rose-wreaths on their heads, remind me less of dancing than of death. They look like little victims. A sad thought for May-day!" A visit from Charles Sumner did little to relieve the gloom. "It is indeed a heavy atmosphere to breathe, the impending doom of a nation," a depressing conviction compounded even further by the steady deterioration of Nathan Appleton, his father-in-law, who "looks death in the face with perfect calmness."

Before long Henry found himself neglecting his work, and he used an Italian phrase—*dolce far niente*, literally "sweet idleness"—to vent his frustration. A good deal of his inactivity, too, was related to the moribund state of publishing. "Nothing alive but the military," he groused after a trip into town to see William Ticknor, who looked "dark and dreary," and James T. Fields, who "was going home ill," the reason for both he surmised with a sparsity of words: "Book-selling dead." Ten days later came more of the same. "Ticknor looks grim and Fields is fierce— business at a standstill. So much for war and books." One bright spot in the Longfellow household was the purchase, after many years of renting, of a roomy cottage on Willow Street in Nahant with gables and a long piazza overlooking the southern shore. Henry had purchased the property with Fanny's brother Tom Appleton for $5,000. A full summer at their newly acquired retreat had been an appealing prospect, but given Nathan Appleton's fragile condition, short stays and periodic day trips would have to suffice, at least for the adults.

As June drew to a close, Henry had a sense of imminence, of what, he could not say. "If one could only foresee one's fate," a gratuitous comment he jotted down that would seem cruelly prophetic a few weeks later, when viewed in retrospect. "We seem on the eve of great events. The two armies are drawing nearer to each other, and a battle somewhere is looked for." June 27 was spent uneventfully at Nahant; the day after that Henry and Fanny were back in Cambridge. A dinner meeting of the Saturday Club at the Parker House included a measure of solemn conversation; the month ended Sunday with a sermon in Appleton Chapel by the biblical scholar Dr. George R. Noyes, followed by a quiet afternoon at home.

July arrived the following morning, a "bright, joyous, triumphant summer's day." Louis Agassiz came to dinner later in the week; Robert Mackintosh, Fanny's brother-in-law, then in the United States by himself, dropped by as well. Between visits with Nathan Appleton in Boston, Henry and Fanny took Alice to see a hippopotamus, "a cumbersome fellow in his tank," brought to Boston from the Royal Zoological Gardens in London for public viewing. That night they all admired "a splendid comet" in the northern sky, "near the Great Bear." There were fireworks on Independence Day, and a visit from Charley, who had been having "a grand time" swimming and boating on Nahant. July 6 was so "sweltering" they all longed for the seashore; the next day was even "hotter and hotter," leaving the ground "parched and sun-burnt."

Henry's entry for Monday, July 8, is concise: "Still, the fervent sunshine and heat with a south wind fanning in at the window. Charley starts again for Nahant." After that appears the heading "9. 10 . . . 13," denoting the span, presumably, of the next five days. Written out beneath that, undated, in Henry's hand, are the last two stanzas of Alfred, Lord Tennyson's touching poem of bereavement, "To J. S."—words of his own, for once, having eluded him:

> Sleep sweetly, tender heart, in peace;
>   Sleep, holy spirit, blessed soul.
> While the stars burn, the moons increase,
>   And the great ages onward roll.
>
> Sleep till the end, true soul and sweet,
>   Nothing comes to thee new or strange,
> Sleep full of rest from head to feet.
>   Lie still, dry dust, secure of change.

LONGFELLOW HOUSE–Washington's Headquarters stands alone among National Park Service sites as a laboratory for American history. It is not just a historically significant building; it also is a research center teeming with archival materials and artifacts that illuminate the larger narrative in ways that are immediate and personal. I examined thousands of documents and objects for this book, a good many of the latter in this place—writing desks, bedroom furniture, paintings, sculptures, curios and knickknacks, books shelved according to their original scheme, rooms where fascinating individuals from the eighteenth and nineteenth centuries gathered, broke bread, sipped wine, smoked cigars, discussed, and in many instances influenced, the events of the day.

But nothing moved me more profoundly—actually made me sit back and pause before proceeding—than to hold in my hands five tiny white envelopes bearing, on the front of each, and in Fanny Longfellow's distinctive handwriting, the words "Edith's hair July 1861." Neatly inserted inside four of them are individual locks of luxurious blond hair—the same "golden hair" made famous in "The Children's Hour,"

Henry's joyful poem of parenthood, published just nine months earlier in the September 1860 issue of *The Atlantic Monthly*. Artifacts cannot speak, of course; they can only point the way—which raises, in this instance, a question: What are we to make of the fifth envelope, which is empty? Does it suggest a domestic task undertaken by Fanny but never completed? Once again, context is everything.

While largely out of fashion today, keeping locks of human hair as relics has deep historical roots, and was popular in Victorian times. It was used, too, in women's jewelry, including several pieces for a young Fanny Appleton, whose elegant hand-tooled jewelry box with the initials "F.E.A." on the lid still contains assorted earrings, bracelets, and brooches inset with strands of her own black hair. The practice figured as well in fictional works of the period. The narrator of Wilkie Collins's 1854 crime novel *Hide and Seek* asserts that a hair bracelet central to the plot was also "one of the commonest ornaments of woman's wear" in England at the time, rendering its evidentiary value marginal. "This literary fascination with the magical power of women's hair coincided in Victorian everyday life with an intense popular preoccupation with hair and hair tokens," a professor emerita of nineteenth-century culture at the John Jay College of Criminal Justice, Elizabeth Gitter, has written. "At the peak of the fad, in the forties and fifties, hair became something of a Victorian culture obsession: whole suites of jewelry were fashioned, as if through alchemy, from the plaited hair of family members, lovers, and friends, living and dead."

There are numerous snippets of hair preserved in Craigie House, including one taken from Little Fanny, who died as a toddler in 1848; the Houghton Library has a lock identified as Henry's that was clipped on his seventy-fifth birthday, snow white, and housed in a red leather pouch. Another packet contains a cutting from Fanny, black with a strand of gray, and dated July 10, 1861—the day of her death. Somewhat unsettling—"creepy" may be the apter way to put it—is a seven-stanza poem by Gustav Pfizer translated years earlier from the German by Henry, and written out by Fanny on a single sheet of paper, and kept with a pair of hair clippings. It is titled "Two Locks of Hair" ("Der Junggeselle," *The Bachelor*); these are the final two stanzas:

Two locks—and they are wondrous fair—
    Left me that vision mild;
The brown is from the mother's hair,
    The blond is from the child.

And when I see that lock of gold,
    Pale grows the evening-red;
And when the dark lock I behold,
    I wish that I were dead.

"IF I COULD HAVE KNOWN the heat would last so long, I should have tried to get down a week sooner," Fanny had written on July 7 to Erny, who was then on Nahant with his brother Charley and uncle Tom. "You are lucky in such hot weather, and we are all sighing for the good sea breeze instead of this stifling land one filled with dust." She mentioned the "very feeble" condition of "Dear Grandpapa," disappointed they could not bring him out to his own summer retreat in nearby Lynn, where "the sea air might strengthen him a little," but he was too weak to travel. "Poor Annie is very droopy with the heat," she continued in this—the last surviving letter she ever wrote—"and Edie has to get her hair in a net to free her neck from its weight."

The only eyewitnesses to what happened in the Craigie House library two days later were Edith Longfellow, seven years old at the time, and her younger sister, Annie Allegra, five. Erny had come home that day for lunch, but left just before Fanny returned from her father's bedside. Charley was still with his uncle Tom in Nahant, Alice was away from the house, visiting with friends. "As I was stepping on the horse-car to go into town to take the boat to Nahant, my mother drove by in a carriage and waved her hand to me," Erny recalled many years later. "That was the last I saw of her alive. She met with the accident that afternoon and the next morning she was dead. This was my first great grief, and my first acquaintance with death, that great mystery."

Outfitted in a hooped summer dress of light muslin, Fanny was seated at the long, carved Italian table that overlooks the eastern piazza. We can fairly well assume that she had done something with Edie's cumbersome folds of heavy blond hair, and taken a few cuttings while she was at it. The lock-snipping process, apparently, was mostly done—the envelopes tell us that—and a candle had been lit to melt some hot wax for use as a sealant. What followed then is uncertain; a gust of wind "fanning in" through the open window, to use Henry's description of the day before, possibly knocking a burning taper onto Fanny's lap, or perhaps an errant drop of molten wax somehow igniting the hem or sleeve of her highly flammable dress? It may have been, too, as one of Henry's biographers has suggested, that one of the girls was playing with matches, though there is no contemporary evidence to support that. Whatever the cause, Fanny's dress was in an instant consumed in flames and she ran toward the study, where Henry was taking an afternoon nap. Jolted to his feet by the commotion, he did what he could, hugging his wife with his arms in a futile attempt to suffocate the flames, losing hold when she broke away in a panic, managing, finally, to snuff out the fire with a small throw rug that proved woefully inadequate to the task.

Someone among the domestic staff was dispatched to get help, someone else tried to calm the hysterical children, others still cut loose the smoldering dress and carried Fanny upstairs to her bedroom. Among the first to arrive on the scene was Cornelius Conway Felton, recently appointed president of Harvard College. A messenger was sent to summon Tom Appleton and the boys on Nahant, someone else took the girls to the home on nearby Berkeley Street of Richard Henry Dana Jr., where they would remain until after their mother's funeral. "This was before the days of telephones or swift-moving vehicles," Henrietta Dana Skinner, one of the children in the Dana house when Edith and Annie arrived, would write of the tragedy in *An Echo from Parnassus: Girlhood Memories of Longfellow and His Friends*. "The family physician, Dr. Morrill Wyman, was out of town; a second doctor summoned was also away; half the houses in Brattle Street were closed, their occupants in the country." Finally, a stranger, Dr. William Otis Johnson, arrived to administer ether to Fanny. "In after years I came to know Dr. Johnson's widow," Mrs. Skinner recalled. "As she described the scene to me, Mrs. Longfellow lay calm and beautiful as if in sleep, her face unmarred by the flames, and wearing an expression so spiritual, so far removed from this world of suffering, that the physician in ministering to her felt a hushed reverence as if in the presence of a martyred saint."

Four lengthy letters Felton wrote to Sumner in the immediate aftermath provide the most thorough reconstruction of the events. He told of Henry's consuming fear that he was "growing idiotic" from what he had witnessed, and how he begged not to "be sent to an asylum," though he began to calm down a few days later. "His sweet and lovely nature never showed itself so beautifully," Felton wrote. "It will be long before he will recover perfectly from his wounds. His hands are badly burned, and give him more pain: but he says he sleeps best when he suffers the most physical pain."

Charles Eliot Norton spared few words in describing Fanny's ordeal for Elizabeth Gaskell, the English novelist and biographer of Charlotte Brontë. "There was nothing to be done but to alleviate her suffering which for an hour or two was intense. She was rendered unconscious by ether,—and when it was discontinued the suffering was over and did not return. Through the night she was perfectly calm, patient and gentle, all the lovely sweetness and elevation of her character showing itself in her looks and words. In the morning she lost consciousness and about eleven o'clock she died."

Norton lauded Fanny as being "very beautiful" in these final hours, her beauty distinguished by "the loveliness and nobility" of her character. "There is nothing in her life that is not delightful to remember. There was no pause and no decline in her." Only those who knew Fanny could fully appreciate "how quick and deep and true her sympathies were, how poetic was her temperament, how pure and elevated her thoughts. Longfellow was worthy of such a wife." The public response to the horror had been overwhelming. "I have never known any domestic calamity so sad and tragic as this. Of all happy homes theirs was in many ways the happiest."

George William Curtis would recall a carriage ride he shared with Oliver Wendell Holmes a few weeks before the accident. As they passed 105 Brattle Street, he noticed that Holmes turned his head abruptly away from the house, explaining later that he had momentarily "trembled to look" at the dwelling, his feeling then that "those who lived there had their happiness so perfect that no change, of all the changes which must come to them, could fail to be for the worst."

John Lothrop Motley, a Boston author, diplomat, and family friend, wrote two lengthy letters about the accident to his wife, Mary Benjamin Motley, then on Nahant. A few weeks after the funeral, he reported that Henry's hands were "becoming serviceable," and that he was now "suffering more feebleness" than pain. "I have never seen any one who bore a great sorrow in a more simple and noble way. But he is very desolate,—and, however manfully and religiously he may bear up, his life must hereafter be desolate. I hope he may find happiness in his children; his three little girls are very dear and charming, and his two boys are just growing into manhood." He shared Felton's concern for Henry's mental stability, confiding guardedly that he was being "spoken of as in almost a raving condition."

Motley was the author of several learned works, one of which—*The History of the United Netherlands*—had been released a few months earlier. Shortly after it was published, he wrote two deeply considered letters to *The Times* of London entitled "The Causes of the Civil War." Reprinted in the United States, they attracted the attention of President Lincoln, who thereupon named him minister to Austria, where he would be credited with persuading the nations of Europe to remain neutral throughout the rebellion. Motley shared with his wife the misery he felt over the senselessness of Fanny's death:

> There is something almost too terrible to reflect upon in this utterly trivial way in which this noble, magnificent woman has been put to a hideous death. When you hear of a shipwreck, or a stroke of lightening, or even a railway accident, the mind does not shrink appalled from the contemplation of the tragedy so utterly as it now does, from finding all this misery resulting from such an invisible cause—a drop of sealing-wax on a muslin dress. Deaths in battle are telegraphed to us hourly, and hosts of our young men are marching forth to mortal combat day by day, but these are in the natural course of events. Fate, acting on its large scale, has decreed that a great war shall rage, and we are prepared for tragedies, and we know

that those who fall have been discharging the highest of duties. But what compensation or consolation is there for such a calamity as this?"

While decidedly gruesome, Fanny's accident was by no means an isolated incident. Serious injury and death in this manner was distressingly common during much of the nineteenth century, the fashion for billowy dresses known as crinolines made with highly flammable open-weave fabrics making for a deadly combination. "Crinoline" was a coinage of the Latin words *crinis* for horsehair, often used as a fabric stiffener essential for the look, and *linum,* for the thread used to fashion the hooped petticoats that made a woman's skirt flare out from the body, creating a bell-shaped cage around the lower torso that functioned as an air duct in the event of fire.

Nine months before Fanny's accident, one of the world's oldest and most prestigious medical journals, *The Lancet,* reported that hundreds of women in Britain were dying each year in an "almost daily holocaust" of accidents resulting from "the combustibility of their dress and the expansion of their crinoline," and cited government inquest figures to back up the claim. "This is a very serious evil, and one which cannot be regarded without a regret deepened by the reflection that such accidents are preventable." *Punch*, the famous satirical weekly, published derisive poems and merciless cartoons in issue after issue condemning what it called "that inflated absurdity, Crinoline," denouncing its existence as a "living institution, which nothing seemingly can crush nor compress." Another *Punch* article called crinoline dresses "the detestable cages which depraved vanity has invented to conceal three-quarters of a woman's figure under a scaffolding for drapery." Yet another appeared under the headline "Suicide by Crinoline."

While this crusade was going on, *The Examiner,* an influential London weekly through most of the nineteenth century, was publishing a continuing log of "crinoline accidents causing death by fire," opening its compilation often with the remark: "We have more to record this week." The circumstances were numbingly similar. A fourteen-year-old girl "catches fire" while standing by the grate in her home, "the only part of her person which escaped unburned being her feet." A twenty-five-year-old female "inmate" at a "lunatic asylum" outside of London is consumed in flames after she "tore down" the "fire-guard" from a stove in her room. A sixteen-year-old domestic servant in Leeds becomes "enveloped in flames" while placing an object on the mantelpiece in her house, and succumbs after two days of intense suffering.

Being the wife of a famous American poet, Fanny attracted international attention with her fatal mishap, but she was by no means the only woman of prominence to be victimized in this manner, and would not be the last. Within three weeks of her accident, *The Spectator* of London reported the death of the thirty-two-year-old wife of a London lawyer under similar circumstances—she had leaned over a candle while writing letters. "Every means was tried to extinguish" the flames, but "the hoops had to be cut off before the fire could be extinguished."

Just two months after Fanny's death, an even more horrifying incident took place in a Philadelphia theater packed with fifteen hundred people waiting for the curtain to go up in an elaborately staged production of Shakespeare's *Tempest*. One of the dancers putting on her costume backstage came in contact with a gaslight that ignited her dress. Several other women in the corps de ballet who came to her aid became enflamed as well, spreading chaos and panic throughout the theater. Six women died, four of them sisters from England, one of whom jumped to her death from a window in the dressing room; eight others were severely injured. *Harper's Weekly* would describe the scene at the Continental Theater on Walnut Street that night as "most piteous and agonizing."

In its coverage of the horror, *Scientific American* cited other instances in which "the dresses of ballet girls have caught fire from the foot lights, causing death in the most terrifying and excruciating form." The magazine repeated a caveat it had issued in its pages following the "death of the wife of Professor Longfellow"—that "all such accidents can be prevented" by simply treating garments with a solution of "tungstate of soda and the sulphate of ammonia," an intervention that effectively serves as a fire retardant, and was already being used in England for Queen Victoria's dresses. "We again urge this subject upon the attention of the public, and we solicit our readers to use their influence to disseminating such humane and useful information."

FANNY'S FUNERAL TOOK PLACE on July 13, 1861, on what would have been her eighteenth wedding anniversary. Services were conducted in the Craigie House library, just a few feet from where she had suffered her fatal injuries. Though private, the ceremonies were attended, according to press accounts, by "most of the clergymen of Boston and Cambridge, the Faculty of Harvard College, and a number of prominent literary gentlemen." Fanny had been placed in a "heavily silvered" casket of "rich rosewood," surrounded by "numberless wreaths of rare flowers and bouquets." Sprigs of fresh orange blossoms, the same arrangement that adorned her wedding bouquet, had been placed on her breast.

The service began shortly after noon, "at which hour the bells in Cambridge were tolling in honor of the deceased," according to the *Lowell Daily Citizen & News*. "Rev. Dr. Peabody was the officiating clergyman, and at the close of the religious ceremonies the body was removed to the family burying place" on Indian Ridge Road in Mount Auburn Cemetery, the rustic burial ground a half mile due west of Craigie House, a quiet place of rural beauty where the Longfellows had enjoyed so many walks and carriage rides through the years of their marriage. The funeral cortege numbered one hundred carriages, thirty of them carrying dignitaries from Boston. The burial preceded by a day the death of Nathan Appleton, who died within hours of being told of Fanny's passing. The *Daily Citizen* reported further that "it was a singular circumstance that the flames in no wise disfigured the beautiful face of their victim."

Many dozens of well-wishers had come calling to pay their respects, a steady outpouring of grief that Henry could only hear, and not witness, as he remained in seclusion, tending to his bodily wounds and battered psyche. His younger brother Sam, a Unitarian minister, was unable to provide any comfort; he was in England, and learned of Fanny's death from the London newspapers. Ernest Longfellow would recall his father's distress with clarity. "I remember his lying in bed and holding up his poor bandaged hands and murmuring, 'Oh, why could I not save her?' It was a terrible blow to him, from which he never recovered." Twelve days after the accident, Felton reported that Henry's face was still swollen, "and he cannot yet shave; the burn to his nose and his left cheek are already healed."

There had been a flood of sympathetic letters, which Henry found nearly impossible to answer fully, though he did send a few notes of acknowledgment. Charles Sumner wrote from Washington immediately upon hearing the devastating news. "Dearest Longfellow," he began. "God bless and comfort you! I am overwhelmed with grief, and long to be with you. Nothing but duties here, which cannot be postponed, prevents me from going on at once!" Sumner's personal anguish at Fanny's loss was expressed even more poignantly ten days later:

> Daily, hourly, constantly I think of you, and my thoughts end with myself; for I cannot forget my own great and irreparable loss. In all visions of life I have always included her, for it never occurred to me that I should be the survivor, and I counted upon her friendship to the last. How strong must be your grief, I know and feel in my heart. But your happiness has been great, and the memories which remain are precious. I long to talk with you, and to enter into all this experience so trying, and help you to bear it, if I can. I must go with you to Mount Auburn. I hear of the children with great interest; they will be to you a comfort and consolation. I wish Charley would write me about you, and tell me how you are doing. I have been unhappy away. I wish I had seen her once more; but duties here stood sentinel in the way. Mr. William Appleton [a cousin of Nathan Appleton's, at that time a member of Congress in the Massachusetts delegation] and myself have been together a good deal to talk of this bereavement. He is well. God bless you!

Julia Ward Howe posted a heartfelt letter the day after the funeral, expressing the inadequacy of "words, human or divine" to give comfort in the "terrible sorrow" that now consumed her close acquaintance of many years, the man she playfully called "Longo" in most letters, my "dear friend" here:

> What is there for any of us in such moments but the one simple word: "Thy will be done." This expresses at once our helplessness

and our hope. My eyes are blinded with bitter tears while I try to write. This tremble is so great that it overflows into the hearts of your friends, filling them like a personal sorrow. The vision of beauty that has passed away from the earth—the mother's heart grown cold with those mighty words of love clinging to it. Oh! This is something in which we all have a part—we can not be human, and not weep for you. I know how darkly this must fall upon you, how long it will be for your kindly nature will become reconciled to such a maiming and mutilation of life. Your children will plead most tenderly with you for its endurance. For their sake you will try now for composure, and hereafter for cheerfulness, but that will take time, much time. May all the sweet comfort that you have flung abroad for others return tenfold to your own bosom. "As ye do unto others, it shall be done unto you." Your words have consoled many—they have embellished suffering to thousands of mourners. May some of them come back home to you with consolation. I know that none of us can do you any good, only but our love . . . God bless you.

That same day, July 14, Nathaniel Hawthorne wrote James T. Fields, the editor both men shared and trusted unconditionally, unable, he admitted, to contact Henry directly, at least not then. "How does Longfellow bear this terrible misfortune? How are his own injuries? Do write, and tell me all about him. I cannot at all reconcile this calamity to my sense of fitness. One would think that there ought to have been no deep sorrow to the life of a man like him; and now comes this blackest of shadows, which no sunshine hereafter can ever penetrate! I shall be afraid ever to meet him again; he cannot again be the man that I have known."

Writing from Italy, the artist Thomas Buchanan Read, whose painting of Henry's three daughters hangs prominently in the dining room, related how "your terrific disaster burst upon us here in Rome, as it did indeed over the whole world, wherever your poetry has endeared your name and made it a household word."

Taking pen to paper finally on August 18, Henry wrote his sister-in-law in London, Mary Appleton Mackintosh, from Nahant, where he had retreated for a few days of solitude by the seashore. "I feel that only you and I knew her thoroughly. You can understand what an inexpressible delight she was to me, always and in all things. I never looked at her without a thrill of pleasure;—she never came into a room where I was without my heart beating quicker, nor went out without my feeling that something of the light went with her. I loved her so entirely, and I know she was very happy."

The magnitude of the loss they both shared, and the inexpressible horror of what he had witnessed the previous month, was central to Henry's thoughts. "How I am alive after what my eyes have seen, I know not. I am at least patient, if not resigned; and thank God hourly—as I have from the beginning—for the beautiful life we led together, and that I loved her more and more to the end." Looking ahead, "I have no plans," he admitted, being unable to "lift my eyes in that direction," managing only to "look backward, not forward. The only question is, what will be best for the children?" He closed by asking Mary to "think of me here, by this haunted sea-shore," where "the sense of her presence upon me" was so strong "that I should hardly be surprised to meet her in our favorite walk, or, if I looked up now to see her in the room. My heart aches and bleeds sorely for the poor children. To lose such a mother, and all the divine influences of her character and care. They do not know their loss, but I do. God will provide. His will be done!"

George William Curtis had written Tom Appleton within days of the accident, assuring him that "many thousand hearts" were mourning for Fanny, people who had reached out to him, a mere acquaintance, with their condolences. He predicted that Henry would one day "feel that every heart he has comforted—and no man living has so personal a relation with his unknown friends—is a friendly heart to him." Speaking for himself, he considered having known Fanny "one of the great blessings" of his life, "and one of its best influences." Reaching out to Henry, finally, on September 7, Curtis described a "dark valley that opened so suddenly" for everyone who knew her. "I see her smiling through it always—as that beautiful light of heavenly womanhood which shone in her, will shine through all our memories forever." He described the devastation he felt when learning the horrible news. "My heart was so loyal to her that there is nothing with which I associate her that does not make me see her and hear her again. Books, the sea, the summer day, the heroic men and the heroic ladies of the time, all bring me into her presence." From all these "scenes she knew," she "cries to me, immortal," her memory "a constant purification" for him.

"In very dangerous and trying moments of my life she was a wonderfully true and controlling friend," he continued. "Those days are long gone, and I have fallen upon the undeserved and serene happiness that so few know in this world—but the great fidelity, the exquisite instinct, the good word in season, how much of my happiness I owe to those, how much of my real life, to her!" He closed with typical grace and elegance: "Good bye, dear heart, and God bless you. You know how I love and honor you, but we can't talk of such things." In a brief reply, Henry thanked Curtis for his "affectionate and touching letter," and apologized for not writing a fuller response. "Even now I can not answer it; I can only thank you for it. I am too utterly wretched and overwhelmed,—to the eyes of others, outwardly, calm; but inwardly bleeding to death. I can not say more. God bless you, and protect your household."

There remained one person Henry felt obligated to contact, his wife's dearest friend through most of her life, and the recipient of at least 225 letters from Fanny over a twenty-five-year period (1836–61), the frequency increasing when Emmeline married in 1846 and moved to Geneseo, in the Finger Lakes region of New York. "Henry is jealous when I tell him this," Fanny once said of their special bond, "but he has his male friends and I can well know the peculiar pleasure their society must give him, while I have no darling Emmeline with whom to chatter and talk as only women can."

Written three months after Fanny's death, Henry's letter to Emmeline came to Harvard University in 1979 from the Wadsworth family, arriving too late to be included in Andrew Hilen's volume of correspondence for that period, and thus unpublished previously anywhere until now. "Your letters I find carefully put away in a box by themselves," he informed her, stressing how they had occupied a special place among his wife's possessions. "I shall keep them safely for you till you come, should you wish to reclaim them." Whether Emmeline ever did take the letters, or if she did, what happened to them, is not known; their fate remains a mystery to this day. The letters Fanny wrote to Emmeline made their way back to Brattle Street, and were an essential resource for this book; fifteen Emmeline sent to Henry between 1850 and 1866 are in the Houghton Library.

The discovery of the cache had given Henry pause to reflect. "When I come upon such things, I have no more fortitude than a child; and it is only little by little that I can bring myself to go through the dear but dreadful task, of opening a closet, or a drawer or a box. I keep everything in the home, exactly as it was—as if she were only absent for a short while, and soon coming back: and do by illusions try to make the ruin of my household less terrible." He apologized for suggesting that the pain of loss was his alone. "I fear I think of my own sorrow only, and forget wholly that of others; and that I shall sadden you rather than comfort you. At first one's grief must have way. My thoughts have worn this channel for themselves, and it is difficult for me to turn them aside; particularly in writing to you, whom she loved most, next to her sister, Dear Mary, with her double weight of woe!" He then reflected on the "unwonted splendor" of autumn then in full color. "I have driven again and again through all the haunted lanes of Brookline and Waltham. It is indescribably painful yet sweet, to revisit often the familiar places. They are full of ghosts, they do not terrify me. No harm can ever come from them. You see how it is. Wherever I begin, I drift and sway back to the same place again, for my mind is troubled and bewildered."

A few weeks later, James T. Fields, who had recently acquired *The Atlantic Monthly* with William Ticknor and succeeded James Russell Lowell as editor, asked Henry to write something, anything, for the January 1862 issue. The answer was respectfully short: "I am sorry to say *No*, instead of *Yes*; but so it must be. I can neither write nor think; and have nothing fit to send you, but my love—which you cannot put into the Magazine." A single entry in Henry's journal for August had taken stock of the situation, a month having passed since his world had been turned upside down. "So closes the Second Act of Life's Drama, and the Third begins," the first two, presumably, having been his marriages to Mary and Fanny. The next would embrace the final twenty-one years of his life—and be a triumphant validation of the first two.

17

Perfect Peace

With snow-white veil, and garments as of flame,
    She stands before thee, who so long ago
    Filled thy young heart with passion and the woe
    From which thy song in all its splendors came;
And while with stern rebuke she speaks thy name,
    The ice about thy heart melts as the snow
    On mountain heights, and in swift overflow
    Comes gushing from thy lips in sobs of shame.
Thou makest full confession; and a gleam
    As of the dawn on some dark forest cast,
    Seems on thy lifted forehead to increase;
Lethe and Eunöe—the remembered dream
    And the forgotten sorrow—bring at last
    That perfect pardon which is perfect peace.

—Henry Wadsworth Longfellow, Sonnet 4,
Divina Commedia

C harley Longfellow, the couple's firstborn child, had been a handful from the day he took his first steps, a robust lad with an independent spirit who had it in him to drive his parents to utter distraction. By the time he was fourteen months old, Fanny was describing her son as an "infant Hercules," while admitting with a touch of exasperation that she would "take more comfort in him if he were quieter."

Both parents had spent considerable time honing their children's reading and drawing skills, the latter a pastime everyone enjoyed. Henry even invented a clever series of illustrated characters for their amusement, one he called Peter Piper, another Little Merrythought. They saved dozens of their children's drawings, the girls making happy pictures of playmates dancing, having parties, opening presents; there is one undated portrait Edith made of Annie Allegra, another of Edith by Annie. Erny gave hints of the professional artist he would one day become, toiling carefully on outdoor scenes and studies of Craigie House, occasionally sketching casual portraits of his parents, one picturing Henry standing at his corner writing desk, another of Fanny seated, relaxing in profile. Charley packed a lot of energy into his images—hand-to-hand combat with Indians, an occasional scalping on the frontier, warships dueling at sea, steam locomotives puff-puffing away, sleds roaring down icy hills. An undated but very early letter he wrote as a boy to Santa Claus asks

Private Charley Longfellow, 1863, photographed the day before he was commissioned a lieutenant in the Union Army

for a soldier's cap, a cartridge box with a silver eagle on it, a sword, and a helmet.

Determined to take part in the Civil War—and with no mother around now to keep him in line—Charley left home on March 9, 1863, three months shy of his nineteenth birthday, destination not disclosed. "On Tuesday, Charley went to town and has not since appeared," Henry wrote in his journal four days later. "This morning comes a letter without place or date, saying he has gone into the army!" The young man's letter was concise and to the point. "Dear Papa, You know for how long a time I have been wanting to go to the war. I have tried hard to resist the temptation of going without your leave but I cannot any longer. I feel it to be my first duty to do what I can for my country and I would willingly lay down my life for it if it would be of any good. God Bless you all. Yours affectionately, Charley."

Surmising from the postmark that Charley had gone up to Portland, Henry wrote a letter to him in care of an acquaintance he believed knew his whereabouts, pleading for a chance to talk. "Your motive is a noble one," Henry reasoned, "but you are too precipitate. I have always thought you, and still think you, too young to go into the army. It can be no reproach to you, and no disgrace, to wait a little longer; though I can well understand your impatience." As a clever diversion, Charley had arranged to have his letter posted from Maine, while in actuality he was taking the train south to Washington DC, where he presented himself to one Captain W. H. McCartney, of the First Massachusetts Artillery, requesting to join his battery.

Recognizing the young man's surname—and confirming that his father was the famous poet—the officer delayed Charley with a ruse, and contacted Henry directly, offering to keep his son occupied until advised otherwise. "I did not consider him the proper person to enlist," McCartney explained, given the "loss of a thumb" that had already occasioned his rejection in the regular infantry. Charley told him that if turned down at this unit, he would just go to yet another and try his luck there, so there was a degree of urgency. Henry wisely chose not to have his son sent home, as he could have, given his age, but took immediate steps instead to see if he might secure a commission for him, reaching out simultaneously to Sumner in Washington and indirectly, through James T. Fields, to Massachusetts Governor John A. Andrew, a graduate of Bowdoin College, class of 1837. Also at play was the likely involvement of Fanny's stepmother, Harriot Sumner Appleton, whose daughter, Hatty—Charley's twenty-one-year-old "half aunt"—was engaged to marry Lieutenant Colonel Greely Curtis, who would be the official to inform Charley of his selection to be a cavalry officer, and telegraph Henry with the news.

Henry responded in jubilation, quipping to Sumner, "I expect to hear next week that he is a Brigadier General!" Given a checklist of necessities a commissioned cavalry officer was required to obtain at his own expense, Henry went to work: a horse, a saddle, blankets, spurs, boots, uniforms, shoulder straps, insignia, foul-weather gear, a Colt revolver, ammunition, a saber, grooming accessories, even a paid personal attendant, along with three volumes of field tactics. While waiting for formal notification of his new status, Charley remained under the watchful eye of Captain McCartney. On March 30, he sat for a tintype portrait, his rank still a private. On April 1, three weeks having passed since he left home, Lieutenant Longfellow was assigned to the First Massachusetts Cavalry, then bivouacked at Potomac Creek, Virginia.

After seeing him off to his new duty station, Captain McCartney wrote Henry with an update. "It affords me much pleasure to say of him: that he exhibits all the characteristics of a thorough soldier. I am also very much pleased to know that I have contributed somewhat to his success—present—and that which awaits him in the future." Deeply grateful, Henry asked Sumner in Washington to kindly "order your wine merchant to send a basket of Champagne to Capt. McCartney, with my compliments." Charley, on his end, could not have been happier. "If I had taken my pick of our whole army I don't think I could have joined anything more to my idea than this Battery," he wrote home of his assignment. He would develop a more nuanced appreciation later, when exposed to combat: "They may talk about the gaiety of a soldiers life but it strikes me as pretty earnest work when shells are ripping and tearing your men to pieces."

On March 16, Henry had made two seemingly unrelated entries in his journal. "A letter from Captain McCartney, of Battery A, Mass. Artillery, says Charley is with him, on the Rappahannock! I shall not send for him. He is where he wants to be, in the midst of it all. Gen. Hooker is a fighting general, and will soon be moving." On the next line, he wrote that he had just begun translating the *Inferno*: "Mean to take a Canto a day till it is finished." Put in sharper focus: Henry began translating Dante's account of a harrowing journey through the circles of hell on the same day he confirmed that his eighteen-year-old son was on his way to fight in a frightfully lethal war. The battles of Shiloh, Antietam, Fredericksburg, Bull Run, and Stones River had already claimed thousands of lives; Chancellorsville, a resounding Union defeat, would be fought in just a few weeks, and Gettysburg, the bloodiest of them all, would follow in July. And yet he did it all—a canto a night—in one sustained burst of creative energy.

Henry's determination to be the first American to do a complete translation of Dante's epic went back two decades. In 1853, he picked up where he had left off ten years before that. "In weariness of spirit, and despair of writing anything original, I turned again today to dear old Dante; and resumed my translation of the *Purgatorio*, where I left it in 1843," he wrote then. "Find great delight in the work. It diffused its benediction through the day." He described his progress to Catherine Eliot Norton, who had been urging him to persevere. "I write a few lines every day before breakfast. It is the first thing I do,—the morning prayer,—the key-note of the day. I am delighted to have you take an interest in it. But do not expect too much, for I really have but a few moments to devote to it daily; yet daily a stone, small or great, is laid on the pile."

Like Catherine Norton, Fanny, too, had been greatly devoted to Dante, evident in the many mentions of him in her journal and correspondence. During a visit to Washington DC in 1840, she described being on a street enveloped in a "thick warm fog" one morning "through which people and horses emerge like spirits in Dante's smoky circles." Reflecting in 1853 on the passing of her dear Aunt Sam, she found solace in the *Paradiso*: "Let us, like the sacred mountain of Dante, tremble with joy and not fear when another joins the happy company and feel lifted higher on our own path by that angelic sympathy." Four years into her marriage, she mentioned to Emmeline how "Henry has gone to college to lecture on Dante, carrying with him my Francesca by Scheffer, to charm the young eyes of his hearers," a delightful little aside offered, perhaps, with an unseen wink. Tom Appleton had given Fanny an engraving of a painting by the Dutch artist Ary Scheffer that pictures a mostly naked Francesca da Rimini embracing her adulterous lover, Paolo Malatesta; the figures of Dante and Virgil consider the condemned couple's plight from a discreet distance.

"It is tempting to visualize the moment—the undergraduate men, barely out of adolescence, staring raptly at Francesca's unclothed figure and tracing the outline of her left breast and buttock," the Longfellow scholar Christoph Irmscher wrote of the impact this show-and-tell session may have had on the teenage students in Henry's all-male literature classes. "Francesca's pose is so suggestive that the viewer forgets why exactly she is pressing herself so closely to Paolo's body"—to shield herself, of course, from the punishing winds of hell that swirl around them, the carnal implications of the embrace notwithstanding. Being a woman, Fanny was not permitted to sit in on any of her husband's classes, leaving her no choice but to enjoy them from a distance: "I am reading along with him in ever-fresh delight."

Print of *Paolo and Francesca* by Luigi Calamatta after Ary Scheffer that Henry borrowed from Fanny for a show-and-tell at Harvard

Now, in 1863, with Fanny gone and Charley in uniform, there was renewed motivation. Harry Dana, the poet's grandson and resident curator at Craigie House, made the perceptive observation that Elizabeth Barrett Browning's death on June 29, 1861—just twelve days before Fanny's passing—had moved Robert Browning to take on a translation of the *Alcestis* of Euripides, "the great drama of a man whose wife had died and had been carried off to the other world." For both Robert Browning and Henry, "the theme of the poem translated was curiously appropriate to the inner mood of the translator, and in both cases the author to be translated was one that had been deeply loved by the departed wife." William Cullen Bryant was similarly dispirited following the death of his wife in 1866. "I am like one cast out of Paradise and wandering in a strange world," he told Richard Henry Dana. Bryant declined an invitation to write something for *The Atlantic Monthly,* having "already formed a project for escaping from his depression of mind by translating the whole of Homer," both the *Iliad* and the *Odyssey,* according to Parke Godwin, his son-in-law and biographer.

Henry confirmed his rationale for having at long last completed the Dante project to his friend and colleague in Germany, Ferdinand Freiligrath, in 1867. "Of what I have been through, during the last six years, I dare not venture to write even to you; it is almost too much for one man to bear and live. I have taken refuge in this translation of the *Divine Comedy,* and this may give it an added interest in your sight." In the months following Fanny's death, Henry found comfort in Dante's exploration of the heavenly spheres, with the idealized Beatrice at his side. "Translated the beautiful Canto XXV of the *Paradiso,*" he wrote just seven months after her accident. It is a passage at the close of this canto, Harry Dana also pointed out, where Dante "speaks of his distress in not being able to see the woman he has loved and lost, although he feels that she is close at hand," a passage that undoubtedly had special resonance for his grandfather. "Another week gone," Henry wrote on March 25, 1862. "All given to Dante."

Several lectures Henry gave at Harvard years earlier survive in manuscript, one of them arguing that the constant presence of Beatrice is essential to comprehending Dante himself. "With all that he wrote," Professor Longfellow impressed upon his students, "the name of Beatrice is interwoven. This passion flows from the sunny clime of his youth. Like the gulf-stream, forever warm through the cold and stormy ocean of his life. With her his song begins and ends." Elsewhere, Henry lauded all of Dante's "female portraits" as being "drawn with exquisite delicacy," adding further that he could not cite in any of his writings "a single sarcasm against women," a tribute that could well apply to Henry himself. With Charley preparing for armed combat, Henry's thoughts had turned to tackling the *Inferno*, where Dante's guide through the horrors of the condemned is the poet Virgil, and where the virtuous Beatrice is conspicuously absent. April 16, 1863, was a rainy day, but noteworthy for the milestone Henry announced having just reached. "Finish the translation of the *Inferno*. So the whole work is done, the *Purgatorio* and *Paradiso* having been finished before. I have written a Canto a day, thirty-four days in succession, with many anxieties and interruptions. Now I must make some Notes."

HENRY HAD MADE being a single parent his chief priority since Fanny's death, the welfare and well-being of his five children his principal concern, but he did not abandon his work, as his revitalized passion for Dante makes clear. Acting, perhaps, at the urging of James Fields, he was also assembling a collection of poems inspired by Geoffrey Chaucer's *Canterbury Tales* and Giovanni Boccaccio's *Decameron,* his theme a series of stories narrated by travelers who meet at a hostelry outside of Boston. For Chaucer, the setting was the Tabard Inn on the road to Canterbury Cathedral and the shrine of Saint Thomas à Becket; Boccaccio had placed his narrators in an isolated villa during the frightful years of the Black Death. Following their example, Henry focused on what he was vaguely calling a "wayside inn," the location to be determined. He and Fields had made plans to see such a place in the countryside, an appointment that the publisher was unable to make. "Waiting, waiting, waiting for Fields, who promised to come out today, and does not come," Henry recorded testily on September 15, 1862. "Beware of making appointments. They weary the spirit, and waste the day."

With no specific setting yet selected, he pressed ahead anyway. "Write a little upon 'The Wayside Inn,' a beginning, only," he logged

on an otherwise "rainy Saturday." Finally, on Halloween—"a delicious
Indian Summer Day"—the two went on a day trip to a tavern twenty
miles west of Cambridge in the town of Sudbury on the old Boston
Post Road, which he learned, when he got there, was "no longer an
inn," but a "rambling, tumble down old building, two hundred years
old; and till now in the family of the Howes, who have kept an inn
for one hundred and seventy five years. In the old time a house of call
for all travellers from Boston westward." Henry deemed the Red-Horse
Tavern, as it was known, ideal for the collection he would title, at the
urging of Charles Sumner, *Tales of a Wayside Inn,* overruling Fields, who
had already announced it as *The Sudbury Tales.* "Everybody who speaks
to me of the book, says, 'A kind of *Canterbury Tales,* I suppose,'" he
explained to Fields. "Probably every criticism in the papers would begin

Studio photograph of Charles Sumner and Longfellow, by Alexander
Gardner, while Henry was in Washington during the Civil War, 1863,
tending to his wounded son

the same way, if any place is connected with the title. So I prefer *Tales of a Wayside Inn,* or simply, *The Wayside Inn.*"

For this project, Henry modeled his storytellers on actual friends and acquaintances; "all the characters are real," he assured George Washington Greene. To open the collection, he repurposed "Paul Revere's Ride" and its already ubiquitous opening line, "Listen, my children, and you shall hear," for "The Landlord's Tale," narrated by a clone of Lyman Howe, whose family owned the Red-Horse Tavern. For the Musician, he used the famous Norwegian violinist and composer Ole Bull, a regular visitor to Craigie House. The Sicilian, in turn, was modeled on Luigi Monti, a political refugee from Italy who taught at Harvard, and by this time one of Henry's most supportive friends. A dabbling interest in spiritual matters made the brilliant physicist Daniel Treadwell, another Harvard colleague, ideal for the Theologian. Similarly, the Poet was modeled on Thomas William Parsons, a dentist and occasional writer who had translated parts of Dante's *Divine Comedy,* and the Student on Henry Ware Wales, a young scholar of promise. For the Spanish Jew, who regales his listeners with exotic tales of the Orient, Henry chose Isaac Edrehi, the son of a Moroccan-born scholar and itinerant preacher who, according to Andrew Hilen, had "inherited a penchant for Oriental robes, and other fancies," and thus was perfect for his purposes.

"FIFTEEN THOUSAND COPIES," Henry wrote in his notebook for November 25, 1863, marking, with those three words, the publication of *Tales of a Wayside Inn,* adding that the publishers had dined with him that night to celebrate. Joining Henry the next day for Thanksgiving dinner were Tom Appleton and Harriot Appleton, whose son Nathan Appleton Jr., like Charley, was a junior officer serving on the front lines. "We drank the health of 'all the Lieutenants in the Army of the Potomac,'" Henry wrote, Charley having recently returned to duty after suffering a bout of "camp fever," a term used for a variety of contagious illnesses endemic to the close-quartered military encampments of the period, most severely typhoid fever, which took the lives of more soldiers during the Civil War than injuries inflicted in combat.

Charley had fallen grievously ill with one of these ailments not long after receiving his commission, word reaching Henry in Portland on June 11, where he was visiting with his sister Anne. Setting off immediately for Washington, he arrived within a day of hearing the news. Charley was assigned a bed in the home of a Unitarian minister; taking a hotel room for himself, Henry spent the next few weeks by Charley's bedside, visiting occasionally with Sumner and a host of government officials eager to meet him. "Yesterday, Sunday, I heard the distant cannonading, mingling in with the sound of the church bells and the chanting of the choir in the church close by," he wrote Erny on June 22, a paradox he would recall six months later when inspired to write "Christmas Bells," adapted many times in the years ahead as a yuletide song, most famously by Johnny Marks in 1956 as "I Heard the Bells on Christmas Day," and recorded that year by Bing Crosby. The opening stanza in the song is the same as in Henry's poem.

> I heard the bells on Christmas Day
> Their old, familiar carols play,
>   And wild and sweet
>   The words repeat
> Of peace on earth, good-will to men!

Two stanzas typically left out of the carol speak directly to the horrors of the Civil War:

> Then from each black, accursed mouth
> The cannon thundered in the South,
>   And with the sound
>   The carols drowned
> Of peace on earth, good-will to men!

> It was as if an earthquake rent
> The hearth-stones of a continent,
>   And made forlorn
>   The households born
> Of peace on earth, good-will to men!

Picking up at the next stanza, the song—and the poem—conclude with hope:

> And in despair I bowed my head;
> "There is no peace on earth," I said:
>   "For hate is strong,
>   And mocks the song
> Of peace on earth, good-will to men!"
>
> Then pealed the bells more loud and deep:
> "God is not dead; nor doth he sleep!
>   The Wrong shall fail,
>   The Right prevail,
> With peace on earth, good-will to men!"

BEFORE REJOINING HIS UNIT that fall, Charley spent six weeks with his family relaxing on Nahant, where—Charley being Charley—he was brought up on charges of "bathing without clothes" at a secluded beach. The case was dismissed when the woman who filed the complaint—the writer Jessie Benton Frémont, wife of the western explorer and Republican candidate for president in 1856, John C. Frémont, who were summer residents—acknowledged having identified the strapping young man from a distance, and only then with the aid of opera glasses. Before the year was out, Henry would travel to Washington once again, summoned this time by a telegram with news that his son had been severely wounded in a skirmish near New Hope, Virginia. "An Enfield bullet passed through both shoulders, just under the shoulder-blades, grazing the back bone, and making a wound a foot long," Henry informed George Washington Greene a few weeks later. "A very narrow and fortunate escape, but so serious is the wound that the surgeons say he will not be able to rejoin his Regiment for six months."

Accompanied this time by Erny, Henry arrived in Washington ahead of Charley, who was still being processed for transfer, and went directly to a depot where he was told his son would be arriving shortly on a freight train. "While I am waiting," he recorded later that night, "a person steps up to me dressed in military overcoat, high boots, and corduroy trousers," and asked if he might be Professor Longfellow. "I am," Henry replied. "Give me your hand. I am Dr. Baalam of Riga; have translated your *Hiawatha* into Russian." The man had come to America to support the Union cause, and directed ambulance services in the nation's capital. During his stay at the Ebbitt House, Henry had a studio photo taken of himself with Charles Sumner, the only known image of the two men together, and reproduced often over the years.

Returning to Massachusetts with his father, Charley would be declared unfit for further military service and given an honorable release from active duty. Henry would follow the course of the war carefully, discuss its conduct periodically with Sumner, express great joy and relief when Robert E. Lee surrendered at Appomattox, and profound sadness when President Lincoln was assassinated. But on a personal level, once Charley was back in Craigie House, the war was effectively over for the Longfellow family. Ernest wrote how heartbroken he was when told by his father that he could not go to West Point, as he had dearly wished, and declined an appointment to the academy secured for him by Charles Sumner. "I was not of age, and as my brother was in the cavalry at the front, he thought one son risking his life was enough."

Over the next thirty years, Charley, a lifelong bachelor, would fill Craigie House with artworks, crafts, curios, and photographs gathered on travels and expeditions he made in many parts of the world, a man on the move to the end of his days. He died at the age of forty-eight from complications of pneumonia, his death, his brother firmly believed, due partly to his war ailments and wounds, although his warp-speed lifestyle undoubtedly had something to do with it too. The only house Charley ever owned was in Yokohama during a twenty-month residence in Japan between 1871 and 1873, immersing himself while there in the culture, posing for photographs in native garb, enjoying the companionship of teahouse girls—all of it duly recorded, however cryptically, in notebooks now among the Longfellow House collections. How Henry may have responded to the huge image of a carp Charley had tattooed on his back while in Japan, or any of the others he had etched elsewhere on his skin, if he ever saw them at all, has not been recorded.

On one level, Henry took vicarious pleasure in his son's far-flung adventures, eagerly opening up the trinkets and curiosities he shipped home from exotic places. On another, he despaired at his son's absences, informing him once that he had burned through half of the inheritance money he had received from his mother and grandfather. In 1869, Henry asked Charley to join him in acquiring a seventy-acre tract facing Craigie House on the other side of the Charles River that was about to be developed for a slaughterhouse. Determined to stave that hideous prospect off, Henry led the effort to purchase the property, known as Brighton Meadows, for $12,000, and give it to Harvard. "Shall I put you down for five hundred dollars, which is what Ernest gives, and each of the girls? I have succeeded in getting control of the land, and if I can fill up the subscription all will be right." Charley signed on—"a capital idea," he wrote back. With the later acquisition of an adjoining tract, the university created Soldiers Field, home to Harvard Stadium, and secured a permanent location for the Harvard Business School.

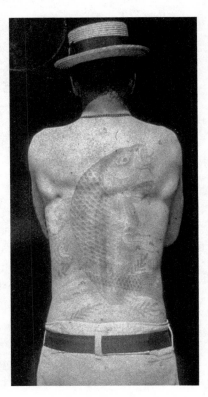

Charley Longfellow, c. 1874, displaying the tattoo of a carp on his back, done while he was living in Japan

Henry and Trap, undated, from an album kept by Alice Longfellow

In that same letter, Henry reassured Charley that his collection of guns was "safely locked up, that we cannot get at them," and that "a scimitar has arrived, with a silver hilt, and a green velvet scabbard. Also a box containing various little matters, horns, flags, and some beautiful photographs. I opened the box to make sure that the contents were not damaged." Finally, there was some bad news to report—Trap, Charley's mixed-breed terrier, who had become a comfort to Henry following Fanny's death, "is no longer among the living," passing away recently "in one of his summer fits. I miss him constantly."

Of Trap's many endearments, few could surpass his stowing away on the yacht *Alice* as it embarked for England in 1866 with Charley aboard as a member of the otherwise professional crew, their goal to set a trans-atlantic speed record for a boat of its class. Instead of turning around and losing time, they handed the pooch over to an inbound schooner with a request he be returned to Henry, for which a five-dollar reward would be forthcoming. Named for Fanny and Henry's eldest daughter, *Alice* had been built to order for Tom Appleton, who did not sail himself, but was happy to indulge his nephew's love of the sport. The fifty-four-foot sloop made landfall eighteen days and eight hours after departing Nahant. On "a lark," Charley paid twenty pounds to send an underwater cable home with the news—they had, as hoped, set a new standard for the crossing. Among the many curios Charley gathered over the years, one item he treasured—the wooden tiller from the *Alice*—is displayed in the guest room on the second floor. Kept in basement storage is an Army officer's hat sporting, just above the brim, the insignia of the First Massachusetts Cavalry, and a blue field jacket, with two holes plainly visible on the back, one just beneath the left shoulder blade, where the projectile fired from a British-made Enfield musket had entered Charley's body, and the other on the right, where it made its exit.

WITH CHARLEY NOW permanently out of the line of fire, Henry turned his full attention once again to the Dante project. He had all three *cantiche* of his translation set into type, and proof sheets pulled of each canto individually, which he would pass around for comment to a group of colleagues he had invited to meet with him regularly in Craigie House. "Lowell, Norton and myself, had the first meeting of our Dante Club," he wrote on October 15, 1865. "We read the XXV *Purgatorio*, and then had a little supper. We are to meet every Wednesday evening at my home." They continued with this routine through June 13, 1866, and from December 19, 1866, to May 1, 1867.

Both Lowell and Norton had taken Henry's Dante course as Harvard undergraduates, and remained close to him in the years that followed. Lowell succeeded him as Smith Professor at Harvard; Norton would found the Dante Society in 1881, with Henry serving as the first president. Two years into the meetings, Norton described the sessions to a colleague, the goal of each "to consider" with Henry "the last touches of his work." The "night's canto" was always followed by "a little supper" in the dining room, "to which generally one or two other friends come in, and at which we always have a pleasant time." A good deal has been written about these confabs, including a best-selling biblio-mystery in 2003 by the Cambridge novelist Matthew Pearl, aptly titled *The Dante Club,* in which the scholars put their heads and wits together to solve a series of grisly crimes being committed in Boston that are disturbingly similar to punishments meted out in the *Inferno.* The novel was inspired by research Pearl conducted as a Harvard undergraduate for an honors thesis on the actual Dante Club.

In real life, the meetings were attended periodically by other friends and colleagues, who included Oliver Wendell Holmes, Thomas Wentworth Higginson, James Fields, George Washington Greene, Tom Appleton, and Louis Agassiz; Henry's younger brother, Alexander Wadsworth Longfellow, a civil engineer for the United States Coast Survey, occasionally participated, too, when he was in town. Henry had already translated the entire epic into English; what he was looking for at this stage was clarity and a sharper tone. Fanny was no longer by his side to comment; neither was Felton, who had died in 1862, and Sumner was away most of the time in Washington. In their absence the Dante Club was born. "They are revising the whole book with the minutest care," James Fields wrote of a meeting he attended. "Lowell's accuracy is surprising and of great value to the work; also Norton's criticisms. Longfellow stands apart at his desk taking notes and making corrections, though of course no one can know yet what he accepts."

Another frequent participant, William Dean Howells, wrote the most extensive treatment of the club's meetings, including a description of the protocol Henry followed. "When Longfellow read verse," he recalled, "it was with a hollow, with a mellow resonant murmur, like the note of some deep-throated horn. His voice was very lulling in quality, and at the Dante Club it used to have early effect with an old scholar who sat in a cavernous armchair at the corner of the fire, and who drowsed audibly in the soft tone and the gentle heat. The poet had a fat terrier who wished always to be present at the meetings of the Club, and he commonly fell asleep at the same moment with that dear old scholar, so that when they began to make themselves heard in concert, one could not tell which it was that most took our thoughts from the text of the Paradise."

The "dear old scholar" of the recollection was George Washington Greene; the "fat terrier" was Trap. Once the scholarly work had been finished for the evening, Henry led the group through the main hallway to the dining room, where everyone was invited to take a seat. "The supper was very plain," Howells wrote, "a cold turkey, which the host carved, or a haunch of venison, or some braces of grouse, or a platter of

One of three miniature volumes of Dante's *Commedia* given to Henry as a gift by George Washington Greene in Europe, 1827

quails, with a deep bowl of salad, and the sympathetic companionship of those elect vintages which Longfellow loved, and which he chose with the inspiration of affection. We usually began with oysters, and when someone who was expected did not come promptly, Longfellow invited us to raid his plate, as a just punishment of his delay."

Henry's explicit intention—and one reason his *Commedia* remains a highly relevant translation prized by critics and other poets—was to be heedful of what the Pulitzer Prize winner and Dante enthusiast James Merrill called its "priceless fidelity" to the original text. Henry stressed the point well before the Dante Club convened its first meeting. "In translating Dante something must be relinquished. Shall it be the beautiful rhyme that blossoms all along the lines, like a honeysuckle in a hedge? I fear it must be, in order to retain something more precious than rhyme, namely fidelity—truth—the life of the hedge itself."

The "beautiful rhyme" scheme Henry found it necessary to sacrifice, known as *terza rima,* consists of three-line stanzas with interlocking rhymes called tercets. Introduced by Dante specifically for the *Commedia,* the form requires that the end word of the second line in each tercet provide the rhyme for the first and third lines in the next, producing a "chain rhyme" throughout the poem. It was ideally suited for the Italian language, which has numerous musical-sounding words ending in vowels, and more versatile than English. By retaining the use of three-line stanzas, and using an iambic-pentameter pattern known as blank terzine that does not require rhyming, Henry was able to respect, as closely as possible, the line breaks of Dante's original. Of singular merit, too, are the copious explanatory notes and illustrative passages drawn from a great variety of sources that he included in each of the three volumes. Henry's old mentor George Ticknor offered this: "I shall always read your translation with the original ringing in my ears."

Of more recent vintage is the view of the late Yale scholar Harold Bloom, author of numerous works of literary criticism and commentary, including the influential *Western Canon* (1994). In an anthology he edited called *The Best Poems of the English Language*—which included four Longfellow poems—Bloom wrote that "Longfellow is a superb lyric poet," and that his "translation of Dante's *Divine Comedy* seems to me undervalued, and compares favorably with the current versions." In an interview for this book, Bloom went further, saying that he preferred the Longfellow translation to "*all* the current versions." His reason: the "fidelity" it shows to Dante's original Italian.

Not long after the edition was published, Henry clarified his general approach to translation for an admirer in England. "The only merit my book has is that it is exactly what Dante says, and not what the translator imagines he might have said if he had been an Englishman. In other words, while making it rhythmic, I have endeavoured to make it also as literal as a prose translation." To that he added: "The business of a translator is to report what the author says, not to explain what he means; that is the work of the commentator. What an author says, and how he says it, that is the problem of the translator."

As modest as Henry may have been with this self-assessment, there was nonetheless a strikingly original feature he had added to his edition. On October 6, 1864—what would have been Fanny's forty-seventh birthday—he recorded that he was writing six original sonnets to introduce his translation, two for each canticle. "Go down to the Printer's with a sonnet, 'On Translating Dante.' Meet Fields and walk half way to town with him. He wants the Sonnet for *The Atlantic*." And then, in the next sentence, this: "Let me not forget today!"

Henry did not otherwise say why he chose to put such a personal stamp on his edition, and to do it with a poetic form he had used sparingly to that point—just four sonnets in the 1840s, one of them the deeply personal "Mezzo Cammin," another his love poem for Fanny "The Evening Star"—and none at all in the 1850s. Resuming with the Dante sequence, he composed them with increasing frequency, thirty-three in the final decade of his life, 75 percent of his entire output. In his interview with me, Harold Bloom called Henry a "master of the sonnet," singling out the six Dante "proems," as they are known, as being "quite remarkable." The first of these appeared in *The Atlantic Monthly* in December 1865; three others followed in the July, September, and November 1866 issues; the remaining two made their first appearance in the hardcover edition.

Henry's sixtieth birthday was observed on February 27, 1867, with "bouquets, and presents from the children." On May 6, the Dante edition, at long last, was "all done," and "the last word and the final corrections" were "in the Printer's hands." The completed work appeared in three uniform volumes later that year, around the time it was learned that Charles Dickens would be coming to the United States for a final round of public performances.

IT WOULD NOT BE too far-fetched to suggest, as some have, that at the time of their reunion in 1867, Charles Dickens and Henry Wadsworth Longfellow stood alone as public figures in the English-speaking world, their fame and popularity cutting across all demographics and social classes. "It was right pleasant to see him again after so many years— twenty five," Henry wrote after calling on his friend at the Parker House. "He looks somewhat older, but as elastic and quick in his movements as ever." Dickens spent four months in the city, giving the two men ample opportunity to meet at least a dozen times. Among several dinners they attended together, one was a "grand banquet" given for Annie Fields; most others were quiet gatherings, a number of them in Craigie House. Henry made it a point, too, to attend every reading his friend gave in the area. A "triumph for Dickens," he enthused after the first. "It is not Reading exactly; but acting, and quite wonderful in its way." Selections that night came from *A Christmas Carol* and *The Pickwick Papers*. "I never saw anything better." He expressed similar superlatives for the other performances.

Booked solid as Dickens was, he set some time aside for a most unusual side trip, as he explained to the writer Wilkie Collins. "I took it into my head to go over the medical school, and survey the holes and corners in which that extraordinary murder was done by Webster. There was the furnace—stinking horribly, as if the dismembered pieces were still inside it—and there are all the grim spouts, and sinks, and chemical appliances, and what not. At dinner, afterwards, Longfellow told me a terrific story. He dined with Webster within a year of the murder, one of a party of ten or twelve. As they sat at their wine, Webster suddenly ordered the lights to be turned out, and a bowl of some burning mineral to be placed on the table, that the guests might see how ghostly it made them look. As each man stared at all the rest in the weird light, all were horrified to see Webster with a rope round his neck, holding it up, over the bowl, with his head jerked on one side, and his tongue lolled out, representing a man being hanged!"

The two men would have one more reunion during Henry's triumphant tour of Europe the following year, made in part to visit with Dickens. Henry would learn of his friend's sudden passing, at the age of fifty-eight, on June 14, 1870, when back in Craigie House. "I can think of nothing else," he lamented, "but see him lying there dead in his house at Gad's Hill; silent, motionless"—the very place where they had so recently bid each other what amounted to their final farewells. There is no way Henry could have known, of course, how similar that response of his was to what Dickens had felt when he joined the Longfellow family in Cambridge for Thanksgiving dinner in 1867. Arriving on that occasion by private coach at two-thirty in the afternoon, Dickens had been pleased to see that three shelves mounted on the wall directly across from where he was seated in the dining room was dedicated to his writings. "Ah," he said to the delight of Henry's daughters, "I see you read the best authors."

If Dickens happened to notice that a first-edition copy of *Great Expectations* was among the titles—which indeed it still is, at eye level, on the middle shelf, to the left—he made no mention. Published around the time of Fanny's death, the novel features a character, Miss Havisham, who dies from injuries suffered in an accident frightfully similar to hers. "I suppose you don't remember Longfellow," Dickens wrote two days later to his eldest son. "He is now white-haired and white-bearded, but remarkably handsome. He still lives in his old house, where his beautiful wife was burnt to death. I dined with him the other day, and could not get the terrific scene out of my imagination. She was in a blaze in an instant, rushed into his arms with a wild cry, and never spoke afterwards."

18

Daybreak Everywhere

Four by the clock! and yet not day;
But the great world rolls and wheels away,
With its cities on land, and its ships at sea,
Into the dawn that is to be!

Only the lamp in the anchored bark
Sends its glimmer across the dark,
And the heavy breathing of the sea
Is the only sound that comes to me.

—Henry Wadsworth Longfellow, "Four by the Clock,"
"NAHANT, September 8, 1880, Four o'clock in the morning"

HENRY'S TRIP TO EUROPE in 1868 had all the pomp and ceremony of a
state visit, one he had shown the greatest reluctance to make in the first
instance, but undertook at the urgings of his family, and possibly with
the encouragement of Charles Dickens, who undoubtedly impressed
upon him the great interest his many admirers in England would have
in hosting his return to their shores after an absence of twenty-five years.
Henry's sisters, Anne Longfellow Pierce and Mary Longfellow Greenleaf,
were eager to come along; so, too, were his three daughters. Also joining
the entourage were Charley and the recently married Ernest, who was
accompanied by his wife, Harriet Spelman Longfellow. Rounding out
the traveling party to an even dozen were Henry's youngest brother, the
Reverend Samuel Longfellow; his brother-in-law Tom Appleton; and

The Longfellow traveling party to Europe, 1868–69, included Henry's three daughters, his brother Samuel Longfellow, his brother-in-law Tom Appleton, and his son Ernest and his wife

Hannah C. Davie, the longtime family governess and teacher for the children, who would spend much of the time abroad with her own family in England. They departed New York aboard the steamship *Russia* on May 27, 1868.

In a regal ceremony featuring formal scarlet robes and Latin orations, Henry was presented with an honorary LLD at Cambridge University on June 16. For the next six weeks, he was fêted and praised by one learned society after another. Among the guests at an elegant dinner given in his honor at the Langham Hotel was William Ewart Gladstone, soon to succeed Benjamin Disraeli as prime minister. That night, the artist Albert Bierstadt presented Henry with a magnificent rendering in oil, *Departure of Hiawatha*, which today is a centerpiece in the Brattle Street dining room, with the menu for that evening's feast affixed on the back.

On the Fourth of July, Henry spent the evening at Gad's Hill with Charles Dickens. He began the day at Windsor Castle, where he was received cordially by Queen Victoria, who favored him with an auto-

The British photographer Julia Margaret Cameron made this
portrait on the Isle of Wight while Longfellow was visiting Lord
Tennyson in 1868.

graphed photograph of herself. That afternoon, Her Royal Highness had
told Sir Theodore Martin, then working on a multivolume biography
of her late husband, Prince Albert, how pleasantly surprised she had
been to see so many members of her household staff maneuvering to
get a closer look at the honored guest. "I wished for you this morning,
for you would have seen something that would have delighted you as a
man of letters. The American poet Longfellow has been here. I noticed
an unusual interest among the attendants and servants. I could scarcely

credit that they so generally understood who he was. When he took leave, they concealed themselves in places from which they could get a good look at him as he passed. I have since inquired among them, and am surprised and pleased to find that many of his poems are familiar to them. No other distinguished person has come here that has excited so peculiar an interest. Such poets wear a crown that is imperishable."

Henry summed up his frenetic pace to John Forster in a letter written from the Isle of Wight, where he had traveled to meet with the poet laureate, Alfred, Lord Tennyson, and be photographed by the famed camera portraitist Julia Margaret Cameron. "I have in my brain a confused memory of London, rattle and road of streets, and 'dreams of fair women,' in drawing rooms, and breakfasts and luncheons and dinners in hopeless entanglement; and an endless procession of people, headed by the Archbishop of Canterbury! But I have a very clear memory of your most cordial welcome and hospitality, and cordially thank you for it once more."

Henry's popularity was such in Britain that he was outselling Robert Browning and Tennyson on their own turf, a circumstance acknowledged by the latter once when bragging to a friend how he earned two thousand pounds a year from his poetry, a goodly sum by any standard, "but Longfellow, alas, receives three thousand." James T. Fields would write that his star author's "currency in Europe is almost unparalleled," with twenty-four publishing houses in England alone issuing editions of his works. "Many of his poems have been translated into Russian and Hebrew. *Evangeline* has been translated three times into German, and *Hiawatha* has not only gone into nearly all the modern languages, but can now be read in Latin. I have seen translations of all Longfellow's principal works, in prose and poetry, in French, Italian, German, Spanish, Portuguese, Dutch, Swedish, and Danish."

From England, the entourage moved on to the Continent, proceeding at a far more leisurely pace for the next twelve months. Charley had gone yachting with friends for the summer, and continued on to India; Sam Longfellow and Tom Appleton, both life-long bachelors, broke away periodically on their own. The group lingered in Paris, Rome, Naples, and Sorrento, taking in operas, concerts, and plays and visiting the various museums. One afternoon Henry led "a grand walk" through the Eternal City that was notable for one bittersweet moment. "Ever since I reached Rome I have searched for the Persianis in vain," he confided to Greene, finally tracking down Giulia's brother, Fabio, in the old neighborhood. "He is shrunken and old, and looks very much as his father did when we were here."

A visit to the studio of the American portrait artist George Peter Alexander Healy, formerly of Boston and at that time based in Rome, occasioned a far more productive encounter. Healy had already painted portraits of several Appleton family members, including one of Fanny when she was seventeen, her tilted head resting on clasped hands, a mane of flowing hair hanging loosely to her shoulders. Given to Henry as a New Year's present in 1846 by Nathan Appleton, it hangs prominently in the dining room. A stately portrait of Henry commissioned in 1862 by James T. Fields for display in his office at the Old Corner Bookshop is now in the Bowdoin College Museum of Fine Arts.

On this visit—vividly recalled by Healy in his memoirs—Henry arranged to sit for a charming father-daughter portrait with Edith, then fifteen, and pictured standing behind him, to his right. Healy told how taken Henry was by a large portrait of the Hungarian composer and virtuoso pianist Franz Liszt that was on an easel in his studio. "I had recently painted it, and I told the poet how, during the sittings, Liszt had played, for hours at a time. I showed him casts I had had taken of the musician's hands; and these greatly interested him, for they were extraordinary,—thin, nervous, and well shaped; revealing much of the man's passionate, unquiet, earnest nature." Liszt was then living at a monastery just outside Rome, having taken minor orders several years earlier, and asking that he be addressed as Abbé Liszt. "Longfellow expressed a desire to see the great musician; and as I had remained on good terms with the sitter, I asked permission to present the American poet to him."

Arrangements were made, and on Christmas Eve, "toward sundown," they took a carriage to the monastery and rang at Liszt's private entrance. "It was already quite dark in the vestibule, the door of which was opened by means of an interior cord," Healy wrote. "No servant was visible. But the Abbé himself came forward to greet us, holding a Roman lamp high up, so as to see his way. The characteristic head, with the long iron-gray hair, the sharp-cut features and piercing dark eyes, the

Portrait of Franz Liszt, painted
for Henry by G. P. A. Healy
in Rome, 1869

tall, lank body draped in the priestly garb, formed so striking a picture
that Mr. Longfellow exclaimed under his breath: 'Mr. Healy, you must
paint that for me!'"

Once inside, Liszt played a number of selections on the piano for his
guest. "I told him how much we had both been struck by his appearance as he came toward us, light in hand," Healy wrote. "He willingly
consented to sit, and I made a small picture, as exact a reproduction as
possible of what we had seen, and which gave great pleasure to Longfellow." It was from that sketch that Healy prepared the dramatic painting that Henry commissioned—the maestro standing in darkness at an
abbey door, candle held high—that hangs in the Craigie House library,
immediately to the left upon entering from the study. Several years later,
Henry wrote Liszt to tell him how much he enjoyed the painting. "Your

portrait, with the light, hangs in my library. It always gives me pleasure to look upon it; and not less to all who see it." As a token of gratitude, on the flyleaf of an 1869 copy of *Evangeline*, he had inscribed, "Franz Liszt with kind remembrances of the Author," and dated it October 20, 1872.

On November 22, 1874, Liszt wrote Henry a warm letter in French reminding him of their most agreeable interactions. Translated, the original, now in the Library of Congress, included a bit of news: "Allow me to continue this sympathetic union by dedicating to you the musical composition of your poem: 'The Bells of Strasbourg Cathedral' with the prelude likewise inspired by one of your poems: 'Excelsior!'" That very word itself—"*Excelsior!*"—Liszt repeated in the next paragraph, "is the motto of poetry and music. Forever they sing the exaltation of the human soul to the ages and to the heavens, and thus accompany the *sursum corda* daily resounding in the churches and their bells." The following year, J. Schuberth & Co. of Leipzig issued *Die Glocken des Strassburger Münsters* in two forms, a piano-vocal score and a full score, with text in German and English. The printed musical score also reads: "Gewidmet dem Dichter H. W. Longfellow"—Dedicated to the poet H. W. Longfellow.

A few months after visiting Liszt in Rome, Henry was ready to call it a day. "I am heartily tired of traveling," he wrote Charley, then in India, "and long to be at home again." There was a brief return to England to receive another honorary degree, a DCL from Oxford University; then it was back to Craigie House, and into a routine that occupied the final thirteen years of his life. On December 31, 1869, to mark the closing of another year, he wrote of taking up "in earnest" *The Divine Tragedy*, a three-part chronicle of Christianity and its virtues that he had initiated with *The Golden Legend* and would see through the press in 1871. The following year he gathered in one volume, *Three Books of Song*, poems comprising a second day of *Tales of a Wayside Inn*, along with a "poetic drama" in five acts, *Judas Maccabaeus*, and a "handful of new translations." Meanwhile, he oversaw publication of a new edition of *The Poets and Poetry of Europe*—the "our book" collaboration with Fanny during their first year of marriage.

It was during this time of readjustment that Martha Ann Cleaveland Chandler, a friend of Henry's first wife and daughter of a onetime colleague on the Bowdoin faculty, invited him up for a commencement, thinking a little fresh air among old friends in familiar surroundings would do him a world of good. "He wrote that he could not go," the woman's son, Horace P. Chandler, recalled in an essay for *Every Other Saturday,* shortly after Henry's death in 1882. His reason: "for there were too many ghosts there."

When Henry finally did return to Brunswick for his fiftieth class reunion in 1875, he stayed in the Cleaveland House, an elegant dwelling just off Federal Street that now serves as the formal residence of the college president. Henry had respectfully declined an offer to stay with then Bowdoin president Joshua L. Chamberlain, whose valor as commander of the Twentieth Maine Volunteer Infantry Regiment at the Battle of Gettysburg earned him a Congressional Medal of Honor, the bayonet charge he led at Little Round Top generally credited with preserving a Union victory in the epic engagement.

"I am rejoiced to hear that you are to visit 'old Bowdoin' with your class this year," Chamberlain had written a month and a half before the scheduled exercises. "My special object in writing is to ask you to make my house your 'base of operations,'" noting further that his residence—today the Joshua Chamberlain Museum at the corner of Maine and Potter Streets, directly across from the church where Henry spoke—had an interesting provenance. "This house was, I think, one of your homes while you were here, and it seems as if you ought to be here while you are in Brunswick." Henry and his first wife, Mary, had in fact lived in a small second-floor suite of the house for a year prior to leaving for Europe. When Henry was shown the rooms by Chamberlain, he recalled having written a few poems while seated by the fireplace, then began to weep, and said no more.

It is thought Henry got the idea to call his ode "Morituri Salutamus" from a well-known painting by the French artist Jean-Léon Gérôme, *Pollice Verso* (1872), that pictures a vanquished gladiator lying helpless on the ground, the victor awaiting a signal from the frenzied crowd—thumbs up or thumbs down, thus the name of the painting ("with a turned thumb")—that will determine whether he lives or dies. Among the lines addressed to the audience assembled in the church to hear his oration were these:

What shall I say to you? What can I say
Better than silence is? When I survey
This throng of faces turned to meet my own,
Friendly and fair, and yet to me unknown,
Transformed the very landscape seems to be;
It is the same, yet not the same to me.
So many memories crowd upon my brain,
So many ghosts are in the wooded plain,
I fain would steal away, with noiseless tread,
As from a house where some one lieth dead.

Thirty-eight undergraduates received degrees in the Bowdoin class of 1825, Henry and Hawthorne being by far the most famous, but there were other high achievers among them, notably Horatio Bridge, a senior government official during the Civil War, and one of the thirteen surviving members of the class, eleven of whom were able to attend the celebration. Each had a seat on a dais at the front of the church. Press coverage the following day was extensive, including a report in *The New York Times*, which ran "Morituri Salutamus" in its entirety, reproduced "from the advance sheets of *Harper's Monthly* for August," which Henry—ever the shrewd manager of his intellectual property—had negotiated beforehand.

One unnamed observer called the scene "indescribably affecting," the audience "hushed to silence" by "the low and pleasant but often tremulous tones of Mr. Longfellow's voice as he read the poem," everything he said "clearly heard in every part of the church." Arguably the best firsthand report was written for *The Bowdoin Orient,* the student newspaper, by an unnamed undergraduate. "The day was theirs," the young correspondent declared of the class of 1825. "They needed no guests, and were each other's own best company." Professor Longfellow's "appearance on the platform," and the insights he shared, were "greeted by vehement and continued" applause, the student continued. "To those of us to whom the poet's verse has long been dear for its own inherent worth, it will be doubly dear now that we have heard it from his own lips. To hear Longfellow is a boon not vouchsafed to many, and those to whom it was granted will not soon forget, will never forget that they heard from the lips of America's greatest poet, the poem on the fiftieth anniversary of the graduation of his College Class."

A phrase from the Latin Henry came across as a young scholar and used as a motto for one of several personal bookplates he had printed—"non clamor sed amor" (not clamor, but love)—typifies in many ways how he comported his life. There was a time when the unqualified highlight of his day would be an evening spent by the fireside with Fanny reading aloud books they had chosen to engage and enjoy as a couple. Those glorious days of old—and that unforgettable, musical voice that had so enchanted him—were gone forever. But books nonetheless remained his constant companions. Andrew Hilen itemized the titles Henry indicated he had read between 1870 and 1872, dozens of works embracing every manner of theme and subject, a daunting assortment that gives "evidence of the diversity of his intellectual interests."

Henry never prepared a catalogue of his holdings, which today total 11,799 volumes still shelved in-house, a number that does not include books of particular scholarly interest transferred to Harvard in 1954 with the literary archive. There were undoubtedly many more than that, with volumes shelved in bookcases and presses and improvised mountings throughout the residence, in several instances in closed-off window openings that had been improvised for that purpose—one quite dramatically in Henry's study, another in an upstairs bedroom. Overflow was squirreled away in cubbyholes on the third floor, where the domestic staff had their rooms; others of lesser merit were piled in the basement. Writings in fifteen languages, each of which he read, and in most cases spoke, with fluency, and dozens of dialects are represented. Of its character, it can be said the contents are cosmopolitan to the extreme. And while there is no formal catalogue, there is a decided sensibility to the arrangement that proceeds associatively from bookcase to bookcase and from room to room—there is nothing haphazard or willy-nilly about the organization.

According to his brother Sam, Henry acknowledged during an 1877 trip to Portland that he had "bought a copy of *Plutarch's Lives,* in Latin, printed in Venice in 1496," which would make it an item printed on paper with moveable metal type during the "incunabulum," or "cradle," period of book publishing in Europe. Henry did not need another copy of Plutarch, and thus had acquired this item for its value as an artifact, not its content. "I believe this is my first purchase of a book on account of its age," he admitted, confirming that its acquisition was driven by an antiquarian impulse. While Henry treasured his books, he was a reader and scholar first, a collector second, and the same can be said of Fanny, whose own library contains numerous materials inscribed to her by friends and authors. "Even closets supposed to be devoted to pails and dust-cloths 'have three shelves for books and one for pails,'"Annie Adams Fields wrote of what she remembered seeing in Craigie House. "In his own bedroom, where the exquisite portrait of his wife by Rowse hangs over the fireplace, there is a small bookcase near his bed which contains a choice collection of the English poets"—that "lovely company of the past." One of these bedside volumes included "Exequy on His Wife" by the seventeenth-century poet Henry King, "exequy" being an archaic word from the French to describe solemn funeral rites. Longfellow had highlighted these lines of the poem in his copy:

> Sleep on, my *Love,* in thy cold bed
> Never to be disquieted!
> My last good night! Thou wilt not wake
> Till I thy fate shall overtake:
> Till age, or grief, or sickness must
> Marry my body to that dust
> It so much loves; and fill the room
> My heart keeps empty in thy Tomb.

Of the sonnets Henry turned to writing at this time with consummate skill, one, written in 1881, the year before he died, was dedicated entirely to his "most intimate friends," and titled, simply, "My Books." It closed with these lines:

> So I behold these books upon their shelf,
> My ornaments and arms of other days;
> Not wholly useless, though no longer used,
> For they remind me of my other self,
> Younger and stronger, and the pleasant ways
> In which I walked, now clouded and confused.

In her 1896 essay for *Cambridge Magazine,* Alice Longfellow acknowledged that while "no catalogue was ever made" of her father's library, it was nonetheless "carefully arranged by subjects," and he "was never at a loss where to look for any needed volume. His books were deeply loved and tenderly handled. Beautiful bindings were a great delight, and the leaves were cut with the utmost care and neatness." Alice—"grave Alice" of her father's poem "The Children's Hour," and the eldest of his adult daughters—never married, and lived in Craigie House her entire life, caring for her father in his elder years and also for her brother Charley, who spent the final thirteen months of his life as an invalid there as well. She took a great interest in philanthropic causes, notably Radcliffe College, even hosted a number of the school's commencements at Craigie House; Longfellow Hall, now part of the Harvard School of Education, is named for Alice, not Henry. Among her numerous projects was establishment of the Longfellow Family Trust, which in 1972 arranged for transfer of the property and its contents to the National Park Service, with the notable exception of the massive literary archive and correspondence, which had already gone over to Harvard.

"In this same old house he passed the remainder of his life," Alice wrote of her father's final years. "Home had great attractions for him. He cared more for the quiet and repose, the companionship of his friends and books, than for the fatigues and adventures of new scenes. Many of the friends of his youth were the friends of old age, and to them his house was always open with a warm welcome. Mr. Longfellow was always full of reserve, and never talked much about himself or his work, even to his family. Sometimes a volume would appear in print, without his having mentioned its preparation. In spite of his general interest in people, only a few came really close to his life. With these he was always glad to go over the early days passed together and to consult with them about literary work."

HENRY WOULD BE mightily amused to think of his study on the first floor as a precursor to what some in twenty-first-century America have come to call a "man cave." But this was his haven and refuge, the special place where he gathered things that defined his life and his interests,

Henry in his study, c. 1872–74, photograph by George K. Warren

where he honored his friendships and achieved professional accomplishment. The sanctity of the room—the very room where George Washington directed the war effort during the Siege of Boston—was not lost on his visitors, a number of whom described the awe they felt at being welcomed inside. It is so appropriate that the only sketch that Fanny is known to have made of her husband pictures him here, reclined in his favorite chair, by the fireplace. And the only sketch we have that Henry made of Fanny? She, too, sits serenely, eyes closed, taking a break, it would appear, from an evening of reading together. Both were done in 1847.

Crowning the tops of glazed bookcases are the busts of towering literary figures, with Dante and Shakespeare occupying the highest reaches. Closer to eye level hang the Eastman Johnson portraits of Henry and four of his friends, all chalk-and-crayon likenesses on paper. A corner by the entry from the hallway is devoted to George Washington; at another, by the window looking south across the front lawn, is the upright writing desk, with the Goethe cast standing sentinel. George Washington

Greene—the only contemporary of the poet to be favored by a cast
of his likeness in this room—wrote a description of the study as he
saw it in 1872 for *The Aldine,* adding a teaser to tempt future scholars.
"Here Vassall gathered his loyal friends around him in Colonial days.
Here Washington met statesmen and generals in the troubled days of
the Revolution. Here most of Longfellow's works were written. Here
the Dante Club held its meetings. What a chapter of American history
opens before us as we cross its threshold—too full a one to be told now,
though we trust it will some day be written with all its details."

On February 27, 1877, his seventieth birthday, Henry took pause,
and did so in this most congenial of places. "My study is a garden of
flowers, salutations and friendly greetings from far and near. I have a
whole box full of letters and poems." George Washington Greene came
to toast the milestone with him, and stayed for ten days. "He is my oldest friend living, and always a welcome guest." Henry could count, and
he knew the clock was ticking. Felton had died in 1862, Hawthorne in
1864, Agassiz in 1873, Sumner in 1874—and he wrote poignant poems of
loss about each of them, Hawthorne in an elegy of nine stanzas, Felton,
Agassiz, and Sumner in a sequence of four sonnets he called, collectively,
"Three Friends of Mine," commencing thusly:

> When I remember them, those friends of mine,
>> Who are no longer here, the noble three,
>> Who half my life were more than friends to me,
>> And whose discourse was like a generous wine,
> I most of all remember the divine
>> Something, that shone in them, and made us see
>> The archetypal man, and what might be
>> The amplitude of Nature's first design.
> In vain I stretch my hands to clasp their hands;
>> I cannot find them. Nothing now is left
>> But a majestic memory. They meanwhile
> Wander together in Elysian lands,
>> Perchance remembering me, who am bereft
>> Of their dear presence, and, remembering, smile.

The ever-observant Annie Fields recalled a dinner party at her Charles Street home on May 1, 1876, where, characteristically, Henry preferred listening to speaking, especially in groups such as this. "He was inclined to be silent, for there were other and brilliant talkers at the table, one of whom said to him in a pause of the conversation, 'Longfellow, tell us about yourself; you never talk about yourself.' 'No,' said Longfellow gently, 'I believe I never do.' 'And yet,' continued the first speaker eagerly, 'you confessed to me once'—'No,' said Longfellow, laughing, 'I think I never did.'"

That gathering was just a few weeks before Henry set off for Philadelphia to attend the Centennial Exposition then opening on the grounds of Fairmount Park. He had been invited to participate in an opening ceremony with President Ulysses S. Grant, but declined, one "occasional" poem in a twelve-month period sufficient, apparently, for his liking. He was suitably impressed nonetheless by what he saw of the brave new world being forecast in Philadelphia, and later acquired two fully illustrated accounts of the many exhibitions that had been gathered there, both kept today in compact shelving in the basement.

Most visitors to the exposition would agree that the unqualified highlight was the seven-hundred-ton, forty-foot-high, fifteen-hundred-horsepower Corliss steam engine that furnished power to two hundred buildings in the complex; but newfangled sewing machines, typewriters, a powered monorail, Alexander Graham Bell's "Speaking Telephone," and radiant prototypes of incandescent lighting made for a strong undercard of impressive attractions. Henry spent a week in the City of Brotherly Love, a few days with acquaintances in nearby Bryn Mawr, "a charming vacation," he felt, "with all the wonders of the Centennial Exhibition" taken in—and that, pretty much, was that, at least as far as his commentary was concerned. Henry did not indicate if he saw any of the many paintings on display, though it would have been an oversight had he missed them, with works by people he knew personally and worked with, including Albert Bierstadt and F. O. C. Darley, well represented. Given a central place in the main hall—and chosen winner of the gold medal for "excellence in landscape painting"—was *The Mountain of the Holy Cross* by the esteemed outdoor artist Thomas Moran. Twelve of Moran's pieces all told were displayed in Philadelphia,

Engraving of Thomas Moran's *Mountain of the Holy Cross* in
the Houghton Library copy of *Picturesque America*

five of them in oil, one in watercolor, and six drawings inspired by scenes
in *Hiawatha*.

On June 5, 1876—a month before the opening of the exposition—
Moran wrote Henry with the hope of showing him the "series of illustrations of *Hiawatha* that I have had in preparation for several years"
when he came to Philadelphia. "I have long desired to show you these
illustrations previous to their publication," he noted, and had hoped to
do so, he added, "during the exhibition of my picture of 'The Mountain
of the Holy Cross'" in Boston a few months earlier, but had been unable

to make that trip—clear evidence that Henry not only knew about the painting, but knew about it directly from the artist. Hearing that Henry would be in Bryn Mawr, Moran asked if "it would be agreeable to you to have me call and show these designs." No response from Henry survives, but we do know he dutifully answered his letters, especially important ones like this, and we know that he attended the exposition.

The likelihood, then, is that Henry did get a good look at the *Hiawatha* drawings, and probably did see Moran's five-foot-by-seven-foot painting as well. There was also a photograph of the mountain taken in 1873 by William Henry Jackson that was widely circulated and available in stereoscopic images, which were a favorite pastime in Craigie House. Moran's painting, moreover, was reproduced in a full-page steel-plate engraving in a later number of *Picturesque America*, a lavishly illustrated, folio-sized publication under the general editorship of William Cullen Bryant, and issued serially by subscription over a two-year period. Complete copies of the noncirculating set were acquired as released by the Boston Athenæum, where Henry was a member, and also Harvard University, where he consulted newly arrived publications regularly—and which holds the first-issue set that I examined. Ease and likelihood of access is important to document here once again, not just for the engraving of the painting itself, but also for the text, which includes a key physical description that had particular resonance with Henry, giving him what in due course would shape the central image of his most powerful sonnet: "The principal peak is composed of gneiss, and the cross fractures of the rock on the eastern slope have made two great fissures, which cut into one another at right angles, and hold snow in the form of a cross the summer long."

BACK HOME IN CAMBRIDGE, Henry resumed his agreeable pace, welcoming for dinner one evening Dom Pedro II, emperor of Brazil, "a hearty, genial, noble person, very liberal in his views," who would honor him by translating several of his poems into Portuguese. Other esteemed visitors would include Mark Twain, Wilkie Collins, Edwin Booth, Prince Albert Edward of England (later King Edward VII), and Sarah Bernhardt, who was reported by Ernest to have given his father a kiss on the forehead. A particular delight was an evening with the Italian actor Tommaso Salvini, famed for performing major Shakespeare roles entirely in Italian while others in the cast delivered theirs in English. Henry attended Salvini's portrayal of Othello, one of the few in the audience able to follow the dialogue in both languages.

Anthony Trollope treasured the bond he established with his American counterpart. "In personal contact with Longfellow," he wrote a year before Henry's death, "the stranger is apt to drop the poet in the gentleman, the distinguished man of letters in the uncommonly pleasant fellow whom he has encountered." An evening in his company, Trollope reflected, was memorable. "His children, his cigars, the dinner he will give you,—or more probably yourself,—are the subjects which are apt to come up with Longfellow in his conversation." The last guest of prominence Henry welcomed in his home was Oscar Wilde, who had lobbied mightily through Sam Ward and other intermediaries to secure an invitation, arranging finally to come by one morning for breakfast.

Anticipating the inevitable request for autographs from total strangers who continued to knock at his door, Henry kept a stack of cards handy, already signed, and dispensed freely, which turn up for sale periodically on eBay. Annie Fields was incredulous at his unwavering equanimity. "Day by day he was besieged by every possible form of interruption which the ingenuity of the human brain could devise; but his patience and kindness, his determination to accept the homage offered him in the spirit of the giver, whatever discomfort it might bring himself, was continually surprising to those who observed him year by year."

Mention of these encounters with total strangers pop up often in Henry's journal, some too good, he obviously felt, to go undocumented. "As I was standing at my front door this morning, a lady in black came up and asked, 'Is this the house where Longfellow was born?'" He answered, honestly, no, Longfellow was not born here. The woman then wondered, "Did he die here?" Henry's answer was equally direct. "Not yet," causing a light to flash over the stranger's head. "Are *you* Longfellow?" With the answer in the affirmative, her closing line made his day: "I thought you died two years ago." Another "traveler" called "and asked me if Shakespeare did not live somewhere about here? I told him I knew no such person in the neighborhood." When he was not answering the door, he was, as always, answering letters, a good number of them exasperating. "A gentleman writes me for 'your autograph in your own handwriting,'" he bemoaned one day. "A lady in Ohio sends me one hundred blank cards, with the request that I will write my name on each, as she wishes to distribute them among her guests at a party she is to give on my birthday," he reported the next. "Letters, letters, letters! Some I answer, but many, and most, I cannot," a few days after that. And this was just one week, in January 1881.

THERE WAS A TIME when 105 Brattle Street was one of the most-visited historic landmarks in the United States. "Next to Mount Vernon," the architectural writer Donald Millar wrote in 1916 of Craigie House, "this is the best-known house in America." Lithographed likenesses of the façade, and the white-bearded poet who lived inside, appeared on every manner of ephemeral surface, from calendars and cigar boxes to postcards and broadsides, from Wedgwood pitchers to decks of playing cards. In 1918, a full thirty-six years after Henry's death, Sears, Roebuck unveiled a self-assembly replica of Craigie House called the Magnolia, available for purchase through 1927.

Inside the mansion, Henry's likeness can be found in every room, be it sculpted in stone, molded in plaster, painted in oil, drawn on paper, or reproduced photographically, some clean-shaven, some fully bearded. A first-floor passageway at the back of the house I like to think of as the "Henry, Henry, Henry" room is dominated by three busts, two of them perched atop adjacent bookcases, one sculpted by Edward Augustus Brackett in 1844, the other by Benjamin Paul Akers in 1851. The third, on a corner pedestal next to the glazed cabinet containing Mrs. Craigie's seventy-five-volume edition of Voltaire, was carved in 1879 by Samuel Kitson. Just outside this room—it is actually an extended hall-way known as the Blue Entry—is a reproduction of the memorial bust installed in Westminster Abbey in 1884.

In the study, a portrait of Henry painted by his son Ernest is mounted on an easel; on a wall nearby is the Eastman Johnson *Five of Clubs* chalk-on-paper portrait. Among a cluster of paintings decorating the rear stair-way to the second floor is the image of a smartly dressed man of letters with intense eyes, painted in 1840 by Cephas Giovanni Thompson—alert and fresh-faced, as both his wives would have known him. Fanny's favorite likeness of her husband—chalk on cream wove paper—was done in 1854 by Samuel Laurence; it occupies a corner of the first-floor parlor near the portal to the front vestibule, facing the Bartolini sculpture on the other side of the room. "He has made a beautiful drawing of Henry which all agree in thinking the best yet taken," she reported to her sister, in recommending the artist's work. "It is full of life and with a very lively, agreeable expression, very different from the woodeny likeness engraved in England." Not displayed in the house—but fully represented in the basement files and as frontispiece images in many of Henry's books—are engraved images executed at different stages of his career. He was photographed formally by the leading practitioners of the medium as well, in the United States by Mathew Brady, in England by Julia Margaret Cameron, and by a host of others—impeccably dressed and groomed in every instance.

Fanny posed for numerous photographs of her own during the years of her marriage, the vast majority in professional studios—about twenty-five, is the best estimate. Most of these picture a stately woman clad in fashionably hooped dresses of the period, her hair pulled back, standing regally in profile. A few show her seated, a number picture her in groups, one or two delightfully lively, but for the most part stiff and rigid, par for the course at a time when excruciatingly long poses were required to get proper exposures.

In 2017, two previously unrecorded ambrotype images of Fanny and Henry were acquired by Bowdoin College from a dealer representing a private collector. Based on other images that came to the library with these two, the evidence suggests they were once possessed by descendants of Henry's brother Alexander Longfellow, and thus not recorded in Craigie House inventories, where logic suggests they should have been, given their importance. Information entered on the back of each picture—both housed in identical gilt frames and taken, it appears, at the same time, and in the same studio, that of C. T. Sylvester of Boston—indicates they were done in 1860, a year before Fanny's death.

Of images of Fanny on view in Longfellow House, the fetching G. P. A. Healy portrait done when she was seventeen is by far the most flattering, and the one reproduced most often. The Bartolini sculpture in the front parlor, and the Isabey miniature in the dining room, came to Brattle Street after the death of Nathan Appleton, and were not on view there while Fanny was alive. The likeness that I suspect comes closest to the woman Henry knew and adored hangs in the master bedroom, front and center above the fireplace. The artist, Samuel W. Rowse, was a friend of Eastman Johnson's and best known for his portraits of Ralph Waldo Emerson and Henry David Thoreau. A dual portrait of their youngest daughters done in 1857 earned special praise from Fanny. "I told you that Rowse has taken a lovely crayon sketch of Alice and Edie," she informed Emmeline, stressing the "grace" the artist exhibited in depicting children. "You ought to have your boys done by him. He is so patient too, catching the child as he can, on a small tablet and working up the real drawing, without a sitting at his room."

Suitably impressed himself, Henry sat for the artist the following year, finding the sessions tedious but productive. "Rowse began yesterday to draw my head in crayons and went on to-day, slowly, slowly. It is no vanity or folly of mine, but his own. So let him work away. He is a very clever artist; a Maine man, born in Bath, brought up in Augusta." A year after that, Tom Appleton commissioned the portrait of Fanny that ultimately made its way to the master bedroom. To affirm the spell it came to cast on the single occupant of that room on a nightly basis, we have the opening lines of the sonnet Henry wrote on July 10, 1879. Structurally, it is a meditation in fourteen lines of two artworks, this one—the one over the fireplace—the other not identified by name, but indisputably the Thomas Moran landscape he had seen in Philadelphia a few years earlier that had electrified viewers worldwide with its unmistakable symbolism. The flow is continuous, from one visual image to the next.

THE CROSS OF SNOW

In the long, sleepless watches of the night,
    A gentle face—the face of one long dead—
    Looks at me from the wall, where round its head
    The night-lamp casts a halo of pale light.

Here in this room she died, and soul more white
  Never through martyrdom of fire was led
  To its repose; nor can in books be read
  The legend of a life more benedight.
There is a mountain in the distant West
  That, sun-defying, in its deep ravines
  Displays a cross of snow upon its side.
Such is the cross I wear upon my breast
  These eighteen years, through all the changing scenes
  And seasons, changeless since the day she died.

—July 10, 1879

Eighteen years, precisely, had passed since the day of Fanny's death, her funeral falling on what would have been the couple's eighteenth wedding anniversary. The two quatrains at the beginning—forming an "octave" of eight lines—present an "argument," which in this instance is the contemplation of Fanny's likeness that hangs over the mantel of the fireplace in his bedroom. The "turn," or shift, in the structure—known as the "volta"—occurs in the ninth line, marking the beginning of the "sestet," comprising two stanzas of three lines each. Henry's transition is powerful, profound, and daringly dramatic, the focus having shifted abruptly to another artistic rendering, this one enormous, public, and familiar to thousands, wherein lies the brilliance of his "resolution"— a declaration from the heart that brings the two together in seamless unity.

Henry's lifelong fascination for Dante is evident, too, the parallels and similarities between Beatrice and Fanny distinctive, the imagery of a "soul more white" and a "martyrdom of fire" informed by the sonnets he had prepared as "proems," or preludes, for his edition of *The Divine Comedy*. The one archaic word in the sonnet that seems forced to some—"benedight"—appears several times in his translation of Dante, and actually has a perfectly appropriate application as an adjective in "Cross of Snow" that goes beyond the convenient circumstance of its rhyming with "white." Synonymous with "blessed," it is derived from the Latin *benedictus* for "benediction" or "blessing," presumably a tribute to Saint Benedict, the founder at Monte Cassino in the fifth century of Western monasticism.

Written neatly in pen on both sides of a single sheet of paper—eight lines on the front, six on the back—the holographic copy is clean and distinctive, executed with a firm hand and no strikeouts or substituted words, suggesting that it is a fair copy and the product of sustained effort. Unlike "Mezzo Cammin" twenty-seven years earlier—just as personal, and unpublished during his lifetime—no drafts were left behind. After entering the date at the bottom, he tucked the sheet inside a yellow envelope and placed it among his private papers, leaving no instructions whatsoever for its disposition. Found by his brother Sam, it was published for the first time in an appendix to the biography he wrote of his brother.

IT WAS SUMMER, and soon Henry was on Nahant, devoting very little time these days to his journal. An entry for September 1, 1879, trumpets, in a single sentence, a milestone in the family. "Born in the southwest chamber of the Craigie House, at ten o'clock, a new Richard Henry Dana; my first grandchild." Daughter Edith had married the "boy next door," Richard Henry Dana III, the previous year; her second son, Henry Wadsworth Longfellow Dana—Harry Dana, the future curator of Craigie House—was born eighteen months after that, giving Henry two grandchildren, one of them a namesake, to enjoy through the remainder of his days.

Henry's youngest daughter, Annie Allegra, would marry Joseph Thorp Jr. in 1885, and have five daughters. One of her great-granddaughters, Frances Appleton Smith Wetherell—"Frankie" to staff past and present at Longfellow House, who treasure her as one of their own—talked with me on several occasions for this book, and provided some wonderful insights on the family heritage. One of these recalled the reenactment in 1953 of the wedding, one hundred and ten years earlier, of Henry and Fanny, in which Frankie wore one of Fanny's surviving gowns, and assumed the role of the bride; another family descendant, according to press clippings in the Boston newspapers she had saved and has since turned over to the archivists, was the groom. The reenactment was staged in the front parlor of the Nathan Appleton residence at 39 Beacon Street, at that time home of the Boston Women's Club, and now a private residence designated a National Historic Site, which my wife, Connie, and I visited in 2017 shortly after new owners—at the reported price of $15.3 million—had taken title to the building.

All three of Henry's married children lived in houses built for them close by, Edith and Annie in homes immediately adjacent to Craigie House on the western border of the property, Ernest directly across Brattle Street to the right of Longfellow Park. Henry never wavered in his work, completed a thirty-one-volume project he had taken on for James T. Fields, a series of anthologies called *Poems of Places*, which gathered compositions from around the world, a number of which he translated. It was not heavy work, but it was busy work, and that was good.

As he advanced in years, his birthdays were celebrated with parades, readings of his poems, orations, the sending of flowers, and formal declarations. His death, on March 24, 1882, after a brief illness believed to have been peritonitis, was reported on the front pages of newspapers throughout the world. Henry understood as well as anyone the vicissitudes of celebrity. He was content to let his oeuvre speak for itself, some 420 poems of every category and genre having appeared in print, not counting numerous other works in foreign tongues he had translated and introduced to English-speaking readers, along with prose works and scholarly essays. His edition of Dante alone is a singular achievement, and his sonnets compare with the best in English, certainly among American writers. That he was fully engaged to the end became evident by a poem he completed barely a week before his death. The creative spark on this occasion came from an extensively illustrated and extremely well-written article by the Connecticut travel writer and novelist William Henry Bishop, titled "Typical Journeys and Country Life in Mexico," displayed handsomely over sixteen successive pages in the March 1882 issue of *Harper's New Monthly Magazine*.

The last of seventeen illustrations to appear in the suite reproduced Bishop's sketch of four antiquated church bells dangling from a make-shift wooden frame in the seaport town of San Blas. The text described the once thriving community on Mexico's Pacific Coast as "hardly more than an extensive thatched village" that had, "on a bluff beside it, the

BELLS OF SAN BLAS.

The drawing of the bells of San Blas that inspired Henry's final poem,
cut from the March 1882 issue of *Harper's New Monthly Magazine*

ruins of a once more substantial San Blas." And then there was this:
"Old bronze bells brought down from it have been mounted on rude
frames a few feet high to serve the purpose of the present poor church,
which is without a belfry, and this is called, in irony, 'the Tower of San
Blas.'"

In a journal he kept for ideas and thoughts he called his "Book of
Suggestions"—sometimes with a single word or catchphrase—Henry
had pasted onto an otherwise blank page Bishop's sketch of the bells,
with no added text of his own. The poem he thereupon wrote was composed with what had to have been the knowledge that his days were
winding down, that the end was near. "The Bells of San Blas" was published shortly after his death in *The Atlantic Monthly*, and later that
year in a collection of his final poems, *In the Harbor*. Bishop's book *Old
Mexico and Her Lost Provinces* appeared the following year, using much
of the material from the *Harper's* article, including an even-larger reproduction of his drawing, with this addendum: "My slight sketch of these

bells, made on a fly-leaf of my note-book in the first instance, came to have importance far beyond its own merits. I have the gratification of knowing that it proved to be the source of nothing less than the last inspiration of Longfellow."

In a superb monographic examination of Longfellow's poetry published in 1963, the National Book Award–winning literary critic Newton Arvin wrote that bells had always spoken to Henry's imagination "with a special force, and these rather pitiful church bells, once so grandly housed and now so meanly exposed, without even a belfry around them, spelled for him the whole grandeur of a proud and powerful past, both in the state and in the realm of faith—a past that one can only look back upon with reverence, but that it is folly to revive."

Henry lamented the desperate condition of the bells in his opening lines, but, "dreamer of dreams" that he was, expressed hope they might someday reclaim their past glory:

> What say the Bells of San Blas
> To the ships that southward pass
>   From the harbor of Mazatlan?
> To them it is nothing more
> Than the sound of surf on the shore,—
>   Nothing more to master or man.
>
> But to me, a dreamer of dreams,
>   To whom what is and what seems
>   Are often one and the same,—
> The Bells of San Blas to me
> Have a strange, wild melody,
>   And are something more than a name.

After finishing his first draft and setting it aside, Henry returned a few days later to add a final stanza, completing it a few days before he died peacefully in his bed, surrounded by his family. His final words of this, his final poem, endure as a coda to a life lived well and lived in full—and one that did not end shrouded in darkness:

O Bells of San Blas, in vain
Ye call back the Past again!
    The Past is deaf to your prayer;
Out of the shadows of night
The world rolls into light;
    It is daybreak everywhere.

Acknowledgments

My first debt of gratitude for this project is to Dr. Diana Korzenik, professor emerita of the Massachusetts College of Art in Boston, one of the scholar-collectors I profiled in my 2001 book, *Patience & Fortitude,* who was tireless in urging me to take a look at the treasures and archives contained within the Longfellow House National Historic Site at 105 Brattle Street in Cambridge. A determined Fanny scholar in her own right—and cofounder of the Friends of Longfellow House—Diana assured me that a wonderfully instructive and inspirational story had yet to be written about the Henry-Fanny relationship, with rich resources readily available to document it.

An essay I subsequently wrote for *Smithsonian* magazine to mark the bicentennial of Longfellow's birth in 2007, and the concurrent opening then of a fabulous exhibition at the Houghton Library, *Public Poet, Private Man,* gave me a taste for just how rich the untapped resources on the subject are. During multiple visits to Longfellow House over a five-year period, James M. Shea, site director from 1992 to 2012, served as my personal guide to the vast holdings he had identified, supervised, and "museumized" (his word) during his tenure, and gave me a renewed appreciation for the role materiality can play in the writing of general nonfiction.

The National Park Service onsite collections specialists have been a pleasure to work with as well, their knowledge and interpretation of the materials entrusted to their care matched only by their eagerness to see them properly consulted and appreciated, and who, to a person, I have come to know very well. I recognize in particular Christine M. Wirth, archives specialist; Kathryn Hanson Plass, museum technician and supervisor of the Fanny Longfellow transcription project; and David Daly, curator of collections. Also: Beth Law, site director during the early stages of my research; rangers Garrett Cloer and Anna M. Christie; and volunteer Patricia Grandieri.

An equally essential component of my research was done in the Houghton Library of Harvard University, repository for the enormous collection of literary manuscripts, diaries, and correspondence of Longfellow and many of the people in his circle; the entire staff was unfailingly helpful, with special thanks to Peter X. Accardo, programs and public service librarian, and Susan Halpert, reference librarian.

Two research trips my wife, Connie, and I made to Bowdoin College in Brunswick, Maine, were productive through the efforts of a most hospitable community of professionals: Kat Stefko, director of special collections and archives in the Hawthorne-Longfellow Library, and Caroline Mosely, archivist; John Cross, secretary of development and college relations; Frank H. Goodyear and Anne Collins Goodyear, codirectors of the Bowdoin College Museum of Art, and Joachim Homann, curator; Cathi Belcher, of the Harriet Beecher Stowe House, and Carmen Greenlee, humanities and media librarian.

The final manuscript has benefited measurably from the close reading given to it by Professor Christoph Irmscher of Indiana University, whose keen eye for detail and nuance helped make for a much stronger book. For their unstinting encouragement and support, my gratitude also to Christian Dupont, Dana Gioia, Bradford Morrow, Joel Silver, Michael Suarez, Susan Jaffe Tane, and the late J. D. McClatchy. Also, my thanks to, in Nahant, Calantha Sears, Kenneth C. Turino, Christopher R. Mathias, and Lynne Spencer; in Portland, John W. Babin of the Maine Historical Society and the Wadsworth-Longfellow House; and in Hiram, Maine, Sue Moulton, direct descendant of General Peleg Wadsworth, for opening up the ancestral house there for our examination, and her son Jim, for making the arrangements.

Once again, my appreciation to the National Endowment for the Humanities, which recognized the worthiness of this project with its award in 2016 of a Public Scholar research grant, without which this book would have not been possible; and to the Vancouver philanthropist Dr. Yosef Wosk, for his continuing support of independent scholarship, and of my work in particular.

For assistance in transcribing a key sequence of letters from Catharine Maria Sedgwick to Fanny Appleton, I gratefully acknowledge Dr. Lucinda Damon-Bach of Salem State University, founding president of the Catharine Maria Sedgwick Society, and author of a forthcoming biography of this important American writer. For translations of key documents: Dr. Iván Jaksić, director of Stanford University's Bing Overseas Studies Program in Santiago, Chile; Niclas Wallin, a former antiquarian bookseller and colleague in Stockholm; and Barbara Basbanes Richter, of Larchmont, New York.

My thanks, as always, to my literary agents, Glen Hartley and Lynn Chu at Writers' Representatives. I shall be forever grateful to them for finding me a welcoming home at Alfred A. Knopf, and the opportunity to work with my editor there, Victoria Wilson, on this, our second book together, and one of the outstanding experiences of my professional life. I greatly appreciate, too, the good work of her assistant, Marc Jaffee, and copy editor Patrick Dillon.

National Park Service ranger Ryan McNabb provided an extraordinary overview of history and tradition during a four-hour walking tour of the Black Heritage Trail on the North Slope of Beacon Hill. Ellen Dunlap, president of the American Antiquarian Society, and Peter Drummey, librarian of the Massachusetts Historical Society, made sure I had all the assistance I needed in perusing their collections.

The Boston Athenæum has been "home base" for me now for ten books, and in all that time the head of circulation, James P. Feeney Jr., has provided courtesies and services too numerous to itemize. When I wondered, way back in 1995, how and why it was that this national treasure of a library had held on to three obscure books for close to a century that nobody before me had ever checked out, it was Jim who said, "We got them for *you*, Mr. Basbanes."

My family continues to be an inspiration: our daughters, Barbara and Nicole; their husbands, Michael Richter and Billy Claire; our granddaughter, Abigail Constance; and, of course, Connie, my wife, and reader of first resort. What's next? Whatever it is, we'll do it together.

Notes

Abbreviations of frequently cited references. Full information given on first usage.

INDIVIDUALS

ALP	Anne Longfellow Pierce
ASM	Alexander Slidell Mackenzie
CAL	Charles Appleton Longfellow
CMS	Catharine Maria Sedgwick
CS	Charles Sumner
EAW	Elizabeth Austin Wadsworth
FEAL	Frances Elizabeth Appleton Longfellow
GWG	George Washington Greene
GWC	George William Curtis
HWL	Henry Wadsworth Longfellow
IAJ	Isaac Appleton Jewett
MLG	Mary Longfellow Greenleaf
MSP	Mary Storer Potter Longfellow
SL	Stephen Longfellow
ZL	Zilpah Longfellow

INSTITUTIONS

HL	Houghton Library, Harvard University
LH	Longfellow House–Washington's Headquarters National Historic Site

FREQUENTLY CITED WORKS

Andrew Hilen, ed. *Letters of Henry Wadsworth Longfellow*	Letters
Andrew Hilen, ed. *The Diary of Clara Crowninshield*	Crowninshield
Samuel Longfellow. *Life of Henry Wadsworth Longfellow*	Life
Journals of Henry W. Longfellow	HWL Journal
Journals of Frances Elizabeth Appleton Longfellow	FEAL Journal
Letters of Frances Elizabeth Appleton Longfellow	FEAL Letters
Longfellow House Catalogued Materials	LONG

AUTHOR'S NOTE

x   "Craigie Edition": Periodic mentions of "Craigie House" and "Longfellow House" are references to the same structure at 105 Brattle Street in Cambridge, Massachusetts, known when built in 1759 as "Vassall House," and formally today as "Longfellow House–Washington's Headquarters National Historic Site."

INTRODUCTION

4   "the last I shall": Henry Wadsworth Longfellow Journal, April 19, 1854, Houghton Library (HL), MS Am 1340 (hereafter HWL Journal). In 1858, Longfellow declined an invitation from Bowdoin College to deliver a poem before a public gathering with this explanation: "I have a positive repugnance to doing this kind of work, probably from not recognizing in myself any capacity for doing it well. For this reason I habitually decline all invitations however urgent." Henry W. Longfellow (hereafter HWL) to Alpheus Spring Packard, April 30, 1858, in Hilen, *Letters* (hereafter *Letters*), vol. 4, 76.

4   "Too many ghosts": [Horace P. Chandler] "Longfellow's First Wife and Early Friends," in *Every Other Saturday,* Jan. 19, 1884, vol. 1, no. 2, 20–21.

4   "Morituri salutamus": It is thought Longfellow got the idea for the premise from a well-known painting by the French artist Jean-Léon Gérôme, *Pollice Verso* (1872), which pictures a vanquished gladiator lying helpless in the arena, the victor looming above, sword poised, awaiting a signal from the crowd—thumbs up or thumbs down—that will determine life or death.

5   "In the repudiation": Aaron, in Maine Historical Society, 65.

6   *damnatio memoriae:* For more on the practice through history—also translated to mean "obliteration of the record"—see the "Ex Libris Punicis" chapter in my book *A Splendor of Letters.*

6   "Anthologists create": Author interview with Joel Myerson, Aug. 6, 2018. See my profile of Myerson, "Transcendentalists in South Carolina," *Fine Books & Collections* (Spring 2019).

6   "Longfellow is to poetry": Van Wyck Brooks, *America's Coming-of-Age* (New York: B. W. Huebsch, 1915), 50.

6   "Who, except wretched": Ludwig Lewisohn, *The Story of American Literature* (New York: Modern Library, 1939), 65 [first Harper & Brothers edition, 1932].

7   "Don't look down": Theodore Roosevelt to Martha Baker Dunn, Sept. 6, 1902, quoted in Carl J. Weber, "Poet and President," *The New England Quarterly*, vol. 16, no. 4 (Dec. 1943), 615–626. Roosevelt was responding to Dunn's essay "Browning Tonic," in *The Atlantic Monthly,* August 1902 (vol. 90, no. 538). For an excellent critical reading of "The Saga of King Olaf," see Matthew Gartner, "Becoming Longfellow: Work, Manhood, and Poetry," in *American Literature,* vol. 72, no. 1 (March 2000), 1-28.

7   "He is already thought": Bliss Perry, "The Centenary of Longfellow," *The Atlantic Monthly,* no. 99 (March 1907) (Boston: Houghton Mifflin, 1907), 379–388.

7   "in the eyes": Steven Allaback, "Longfellow Now," in National Park Service, *Papers Presented.*

8   "new poetry": Lawrance Thompson, *Robert Frost: The Years of Triumph, 1915–1938* (New York: Henry Holt, 1966), 291.

8   "I never was": Lawrence Buell, author interview, March 28, 2017.

8   "all that silliness": Harold Bloom, author interview, March 30, 2016. See my profile of Bloom in *Every Book Its Reader,* 228–237, and his obituary, "Harold Bloom, Critic, Who Championed Western Canon, Dies at 89," *The New York Times,* Oct. 14, 2019.

9   Library of America: In a June 23, 2016, interview with me, J. D. "Sandy" McClatchy said one immediate result of the publication of his edition of Longfellow's poetry in 2001 was to hear from academics informing him they would be "putting Longfellow back into the curriculum of American literature. It was amazing how they woke up, saying, 'This stuff is better than I thought it was,' or 'It's more important than I thought it was.'" See my profile of McClatchy in *Fine Books & Collections* (Winter 2017) and obituary "J. D. McClatchy, Poet of the Body, in Sickness and Health, Dies at 72," *New York Times,* April 11, 2018.

9   "He is back": Christoph Irmscher, in Irmscher and Barbour, *Reconsidering Longfellow,* 1.

9   "Longfellow is back": Christoph Irmscher, in "Henry Wadsworth Longfellow," *Oxford Bibliographies in American Literature,* ed. Jackson Bryer (New York: Oxford University Press, 2013). Available online through Oxford Bibliographies Online.

10   "The United States today": Interview by telephone and subsequent exchange of emails with Andrew C. Higgins, March 8, 2019. My thanks to Professor Higgins also for allowing me to read an advance text of his essay "Prospects for the Study of Henry Wadsworth Longfellow," accepted for publication in *Resources for American Literary Studies,* and still in production at the time of this writing.

I · THE WIND'S WILL

13   "His grandchildren looked": Samuel Longfellow, *Life of Henry Wadsworth Longfellow* (hereafter *Life*), vol. 1, 21.

14   "a lady of eminent piety": Horace Wadsworth, *Two Hundred and Fifty Years of the Wadsworth Family in America* (Lawrence, MA: privately printed, 1883), 43. Peleg Wadsworth's Harvard classmates included Alexander Scammell, who died in the Revolution, and was namesake for one of his sons, and Theophilus Parsons, who became chief justice of the Massachusetts Supreme Court. The house in Hiram, known as Wadsworth Hall, is still owned by Peleg's direct descendants.

14   Congress Street: An extensive summary of Peleg Wadsworth's service during the Revolution and his life afterwards, including the construction of his house in Portland and his move later to Hiram, is chronicled by William Goold, "General Peleg Wadsworth, and the Maternal Ancestry of Henry Wadsworth Longfellow," in the "Seventy-Fifth Birthday" special issue of the *Proceedings of the Maine Historical Society* (Portland: Hoyt, Fogg, and Donham, 1881), 52–81.

14   "fell before the walls": Text of the cenotaph, and details of the naval battle, in Horace Wadsworth, 48–49.

14   "We are in daily expectation": Shipboard diary of Henry Wadsworth, in Longfellow House archives. The actions of Lt. Wadsworth and his shipmates were more formally memorialized in 1806 by the erection in Washington, DC, of the Tripoli Memorial, a sculpture of Carrara marble carved in Italy and brought to the United States aboard the USS *Constitution;* regarded as the nation's first military memorial, it was moved to the US Naval Academy at Annapolis in 1860.

15   "one moment": Full text of formal death notice of Lt. Wadsworth written by Zil-

pah Longfellow, reprinted in *MHS,* the official publication of the Maine Historical Society (Fall 2011), 5.

16 "one of the most imposing": William Willis, *History of Portland from 1632 to 1864* (Portland, ME: Dailey & Noyes, 1865), 760.

17 Wadsworth-Longfellow House: 489 Congress St., Portland, ME, was the first building in the state to be designated a National Historic Landmark, according to the Maine Historical Society. It is open to the public.

17 "Henry is remembered": Quoted in *Life,* vol. 1, 21.

18 Lafayette visit to Portland: A bouquet of flowers was presented to the general on this occasion by thirteen-year-old Mary Storer Potter, daughter of a prominent local judge, and from 1831 to her death in 1835 the wife of Henry Wadsworth Longfellow.

18 "Master Henry Longfellow": Quoted in *Life,* vol. 1, 17.

19 Portland Academy: See Samuel Longfellow, "The Old Portland Academy: Longfellow's 'Fitting School,'" *New England Quarterly,* vol. 18, no. 2 (June 1945), 247–251.

19 The Reverend Samuel Longfellow: Henry's youngest brother's close personal and professional friendship with Samuel Johnson dated from their years as classmates at Harvard Divinity School. See the excellent biographical essay and chronology in the finding aid for the Reverend Samuel Longfellow (1819–1892) Papers, LONG 33705, which includes his outgoing and incoming correspondence. See also Abdo, passim.

19 "If you desire . . . say any more": HWL to Zilpah Longfellow (hereafter ZL), March 7, 1844, Hilen, *Letters,* vol. 1, 79–81. See also Abdo, passim.

20 "indolence": ZL to Stephen Longfellow (hereafter SL), Jan. 10, 1824. Zilpah's letters to her husband during his years in Congress, and his letters to her, are to be found in seven folders of correspondence in Series V, Stephen Longfellow (1776–1849) and Family Papers, Subseries B, and Zilpah Wadsworth Longfellow, Correspondence, Outgoing, in the Wadsworth-Longfellow Family Papers, 1610–1971 (LONG 27923), Longfellow House—Washington's Headquarters National Historic Site. For extended discussions of Henry's undergraduate years at Bowdoin, see Thompson, 23–73, and Calhoun, 26–38.

20 "disturbing to the quietness": Information and quotations relating to the behavior of Stephen Longfellow at Bowdoin College in "Records of the Executive Government, 1805–1875," box 2 (1.7.1), Hawthorne-Longfellow Library, Bowdoin College, Brunswick, ME.

20 Acquaintance with Stephen: Writing to Henry on March 27, 1848, Hawthorne stressed how "I want to see Stephen very much," and expressed hope that he might make a visit to Concord when another Bowdoin classmate and mutual friend of theirs, Horatio Bridge, would be visiting. "It would give me great satisfaction to receive him here." HL, bMS AM 1340.2 (2616). Hawthorne drew on his years as a Bowdoin undergraduate for *Fanshawe,* his first published work, printed at his own expense and issued anonymously in 1828 by Marsh and Capen of Boston; the fictional institution was called Harley College.

21 "After life's fitful fever": HWL Journal, Sept. 20, 1850.

21 "sacrificed his cherished . . . awaited him": Nehemiah Cleaveland, *History of Bowdoin College, with Biographical Sketches of Its Graduates* (Boston: James Ripley Osgood, 1882), 308–309.

21 "What can have made": ZL to SL, Feb. 20, 1825.

22 "a few pages": HWL to ZL, April [no day] 1823, *Letters,* vol. 1, 43–44.

22 "I am not very conversant": ZL to HWL, April 23, 1823, quoted ibid., vol. 1, 44, footnote 1; also Thompson, 37.

22 "I have a strong . . . notwithstanding": HWL to ZL, April 25, 1823, *Letters,* vol. 1, 45.

23 "Chemical Lectures": HWL to SL, March 13, 1824, ibid., 83–84.

24 "In thinking to make": HWL to SL, April 30, 1824, ibid., 89–90.

24 "I would attach myself": HWL to SL, Dec. 5, 1824, ibid., 94–96.

24 "A literary life": SL to HWL, Dec. 26, 1824, HL, Am 1340.2 (3516).

25 "Went to my father's": HWL Journal, Aug. 9, 1849.

25 "Will you permit": Theophilus Parsons to HWL, Nov. 17, 1824, HL, bMS Am 1340.2 (4287).

25 "of all the numerous": William Cullen Bryant, *The New-York Review and Atheneum Magazine,* vol. 1 (Aug. 1825) (New York: E. Bliss & E. White, 1825), 219–220.

25 "exceedingly difficult": Theophilus Parsons to HWL, Aug. 16, 1825, HL, bMS Am 1340.2 (4287).

26 Commencement address: The switch in subject titles was entered by pen in every copy of the printed program by Parker Cleaveland, an esteemed professor whom Henry would honor fifty years later with a sonnet written in his memory. See C. Wilbert Snow, "Longfellow—A Reappraisal," in *Bowdoin College Bulletin, Henry Wadsworth Longfellow Sesquicentennial Issue,* no. 327 (Dec. 1957), 9.

26 "But as yet": HWL Bowdoin Oration, "Our Native Writers," in Higginson, 30–36.

26 Benefactor of Modern Languages chair: Sarah Bowdoin (1761–1826), widow of James Bowdoin III (1752–1811), first patron of the college.

27 "a love for ancient . . . self-instruction": Hillard, vol. 1, 9–11. For more on George Ticknor, see Tyack, passim, and Long, 3–62.

28 "you would splendidly fill": Thomas Jefferson to George Ticknor, Oct. 25, 1818, in Hillard, vol. 1, 302.

29 "the first noteworthy": Henry Grattan Doyle, "George Ticknor," in *The Modern Language Journal,* vol. 22, no. 1 (Oct. 1937), 3–18.

29 "The fortune he inherited": Hillard, vol. 1, 335.

29 "I dined to-day": HWL to ZL, May 2, 1826, *Letters,* vol. 1, 151–152.

30 "this great Babylon": HWL to SL, June 20, 1826, ibid., 162–164.

30 "I have not yet": HWL to his "dear parents," July 11, 1826, ibid., 169–171.

30 "I have settled down": HWL to his brother Stephen, July 23, 1826, ibid., 173–175.

30 "You will allow me": SL to HWL, Sept. 24, 1826, HL, Am 1340.2 (3516).

31 "perfectly at home": HWL to SL, June 20, 1826, *Letters,* vol. 1, 162–164.

31 Hike through the Loire: Henry carried with him a copy of *Itinéraire abrégé du Royaume de France* by Hyacinthe Langlois père, an all-purpose guidebook with a foldout map offering advice on points of interest, transportation, cuisine, and wines. Heavily annotated, the copy is signed by Henry and dated October 1, 1826.

31 "Henri": HWL to ZL, Oct. 19. 1826, *Letters,* vol. 1, 189–192.

31 "The question then": HWL to SL, Oct. 19, 1826, ibid., 185–189.

31 "If the state of Spain": SL to HWL, Dec. 3, 1826, HL, Am 1340.2 (3516).

32 "I shall leave Paris": HWL to SL, Feb. 13, 1827, *Letters,* vol. 1, 211–213.

2 · AWAKENING

33 "A restless spirit": HWL, chapter 1, *The Schoolmaster,* published without attribution, in *The New-England Magazine,* July 1831.

33   "Tell me": HWL, *Outre-Mer: A Pilgrimage Beyond the Sea,* 2 vols. (New York: Harper & Bros., 1835), vol. 1, 215.

34   Longfellow and multiculturalism: See Christoph Irmscher, "Cosmopolite at Home," in *Cambridge Companion to the Literature of the American Renaissance,* ed. Christopher N. Phillips (Cambridge: Cambridge University Press, 2018), 66–79.

34   "If not": HWL to his sisters, Sept. 1, 1828, *Letters,* vol. 1, 278–280.

34   "As many languages": HWL, Harvard lecture, "History of the Modern Languages," Sept. 11, 1844, HL, MS Am 1340 (49).

34   "Like all other people": HWL to ZL, Nov. 27, 1828, *Letters,* vol. 1, 281–283. For more on Goldsmith's "The Traveler," see Lee Storm, "Conventional Ethics in Goldsmith's 'The Traveler,' " *Studies in English Literature, 1500–1900* (Summer 1977), 463–476.

34   "Every reader has": "Remarks in Presenting the Resolutions Upon the Death of Irving at a Meeting of the Massachusetts Historical Society," Dec. 15, 1859, in *Life,* vol. 1, 12.

34   *Sketchbook of Geoffrey Crayon*: See Jeffrey Rubin-Dorsky, "The Value of Storytelling: 'Rip Van Winkle' and 'The Legend of Sleepy Hollow' in the Context of 'The Sketch Book,' " in *Modern Philology,* vol. 82, no. 4 (May 1985), 393–406.

35   "Europe was rich": Washington Irving, *History, Tales and Sketches,* ed. James Tuttleton (New York: Library of America, 1983), 744.

35   "To horse": HWL Spanish Journal, HL, MS Am 1340 (172).

35   *Childe Harold* left in Rome: HWL to George Washington Greene (hereafter GWG), Dec. 18, 1828, *Letters,* vol. 1, 283–286. Longfellow even advised Greene to read the book: "It will serve you, when you come on here."

35   Lord Byron's gondolier: HWL to ZL, Dec. 20, 1828, *Letters,* vol. 1, 288–291. See also Paul R. Baker, "Lord Byron and the Americans in Italy," in *Keats-Shelley Journal,* vol. 13 (Winter 1964), 61–75.

36   "famoso poeta": HWL Italy Journal, HL Am MS Am 1340 (178). For more on Toni Toscan, and his relationship with Lord Byron, see Irmscher, *Longfellow Redux,* 160–174.

36   "I will not say . . . every temptation": ZL to HWL, May 7, 1826, HL, bMS Am 1340.2 (3520).

36   "It is impossible": SL to HWL, undated, quoted in Thompson, 85–86. Original in HL, bMS Am 1340.2, (3516).

37   "all of which": HWL to SL, March 20, 1827, *Letters,* vol. 1, 216–223.

37   "a huge covered wagon": HWL to ZL, May 13, 1827, ibid., 223–227.

37   "The family with whom": HWL to SL, March 20, 1827, ibid., 216–223.

37   "one of the sweetest": HWL letter to ZL, May 13, 1827, ibid., 223–227.

38   "A year today": HWL Journal, May 15, 1827.

38   "Thus I have seen": Ibid., June 6, 1827.

38   "for although": HWL to SL, July 16, 1827, *Letters,* vol. 1, 225–228.

39   "a young countryman": [Alexander Slidell Mackenzie] *A Year in Spain by a Young American,* 2 vols. (London: John Murray, 1831), vol. 1, 335.

39   "I did not like . . . only at Florencia": Ibid., 190–192.

40   "in the hired house": *Outre-Mer,* vol. 1, 214.

40   "a beautiful girl . . . confidence": Ibid., 217–218.

41   "from my memory": Alexander Slidell Mackenzie (ASM), *Spain Revisited,* 2 vols. (London: Richard Bentley, 1836), vol. 1, 203–204.

41   "the mules": ASM to HWL, June 30, 1828, HL bMS Am 1340.2 (3661).

42 "I hope you were not": ASM to HWL, Feb. 15, 1829, HL bMS Am 1340.2 (3661).

42 "My dear Don Enrique": ASM to HWL, Nov. 17, 1829, ibid.

42 "You say little": ASM to HWL, Feb. 20, 1830, ibid.

43 "a very intelligent": ASM to HWL, June 10, 1843, ibid.

43 José Cortés y Sesti: Fifty letters to Henry in Houghton Library, Letters to Henry Wadsworth Longfellow bMS Am 1340.2–1340.7, bMS Am 1340.2 (1319), all in Spanish, several with postscripts added by Florencia González. None of the letters sent by Henry to him—or possibly, by extension, through him to Florencia—have been recovered, according to Professor Iván Jaksić: especially unfortunate since their friendship covered a thirty-year period. For more on Longfellow's time in Spain, see also Whitman, passim.

43 "Florencia's *modus operandi*": Author email exchange with Iván Jaksić, Nov. 7, 2018. For more on José Cortés y Sesti, and the mutual friendship with Florencia González, see Jaksić, 95–96.

43 "with pleasure": Florencia González to HWL, 1835, HL bMS Am 1340.2 (2298). My gratitude to Professor Jaksić for his full translation of this letter from the Spanish.

45 Nicholas Trübner, James Lenox, John Carter Brown: See Basbanes, *A Gentle Madness,* 157–160.

45 "I have a box": Alexander Everett to HWL, undated ["1827" added in pencil], HL, bMS Am 1340.2 (1879).

45 "how much satisfaction": Lucretia Everett to Mrs. Daveis, quoted in *Life,* vol. 1, 127.

45 "I think it a very good sign": ZL to HWL, April 12, 1828, HL, bMS Am 1340.2 (3520).

46 "I thought Longfellow's": George Ticknor letter recommending Henry to fill a teaching position in New York, which he did not get; June 18, 1834, HL bMS 1340.2 (1035).

46 "I am traveling": HWL to ZL, Jan. 23, 1828, in *Letters,* vol. 1, 253.

47 "played 'Yankee Doodle' ": HWL to ZL, Jan. 23, 1828, ibid., 253.

47 "We breakfast at noon": *Outre-Mer,* vol. 1, 153.

47 "There are three": HWL to ZL, March 26, 1828, *Letters,* vol. 1, 256–258.

47 "antiqua flamma": HWL to GWG, Aug. 2, 1842, Ibid., vol. 2, 450–2. This letter was written to Greene from Germany, where Longfellow was spending several months taking a water cure for various unspecified ailments. He was hoping to spend some time in Paris, where he understood Giulia Persiani was living. The full quote: "Please send me in your next the name of Julia's husband, and their address in Paris. I want to see once more my *antiqua flamma.*" Greene wrote back on Aug. 16, 1842: "You will find Julia here with all her family. The old lady is dead: the girls still unmarried and with precious little chance of ever getting husbands, unless their faces should change or some old codger leave them an attractive dowry." In HL, MS Am 1340.2-1340.7, MS Am 1340.2 (2379). Henry was probably inspired to use the phrase from Dante, who refers to Beatrice in *Purgatorio* XXX as *l'antica flamma,* "the ancient flame" of his youth. See Alan Tate, "The Symbolic Imagination: A Meditation on Dante's Three Mirrors," in *The Kenyon Review,* vol. 14, no. 2 (Spring, 1952), 256–277.

48 "violent cold": *Life,* vol. 1, 149.

49 "brought the story": HWL to GWG, Oct. 1, 1839, *Letters,* vol. 2, 177–179.

49 "solitary supper": HWL to GWG, Jan. 2, 1840, ibid., 200–205.

49 "imperishable beauty . . . best flowers": These quotations from Nicander's personal journal were translated from the Swedish for me by Niclas Wallin, a former anti-

quarian bookseller, of Stockholm. They appear in a chapter on Nicander's relationship with Giulia Persiani, and his friendship with Longfellow, in Gunnar Lokrantz, *Karl August Nicander* (Uppsala: Almqvist & Wiksells Boktryckeri—A.—B., 1939), 241–255. My gratitude to James Feeney, circulation director at the Boston Athenæum, for locating a copy of this scarce book for my examination.

50 "We wandered . . . mural crown": Quoted in Amandus Johnson, "The Relation of Longfellow to Scandinavian Literature," *The American Scandinavian Review*, vol. 3, no. 1 (Jan. 1915), 39–43. Henry's lengthy description of their evening at the Colosseum—he spells it "Coliseum"—is in *Outre-Mer*, vol. 2, 168–172, which begins: "I have just returned from the Coliseum, whose ruins are so marvellously beautiful by moonlight."

51 "I assure you . . . desire the situation": HWL to SL, *Letters*, vol. 1, 286–288.

52 "young, lovable Longfellow": Nicander journal.

53 "The March of Mind in the East": "The Old Dominion," in HL, MS Am 1340.2.

54 Support for Greene: In addition to underwriting the publication of Greene's biography of his grandfather, and providing occasional assistance for his family, Henry's account book shows that he gave his friend a monthly stipend of fifty dollars over the final four years of his life, the initials "GWG," and the amount, always at the top of each month's summary of payments.

54 "What a devourer of books": HWL to GWG, April 29, 1877, *Letters*, vol. 6, 268.

3 · THE HOLY ONES

55 "I think I have formed": HWL to Judge Barrett Potter, Sept. 26, 1830, *Letters*, vol. 1, 348.

55 "Yesterday I was at": HWL to GWG, May 21, 1837, ibid., vol. 2, 28.

56 "an infected incomplete miscarriage": Hilen, in *Diary of Clara Crowninshield* (hereafter *Crowninshield*), 177.

56 "I have a great desire": Clara Crowninshield letter to Lydia Nichols Pierce, wife of her legal guardian, Jan. 30, 1835, original in Peabody-Essex Museum, Salem, MA, quoted in *Crowninshield*, xxiii.

56 "Mr. and Mrs. Carlyle": Mary Storer Potter Longfellow (MSP) to ZL, "New Longfellow Letters, with Commentary by Mary Thacher Higginson," *Harper's Monthly Magazine*, April 1903, 779–786.

57 "a young and rather raw": HWL Journal, May 25, 1835.

57 "an unused repository": Roger Michener, "Henry Wadsworth Longfellow: Librarian of Bowdoin College, 1829–35," *The Library Quarterly*, vol. 43, no. 3 (July 1973), 215–226.

57 Italian reading book: See *Bibliography of American Literature* (BAL), 474–475; also HWL to Gray & Bowen, the Boston publisher, March 29, 1832, in *Letters*, vol. 1, 370–371.

57 *Catalogue of the Library of Bowdoin College* (Brunswick, ME: Griffin's Press, 1821). Bowdoin College Special Collections, MZ90:J5, 1821, interleaved.

58 "This compendious": H. W. Longfellow, *Syllabus de la Grrammaire Italienne* (Boston: Gray & Bowen, 1832), copyright page.

58 "double": Austin, 177.

58 "His heart": Samuel Longfellow, *Life*, vol. 1, 187.

58 "Portland young men": Mary Thacher Higginson, "New Longfellow Letters, with

Commentary by Mary Thacher Higginson," *Harper's Monthly Magazine,* April 1903, 779–786.

59 Mary Storer Potter: [Horace P. Chandler], "Longfellow's First Wife and Early Friends," in *Every Other Saturday,* Jan. 19, 1884, vol. 1, no. 2, 20–21.

59 "I most ardently": HWL to Barrett Potter, in *Letters,* Sept. 26, 1830, vol. 1, 348.

59 "I certainly never": MSP to Anne Longfellow (hereafter ALP), June 20, 1831, in Mary Thacher Higginson, 799–786.

59 "Her character": *Life,* vol. 1, 187–188.

59 "My first impression": Quoted in Higginson, 61–62.

60 "His intercourse with": Quoted in *Life,* vol. 1, 182. Cyrus Hamlin (1811–1900), missionary, educator, college president, author, and inventor of the first functional steam engine in the state of Maine, which is still preserved at Owls Head Transportation Museum in Rockland.

60 "I am sorry to find": ASM to HWL, Nov. 17, 1829, HL bMS Am 1340.2 (3661).

60 "this miserable": HWL to James Berdan, *Letters,* vol. 1, Jan. 4, 1831, 351–352.

60 "You call it a dog's life": HWL to ALP, Aug. 21, 1831, ibid., 383.

60 "I have been laboring": HWL to GWG, June 2, 1832, ibid., 373–376.

61 "You will excuse me": HWL to Alexander H. Everett, July 16, 1833, ibid., 419–420.

62 "I suppose you think": HWL to GWG, Feb. 13, 1834, ibid., 429-431.

62 "The Wondrous Tale": James Taft Hatfield, "An Unknown Prose Tale by Longfellow," in *American Literature,* vol. 3, no. 2 (May 1931), 136–148. Supporting correspondence: the clincher being a letter to Longfellow from Clark, dated Dec. 10, 1834: "Haven't you got $50 from Greeley through your *nom de guerre,* in Boston? Please let me know."

63 "from the pen": *The American Monthly Review,* no. 20 (August 1833) (Boston: Russell, Odiorner & Co., 1833), 157–160; see also Loring E. Hart, "The Beginnings of Longfellow's Fame," *New England Quarterly,* vol. 36, no. 1 (March 1963), 63–76.

63 "It is not unreasonable": Higginson, 60.

64 Josiah Quincy: Josiah Quincy to HWL, Dec. 1, 1834, quoted in *Letters,* vol. 1, 459.

64 "Good fortune": HWL to SL, Dec. 2, 1834, ibid.

64 "While my little boy": George Ticknor to C. S. Daveis, Aug. 20, 1834, in Hillard, 398–399.

65 "become the standard": Thomas R. Hart Jr., "George Ticknor's History of Spanish Literature: The New England Background," in *PMLA,* vol. 69, no. 1 (March 1954), 76–88.

65 George Ticknor as bibliophile: See my books *A Gentle Madness* and *Patience & Fortitude.*

65 "With respect": SL to HWL, Dec. 8, 1834, HL, Am 1340.2 (3516).

65 "How often": Mary Potter Longfellow to Barrett Potter, Sept. 13, 1835, in "New Longfellow Letters, with Comment by Mary Thacher Higginson," *Harper's Monthly,* vol. 106, no. 635 (April 1903), 779–786.

66 *Kalevala*: See Waino Nyland, "Kalevala as a Reputed Source of Longfellow's Song of Hiawatha," in *American Literature,* vol. 22, no. 1 (March 1950), 1–20.

66 "far different": Mary Potter Longfellow to Stephen and Zilpah Longfellow, July 14, 1833, in "New Longfellow Letters," *Harper's Monthly Magazine,* April 1903. For more on Henry's work with Scandinavian languages, see George L. White, "Longfellow's Interest in Scandinavia During the Years 1835–1847," in *Scandinavian Studies,* vol. 17, no. 2 (May 1942), 70–82.

66 "Thank you for the acquaintanceship": Quoted by Hilen, in Crowninshield, 98.

67 "Just before I sailed": HWL to Margaret Potter Thacher, Feb. 15, 1843, *Letters,* vol. 2, 505–506. With the exception of a diary Henry kept during his six-month trip to Europe in 1842, there is a four-year gap in his private journal (May 7, 1840, to July 14, 1844); whatever entries he may have recorded then were likely among the personal materials he admits in this letter to having destroyed at this time.

68 "Though her sickness . . . unspeakable": HWL to Barrett Potter, Dec. 1, 1835, *Letters,* vol. 1, 526–528.

68 "Henry has given up": Mary Potter Longfellow to Barrett Potter, Sept. 13, 1835, in "New Longfellow Letters," *Harper's Monthly Magazine,* April 1903.

69 "How everything": Crowninshield, 296.

69 "What a prisoner's life": Ibid., 165.

70 "worst symptom": Ibid., 182.

70 "Little Mary is slowly recovering": HWL Journal, Nov. 1, 1835.

70 "Mary is better": Ibid., Nov. 25, 1835.

70 "This morning": Ibid., Nov. 29, 1835.

70 "Her face . . . resignation": Crowninshield, 183–184.

71 "She was very much changed": Ibid., 184.

71 Henry ("Harry") Wadsworth Longfellow Dana (1881–1950): The son of Richard Henry Dana III and Edith Longfellow Dana; his paternal grandfather, Richard Henry Dana Jr., was the author of *Two Years Before the Mast.* Harry Dana was the resident curator of Longfellow House for thirty-three years. See the excellent biographical essay and chronology in the finding aid to his papers, LONG 17314, which comprise 114 linear feet of archival material.

71 "It was not a fortunate one": Crowninshield, 95.

73 Portrait of Mary in basement storage: LONG 4423-1.

73 "Professor Longfellow": Will of Elizabeth Craigie, in the hand of Lemuel Shaw, collections of the Cambridge Historical Society, in Craigie Family archive.

73 Elizabeth Melville Thomas Metcalf: For more on her work as Melville scholar, editor, and custodian of archival materials, see Wyn Kelley, "Out of the Bread Box: Eleanor Melville Metcalf and the Melville Legacy," *Leviathan,* vol. 13, no. 1 (March 2011): 21–33, available online through MIT Open Access Articles.

74 "Mrs. Metcalf remembers": Harry Dana's one-page accession notes for the Potter painting, LONG 4423-1.

74 "The world considers grief": HWL letter to Eliza Potter, Cambridge, Sunday Evening [1836], in Higginson, 113–115, and *Letters,* vol. 1, 568–569.

000 an evening visitation: HWL Journal, March 26, 1839.

76 "Oh, give details": Ibid., Aug. 5, 1838.

4 · CHILD OF THE TEMPEST

78 "She kept her eyes": Journal that Fanny and Mary kept jointly, LONG 21578 FEAL-MAM Journal (June 17, 1832–July 14, 1833), Feb. 10, 1832.

78 "This evening Father arrived": Mary Appleton, ibid., Feb. 11, 1833.

78 Thomas Gold Appleton (1812–1884): Like his sister Fanny, Tom had artistic aspirations, and dabbled as a painter, writer, and poet. He published several books in his lifetime, most notably *Faded Leaves* (1872), a collection of poems; *A Sheaf of Papers* (1875), a collection of essays; and *A Nile Journal* (1876), the record of one of his

many trips abroad. The Massachusetts Historical Society has an extensive archive of his personal papers, in Ms. N-1778. For a full biographical treatment, see Tharp, passim.

79   Niagara Falls and New England: For discussion of Fanny's art on this trip, see Diana Korzenik, "Face to Face: Fanny Appleton and the Old Man of the Mountain," in *Historical New Hampshire,* vol. 63, no. 2 (Fall 2009), 121–139. For more on the trip itself, see Tharp, 141–153.

79   "We are now": Frances Elizabeth Appleton (hereafter FEAL) to Robert Apthorp, Oct. 29, 1835, B2-F5-I8.

80   "Flowers and kind wishes": Frances Elizabeth Appleton Journal FEAL 21857 (hereafter FEAL Journal), Nov. 16, 1835.

81   "SKETCHES": Green leather volume, with FEA on the back. LONG 18490.

81   "Reclined on a coil": Ibid., Nov. 16, 1835.

81   "We are off Sandy Hook": Ibid., Nov. 17, 1835.

81   "We are agreeably": Ibid.

82   "I am now": Ibid.

82   Cleaveland Alexander Forbes: Forbes Family Papers (Manuscript Collection 293), G. W. Blunt Library, Mystic Seaport Museum, Mystic, CT; folder 1 includes biographical information on the captain, his seagoing family, and historical information on the *Francis Depau.*

82   "truly 'mountain high' ": FEAL to Robert Apthorp, Dec. 3, 1835, FEAL B2-F5-I10.

83   "called upon deck": FEAL Journal, Nov. 17, 1835.

83   "radiant with a clear": Ibid., Nov. 20, 1835.

83   "I have longed": FEAL letter to Robert Apthorp, Dec. 3, 1835, FEAL-B2-F5-I10.

83   "crawled up": FEAL Journal, Nov. 22, 1835.

84   "The lovely": Ibid., Dec. 5, 1835.

84   traveling desks: with label for T. Dalton of Great Ormond St., LONG 18564; with "Frances E. Appleton, 1832" engraved inside, LONG 36537.

84   "Today we surmise": FEAL to Robert Apthorp, Dec. 3, 1835. FEAL-B2-F5-I10.

84   Nathan Appleton and Maria Theresa Gold Appleton: See Gregory, passim; Winthrop, passim; Tharp, passim.

85   "a man of elegant": J. E. A. Smith, *The History of Pittsfield (Berkshire County), Massachusetts* (Springfield, MA: C. W. Bryan, 1876), 70.

85   Berry Street Academy: Grace Overmyer, *America's First Hamlet* (New York: New York University Press, 1957), a biographical study of John Howard Payne and his family, with a segment on the school, 33–39. See too Katharine H. Rich, "Beacon," in *Old-Time New England,* vol. 66, no. 243 (Winter/Spring 1976), 42–60.

86   Gilbert Stuart and Boston: George C. Mason, *The Life and Works of Gilbert Stuart* (New York: Charles Scribner's Sons, 1894), 28.

86   "The sentiment": Quoted in Diana Korzenik, "Becoming an Art Teacher c. 1800," in *Art Education,* vol. 52, no. 2 (March 1999), 6–13.

88   "hub of the solar system": The phrase first appeared in an "Autocrat of the Breakfast Table" essay Oliver Wendell Holmes wrote for the October 1858 issue of *The Atlantic Monthly:* "Boston State-House is the hub of the solar system. You couldn't pry that out of a Boston man, if you had the tire of all creation straightened out for a crowbar."

88   Boston Athenæum: For more on this remarkable cultural institution, see my book *A Gentle Madness,* 154–157.

88 "I urged him": Nathan Appleton, *Introduction of the Power Loom and Origin of Lowell* (Lowell, MA: B. H. Penhallow, 1858), 7. See also Robert F. Dalzell Jr., *Enterprising Elite: The Boston Associates and the World They Made* (Cambridge, MA: Harvard University Press, 1987).

90 "a very intelligent": Catharine Maria Sedgwick, quoted in Marshall, 179–180.

90 "Her chief difficulty . . . immediate improvement": Elizabeth Palmer Peabody to Nathan Appleton, Feb. 12, 1827, Series I, Nathan Appleton Correspondence in the Appleton Family Papers, Longfellow House—Washington's Headquarters National Historic Site (LH), LONG 20256.

91 "I now go": FEAL to Thomas Gold Appleton (hereafter TGA), Feb. 20, 1827, FEAL-B2-F1-I3.

91 "my intentions respecting . . . health of her mind": Elizabeth Palmer Peabody to Nathan Appleton, undated, but internal evidence establishes 1827, in Bruce A. Ronda, ed., *Letters of Elizabeth Palmer Peabody, American Renaissance Woman* (Middletown, CT: Wesleyan University Press, 1984), 78–82.

93 "Mademoiselle Frances": French notebook with tutor George Barrell Emerson, in Frances Elizabeth Appleton Longfellow Papers, LONG 21583.

93 "a gentleman who": Elizabeth Peabody, in the preface to the second edition of *Record of a School* (Boston: Russell, Shattuck & Co., 1836), xxii.

93 Lorenzo Papanti: See Crawford, 314–315.

93 Frances Erskine Inglis (1804–1882): In 1836, Fanny's former music teacher married the Spanish nobleman and politician Ángel Calderón de la Barca y Belgrano and became known as Marquesa Calderón de la Barca. In 1843, she wrote *Life in Mexico*, an influential travel narrative of the period. She retained close contact with her Boston friends, notably the historian William Hickling Prescott, who kept her up to date on local happenings. See Marion Hall Fisher, passim.

93 "in every branch of learning": For more on the Inglis school in Boston, see Fisher, 167–175.

94 "Fanny Calderón was here": FEAL to EAW, April 19, 1842, FEAL-B3-F13-I73.

94 Francis Lieber: See Freidel, passim.

95 "the heroine of the world": Frances Elizabeth Appleton Longfellow Journal, LONG 21587 (Nov. 16, 1835–Jan. 31, 1836), Dec. 6, 1835. Hereafter FEAL Journal.

95 "lullabies of creaking masts": Ibid.

95 "mirrored and curtained": Ibid., Dec. 12, 1835.

96 "I cannot attempt": Ibid., Dec. 17, 1835.

96 "the atmosphere of poetry": Ibid., Dec. 18, 1835.

96 Dual portrait by Isabey: LONG 4152.

96 "He is a charming": Ibid., Dec. 29. 1835.

96 "The largest is a sort": Ibid., Jan. 22, 1836.

97 "We left Paris": Ibid.

98 Fanny's writing interests: "Would I not gain a living as authoress of 'Tourist's Guides'?", FEAL to Robert Apthorp, Nov. 17, 1836, FEAL-B2-F6-I4; "I remember, in my despair, I often thought of writing some [children's books] myself knowing so well what pleased best my own children." FEAL to EAW, April 16, 1852, FEAL-B3-F2-I10.

98 "You know how I love": FEAL to Robert Apthorp, Aug. 20, 1835, FEAL-B2-F5-I6.

98 "Coining words": FEAL to Isaac Appleton Jewett (IAJ), Aug. 26, 1838, FEAL-B2-F8-I3. A lawyer by training, Jewett (1808–1853) was the son of Nathan Appleton's

youngest sister, Emily. He aspired to be a writer, and published a two-volume travelogue based on the European trip he made with his cousins in 1835–37, *Passages in
Foreign Travel* (Boston: Little, Brown, 1838). His disapproval of Fanny's decision to
marry Henry effectively ended what had been a rich and fruitful correspondence.

5 · MOVING ON

100   "A beautiful morning": HWL Journal, Nov. 24, 1835.

100   "Clara is still": Ibid., Dec. 2, 1835.

101   "just at the moment": Ibid.

101   "I could not get him": Ibid., Dec. 7, 1835.

101   "ignorant of everything": Henry Wadsworth Longfellow, *Hyperion, a Romance*, 2
       vols. (New York: Samuel Colman, 1839), vol. 2, 110.

101   "She says you have": Ibid., vol. 1, 109.

101   "They are the best": HWL to SL, May 8, 1836, *Letters*, vol. 1, 550–551.

102   "buried himself in books": *Hyperion*, vol. 2, 93.

102   "I will read and write": Crowninshield, 210.

102   "no mean mastery": Hatfield, 38.

102   "The clock is even now": HWL Journal, Dec. 17, 1835.

103   "the sense of my bereavement": HWL to SL, Jan. 24, 1836, *Letters*, vol. 1, 538–540.

103   "I like them all": Crowninshield, 213.

103   "I feel far happier": Ibid., 215.

103   "Called on Bryant": HWL Journal, Dec. 11, 1835.

104   "expired with perfect": HWL to George Ticknor, Dec. 19, 1835, *Letters*, vol. 1,
       529–531.

104   "Monsieur le Professeur": George Ticknor to HWL, Dec. 25, 1835, HL bMS Am
       1340.2 (5546).

104   "a journey of sentiment": Edward C. Steadman, *The Century Illustrated Monthly
       Magazine*, vol. 26, 1883.

104   "Henry has become quite": Quoted in Higginson, 99.

104   "We compared it": HWL Journal, Aug. 13, 1835.

105   *Frithiof's Saga*: Hatfield, 36–37.

105   "rather unkind and unnatural": Crowninshield, 221.

105   Clara's share of the expenses: HWL Account Book, 1835–1840, in HL, MS Am 1340
       (150), entries on pages 115–117, "Miss Crowninshield's Account," and also 127, 129.

106   literary history of the Middle Ages: bound manuscript of this unpublished work,
       HL, Am MS 1340 (8).

106   "I have a blank book": HWL to GWG, Feb. 1836, *Letters*, vol. 1, 540–544.

106   book purchases for Harvard: See Johnson, 16–21. Henry would later learn that
       three trunks of books he had shipped to Boston from Rotterdam had been lost with
       the sinking of the brig *Hollander* "in sight of her port," the titles "rare and curious
       Dutch books; the harvest of a months toil among the book-stalls of Amsterdam."
       He found their loss lamentable. "The books were really too good to be sunk;—they
       were food for worms—not fishes. And so goes the entire collection of Dutch litera-
       ture." HWL to George Ticknor, May 9, 1836, *Letters*, vol. 1, 552–554.

106   "I am sorry": George Ticknor to HWL, March 29, 1836, quoted in full in Johnson,
       19–20. Ticknor's manuscript letters to HWL are in HL bMS Am 1340.2 (5546).

106   "The part relevant": HWL Journal, Feb. 20, 1836.

106 "nearly froze myself to death": Ibid., Feb. 19, 1836.

107 "The winter . . . upon themselves": Ibid., Feb. 20, 1836.

107 Samuel Ward: See Lately Thomas, *Sam Ward: "King of the Lobby"* (Boston: Houghton Mifflin, 1965).

107 "He knows many": HWL Journal, March 17, 1836.

107 "desultory tatter": Ibid., March 18, 1836.

108 "the most remarkable": Cornelius Conway Felton to HWL, June 15, 1842, Hl, bMS Am 1340.2 (1941).

108 "Longfellow had . . . ever since": Samuel Ward, "Days with Longfellow," *North American Review,* vol. 134, no. 306 (May 1882), 456–466.

108 "no interest": Crowninshield, 218.

109 "a miscellaneous youth": *Hyperion,* vol. 1, 55.

109 "It is strange how soon": Ibid., 186.

109 "perfectly faithful representation": In Henry Wadsworth Longfellow, *Hyperion: A Romance,* illustrated by Birket Foster (London: David Bogue, 1853), artist's note to the reader. Longfellow wrote approvingly of the artist's work in an itemization of paintings contained in Craigie House, including two original scenes from *Hyperion* Foster sent to him personally as gifts.

109 "The clock is just striking": HWL Journal, June 4, 1836.

110 "At table": Crowninshield, 283.

110 "It is certainly": Ibid., 286.

110 "I have a proposition": HWL to GWG, June 5, 1836, *Letters,* vol. 1, 554–557.

110 "if we can find": HWL to George Ticknor, May 9, 1836, ibid., vol. 1, 552–554.

110 "I think you must be crazy": HWL to Samuel Ward, June 22, 1836, ibid., vol. 1, 558–560.

111 "So once more": HWL Journal, June 19, 1836.

111 "The day is bright": HWL Journal, June 23, 1836.

111 "It is now nearly": HWL Journal, June 24, 1836.

112 "companion": *Life,* vol. 1, 212. Elsewhere in this chapter, Sam Longfellow refers to Henry and Clara simply as "our travelers."

112 "You always say": Crowninshield, xxvii.

112 "What this paragraph means": Andrew Hilen, in Crowninshield, xxvii. In *Longfellow in Love: Passion and Tragedy in the Life of the Poet* (Jefferson, NC: McFarland, 2018), 90–92, independent scholar Edward M. Cifelli offers as suggestive evidence of a brief affair between Longfellow and Crowninshield diary entries made by Frances Bryant, the wife of William Cullen Bryant, who deeply resented Henry's abrupt decision to leave Clara in her care in Heidelberg, and travel by himself to Switzerland; there are no other such contemporary speculations.

112 "Went to find my good": HWL Journal, March 24, 1838. One folder of miscellaneous materials in Craigie House contains a business card with Henry's name engraved on the front, a brief note to Clara Crowninshield scribbled on the back to accompany his gift to her of a book in German.

113 "But a trifle": *Life,* vol. 1, 227.

114 "A private journal": HWL Journal, May 21, 1835–July 17, 1836, HL, MS Am 1340 (188).

114 HWL study of languages: see Frederick Burwick, "Longfellow and German Romanticism," *Comparative Literature Studies,* vol. 7, no. 1 (March 1970), 12–42;

W. A. Chamberlin, "Longfellow's Attitude Toward Goethe," *Modern Philology*, vol. 16, no. 2 (June 1918), 57–76.

6 · BELLISSIMA ITALIA

115 "I sat down upon": LONG 21588, FEAL Journal (Feb. 1, 1836–May 9, 1836), Feb. 2, 1836. Hereafter FEAL Journal.

115 laurel leaf: Ibid., Feb. 1, 1836.

115 "pretty little garden . . . eddies": Ibid., Feb. 2, 1836.

116 "a little Eden": FEAL to Robert Apthorp, Feb. 2, 1836, FEAL-B2-F6-I1.

116 "so rich and heavenly . . . made to sketch": Ibid., Feb. 6, 1836.

116 "forest of masts": FEAL Journal, Feb. 5, 1836.

117 "You express": FEAL to Susan Benjamin, Feb. 18, 1836, FEAL-B2-F6-I2.

118 "It is of most singular": FEAL Journal, Feb. 19, 1836.

118 "looked like": Ibid., Feb. 16, 1836.

118 "procession of beautiful . . . of our dreams": Ibid., Feb. 21, 1836.

119 "chisels and hammers . . . in his Court": Ibid., Feb. 22, 1836.

119 "Can I believe . . . What rapture": Ibid., March 1, 1836.

120 "Hardly knew . . . live fast": Ibid., March 3, 1836.

121 "I saw it would . . . 'folly of feeling' ": Ibid., March 4, 1836.

122 Beatrice Cenci (1577–1599): An Italian noblewoman who murdered a highly abusive father after repeated pleas to authorities for help went unheeded. Condemned to death in a lurid trial, her resistance to an arrogant aristocracy has been celebrated in numerous literary, musical, and artistic works as an example of heroic womanhood, and was especially appealing to Fanny Appleton.

122 "a small collection . . . fine it is": FEAL Journal, March 5, 1836.

122 "the lovely little": Ibid., March 7, 1836.

122 "rush and whirlpool . . . pedestal": Ibid., March 9, 1836.

123 "a lovely morning": Ibid., March 11, 1836.

123 "There was something": Ibid., March 18, 1836.

123 "lovely spot": Ibid., April 7, 1836.

123 "take the veil": Ibid., March 13, 1836.

124 "sit, and study": Ibid., March 14, 1836.

124 "a long row": Ibid., March 15, 1836.

124 "Sweetest Emmelina . . of the ruins": FEAL to EAW, March 22, 1836.

125 "Many a Niobe glance": FEAL Journal, April 11, 1836.

126 "if a Circe": Ibid., April 13, 1836.

126 "They are black strips . . . million years": Ibid., April 15, 1836.

126 "At a first glance": Ibid., April 26, 1836.

127 "Our situation": Ibid., May 8, 1836.

128 "bought gloves": LONG 21591 (May 9, 1836–Aug. 21, 1836), May 19, 1836.

128 "met beaux . . . soul sleeps": Ibid., May 20, 1836.

128 "Made a short": Ibid., May 28, 1836.

129 "a quiet I always": Ibid., June 19, 1836.

129 "after such": Ibid., May 19, 1836.

129 "Driving along": Ibid., May 23, 1836.

129 "I sit": Ibid., May 24, 1836.

129   "He gets very much": Ibid., May 28, 1836.

130   "He was the most peace-loving": Ibid., May 23, 1836.

130   "It is hard": Ibid., May 28, 1836.

130   "to look my last": Ibid., June 2, 1836.

131   "ran thro'": Ibid., June 1, 1836.

131   "I should so like": Ibid., June 7, 1836.

131   "It must have been": Ibid., June 8, 1836.

132   "a long chat": Ibid., June 9, 1836.

132   "Seated ourselves": Ibid., June 10, 1836.

132   "we tried to believe": Ibid., June 11, 1836.

132   "more perfect": Ibid., June 14, 1836.

132   "tolerable . . . from marble": Ibid., June 18, 1836.

133   "Addio bello Milano": Ibid., June 19, 1836.

133   "There was a magic": Ibid., June 22, 1836.

133   "farewell row": Ibid., June 23, 1836.

7 · SWITZERLAND

134   "Perhaps the best": William Hazlitt, "On the Fear of Death," in *Table Talk; or Original Essays on Men and Manners* (London: Henry Colburn, 1824), vol. 2, 381–401. See also W. P. Albrecht, "Hazlitt's 'On the Fear of Death': Reason Versus Imagination," in *The Wordsworth Circle*, vol. 15, no. 1 (Winter 1984), 3–7.

134   "noble mountains . . . his *Outre-Mer*": LONG 21591, FEAL Journal, May 9, 1836–Oct. 26, 1836, July 20, 1836.

135   "a young man": Ibid., July 31, 1836.

135   "At the Hotel Bellevue": HWL Journal, July 20, 1836.

136   "As I have neither": Ibid., July 24, 1836.

136   "pleasant": Ibid., July 28, 1836.

136   "found the Appletons . . . quiet sleep": Ibid., July 31, 1836.

136   "After breakfast": Ibid., Aug. 1, 1836.

136   "Since I have": Ibid., Aug. 2, 1836.

136   "a large party": Ibid., Aug. 3, 1836.

136   "A day of true and quiet": Ibid., Aug. 4, 1836.

137   "to the old bridge . . . our absence": FEAL Journal, Aug. 2, 1836.

138   "Mr. L, William": Ibid., Aug. 4, 1836.

138   "Mr. L's journal": Ibid., Aug. 5, 1836.

138   "wilted and weary": Ibid., Aug. 6, 1836.

138   "waiting at the door": HWL Journal, Aug. 7, 1836.

138   "in the deep": Ibid., Aug. 10, 1836.

139   "dip into . . . for itself now": FEAL Journal, Aug. 10, 1836.

139   "very coy": Ibid., Aug. 8, 1836.

139   "some of the best lines": HWL Journal, Aug. 9, 1836.

139   "Appletoniana": LONG 8011.

139   top billing: The Houghton Library copy of Fanny's translation of the Uhland poem "*Das Schloss am Meer*" (The Castle by the Sea), MS Am 1340 (72).

140   "soul-thrilling": FEAL Journal, July 11, 1836.

140   "I sat by him": Ibid., July 14, 1836.

140   "talk about clouds . . . Everything had": Ibid., Aug. 11, 1836.

141 "The scene was perfectly": HWL Journal, Aug. 11, 1836.

141 "to hunt up . . . precious indeed": FEAL Journal, Aug. 12, 1836.

141 "It seems impossible": HWL Journal, Aug. 12, 1836.

141 "a young American": FEAL Journal, Aug. 12, 1836.

141 "While we were at dinner": HWL Journal, Aug. 12, 1836.

141 "Saw a pretty . . . birth-right": Ibid., Aug. 13, 1836.

142 "under shady trees": FEAL Journal, Aug. 14, 1836.

143 "Received a letter": HWL Journal, Aug. 17, 1836.

143 "Mr. L gets one": FEAL Journal, Aug. 17, 1836.

143 "gloomy": HWL Journal, Aug. 29, 1836.

144 "ravages of his disease": FEAL Journal, Aug. 21, 1836.

144 "He desired me": TGA to HWL, Aug. 25, 1835, in HL, Am 1340.2 (182).

144 "sweet youth . . . six weeks": Nathan Appleton, in Webster, 49–50.

144 "never did I love": FEAL to Robert Apthorp, Nov. 17, 1836, FEAL-B2-F6-I4.

8 · PENT-UP FIRE

147 "roared through . . . downcast eyes": HWL Journal, July 22, 1837.

147 "How much": HWL Journal, Feb. 27, 1838. For more on Nathan Appleton and Lowell, MA, see my book *On Paper*, 293–297.

148 "My earliest . . . Golden Legend": Charles Eliot Norton, "Reminiscences of Old Cambridge," in *Proceedings of the Cambridge Historical Society*, vol. 1, 1906, 11–34.

148 "I am now . . . mingled": HWL to GWG, Feb. 1, 1837, *Letters*, vol. 2, 12–15.

148 "To go down": HWL Journal, Sept. 3, 1838.

149 Craigie House journal: Longfellow's recollections of his earliest encounters with Mrs. Craigie, for whom he expresses a special affection, are to be found in this notebook, which includes a number of miscellaneous materials, including an annotated map in his hand of the grounds and premises, and numerous newspaper clippings from the period on its history and other occupants. HL, MS Am 1340 (159).

149 "I have found": HWL to SL, May 25, 1837, *Letters*, vol. 2, 38–40.

149 "delightfully": HWL to George Ticknor, Sept. 28, 1837, ibid., 40–42.

150 "In my new abode . . . handkerchiefs": HWL to ALP, Sept. 21, 1837, ibid., 38–41. In a March 22, 1837, letter to his father (*Letters*, vol. 2, 15–16), Henry passed on thanks to Anne "for her note and *flannel breastplates*."

150 "an abundant supply": HWL to SL, Dec. 7, 1836, ibid., vol. 1, 567–568.

150 "Just twig the Professor": verse and recollections of Phillips Brooks in *Harvard Graduate*, a university periodical, 1908, 219.

151 "Samuel Longfellow . . . and the undergraduates": Edward Everett Hale, *Memories of a Hundred Years* (New York: Macmillan, 1904), 241–247.

151 "To Boston I go . . . object in view": HWL to GWG, Feb. 1, 1837, *Letters*, vol. 2, 11–12.

152 "The Bridge": The half-mile wooden bridge across the Charles River would be replaced in 1909 by a stone-arch span the locals often call the "Salt and Pepper Bridge" for the turretlike shape of its four towers—though its formal name for more than a century has been the Longfellow Bridge. A five-year renovation project was completed in May 2018; part of the restoration involved installation of a companion walkway for foot and bicycle traffic at Charles Circle across Storrow Drive, named by order of the General Court of the Commonwealth the Frances "Fanny"

Appleton Pedestrian Bridge, "in recognition of the celebrated courtship and marriage of Frances Appleton and Henry Wadsworth Longfellow." Acts (2013–2014), chapter 108 (House Bill No. H2904).

152 "The professor called": Mary Lekain Gore Appleton to FEAL, Feb. 4, 1837, Frances Elizabeth Appleton Longfellow Papers, 1011/002.002.

152 "the attention and flattery": Ibid., April 27, 1837, box 4, folder 4, item 22.

153 "as soft and gentle": Ibid., June 25, 1837, box 4, folder 4, item 2.

153 "by the margins": HWL to FEAL, Jan. 8, 1837, *Letters*, vol. 2, 6.

153 "And now the favor": HWL to TGA, Jan. 23, 1837, ibid., 8–11.

153 "2 doz. gloves": Notebook of Nathan Appleton for miscellaneous expenses, Massachusetts Historical Society (MHS), Appleton Family Papers, Ms. N-1778, box 12.

154 "the liberty . . . may please you": HWL to FEAL, October 1837 [date approximate], *Letters*, vol. 2, 47–48.

154 "Hoping you will": HWL to FEAL, Dec. 14, 1837, ibid., 54.

154 "trusty friend-at-court": Hatfield, 50.

154 Mary Appleton Mackintosh: Four folders of letters she wrote to HWL, HL, bMS Am 1340.2-1340.7, bMS Am 1340.2 (3669).

154 "at some future day . . . very sad": HWL to MAM, Dec. 10, 1837, *Letters*, vol. 2, 50–51; full translation of German segment, 52.

155 "without delay": HWL to George Hillard, Dec. 21, 1837, ibid., 55–56.

155 "The precious lining": George Hillard to HWL, Dec. 24, 1837, HL, bMS Am 1340.2–1340.7 (2733).

156 "A leaden . . . her affection": HWL to GWG, Jan. 6, 1838, *Letters*, vol. 2, 58–60.

157 "This closely written": Thompson, 403.

157 Lawrance Thompson and Harry Dana: Craigie House documents discussing Thompson's access to materials for his work on the book *Young Longfellow* cover ten years, 1932 to 1942, and are kept in two onsite collections; four folders of miscellaneous materials are in Longfellow House Trust (1913–1974) Records (LONG 16174), three additional folders of correspondence are in Series IV, Anne Allegra Longfellow Thorp (1855–1934) Family Papers (LONG 27930).

157 Lawrance Thompson: See his obituary in *The New York Times*, "Lawrance Thompson, 67, Dies; Frost Biographer Won Pulitzer," April 16, 1973.

158 Samuel Longfellow's biography: Unable to document his criticism of Henry's brother fully in the text of *Young Longfellow*, Thompson vented his grievances in endnotes, most notably a lengthy complaint that included this: "I am particularly dissatisfied with Samuel Longfellow's handling of this period, not because he omitted, but because he concealed, in such a way as to distort the plain truth." And this: "He emphasized the externals, by means of editorial manipulation, omission, and deletion" (361–362).

159 "emotional and physical collapse": Hilen, in introduction to *Letters*, vol. 2, 5. Harry Dana's correspondence and materials related to Lawrance Thompson are filed in Longfellow House under "H.W.L. Dana Papers, Series IX. Collected Materials."

159 "Met Lady Fanny": HWL Journal, May 19, 1838.

159 "I hear you have grown": Clara Crowninshield to Henry, and his response, May 31, 1838, in *Letters*, vol. 2, 78–79.

159 "Lay upon the sofa": HWL Journal, June 10, 1838.

160 Influence of Goethe: See Frederick Burwick, "Longfellow and German Romanticism," in *Comparative Literature Studies*, vol. 7, no. 1 (March 1970), 12–42; W. A.

Chamberlin, "Longfellow's Attitude Toward Goethe," in *Modern Philology*, vol. 16, no. 2 (June 1918), 57–76.

160 "And first of the 'Dark Ladie' . . . all the morning": HWL to GWG, Oct. 22, 1838, *Letters,* vol. 2, 106–112.

161 "Perhaps the worst": HWL Journal, Sept. 10, 1838.

161 "Lecturing is all well": Ibid., Sept. 12, 1838.

161 "Looked over my notes": Ibid., Sept. 13, 1838.

161 "I have so many": Ibid., Oct. 23, 1838.

161 "and wrote half": Ibid., Oct. 29, 1838.

161 "I feel better . . . open to the world": Ibid., Nov. 5, 1838.

162 "A rainy day": Ibid., Nov. 8, 1838.

162 "a beautiful idea": Ibid., Dec. 4, 1838.

162 "A beautiful holy morning": Ibid., Dec. 6, 1838.

162 "long talk": Ibid., April 28, 1838.

163 "Has it not": HWL to Lewis Gaylord Clark, Aug. 3, 1838, *Letters,* vol. 2, 90–91.

164 "It is raining": HWL Journal, May 3, 1839.

164 "Then it shall stand": Ibid., Dec. 4, 1839.

164 "first appearance": Ibid., Dec. 11, 1839.

165 "wish": Charles Sumner (hereafter CS) to HWL, Jan. 24, 1839, *Letters of Charles Sumner,* vol. 1, 54–55.

165 "I wanted to tell you": HWL to Sam Ward, Nov. 24, 1838, *Letters,* vol. 2, 115–117.

165 "It will look well": HWL Journal, June 11, 1839.

165 "I cannot . . . be *dished*": HWL to Sam Ward, July 13, 1839, *Letters,* vol. 2, 155–156.

165 "I have . . . pent-up fire": HWL to GWG, July 23, 1839, ibid., 158–163.

9 · MUTUAL ADMIRATION SOCIETY

166 "It is of great importance": HWL to GWG, June 5, 1836, in *Letters,* vol. 1, 554–557.

166 "I called it *Hyperion*": HWL to GWG, Jan. 2, 1840, ibid., vol. 2, 200–204.

166 "This book": HWL to GWG, July 23, 1839, ibid., 158–163.

167 "Some one has": *Boston Evening Mercantile Journal,* Sept. 27, 1839. Also quoted in *Letters,* vol. 2, 180, fn. 2.

167 "What care I?": HWL Journal, Oct. 1, 1839.

167 "Of a truth": Ibid., Dec. 8, 1846.

168 "We have no design": [Edgar Allan Poe], "Review of New Book," *Burton's Gentleman's Magazine,* Oct. 1839.

168 "I should be overjoyed": Edgar Allan Poe to HWL, May 3, 1841, HL, bMS Am 1340.2 (4450). "The Beleaguered City" had appeared in *Voices of the Night;* "The Skeleton in Armor" had been published in *The Knickerbocker* just four months earlier by Lewis Gaylord Clark, and would appear in *Ballads and Other Poems* the following year.

168 "I am so much": HWL to Edgar Allan Poe, May 19, 1841, *Letters,* vol. 2, 302.

169 "The amplest funds": Edgar Allan Poe to HWL, June 22, 1841, HL, bMS Am 1340.2 (4450).

169 *The Spanish Student:* First published in the September, October, and November 1842 issues of *Graham's Magazine;* revised, it was issued in hardcover by Edward Moxon, London, in 1843.

169 "If he goes on": HWL Journal, Dec. 7, 1845.

169　"moderate powers": Margaret Fuller, review of Longfellow's poems, in *New-York Daily Tribune*, Dec. 10, 1845, reprinted in Judith Mattson Bean and Joel Myerson, eds., *Margaret Fuller, Critic: Writings from the New-York Tribune, 1844–1846* (New York: Columbia University Press, 2000), 288. See Paula Kopacz, "Feminist at the 'Tribune': Margaret Fuller as Professional Writer," in *Studies in the American Renaissance* (1991), 119–139.

169　"It is what": HWL Journal, Dec. 11, 1845.

169　"We hear that": Ibid., Oct. 11, 1849.

170　"succeeding famously well": Ibid., Dec. 30, 1845.

170　Francis Frith: The noted English landscape photographer was among the first to use the glass-negative and albumen print process. See *Encyclopedia of Nineteenth-Century Photography*, ed. John Hannavy (London: Routledge, 2013), 558–559.

170　"foremost interpreter": W. A. Chamberlin, "Longfellow's Attitude Toward Goethe," in *Modern Philology* (Chicago: University of Chicago Press, 1919), vol. 16, no. 2, 1–20.

170　twenty-five German authors: Hatfield, 74.

170　Felton review of *Hyperion*: *North American Review*, vol. 50 (Jan. 1840), 145–161.

170　"pursuing his way": *Hyperion*, vol. 1, 5.

171　"female figure": Ibid., vol. 2, 28.

171　"with the soft voice": Ibid., 29–30.

171　"They did her wrong": Ibid., 35.

171　"The lady's figure": Ibid., 36.

171　"He conversed": Ibid., 41.

172　"reclining on the flowery": Ibid., 90.

172　"He walked": Ibid., 86–87.

172　"I love this woman": Ibid., 105.

172　"bright eyes": William Hickling Prescott to Fanny Calderón de la Barca, Aug. 15, 1840, in Prescott, *Letters*, 147. Prescott had an admitted crush on Fanny, calling her in another letter (Jan. 3, 1842, 277–278) "the dove in feminine attractions" of softness and beauty, "and the queen of birds in dignity."

173　"for he is now": CS letter to John Jay, May 25, 1843, in Pierce, vol. 2, 261. This John Jay was the son of Judge William Jay of New York, and grandson of the Founding Father and first US Supreme Court chief justice, John Jay (1745–1829).

173　"the supposed prototype": Julia Ward Howe, "Reminiscences of Longfellow," in *The Critic*, 1882, vol. 2, 115.

174　"Once your friend": William Dean Howells, "The White Mr. Longfellow," first published in *Harper's New Monthly Magazine*, August 1896, reprinted in *Literary Friends & Acquaintances*, 178–211.

174　"A part of Mr. Longfellow's charm": Sherwood, 131.

174　"struck by the great": Wyatt Eaton, "Recollections of American Poets," *Century Magazine*, vol. 64 (1902), 844.

174　"too timid": Ernest Longfellow, 47.

174　"You are at the beginning": Winter, 223.

175　Maria Clemm: Letters to Henry Wadsworth Longfellow, HL, bMS Am 1340.2–1340.7, bMS Am 1340.2 (1188). Two of Henry's letters to Clemm survive: see *Letters*, vol. 4, Jan. 12, 1860, 183, and May 4, 1863, 325. Sums of money were enclosed with both, the former also including "the signatures which you request." The complimentary closing and signature on the latter has been cut out, presumably to sell as an autograph with the others. Henry's account book contains four entries for sums sent to her, filed under "moneys given" and "charities," HL, MS Am 1370 (152).

175 "concerned Longfellow": Edwin D. Mead, "Memories of Dickens in Boston," in *Journal of Education*, vol. 101, No. 24 (2534) (June 11, 1925), 667–671.

175 "As a Greek scholar": Thomas Dwight Woolsey, *Eulogy of Cornelius Conway Felton* (Washington: Smithsonian Institution, 1862), 5.

176 Outis: Kent Ljungquist and Buford Jones, "The Identity of 'Outis': A Further Chapter in the Poe-Longfellow War," in *American Literature,* vol. 60, no. 3 (Oct. 1988), 402–415, suggest a New York editor, Lawrence Labree, as Outis; Anne Whitehouse, "Poe vs. Himself," in *New England Review*, vol. 39, no. 1 (2018), 98–107, supports the theory put forth by Burton R. Pollin in "Poe as Author of the 'Outis' Letter and 'The Bird of the Dream'" in *Poe Studies,* vol. 20 (June 1987), that Outis was actually an invention of Poe himself. For a supportive view of Poe's critical attacks on the Boston-Cambridge-Concord writers, see Eric W. Carlson, "Poe's Ten-Year Frogpondian War," in *The Edgar Allan Poe Review,* vol. 3, no. 2 (Fall 2002), 37–51. Kenneth Silverman gives a critically balanced examination in *Edgar A. Poe: Mournful and Never-ending Remembrance* (New York: HarperCollins, 1991). A scholarly monograph by Sidney P. Moss, *Poe's Literary Battles* (Durham, NC: Duke University Press, 1963), includes an excellent chapter on the episode, "Culmination of a Campaign," 132–190.

176 "ironical lady": Julia Ward Howe, "Reminiscences," *Atlantic Monthly*, vol. 80 (1899), 339.

177 "sweet": Hillard, in Cleveland, 1844, xxiii.

177 Julia Ward introduced to Samuel Gridley Howe: see Maud Howe and Florence Howe Hull, in *Dr. Howe's Famous Pupil and What He Taught Her* (Boston: Little, Brown, 1903), 87–88.

177 Letters to Greene: The Houghton Library holds 576 letters Greene wrote to Longfellow, MS Am 1340.2–1340.7, MS Am 1340.2, (2379).

177 Bowdoin classmates: On the evening of Oct. 29, 1824, Longfellow and Hawthorne gave presentations in the same academic program, with Henry delivering a "Salutatory Oration in Latin" on the English Poets ("*Angli Poetae*"), Hawthorne a dissertation, also in Latin, on the Roman Senators ("*De Patribus Conscriptis Romanorum*"). "I have been very much engaged of late in writing my Latin Oration, which is to be delivered at the Exhibition, on Friday next," Henry wrote his sister Anne (Hilen, *Letters,* Oct. [no day] 1824, vol. 1, 92–93, and footnote). "I made a very splendid appearance in the chapel last Friday evening, before a crowded audience," Hawthorne boasted to his sister Elizabeth: "I would send you a printed list of the performances if it were not for the postage" (*Works of Nathaniel Hawthorne,* Boston: Houghton Mifflin, 1884, vol. 27, 113).

177 "no two young men": Nathaniel Hawthorne, quoted by Annie Fields, in "Glimpses of Longfellow in Social Life," *The Century Illustrated Monthly Magazine* (New York: The Century Co., 1886), vol. 31 (new series vol. 9), 884–893.

177 "We were not": Hawthorne to HWL, March 7, 1837, HL, bMS Am 1340.2 (2616). See Wineapple, 94–95.

178 "When a star rises": HWL in *North American Review,* vol. 45 (July 1837), 59.

179 "How can I give you": Charles Dickens to John Forster, in Forster, *The Life of Charles Dickens* (Philadelphia: J. B. Lippincott & Co., 1882), vol. 1, 301.

179 "engaged three deep": HWL to SL, Jan. 30, 1842, *Letters,* vol. 2, 380–381.

180 Seamen's Bethel Church: Dickens wrote about Father Taylor in *American Notes* and quoted extensively from his fiery remarks. It is thought that Herman Melville based the Father Mapple character in *Moby-Dick* (1851) on the famous Methodist preacher.

180 Paul Revere's house and the Old North Church: Henry Wadsworth Longfellow Dana, in "Longfellow and Dickens: The Story of a Trans-Atlantic Friendship" (*Proceedings of the Cambridge Historical Society*, vol. 28, no. 55, 1942, 55–104), speculated that it could have been during this excursion through the North End that Henry conceived the framework for what twenty years later would become "Paul Revere's Ride," though there is nothing in the surviving paperwork to document that assertion.

180 "When shall you be here": HWL to Samuel Ward, Jan. 30, 1842, *Letters*, vol. 2, 382–383.

180 Craigie House: Henry at that time was sharing the house with one other boarder, Joseph Emerson Worcester, a lexicographer and compiler of a dictionary that for a time went head to head with a rival compendium produced by his onetime employer Noah Webster, in a publishing brouhaha called "the Dictionary Wars."

180 "bright little breakfast": *Life*, vol. 1, 268.

180 "My dear Longfellow": Charles Dickens to HWL, Feb. 3, 1842. Henry made an exact facsimile of the Dickens letter by hand, including the exuberant sixfold flourish under the signature, and mailed it off to his father in Maine. Both reproduced fully in *Letters*, vol. 2, 387–388. Originals in Houghton Library.

181 Ailments and treatments: For a full discussion of Longfellow's lifelong battles with conditions both specific and imprecisely described, and the many remedies he sought, see Hilen, *Letters*, vol. 6, 3–6.

181 Continuing litany of ailments: Henry began his journal on Sept. 1, 1838, a Saturday, with this dour comment: "A new month, a new College year, and a new book in my journal begin today. I am neither in good health nor good spirits;—being foolishly inclined to indigestion and the most unpleasant melancholy. It is a kind of sleepiness of the soul, in which I feel a general indifference to all things." On Sept. 20, there was this: "I was literally tired out today with my College labors. I believe I am not well. I hate to break down so near the beginning of the term."

181 "In this time": HWL letter to Harvard Corporation, Jan. 24, 1842, *Letters*, vol. 2, 380.

181 "Mezzo Cammin": holographic copy, HL, MS Am 1340 (72).

182 "dispatched": HWL to CS, Sept. 17, 1842, *Letters*, vol. 2, 469–470.

182 "Oh, I long": CS to HWL, May 15, 1842, in Pierce, vol. 2, 207–208.

182 "There is no inspiration": HWL to CS, Aug. 8, 1842, *Letters*, vol. 2, 456–459. Longfellow documented his days in Marienburg in MS Am 1340 (196).

182 "Your bed is waiting": Charles Dickens to HWL, Sept. 28, 1842, HL, bMS Am 1340.2 (1579).

182 "I write this from": HWL letter to CS, Oct. 16, 1842, *Letters*, vol. 2, 473–474.

183 "Shakespeare on the stage": Charles Dickens letter to HWL, Sept. 28, 1842, HL, bMS Am 1340.2 (1579). See also Valerie L. Gager, *Shakespeare and Dickens: The Dynamics of Influence* (Cambridge, UK: Cambridge University Press, 1996), 70.

183 "the tramps and thieves": John Forster, *The Life of Charles Dickens*, vol. 2 (New York: Lippincott, 1873), 22–23.

183 "McDowell, the boot maker": Charles Dickens to HWL, Dec. 29, 1842, HL, bMS Am 1340.2 (1579).

183 "I have read": HWL to CS, Oct. 16, 1842, *Letters,* vol. 2, 440–441.

183 "The great waves struck": HWL to Ferdinand Freiligrath, Jan. 6, 1843, ibid., 495–498.

184 "hunted Negro . . . the Witnesses": *Poems on Slavery* (Cambridge: John Owen, 1842). The seven poems written at sea were dedicated "To William E. Channing." An eighth poem included in the published edition, "The Warning," was taken in part from "The Soul," which had appeared in the *Knickerbocker Magazine* in January 1835. For more on their content, publication, and reception, see Janet Harris, "Longfellow's Poems on Slavery," in *Colby Quarterly,* vol. 14 (June 1978), 84–92.

184 "the thinnest": Margaret Fuller, in the *Dial,* quoted in Charles Capper, *Margaret Fuller: An American Romantic Life, The Public Years* (Oxford/New York: Oxford University Press, 1992), 59. Fuller had previously written Ralph Waldo Emerson, founder of the *Dial,* which she edited: "Longfellow sent us his poems. If you have toleration for them, it would be well to have a short notice written by some one (*not* me)."

184 "so mild": HWL to IAJ, May 23, 1843, ibid., 537–538.

184 "I was never more surprised": Nathaniel Hawthorne to HWL, Dec. 24, 1842, HL, bMS AM 1340.2 (2616).

184 "Though a strong": HWL to John Greenleaf Whittier, Sept. 6, 1844, *Letters,* vol. 3, 44–45.

185 "I am glad": HWL Journal, Nov. 30, 1850.

185 "I think no one": HWL to Susan Farley Porter, June 8, 1852, *Letters,* vol. 3, 348; a Rochester, NY, activist, Porter had asked for a contribution of "four to five pages" to an antislavery book then being prepared for publication.

185 "hated excess": Ernest Longfellow, 29.

185 "My Etna *is* burnt out": HWL to Sam Ward, March 2, 1843, *Letters,* vol. 2, 511–513.

185 Catherine Eliot Norton: Letters to HWL in the Houghton Library, bMS Am 1340 (4147).

186 "the day and evening": HWL Journal, April 13, 1844.

10 · CASTLES IN SPAIN

187 "Must I say": FEAL Journal, Aug. 31, 1835, LH, LONG 21586.

187 "I would fain": FEAL to EAW, 1838, no month or day indicated, FEAL-B3-F13-I39.

187 "I pity you": FEAL to TGA, July 5, 1839, FEAL B2-F9-I5.

188 "delightfully un-cityfied . . . 'Holy of Holies'": FEAL Journal, July 13, 1835.

188 "Lake District": See Richard D. Birdsall, "Berkshire's Golden Age," in *American Quarterly,* vol. 8, no. 4 (Winter 1956), 328–355.

188 Berkshire authors: See Bernard A. Drew, *Literary Luminaries of the Berkshires: From Herman Melville to Patricia Highsmith* (Charleston, SC: History Press, 2015), and Cornelia Brooke Gilder, with Julia Conklin Peters, *Hawthorne's Lenox* (Charleston, SC: History Press, 2008).

190 "Let me write": FEAL, Spiritual Journal, May 13, 1834, LONG 21598.

190 "Does thy sainted Spirit . . . loneliness and misery": Ibid., Oct. 1, 1836.

191 "Dearest Aunt Kitty . . . Aunt Kitty": FEAL letter to Catharine Maria Sedgwick

(hereafter CMS), June 15, 1835, in MHS, Catharine Maria Sedgwick Papers, microfilm collection of correspondence (hereafter CMS letters).

192   "Most gladly": CMS to FEAL, June 26, 1835, and FEAL letter to CMS, June 15, 1835, in MHS, CMS letters, reel 7, box 9, folder 2.

192   Highly successful proto-feminist: Other books include *Redwood* (1824), *Hope Leslie* (1827), *Clarence, or a Tale of Our Own Times* (1830), and *The Linwoods, or 'Sixty Years Since' in America* (1835), For more on the life, work, and rediscovery of Catharine Maria Sedgwick, see Damon-Bach and Clements, passim. Also Mary Kelley, "A Woman Alone: Catharine Maria Sedgwick's Spinsterhood in Nineteenth-Century America," in *New England Quarterly*, vol. 5, no. 2 (June 1978), 209–225.

192   "one of the first": George William Curtis, unsigned but attributed to him, in *Homes of American Authors*, 160.

192   "Thank you": CMS to FEAL, July 21, 1841, MHS, CMS letters, reel 7, box 9, folder 4.

193   "Miss Sedgwick": Anna Jameson, *Letters & Friendships*, ed. Mrs. Steuart Erskine (London: T. Fisher Unwin, Ltd., 1915), 160.

194   "My head swelled": FEAL Journal, July 17, 1835.

194   Fanny Kemble: The celebrated British actress and writer Frances Anne "Fanny" Kemble (1809–1893) was at this time using her married name, Butler, which she would abandon after a contentious divorce in 1848 from Pierce Butler, a South Carolina slaveholder, a practice she found, as an abolitionist, to be abhorrent.

194   "To me such Nature": FEAL to IAJ, Aug. 26, 1838, FEAL-B2-F8-I3.

194   "I am enjoying myself": FEAL to EA, Sept. 5, 1838, FEAL-B2-F8-I4.

194   "Thank you, again and again": CMS letters to FEAL, Nov. 25, 1838; MHS, CMS letters, reel 7, box 9, folder 3.

195   "Once more my thanks": CMS to FEAL, July 26, 1839, MHS, CMS letters, reel 7, box 9, folder 3.

195   "been reading": FEAL to IAJ, Dec. 29, 1839, FEAL-B2-F9-I19.

195   "The prosperity and beauty": [George W. Curtis], in *Homes of American Authors*, 171.

196   "We are whiling away . . . spinsters of Llangollen!": FEAL to IAJ, Aug. 26, 1838, FEAL-B2-F8-I3. The two women being referenced were Lady Eleanor Butler of Kilkenny Castle (1739–1828) and Sarah Ponsonby (1755–1831) of Woodstock House, Inistioge. Robert Southey, Lord Byron, and William Wordsworth dedicated poems in their honor; Sir Walter Scott and Lady Caroline Lamb were among their many visitors. See Elizabeth Mavor, *The Ladies of Llangollen* (New York: Penguin, 1973), passim.

196   "the two most celebrated": Eugene Coyle, "The Irish Ladies of Llangollen," in *History Ireland*, issue 6 (November/December 2015), vol. 23.

196   "Italian villas": FEAL to EAW, Sept. 5, 1838, FEAL-B2-F8-I4.

197   "We are independent . . . what they are": FEAL to EAW, June 16, 1839. FEAL-B2-F9-I10.

197   Oxbow property: Documents recorded in Berkshire County Registry of Deeds conveying two parcels of land in Stockbridge, Mass., totaling thirty-five acres, to Nathan Appleton: Feb. 2, 1839, from Oliver Partridge, $1,000 (book 98, page 101); March 26, 1839, from Allen L. Yale, $1,800 (book 98, page 181).

198   Mrs. Sedgwick's School for Young Ladies: See Carole Owens, "Connections: Eliza-

beth Sedgwick's Lenox 'Culture Factory,'" *The Berkshire Eagle,* Dec. 1, 2015, and Bernard A. Drew, *Literary Luminaries of the Berkshires,* 23–24.

198 Jennie Jerome: see Anne Sebba, *Jennie Churchill: Winston's American Mother* (London: John Murray, 2008).

198 Harriet Hosmer: See Kate Culkin, *Harriet Hosmer: A Cultural Biography* (Amherst, MA: University of Massachusetts Press, 2010).

198 "Have you seen the Prof's novel": FEAL to EAW, July 7, 1839, FEAL-B3-F13-I19.

199 "She is now absent": HWL to GWG, July 29, 1839, *Letters,* vol. 2, 158–163.

199 "There are really . . . of some name": FEAL to EAW, Aug. 9, 1839, FEAL-B2-F9-I9.

199 "old ideas": See Hatfield, 68–79; "nearly one half" of the chapter on Goethe alone, he noted, "was taken from the Harvard lecture of June, 1838" (74).

199 "The Professor has": FEAL to EAW, Dec. 24, 1841, FEAL-B3-F13-I42.

200 "a bitter-sweet . . . spinsterhood": FEAL to IAJ, Dec. 29, 1839, FEAL-B2-F9-I19.

200 Trip to Washington: In 1842, Nathan Appleton agreed to serve out the unexpired term of Robert Winthrop in Congress.

200 "I have left myself": FEAL to EAW, Feb. 7, 1840, FEAL-B2-F10-I7.

200 "blown that fair castle": FEAL to IAJ, Feb. 25, 1840, FEAL-B2-F10-I10.

201 Stockbridge land: Longfellow sold the seventy acres of pristine countryside off Glendale Middle Road in Stockbridge in 1867, which became the site of a Gilded Age mansion known as Southmayd Farm. Still largely undeveloped, the property was subdivided into two parcels, one of them with a mile of frontage on the Housatonic River, which sold in December 2017 for $6.25 million; the other, undeveloped parcel, was listed for $1.75 million. See *The Berkshire Eagle,* Jan. 8, 2018. My thanks to Cindy Welch, the realtor who brokered the sales, for showing my wife and me around the property.

201 "Passed an hour at the Ox-bow": HWL Journal, July 22, 1848.

202 "very agreeable": FEAL to IAJ, May 9, 1840, FEAL-B2-F10-I13.

203 "Once more the sheltering night": HWL Journal, May 2, 1840.

203 "beyond comparison . . . *Apology* for my madness": HWL letter to GWG, Sept. 4, 5, and 6, 1840 [one letter], in *Letters,* vol. 2, 244–248.

204 "I am much . . . single women": FEAL to IAJ, Nov. 8, 1840, FEAL-B2-F10-I25.

205 Lawrance Thompson mention of Alleyne Otis: Thompson, 333–334.

205 "little party . . . blankets to me.": Typed transcription of letter from Alleyne Otis to Joshua Francis Fisher, March 3, 1840, LONG 20527, Series II, Correspondence. FEAL B7-F5.

206 "decided that work . . . stupid": Morison, 287–292.

206 "*did* nothing": Henry James, *William Wetmore Story,* vol. 2, 186–187.

206 "listening to tortured": FEAL to EAW, July 6, 1840, FEAL-B2-F10-I15.

207 "I can't help": FEAL Journal, Aug. 19, 1836.

207 "I *feel* . . . of ourselves open": CMS to FEAL, May 11, 1840, MHS, CMS letters, reel 7, box 9, folder 3.

208 "passed several weeks": GWG to HWL, May 5, 1840, HL, MS Am 1340.2–1340.7, MS Am 1340.2 (2379).

208 "Fanny, my dear child": CMS to FEAL, Aug. 20, 1840, MHS, CMS letters, reel 7, box 9, folder 1.

208 miniature notebook: FEAL Journal, May 1 to June 28, 1841, aboard steamship *Columbia,* LONG 27596.

209 "I saw Prof—L.": CMS to FEAL, undated, MHS, CMS letters, box 9, folder 2. My gratitude to Lucinda Damon-Bach, professor of English at Salem State University, founding president of the Catharine Maria Sedgwick Society, editor of Sedgwick's correspondence, and author of a forthcoming biography of the author, for her assistance in transcribing these letters to Fanny Appleton, and to Kathryn Hanson Plass, museum technician at Longfellow House, for transcribing Fanny's introductory letter to Sedgwick.

209 "temple": CMS letter of May 11, 1862, quoted in James Turner, *The Liberal Education of Charles Eliot Norton* (Baltimore: Johns Hopkins University Press, 2001), 174.

11 · MAGIC CIRCLE

210 "Oh come to me": FEAL to HWL, May 10, 1843, FEAL-B2-F13-I3.

211 "What a year": 1844 FEAL Journal, LONG 21575, Jan. 1, 1844.

211 "Dear friend": FEAL to HWL, April 19, 1843, HL, MS Am MS Am 1340.2 (3507).

212 "surrendered unconditionally . . . with his name": Andrew Hilen, in *Letters,* vol. 2, 487. Fanny's May 10, 1843, acceptance of Henry's proposal was not quoted in *The Appletons of Beacon Hill* (1976) by Louise Hall Tharp, or by Charles Calhoun in *Longfellow Rediscovered* (2004), though both included her less passionate letter of rapprochement from three weeks earlier. The May 10 letter, unlike the April 19 letter, is not in the Houghton Library collections, but in the Longfellow House archives, where I examined it, FEAL-B2-F13-I3.

212 Lawrance Thompson correspondence: Longfellow House Trust (1913–1974) Records, (E) Researcher Materials, LONG 16174 (box 22).

212 "reluctant to give": Henry Wadsworth Longfellow Dana to Lawrance Thompson, quoted verbatim by Thompson in letter to Anne Longfellow Thorp, Feb. 8, 1938, LONG 16174.

213 "It isn't likely": Lawrance Thompson to Anne Longfellow Thorp, Aug. 19, 1937, LONG 16174.

213 "traveling to England": HWL to Robert Bigsby, Sept. 11, 1849, *Letters,* vol. 3, 213.

213 "Henry and I were among": FEAL to EAW, March 15, 1847, FEAL-B2-F16-I32.

214 "to George Sand's provocative": Irmscher, *Public Poet,* 190.

214 "Mr. McLane": Henry wrote further that "McLane left Cambridge in August and I took possession of his room, making use of it as a library or study, and having the adjoining chamber as my bedroom." HWL, Craigie House Journal, HL, MS Am 1340.2 (159).

215 "This news will": FEAL to Martha Gold, May 16, 1843, FEAL-B2-F13-I5.

215 "Fanny was in all respects": ALP to Elizabeth Poor, Aug. 15, 1843, FEAL Papers, LH, LONG 20257, Series I, Personal Materials.

215 "garland worn by Miss Appleton": FEAL Papers, Series 7, Natural History Specimens, box 8, folder 1. Another flora, a rose petal "worn by Fanny at the Ball Feb. 28, 1844," is in the same box, folder 2.

215 wedding excursion: Fanny's Sketchbook with the inscription "Mary Ashburton to Paul Flemming," LONG 19088.

216 "I wish you could see": FEAL to TGA, Aug. 30, 1843, FEAL-B2-F13-I16.

216 "We have got to love": FEAL to Matilda Lieber, Sept. 4, 1843, FEAL-B2-F13-I17.

216 "If you decide": FEAL to Nathan Appleton, Sept. 1843 [no day], FEAL-B2-F13-I18.

216 household purchases: See *Historic Furnishings Report,* Appendix A (535–558) for

facsimiles of receipts for wedding gifts from Nathan Appleton between 1843 and 1844. See also Tharp, 243–245.

216 "It is a fine thing": ZL to SL, Oct. 13, 1843. Having just met Fanny for the first time in Portland—neither of Henry's parents made the trip to Boston for the wedding—Zilpah had this to say about her new daughter-in-law: "Every one to whom she was introduced seemed delighted with her, such a quiet and gentle manner, such perfect propriety of demeanor, so perfectly ladylike." And she was especially taken by Fanny's eyes: "so beautiful and so brilliant when she is engaged in conversation" (FEAL, Box 1, with correspondence of Zilpah Longfellow).

217 "maelstrom . . . have I seen": FEAL to CS, Oct. 13, 1843, FEAL-B2-F13-I25.

217 "Willis I half like": FEAL to EAW, Sept. 1843 [no day], FEAL-B2-F13-I21.

217 "We have but just returned": FEAL to Samuel Longfellow, Oct. 20, 1843, FEAL-B2-F13-I27.

218 "in a broken . . . be critical": FEAL Journal, Jan. 1, 1844. For more on Mount Auburn Cemetery, see John Harrison and Kim Nagy, eds., *Dead in Good Company: A Celebration of Mount Auburn Cemetery* (Medford, MA: Ziggy Owl Press, 2015).

219 "How much time": FEAL Journal, Feb. 2, 1844.

219 "get on bravely": FEAL to GWG, March 31, 1844, FEAL B2-F14-I7.

219 "*our* book": FEAL Journal, Feb. 10, 1844.

219 "read him into": Ibid., Jan. 2, 1844.

219 "Young Lowell": Ibid., Jan. 21, 1844.

219 "sickened at heart": Ibid., Jan. 13, 1844.

219 "making a great noise": HWL to Sam Longfellow, Jan. 12, 1844, *Letters*, vol. 3, 21.

220 "Danish ballads to Henry": FEAL Journal, Jan. 5, 1844.

220 "H. is so careful": Ibid., Jan. 11, 1844.

220 "I have proposed": FEAL to MLG, March 22, 1844, FEAL-B2-F14-I6.

220 "How I wish": FEAL Journal, Jan. 24, 1844.

220 "Enjoy . . . his rich mind": Ibid., Jan. 19, 1844.

220 "Since last summer": HWL to Samuel Longfellow, Jan. 12, 1844, *Letters*, vol. 2, 21–23.

221 "the shilling edition . . . heart and person": HWL letter to Joseph Bosworth, Feb. 28, 1844, ibid., vol. 3, 26–27.

221 "Such things seem . . . happy hearts and hours": FEAL Journal, Jan. 18, 1844.

221 "Washington's Headquarters at Cambridge": Boston *Evening Transcript*, March 23, 1844, quoted in *Letters*, vol. 3, 29.

222 "Some of the Boston papers": HWL to SL, March 24, 1844, ibid.

222 "Dexter, the architect": HWL Journal, June 9, 1844.

222 "On taking off the old shingles": Ibid., Aug. 14, 1844.

223 "Expected dearest Em": FEAL Journal, Jan. 21, 1844.

223 "rather tough": Ibid., Jan. 30, 1844.

223 "tea and strawberries": HWL Journal, June 8, 1844.

223 "oppressively warm": FEAL Journal, April 14, 1844.

223 "the latter overflowing": Ibid., Jan. 17, 1844.

223 "celery sauce": recipes in Fanny notebook, LONG 21612. Another notebook, LONG 21616, includes ten recipes in Fanny's hand, in French, including "soufflet de ris," "soufflet de chocolat," "Isalmis de perdux," and "un poulet a la casserole."

223 "the evil times": FEAL to MAM, Nov. 15, 1858, FEAL-B3-F9-I11. In his account book for 1865, MS Am 1340 (152), Henry lists wage payments for "cook," "cham-

bermaid," "parlor girl," "outofdoors man," and "gardener," further identified as "indoor servants" and "outdoor servants." A copy of "Shadow of Fame: Documenting Domestic Service at the Craigie House" (2014), a master's thesis by Mirit Lerner Naaman for Harvard University Extension School, is in the Longfellow House archives.

224 "fever flush": FEAL Journal, Jan. 24, 1844.

224 "very magnifique affair": Ibid., Feb. 28, 1844.

225 "Oh Father . . . of my child": Ibid., Feb. 21, 1844.

225 "very agreeable": Ibid., Feb. 2, 1844.

225 "and tried to enlighten": Ibid., Aug. 8, 1843. The Springfield Armory operated from the time of the American Revolution through 1968, and today is a National Park Service Historic Site.

225 "has already a spirit-stirring": Ibid., Feb. 6, 1844.

225 "a more ferocious verse": Ibid., Feb. 19, 1844.

226 "peace poem is fully cast": Ibid., March 6, 1844.

226 "Lined a basket": FEAL Journal, May 4, 1844.

226 "diverse Lilliputian": Ibid., May 28, 1844.

227 "our first in the dining room": Ibid., July 13, 1844.

227 Independence Day oration: Charles Sumner, *The True Grandeur of Nations: An Oration* (London: William Smith, 1846); reference to "The Arsenal at Springfield," 49–50. For more on the negative reception to the speech, see Donald, 110–117.

228 "Got my last proof": HWL Journal, Nov. 24, 1845.

229 "my idyll in hexameters": Ibid., Nov. 28, 1845.

229 "I have nothing . . . in verse": Details of the dinner party, including excerpts from Nathaniel Hawthorne's notebook, quoted by Manning Hawthorne and Henry Wadsworth Longfellow Dana, in "The Origin of Longfellow's *Evangeline*," in *The Papers of the Bibliographical Society of America*, vol. 41, no. 3 (Third Quarter 1947), 165–203.

230 "I owe entirely": HWL to Nathaniel Hawthorne, Nov. 29, 1847, *Letters*, vol. 3, 145–146.

230 "A friend consulted": Anthony Trollope, "Henry Wadsworth Longfellow," *The North American Review*, vol. 132, no. 293 (Apr. 1881), 383–406.

12 · CAMELOT ON THE CHARLES

231 "Once, ah once": A framed copy of this stanza from the poem "To a Child," in Longfellow's hand, hangs in the second-floor room once occupied by General Washington during his residence, and later by Henry when he first moved in as a tenant. The poem was written to note the birth of Charles Appleton Longfellow in 1844.

231 anxiety about using hexameters: On April 4, 1847, Longfellow wrote in his journal: "Sumner and Felton came to tea, and we discussed the first canto of *Evangeline*. I think Sumner is rather afraid of it still; and wants me to let it repose for six months and come to it again with a fresh eye."

232 publication history of *Evangeline*: William Charvat, "Longfellow's Income from his Writings, 1840–1852," in *The Papers of the Bibliographical Society of America*, vol. 38, no. 1 (First Quarter 1944), 9–21.

232 stereotype plates: A solid plate of type metal cast from a papier-mâché or plaster mold, and used for printing instead of the original blocks of handset type. By creating a stereotype, printers could reprint books and documents on demand, and free their equipment for other work.

232 "His own method": Charvat, "Longfellow's Income from his Writings," 15. See also "Income from Books," Henry's record of earnings, itemized by titles, editions, and translations, from 1840 to 1852, in HL, MS Am 1340 (148).

232 Annie Adams Fields: See Gollin, passim, and Roman, passim.

233 ether controversy: See Stephanie Browner, "Ideologies of the Anesthetic: Professionalism, Egalitarianism and the Ether Controversy," in *American Quarterly*, vol. 51, no. 1 (March 1999), 108–143; Judith Walzer Leavitt, "Science Enters the Birthing Room: Obstetrics in America Since the Eighteenth Century," in *The Journal of American History*, vol. 70, no. 2 (Sept. 1983), 281–304; Irving A. Watson, ed., *Physicians and Surgeons: A Collection of Biographical Sketches of the Regular Medical Profession* (Concord, NH: Republican Press Association, 1896), 804.

233 "No physician has tried": HWL Journal, April 6, 1847.

233 "desirable . . . destruction": Dr. James Pickford, *Edinburgh Medical and Surgical Journal*, July 1847, 258.

234 divine punishment: "I will make your pains in childbearing very severe; with painful labor you will give birth to children. Your desire will be for your husband, and he will rule over you." Genesis 3:16, New International Version.

234 "This morning was born": HWL Journal, April 7, 1847.

234 Medical history: See William Channing, *A Treatise on Etherization in Childbirth* (Boston: William D. Ticknor & Co., 1848), 27, and Appendix B, "First case of labor in which etherization was used in America, by N. C. Keep, M.D.," 397, which reprints full text of notice that appeared in *Boston Medical and Surgical Journal*, April 14, 1847.

235 "a double tooth extracted": HWL Journal, April 8, 1847. Among the many objects preserved in the Craigie House storage cabinets is a pair of handcrafted front false teeth set on a gold plate and kept in a leather case; though not otherwise identified, they were likely made for Henry by Dr. Nathan Cooley Keep to replace the two extracted during this procedure. LONG 17229.

235 "I am very sorry . . . gift of god": FEAL to ALP, dated to May 1847 by internal evidence, FEAL B2-F17-l15.

235 "Women have so much to suffer": HWL Journal, April 9, 1847.

235 Little Fanny's scuffed shoes: LONG 13991.

236 "My courage is almost broken": "Chronicle of the Children of Craigie Castle," 1848 (LONG 21576), Sept. 8, 1848, in the Frances Elizabeth Appleton Longfellow Papers (LONG 20257), Series VIII, Diaries, Books, and Albums. Also "Chronicle of the Children of Craigie Castle—Continued," 1849–1858 (LONG 21573).

236 "Our little child": HWL Journal, Sept. 12, 1848. "Via Dolorosa" is Latin for "Way of Grief," the name of a street within the Old City of Jerusalem believed to be the path that Jesus walked on the way to his crucifixion. For an in-depth consideration the death of Little Fanny had on Henry, and his writing of "Resignation," a poem mourning her loss, see Christoph Irmscher, "Longfellow's Sentimentality," in *Soundings: An Interdisciplinary Journal*, vol. 93, no. 3/4 (Fall/Winter 2010), 249–280.

236 "parental public": James T. Fields to HWL, Aug. 1, 1860. Houghton 1340.2 (1972).

238 pendant recovered at Gettysburg: "Henry W. Longfellow's daughters, ca. 1863," Maine Historical Society A85-727-1.

238 "I am sure": FEAL to CS, July 1843, FEAL-B2-F13-I11.

238 "proud and happy": FEAL to Matilda Lieber, June 10, 1843, FEAL 1843-06-10.

239 "Sumner realized": Author interview with John Stauffer, Aug. 2, 2017.

239 "Your New Year's gift": FEAL to CS, Jan. 1, 1844, FEAL-B2-F14-I1. The "Psalm of Life" manuscript, along with Sumner's letter, in Houghton MS Am 1340 (71).

240 "I am alone . . . ills of life": CS to Francis Lieber, July 13, 1843, Pierce, *Memoir and Letters*, vol. 2, 263. See also Moorfield Storey, "Memoir of Charles Sumner," in *Proceedings of the Massachusetts Historical Society*, second series, vol. 20 (1907), 538–549.

241 annexation of Texas and Mexican War: See Frederick Merk, "Dissent in the Mexican War," in *Proceedings of the Massachusetts Historical Society*, third series, vol. 81 (1969), 120–136.

241 "gross disloyalty": Sumner made this allegation under the pseudonym "Boston" in the *Boston Daily Whig*, July 22, 1846, but his identity was quickly determined, and acknowledged; the Pontius Pilate reference was made in the *Boston Courier*, Aug. 13, 1846. See Donald, 142–146.

241 strain on Five of Clubs: In his journal for Dec. 27, 1845, Henry remarked how the group had "supped" that night for "the first time we have been together for many months. A pity these meetings should be so interrupted, as much good comes of our discussions and friendly comparison of opinions."

241 "To be admitted": Charles L. Pierce, *Memoirs and Letters*, vol. 3, 10.

241 Harvard Law School: Institutional conservatism and opposition to abolition at this time was such that in the twenty years preceding the Civil War, at least 392 students enrolled in the Harvard Law School were from the eleven Confederate states, and 191 from the border states, and at least 223 fought for the Confederacy. Among degree-granting institutions, only West Point educated more high-ranking officers for the Confederacy than Harvard Law, including three major generals, eight brigadier generals, and forty colonels. Source: Daniel R. Coquillette and Bruce A. Campbell, *On the Battlefield of Merit: Harvard Law School, the First Century* (Cambridge, MA: Harvard University Press, 2015), 273. See also Carla Bosco, "Harvard University and the Fugitive Slave Act," in *New England Quarterly*, vol. 79, no. 2 (June 2006), 227–247.

241 "Have I not answered": CS to NA, Aug. 18, 1845, in Pierce, vol. 3, 375–376.

242 "Charles Sumner was": William Appleton, "The Whigs of Massachusetts," in *Proceedings of the Massachusetts Historical Society*, second series, vol. 11 (1896–97), 278.

242 Free Soil: The name for the breakaway political party was derived from a slogan used by opponents to the extension of slavery in the western territories that demanded "free soil, free speech, free labor, and free men."

242 Conscience Whigs and Cotton Whigs: John Quincy Adams described the dichotomy in his diary: "There are two divisions in the party, —one based upon public principle, and the other upon manufacturing and commercial interests." John Quincy Adams Diary, Sept. 23, 1846, Adams Papers, Massachusetts Historical Society. See also Frank Otto Gatell, " 'Conscience and Judgment': The Bolt of the Massachusetts Conscience Whigs," *The Historian*, vol. 21, no. 1 (Nov. 1958), 18–45.

242 "an unhallowed union . . . lords of the loom": Quoted in Shotwell, 192. See also O'Connor, passim.

242 "I have regretted": NA to CS, Sept. 4, 1848, in Pierce, vol. 3, 181.

243 "Please do not come": HWL to CS, June 19, 1849, *Letters,* vol. 3, 204.

243 "dissuading him": HWL Journal, March 26, 1848.

243 "Sumner passed the afternoon": HWL Journal, Sept. 17, 1848.

244 "Went to church": FEAL, "Chronicle of the Children of Craigie Castle," vol. 1, Sept. 17, 1848, LONG 21576.

244 "Ah me!": HWL Journal, Oct. 26, 1848.

244 "truly thankful . . . motives": FEAL to Samuel Longfellow, Nov. 11, 1848, FEAL B2-F17-I33, FEAL-B3-F14-I14.

244 "Read Papa's . . . till midnight": FEAL, "Chronicle of Children of Craigie Castle," Dec. 3 and Dec. 5, 1848, LONG 21576.

245 "How I long": FEAL to HWL, July 9, 1849, FEAL-B2-F19-I19.

245 "thrilled . . . the sword'": FEAL to CS, July 19, 1849, FEAL 1849-07-19. According to the *Oxford Dictionary of Quotations,* the phrase "the pen is mightier than the sword" was introduced in 1839 by the British author Edward Bulwer-Lytton in *Cardinal Richelieu,* a historical play.

246 *Sarah C. Roberts v. the City of Boston*: See Stephen Kendrick and Paul Kendrick, *Sarah's Long Walk: The Free Blacks of Boston and How Their Struggle for Equality Changed America* (Boston: Beacon Press, 2006).

246 "twenty bodies washed ashore": HWL Journal, Dec. 17, 1839. "I must write a ballad on this," he declared, and finished "The Wreck of the Hesperus" two weeks later. After retiring for the night, he could not sleep. "New thoughts were running through my head and I got up to add them to the ballad." HWL Journal, Dec. 30, 1839.

247 Abraham Lincoln: In "Lincoln's Imagination," an August 1879 essay for *Scribner's Monthly,* the journalist Noah Brooks recalled having recited from memory "The Building of the Ship" for the president. "As he listened to the last lines . . . his eyes filled with tears, and his cheeks were wet. He did not speak for some minutes, but finally said, with simplicity: 'It is a wonderful gift to be able to stir men like that.'"

247 Franklin Roosevelt: The original copy of FDR's letter to Churchill, signed and dated Jan. 20, 1941, is in the Churchill Archives at Cambridge University. A facsimile can be seen on the Library of Congress online exhibition Churchill and the Great Republic. One of two broadside copies signed by both men sold at a 2001 Christie's auction for $64,625.

247 "The Building of the Ship": See Hans-Joachim Lang and Fritz Fleischmann, "'All This Beauty, All This Grace': Longfellow's 'The Building of the Ship' and Alexander Slidell Mackenzie's 'Ship,'" *The New England Quarterly,* vol. 54, no. 1 (March 1981), 104–118. The poem first appeared in *The Seaside and the Fireside,* a collection of twenty poems and two translations (November 1849).

247 "Mackenzie and his wife": FEAL to CS, Oct. 13, 1843, FEAL-B2-F13-I25.

249 The crew of the *Somers*: Alexander Slidell Mackenzie, in *Case of the Somers' Mutiny: Defence of Alexander Slidell Mackenzie, Commander of the U.S. Brig Somers, Before the Court Martial Held at the Navy Yard, Brooklyn, New York* (New York: Tribune Office, 1843), 14. For more on the court martial, see Buckner F. Melton, Jr., *A Hanging Offense: The Strange Affair of the Warship Somers* (New York: Free Press, 2003).

249 "This officer": *Proceedings of the Naval Court Martial in the Case of Alexander Slidell Mackenzie, a Commander in the Navy of the United States, &c: Including the Charges*

and Specifications of Charges Preferred Against Him by the Secretary of the Navy. To Which Is Annexed, an Elaborate Review, by James Fennimore [sic] *Cooper* (New York: Henry G. Langley, 1844), 265.

249 "The voice of all upright men": HWL to Alexander Slidell Mackenzie, July [no day] 1843, *Letters,* vol. 2, 546–547.

249 "passed the night": HWL Journal, Nov. 11, 1846.

249 "I like him in the main": FEAL to EAW, Dec. 23, 1846, FEAL-B2-F16-I18.

250 Herman Melville: See Charles Roberts Anderson, "The Genesis of Billy Budd," in *American Literature,* vol. 12, no. 3 (Nov. 1940), 329–346. For a discussion of the legal issues raised in the novella by Melville, see Tom Goldstein, "The Law, Once Again, 'Billy Budd' Is Standing Trial," *The New York Times,* June 10, 1988.

250 *Encyclopædia Americana*: Vol. 11, with the "Ship" essay, Longfellow House copy, LONG 8592.

250 "object . . . a mystery": [Alexander Slidell Mackenzie], "Ship," in Francis Lieber, ed., assisted by E. Wigglesworth, and T. G. Bradford, *Encyclopædia Americana. A Popular Dictionary of Arts, Sciences, Literature, History, Politics and Biography* (Philadelphia: Carey & Lea, 1832), vol. 11, 363–378. Vol. 9, also in Longfellow House, includes the two other essays contributed by Slidell Mackenzie, "Navigation" and "Navy."

250 "a charming visit": HWL Journal, Sept. 18, 1845.

251 "the author of": First quoted in Samuel Longfellow, *Final Memorials,* 121–122, later in Hans-Joachim Lang and Fritz Fleischmann, " 'All This Beauty, All This Grace': Longfellow's 'The Building of the Ship' and Alexander Slidell Mackenzie's 'Ship,' " in *The New England Quarterly,* vol. 54, no. 1 (March 1981), 104–118. For other contemporary comment on the technical fidelity of the poem, see Underwood, 152–161.

251 change on proof sheet: Henry Wadsworth Longfellow Dana, " 'Sail On, O Ship of State!': How Longfellow Came to Write These Lines 100 Years Ago," *Colby Library Quarterly,* 2d series, no. 13 (February 1950), 1–5.

251 "Urged him": HWL Journal, Nov. 4, 1849. For more on the political forces suggesting the change, see John Frederick Bell, "Poetry's Place in the Crisis and Compromise of 1850," in *Journal of the Civil War Era,* vol. 5, no. 3 (Sept. 2015), 399–421.

251 "What think you": HWL to James T. Fields, Nov. 15, 1849, *Letters,* vol. 3 (1071), 225. For more on the 1849 election, which none of the candidates for the Fourth Congressional District won for lack of a majority (required at that time), see Frank Otto Gatell, *John Gorham Palfrey and the New England Conscience* (Cambridge: Harvard University Press, 1963), 160–193.

252 "upon the platform": HWL Journal, Feb. 12, 1850. Henry reported the audience as "more than three thousand people."

252 "She stood forth": FEAL to Matilda Lieber, Feb. 23, 1850, FEAL-B2-F20-I4.

13 · AT THE SUMMIT

253 "turning . . . at the touch of a finger": The seemingly effortless movement of the "immense bulk," as Henry put it in his journal, of the Harvard Observatory telescope was explained in "Sketch of William Cranch Bond," *The Popular Science Monthly* (New York: D. Appleton, 1895), vol. 47, 400–408, to wit: "The chief peculiarity of its mechanism is in the method of rotation by means of smoothly-turned

spheres of iron. The dome rests on these at equidistant points, and, being set in motion by suitable gearing, the iron balls sustaining its weight roll along a level circular track of iron, the circumference of which is equal to that of the dome."

254 "grand introduction": HWL Journal, Oct. 25, 1848.

254 "It is luxurious": FEAL to TGA, Feb. 18, 1850, FEAL-B2-F20-I3.

254 "Bought one or two books": HWL Journal, Jan. 16, 1850.

254 "a telegraphic dispatch from Portland": FEAL to EAW, March 18, 1851, FEAL-B3-F1-I9.

254 "curious sight": HWL Journal, Dec. 13, 1862.

254 Sumner in the shower: Ernest Longfellow, 22. Known as a shower-bath, the novelty device was among Nathan Appleton's numerous wedding gifts to Henry and Fanny. See *Historic Furnishings Report*, 135; also appendix A, "receipts for wedding gifts" from Nathan Appleton.

255 "with my soul": Laura Bridgman to HWL, Feb. 8, 1852, HL, bMS Am 1340.2 (723).

255 "bends and bayous": Boston *Journal*, Dec. 5, 1846. See also "John Banvard's Great Picture—Life on the Mississippi," in *Littell's Living Age*, Dec. 11, 1847, 511–515.

255 "I see a panorama": HWL Journal, Dec. 17, 1846.

255 "In materials for this": HWL Journal, Dec. 15, 1846.

256 "Murmuring pines" and "hemlocks": See John Frederic Herbin, *Grand-Pré: A Sketch of the Acadian Occupation of the Shores of the Basin of Minas* (Toronto: William Briggs, 1900). While noting "a few discrepancies" in Henry's description of Grand-Pré topography and history, Herbin deemed the poem to be "in the main, correct" (151).

256 Ten thousand photographs: See Jack Naylor, "The Photographic Discovery of a Lifetime," *New England Journal of Photographic History*, nos. 148/149 (1996), 27–36, 55, a feature on the photograph collection at Longfellow House, which had just recently come to light: "The thousands of photographs have always been in the house. They were in some of the fifty trunks in the attic, in closets and in the basement where they presently have accumulated."

256 "Very good": HWL Journal, Dec. 19, 1846. Fanny wrote this of the presentation to Emmeline: "I sailed down the Mississippi the other day, witnessing Banvard's painting unrolled from three miles of canvas, and felt almost consoled for never having seen it it seemed so like reality." Jan. 19, 1847, FEAL-B2-F17-I3. The advertised length of the canvas was three miles, but was probably about half a mile, according to modern estimates. See Paul Collins, *Banvard's Folly* (New York: Picador, 2001), 1–24.

256 "*Evangeline* is ended": HWL Journal, Feb. 27, 1847.

256 "a national literature": Henry Wadsworth Longfellow, *Kavanagh: A Tale* (Boston: Ticknor, Reed and Fields, 1849), 92–93. For a discussion of the goal to establish a "national literature" during this period, with close attention given to *Kavanagh*, and this quotation in particular, see John T. Frederick, "American Literary Nationalism: The Process of Definition, 1825–1850," *The Review of Politics*, vol. 21, no. 1 (Jan. 1959), 224–238.

258 Andrew Craigie: See Pratt, passim; Maycock, 15–34; Anthony J. Connors, "Andrew Craigie: Brief Life of a Patriot and Scoundrel: 1754–1819," in *Harvard Magazine*, November-December 2011. His role as the "first pharmacist" is recognized each year with presentation of the Andrew Craigie Award for the advancement of professional pharmacy in the federal government.

258 "almost the whole": Lucius R. Paige, *History of Cambridge, Massachusetts, 1630–1877* (Boston: H. O. Houghton, 1877), 204. Paige wrote that Craigie's earliest transactions in the Lechmere Point section of Cambridge were conducted "with much skill and secrecy. His name does not appear on the records until the whole scheme was accomplished" (183).

258 "eccentric to the last": HWL, Craigie House journal in his hand, with clippings inserted, HL, MS Am 1340.2 (159).

259 The Craigies: See Pratt, passim.

259 Jared Sparks: *The Writings of George Washington: Being His Correspondence, Addresses, Messages, and Other Papers, Official and Private,* 12 vols. (Boston: American Stationers' Company/John B. Russell, 1833–1837).

259 Harvard Observatory: Factual information drawn primarily from Solon I. Bailey, *The History and Work of Harvard Observatory, 1839–1927,* no. 4 in the Harvard Observatory Monographs series (New York: McGraw Hill, 1931). For an early account, see "The Astronomical Observatory of Harvard University," in *Christian Examiner & Religious Miscellany,* March 1, 1851, 264–279.

259 "rejoice": Daniel W. Baker, *History of the Harvard College Observatory During the Period 1849–1890* (Cambridge, MA: Boston Evening Traveler, 1890), 15. The first Harvard Observatory operated from 1839 to 1847 with a much smaller telescope in a house just off Harvard Yard formerly owned by Richard Henry Dana, father of the author of *Two Years Before the Mast,* and today the site of Lamont Library. *The Glass Universe* (New York: Penguin, 2016), by Dava Sobel, examines the work of a group of African American women during the late nineteenth and early twentieth centuries who studied, compared, classified, and catalogued data that had been photographed at the observatory on thousands of glass plates.

259 Nineteenth-century wizardry: My gratitude to Dr. Owen J. Gingerich, professor emeritus of astronomy and of the history of science at Harvard University, and a senior astronomer emeritus of the Smithsonian Astrophysical Observatory, whose office in Cambridge is located within feet of the historic telescope, for showing me the wondrous device, and allowing me a hands-on appreciation of the mechanics involved. For more on his writing and his extraordinary collection of books relating to the history of astronomy, see my profile "Mighty Heavens: An Astronomer Casts His Gaze on Rare Ephemerides," in *Fine Books & Collections,* Summer 2012.

260 "over the fields": HWL Journal, April 4, 1844.

260 "Prof. Longfellow [and his] Lady": William Cranch Bond and George Phillips Bond, Harvard Observatory guest book, Oct. 30, 1847, quoted in *Sky & Telescope,* June 2001, 75. Fanny was equally excited about visiting the new marvel located near their property. "I intend, some fine night, to take a peep thro' our noble telescope at the worlds beyond the clouds," she wrote Emmeline in an undated letter. "So fine an instrument in our clear atmosphere is to astonish the world perhaps by many discoveries. It has already resolved the nebulae of Orion into stars which was never done before." FEAL to EAW, FEAL-B2-F18-I52.

261 "immense and awful idea": HWL Journal, Oct. 30, 1847.

261 "a weak, watery": Ibid.

261 "gash": Ibid., Nov. 3, 1848.

261 "The soul": Ibid., Jan. 7, 1848.

261 "I like to look": Ibid., May 11, 1850.

261 "a poet of the Night": Arvin, 64.

261 "Hymn to the Night": Other poems in Henry's oeuvre that heavily use imagery of the night include: "The Light of Stars," 1839; "Excelsior," 1842; "Endymion," 1842; "The Evening Star," 1845; "Pegasus in Pound," 1850; "The Galaxy," 1875; "The Hanging of the Crane," 1875; "The Harvest Moon," 1878; "Night" 1880; and "Moonlight," 1882.

262 "Manuscript Gleanings and Literary Scrap Book": HL, MS Am 1340 (146).

262 "Occultation of Orion": For a close critical reading of the poem, including the veracity of Longfellow's astronomical details, see Michael Zimmerman, "War and Peace: Longfellow's 'The Occultation of Orion,'" in *American Literature*, vol. 38, no. 4 (Jan. 1967), 540–546.

262 "Astronomically speaking": HWL, *The Complete Works of Henry Wadsworth Longfellow*, revised edition (Boston: James Osgood and Co., 1876), vol. 2, 272.

263 John White Webster letters to HWL: Houghton, bMS Am 1340.2 (5894).

263 wives well acquainted: Three months before the murder, Fanny mentioned "Our friends, the Websters in Cambridge" in a letter to her sister Mary Appleton Macintosh, Aug. 6, 1849, FEAL-B2-F19-I21.

263 "Matinée Musicale": HWL Journal, Oct. 30, 1849.

264 "a good natured Don Quixote": FEAL to EAW, Nov. 26, 1849, FEAL-B3-F14-I7 and FEAL-B3-F13-I77.

264 "You will see": FEAL to EAW, Dec. 4, 1849, FEAL-B2-F19-I29.

265 "Nothing talked of": HWL Journal, Nov. 2, 1849.

265 "rainy, cold, bleak": Ibid., Dec. 3, 1849.

265 "It seems . . . with you": FEAL to EAW, Dec. 3, 1849, FEAL-B3-F14-I7, FEAL-B3-F13-I77.

266 "dark horror": FEAL to Mary Longfellow Greenleaf, Dec. 4, 1849, FEAL-B2-F19-I29.

266 "beyond a reasonable doubt": *Commonwealth of Massachusetts v. John White Webster* has been the subject of numerous books, monographs, and journal articles, Simon Schama's *Dead Certainties: Unwarranted Speculations* (New York: Alfred A. Knopf, 1991) and Paul Collins's *Blood & Ivy: The 1849 Murder That Scandalized Harvard* (New York: Norton, 2018) among them.

266 "This horrid murder": HWL Journal, Dec. 7, 1849.

267 "whitewashed cell": Ibid., Dec. 12, 1849.

267 "They brought": Ibid., March 31, 1850.

267 "We have survived . . . public executions": FEAL to NA, April 8, 1850, FEAL-B2-F20-I10.

268 "Poor Dr. Webster": HWL Journal, Aug. 30, 1850.

268 "too good": Ibid., Jan. 14, 1851.

268 "hanging still": FEAL to EAW, Jan. 18, 1851, FEAL-B3-F1-I2.

269 "dearest Papa . . . impartiality": FEAL to NA, May 4, 1851, FEAL-B3-F1-I15.

269 donations: Included in HWL account books in Houghton Library, which also itemize income from writing and teaching, 1835–1840, MS Am 1340 (150); 1840–1882 MS Am 1340 (152); Book of Donations 1874–1880 (152); HWL book of donations, MS Am 1340 (155). For more on Longfellow's response to slavery and donations, see Irmscher, *Public Poet, Private Man,* 109–119.

270 "public opinion in Massachusetts": William Craft, *Running a Thousand Miles for Freedom; or, the Escape of William and Ellen Craft from Slavery* (London: William Tweedie, 1860), 82.

270 Boston free black community: See Horton and Horton, passim.

270 Fredrika Bremer's American trip: See Adolph B. Benson, "American Appreciation of Fredrika Bremer," in *Scandinavian Studies and Notes*, vol. 8, no. 1 (Feb. 1924), 14–33. Called "the Swedish Jane Austen" in some circles, her *Sketches of Everyday Life* were wildly popular in Britain and the United States during the 1840s and 1850s.

270 "surprised to find . . . agreeable wife": Fredrika Bremer, tr. Mary Howitt, *The Homes of the New World: Impressions of America* (New York: Harper & Brothers, 1853), vol. 1, 133–135.

271 "whole table full": HWJ Journal, Dec. 20, 1849.

271 "Longfellow is an agreeable": Bremer, *The Homes of the New World*, 135.

271 "among the most": Ibid., 138.

272 "On Monday": Ibid., 220.

272 "She has given me": FEAL to Matilda Lieber, Feb. 23, 1850, FEAL-B2-F20-I4. Plaster cast of Fredrika Bremer's hand: LONG 17849.

272 "Longfellow, the author": Bremer, *The Homes of the New World*, 43.

273 "though I do not think": Fredrika Bremer to HWL, Sept. 9, 1850, HL, bMS Am 1340.2 (711).

273 "She is very feminine": HWL Journal, Sept. 27, 1850.

273 "Jenny came in": Ibid., Oct. 1, 1850.

273 "There is something": Ibid., June 26, 1851.

273 "I congratulate you": HWL to Harriet Beecher Stowe, Jan. 29, 1853, *Letters*, vol. 3, 371.

273 "I hope that I": Harriet Beecher Stowe to HWL, Feb. 1, 1853, HL bMS Am 1340.2 (5361).

273 "How she is shaking": HWL Journal, Feb. 24, 1853.

273 "Henry, as you have doubtless": FEAL to Samuel Longfellow, Feb. 22, 1854, FEAL-B3-F4-I2. Henry's eighteen-year professional relationship with Harvard is examined at length by Carl Johnson in *Professor Longfellow of Harvard*, including a full examination of the factors that contributed to his resignation aside from the desire to spend more time writing, notably his disagreements with the college administrators over policy and the curriculum.

274 "on the last": HWL Journal, April 19, 1851. When Henry concluded a similar course four years earlier (June 16, 1851), "I told the class that they had finished the *Inferno* perhaps in more senses than one; but they must not think immediately to enter *Paradiso*. The next canto of the poem and of life would be the *Purgatorio*, of which they would have a prelude in the examination on Wednesday. How glad most of them must be to see the end of this drilling."

14 · PERICLES AND ASPASIA

275 "The sea was glorious": FEAL to EAW, July 28, 1851, FEAL-B3-F1-I33.

275 "You can not escape": George William Curtis, *Lotus-Eating: A Summer Book* (London: Richard Bentley, 1852), 139–140.

276 "low, long house": HWL Journal, July 5, 1850.

276 "Boston in Summer clothes": FEAL to ALP, Aug. 25, 1847, FEAL-B2-F18-I17.

276 "No city has": Curtis, *Lotus-Eating*, 137.

276 George William Curtis: See Winter, 264–266.

277 Charles Eliot Norton recalled meeting the "long-haired and sweet-visaged George Curtis" at the Café de Paris, and that it was "the beginning of the friendship which

was to mean much to me during the remainder of my life." In Sara Norton, *Letters of Charles Eliot Norton*, 68.

277 "very nice supper": HWL Journal, March 24, 1851.

277 "A very pleasant . . . remarkable book": Ibid., March 27, 28, 1851.

277 "very learned and original": Ibid., March 23, 18, 1851.

277 "a very summery book": FEAL to Sam Longfellow, March 31, 1851, FEAL-B3-F1-I13.

278 "lulled": FEAL to TGA, March 31, 1851, FEAL-B3-F1-I12.

278 "We take long walks": FEAL to IAJ, July 20, 1851, FEAL-B3-F1-I25.

278 "spacious . . . complete our number": FEAL to ALP, July 17, 1852, FEAL-B3-F2-I18.

279 "a singular damsel": FEAL to TGA, Sept. 13, 1852, FEAL-B3-F2-I21. The Houghton Library collection of incoming letters to HWL includes six from Faustina Hesse Hodges. BMS Am 1340.2 (2755).

280 sheet music collection, 1846–1947: LONG 23207. The LiederArchive Net is an online compilation of texts to more than 150,000 settings of Lieder (art songs: German plural of *Lied, song*) and other vocal pieces such as choral works, madrigals, and part songs, in 125 languages. As of this writing, 1,160 musical compositions based on a Longfellow poem have been documented, the most for any American writer. Of the dozen poets writing in English inspected by the author for comparison, only Shakespeare (1,902) and William Blake (1,383), neither of them American, had more citations. Others examined include Emily Dickinson (1,084), Walt Whitman (778), Tennyson (795), Coleridge (690), Keats (203), and Wordsworth (167).

280 "We went and sat": HWL Journal, July 5, 1852.

280 "a shady nook": Ibid., July 9, 1852.

280 Sephardic community in Newport: See John J. Appel, "Henry Wadsworth Longfellow's Presentation of the Spanish Jews," in *Publications of the American Jewish Historical Society*, vol. 45, no. 1 (Sept. 1955), 20–34, and Hammett W. Smith, "A Note to Longfellow's 'The Jewish Cemetery at Newport,'" in *College English*, vol. 18, no. 2 (Nov. 1956), 103–104. For a factual reading of the poem, and the highly critical response to it in verse by the Jewish American poet Emma Lazarus (1849–1887), see Max Cavitch, "Emma Lazarus and the Golem of Liberty," in *American Literary History*, vol. 18, no. 1 (Spring 2006), 1–28.

281 "great charm of manner": Ernest Longfellow, 40–41.

281 "most radiant": Alice Longfellow, undated typescript of "The Old Order Changes: Morituri Salutamus," text of an address prepared for members of the Cambridge Historical Society, Longfellow House archives.

281 "the acquaintanceships and friendships": FEAL to TGA, Sept. 13, 1851, FEAL-B3-F2-I287.

281 "lithe, slender . . . without a manuscript": Winter, 224, 246.

281 Thucydides and Pericles: See Lowell Edmunds and Richard Martin, "Thucydides 2.65.8: ελευθερως," *Harvard Studies in Classical Philology*, vol. 81 (1977), 187–193.

281 Aspasia of Miletus: Factual details and quotations for this segment drawn from Madeleine M. Henry, *Prisoner of History: Aspasia of Miletus and Her Biographical Tradition* (New York and Oxford: Oxford University Press, 1995); Cheryl Glenn, "Sex, Lies, and Manuscript: Refiguring Aspasia in the History of Rhetoric," in *College Composition and Communication*, vol. 45, no. 2 (May 1994), 180–199; and *Plutarch's Lives, the Translation Called Dryden's*, corrected from the Greek and revised by A. H. Clough, 5 vols. (Boston: Little, Brown and Co., 1906).

283 paper trails: I express herewith my gratitude to Dr. Diana Korzenik, professor emerita at Massachusetts College of Art and cofounder in 1994 of the Friends of Longfellow House, for pointing out to me the Aspasia segment in *Lotus-Eating,* and the Curtis dedication to Fanny in *Prue and I,* which includes the phrase "Castles in Spain."

283 "fashionable life": William Dean Howells, review of six books by George William Curtis, in *North American Review,* vol. 107 (Boston: Ticknor and Fields, 1868), 104–117.

284 "Do you ever see": FEAL to EAW, Oct. 1, 1861, FEAL-B3- F1-I37.

284 epistolary novel: Walter Savage Landor, *Pericles and Aspasia,* 2 vols. (London: Saunders and Otley, 1836), shelved in Craigie House library, "H. W. Longfellow" bookplate on front pastedown, LONG 5664-5665.

284 histories: Oliver Goldsmith, *History of Greece,* 2 vols. (1812), LONG 255–256; William Mitford, *History of Greece,* 8 vols. (1838), LONG 2567–2574; William Smith, *History of Greece, from the Earliest Times to the Roman Conquest* (1855), LONG 12079.

284 "Rappaccini's Daughter": First published in the December 1844 issue of *The United States Magazine and Democratic Review.* See *The Complete Works of Nathaniel Hawthorne: Mosses From an Old Manse* (Boston: Houghton Mifflin, 1882), vol. 2, preface 107–109, "from the writings of Aubépine."

284 "with capital sketches": FEAL to TGA, Nov. 15, 1852, FEAL-B3-F2-I25.

285 "There is much readable": FEAL to EAW, July 20, 1840, FEAL-B2-F10-I21. Fanny was less charitable about the journal in a letter to her cousin Isaac Appleton Jewett: "The last number of the *Dial* is out—more absurd if possible than the other—'tis like reading thro' cobwebs." Oct. 3, 1840, FEAL-B2-F10-I24.

285 "Gastric Sayings" and "train of fifteen railroad cars": Cited by Adam D. Shprintzen, in *The Vegetarian Crusade: The Rise of the American Reform Movement, 1817–1921* (Chapel Hill, NC: The University of North Carolina Press, 2013), 48.

285 "Orphic Alcott—or Plato Skimpole": [George William Curtis], *Homes of American Authors,* 245; other uses of the nickname appear in the essay on pp. 246, 249, and 250. For a thorough discussion of the Dickens character, with full historical context, see Stephen F. Fogle, "Skimpole Once More," in *Nineteenth-Century Fiction,* vol. 7, no. 1 (June 1952), 1–18; Brahma Chaudhuri, "Dickens and the Critic: 1852–53," in *Victorian Periodicals Review,* vol. 21, no. 4 (Winter 1988), 139–144; and Eleanor M. Gates, "Leigh Hunt, Lord Byron, and Mary Shelley: The Long Goodbye," in *Keats-Shelley Journal,* vol. 35 (1986), 149–167.

286 "Plato Skimpole was": George Willis Cooke, ed., *Early Letters of George William Curtis to John S. Dwight: Brook Farm and Concord* (New York: Harper & Brothers, 1898), 96.

286 "for someone else's witticism": *New York Times Saturday Review,* Sept. 10, 1898.

286 "I should . . . This Aspasia": Ibid., Sept. 17, 1898.

286 "acquainted . . . self-possession": FEAL to MAM, June 19, 1854, FEAL-B3-F4-I8.

286 "A feeling": HWL Journal, June 24, 1854.

287 "I am staying now": George William Curtis letter to Charles F. Briggs, June 8, 1854, quoted in Cary, 86.

287 "a kind reception . . . guessed it": CMS to HWL, Aug. 27, 1853, Houghton bMS Am 1340.2 (4988).

287 "Now that the vein": FEAL to GWG, March 31, 1844, FEAL B2-F14-I7.

287 "I am a pretty active": FEAL to ZL, April 3, 1844. FEAL B2-F14-I111.

288 "I suppose I can": FEAL to EAW, July 2, 1847, FEAL-B2-F17-I116.

288 "I hope you will like": FEAL to Sam Longfellow, Nov. 5, 1855, FEAL-B3-F6-I114.

288 "Henry has been writing": FEAL to MLG, May 24, 1858, FEAL-B3-F9-I4.

289 "How brief this chronicle": HWL Journal, Oct. 14, 1853.

289 Curtis letters to HWL: In five folders, Houghton, bMS Am 1340.2 (1395); the two Curtis letters to Fanny are in FEAL, Incoming Correspondence, dated July 25, 1854, and Nov. 5, 1855, LONG 1011-2-2-51-15. I was able to locate no letters Fanny may have written to Curtis in any of the institutions that collect either of their correspondence.

289 "My dear Mrs. Longfellow": George William Curtis letter to FEAL, Nov. 5, 1855, FEAL Incoming Correspondence, LONG 1011-2-2-51-15.

289 "A generous box": FEAL to TGA, Dec. 1, 1856, FEAL-B3-F7-I116.

290 "the tacitness of the period": Author interview with Lawrence Buell, March 28, 2017.

290 "which may possibly be": FEAL to EAW, Jan. 13, 1857, FEAL-B3-F13-I63.

290 books inscribed by George William Curtis to Mrs. Longfellow in the Houghton Library: *Lotus-Eating: A Summer Book* (New York: Harper & Brothers, 1852), AC85. L8605.Zy852c; *The Potiphar Papers* (New York: G. P. Putnam & Co., 1854), AC85. L8605.Zy853c; *Prue and I* (New York: Dix, Edwards & Co., 1856), AC85.L8605. Zy856c.

291 "A man must have": Curtis, *Prue and I*, xix–xx. For an excellent biographical sketch of Curtis and a detailed discussion of the novel, see the introduction to the 1899 edition (in bibliography) by M. A. DeWolfe Howe, v–xv. See also William Dean Howells, *North American Review*, vol. 107, no. 220 (July 1868), 104–117 [untitled review of six books by Curtis]; and Florence A. Blanchard, "In Memoriam: George Wm. Curtis," in *Journal of Education*, vol. 36, no. 11, Sept. 22, 1892, 186–187.

15 · BALANCE AND HARMONY

293 "I could not": HWL Journal, June 25, 1854. A month after *Hiawatha* was published, Longfellow sent a complimentary copy to Henry Schoolcraft as "an acknowledgment of my obligation to you; for without your books, I could not have written mine," noting in particular how he had "adhered very faithfully to the old myths, and you will be amused to hear that a critic in the *National Intelligencer* accuses me of drawing many of these legends from the Finnish Poem *Kalevala*" (*Letters*, vol. 3, Dec. 14, 1855, 509).

293 "three huge quartos": HWL Journal, June 26, 1854.

293 "a few lines": Ibid., June 27, 1854.

293 "I think I shall call it": Ibid., June 28, 1854.

293 "I chose it instead": HWL to Freiligrath, Jan. 11, 1856, *Letters*, vol. 3, 517. The point was especially pertinent in this instance, as Freiligrath was translating *Hiawatha* into German.

293 "one hundred hands": HWL Journal, July 28, 1854.

293 nonstop flow of letters: "I thought that when I left College, I should have some leisure; but I have none. A hundred other claimants now take possession of my time; and I am as poor as ever in golden leisure!" (HWL Journal, Jan. 5, 1855).

293 "occupies and delights": HWL Journal, Oct. 19, 1854.

293 Alexander Hesler and collodion-on-glass plates: See Mary A. Foresta, *American Photographs in the First Century* (Washington: National Museum of American Art/ Smithsonian Institution Press, 1996), 131.

295 Minnesota Historical Society: Henry made no mention at all of this in either his journal or his correspondence, but it falls in line with the considerate way he typically went about doing things. In addition to this image, he acquired nine other contemporary photographs of the Minnehaha Falls taken from various vantage points, several of which could be viewed on his stereoscopic device. They are in the Longfellow House archives.

295 Ojibwa chief, Kah-ge-ga-gah-bowh: For an in-depth historical and critical assessment, see Christoph Irmscher, "The Song of Hiawatha," in *American History Through Literature, 1850–1870*, ed. Robert Sattelmeyer and Janet Gabler-Hover (Detroit: Charles Scribner's Sons, 2006), 1106–1112.

295 The Wounded Indian: HWL Journal, Jan. 27, 1851.

295 Louis Agassiz: See Irmscher, *Louis Agassiz*, passim; also Edward Lurie, "Louis Agassiz and the Races of Man," in *Isis*, vol. 45, no. 3 (Sept. 1954), 227–242, to wit: "Agassiz's position demonstrated the manner in which a scientific theory was made to serve a social doctrine, thus illustrating the important relationship between science and society in nineteenth-century America." His argument, now thoroughly discredited, "supported a plural belief in the origin of mankind."

295 "We went together": HWL Journal, June 13, 1850.

296 "right and only measure": Daniel Aaron, introduction to the Everyman Edition of *The Song of Hiawatha* (London: J. M. Dent, 1992), xi–xix. See my profile of Aaron in *Every Book Its Reader*, 208–222. For more on Aaron and the literary canon, see also Kenneth M. Price and Daniel Aaron, "An Interview with Daniel Aaron on the Library of America," *South Central Review*, vol. 5, no. 4 (Winter 1988), 60–71.

296 "pleasing series of pictures": Henry R. Schoolcraft, *The Myth of Hiawatha, and Other Oral Legends, Mythologic and Allegoric, of the North American Indians* (Philadelphia: J. B. Lippincott & Co., 1856), 1.

296 *Hiawatha* in translation: See Joe Lockard, "The Universal Hiawatha," in *American Indian Quarterly*, vol. 24, no. 1 (Winter 2000), 110–125.

296 "From his shoulder": Lewis Carrol's "Hiawatha's Photographing" first appeared in *The Train*, an English periodical, in December, 1857.

297 "*Hiawatha's* metre": FEAL to MAM, Jan. 14, 1856, FEAL-B3-F9-I11.

297 Creative works inspired by *Hiawatha*: See Cynthia D. Nickerson, "Artistic Interpretations of Henry Wadsworth Longfellow's 'The Song of Hiawatha,' 1855–1900," *The American Art Journal*, vol. 16, no. 3 (Summer 1984), 49–77.

298 "was adapted into": Dana Gioia, in Parini, 65.

299 Three operas: *I Puritani*, Jan. 15; *Lucrezia Borgia*, Jan. 17; *Norma*, Jan. 22.

299 "This music for a season": HWL Journal, Jan. 17, 1855.

299 "She read us": Ibid., March 9, 1855.

299 "Over here": James Russell Lowell letter to William Wetmore Story, July 16, 1856, in Henry James, vol. 1, 327.

299 "which has brought me": Charles Eliot Norton to HWL, Oct. 21, 1849, in Sara Norton, *Letters of Charles Eliot Norton*, vol. 1, 40.

299 "is crammed . . . hinted at in them": FEAL to MAM, Dec. 1, 1857, FEAL-B3-F8-I14.

300 "quiet evenings": HWL Journal, Jan. 30, 1855.

300 "charming": Ibid., Jan. 27, 1855.

300 "Society and hospitality . . . and thoughtfulness": Alice M. Longfellow, "Longfellow in Home Life," in *The Cambridge Magazine*, vol. 1, no. 2, New Series (March 1896), 73–82.

301 "very methodical": Ernest Longfellow, 13. For more on the use of cartridge paper by writers and artists, see the "Fiery Consequences" chapter in my book *On Paper*.

301 Havana cigars: LONG 18456.

301 "bit of an anvil": LONG 7203.

302 "If Socrates were here": Ralph Waldo Emerson, in *Emerson in His Journals*, ed. Joel Porte (Cambridge: Belknap Press of Harvard University Press, 1982), 447.

302 "At dinner": HWL Journal, Nov. 23, 1848.

302 Charley's shattered musket: LONG 13823.

302 "the curators of their own lives": One of many author conversations and interviews over a ten-year period with James M. Shea, director emeritus of the Longfellow House—Washington's Headquarters National Historic Site.

302 "slow to acquire": FEAL to ZL, Feb. 19, 1847, FEAL-B2-F17-I8.

303 "disobedient": "Chronicle of the Children of Craigie Castle (Continued)" (1849–1858), LONG 21573, Aug. 3, 1849.

303 "very active": "Chronicle of the Children of Craigie Castle" (1848), LONG 21576, Jan. 1, 1848.

303 "after an ebullition": Ibid., Feb. 7, 1848.

303 "I know not": "Chronicle of the Children of Craigie Castle (Continued)" (1849–1858), LONG 21573, Aug. 3, 1849.

303 "I get very tired": "Chronicle of the Children of Craigie Castle" (1848), LONG 21576, March 1, 1848.

303 "Charley struck me": Ibid., Oct. 30, 1848.

303 "a very good little boy": FEAL to ZL, Feb. 19, 1847, FEAL-B2-F17-I8.

303 "He was at Fresh Pond": HWL Journal, April 10, 1856.

304 "He bought": FEAL to MLG, May 2, 1856, FEAL-B3-F7-I4. The percussion musket in two pieces: LONG 13823.

304 "conspicuous": HWL Journal, June 29, 1854.

304 "We are all greatly": FEAL to Samuel Longfellow, Feb. 22, 1854, FEAL-B3-F4-I2. The line Fanny quoted from John Milton, in context: "So dear to Heaven is saintly chastity / That, when a soul is found sincerely so, / A thousand liveried angels lackey her, / Driving far off each thing of sin and guilt," (*Comus*, lines 453–456).

304 "The Crime against Kansas": See Donald, 281–288.

305 "this damn fool": quoted in Donald, 286.

305 caning of Sumner: Ibid., 288–297.

306 "Sumner's health": FEAL to TGA, July 12, 1856, FEAL-B3-F7-I6, FEAL-B3-F14-I19.

306 "Burlingame has had": FEAL to TGA, July 29, 1856, FEAL-B3-F7-I7. See also Manisha Sinha, "The Caning of Charles Sumner: Slavery, Race, and Ideology in the Age of the Civil War," *Journal of the Early Republic*, vol. 23, no. 2 (Summer 2003), 233–262.

306 "Perfect intellectual rest": FEAL to Samuel Longfellow, Feb. 5, 1857, FEAL-B3-F8-I6.

307 "no personal feeling": HWL Journal, Jan. 28, 1857.

307 Saturday Club: For an account of the organization's first fifteen years, including vignettes of its members, see Edward Waldo Emerson, *The Early Years of the Saturday Club, 1855–1870* (Boston: Houghton Mifflin, 1918).

307 "Lowell was here": HWL Journal, April 29, 1857.

308   chestnut tree: Henry thanked the "dear children" of Cambridge for their gift in a
       poem, "From My Arm-Chair," published in *Ultima Thule* (1880).

308   letter announcing Nightingale poem: FEAL to MAM, Nov. 2, 1857, FEAL-B3-
       F8-I13.

308   "Tom had a beautiful": FEAL to EAW, Jan. 28, 1846, FEAL-B2-F16-I2.

308   "remarkable letter": FEAL to EAW, Feb. 6, 1846, FEAL-B2-F16-I4.

308   Parthenope Nightingale: Letter of thanks from Florence's sister to HWL, HL, MS
       Am 1340.2–1340.7 (4127).

309   "Wherever there is": *The Times,* February 1855, quoted in Sarah A. Tooley, *The Life
       of Florence Nightingale* (London: Cassell and Co., 1914), 175–176.

310   "Santa Filomena": First appearance in *The Atlantic Monthly,* November 1857; first
       book appearance, *Birds of Passage* (1858).

310   "Early in the war": Mark Bostridge, *Florence Nightingale: The Making of an Icon*
       (New York: Farrar, Straus & Giroux, 2008), 254.

310   "Longfellow was the poet": Author interview with Christoph Irmscher, Sept. 6,
       2018.

311   "pass the summer": FEAL to EAW, March 6, 1860, FEAL-B3-F11-I7.

311   "The Barbarism of Slavery": *Speech of Hon. Charles Sumner, on the Bill for the
       Admission of Kansas as a Free State, in the United States Senate, June 4, 1860* (Boston:
       Thayer and Eldridge, 1860).

311   "Allow me": FEAL to CS, June 6, 1860, FEAL-B3-F11-I13.

16 · HOUR OF DARKNESS

312   "very pretty": FEAL to MAM, Dec. 16, 1860, FEAL-B3-F11-I29.

313   "hour of darkness and peril and need": Henry accepted a suggestion from James
       T. Fields to go with this particularly powerful line in the poem. His original ver-
       sion had read, "In the hour of peril men will hear," prompting his editor to rec-
       ommend the alternate construction; he also proposed a variant for the final line,
       which Henry adopted as well. See James C. Austin, "J. T. Fields and the Revision
       of Longfellow's Poems: Unpublished Correspondence," in *New England Quarterly,*
       vol. 24, no. 2 (June 1951), 239–250.

313   "expedition": HWL Journal, April 5, 1860.

313   "I wrote a few": Ibid., April 9, 1860.

313   Paul Revere (1735–1818): See "Early American Artists and Mechanics, No. 11, Paul
       Revere," ed. J. T. & E. Buckingham, *New England Magazine,* vol. 3 (Boston, 1832),
       305–314. Paul Revere's letter to Jeremy Belknap was first published in *Collections
       of the Massachusetts Historical Society,* 1st series, vol. 5 (1798). A full, open-access
       facsimile of Revere's eight-page letter to Belknap (1798), along with side-by-side
       transcriptions of each individual page, can be viewed at the website of the Mas-
       sachusetts Historical Society (MHS Collections Online). For more on the factual
       basis for the poem, see "New Research on 'Paul Revere's Ride' Marks the Poem's
       150th Anniversary," *Longfellow House Bulletin,* vol. 11, no. 2 (Dec. 2009), 1, 3–5. For
       more on Jeremy Belknap, the Massachusetts Historical Society, and its collection
       of 12 million manuscripts, see my books *A Gentle Madness,* 142–144, and *On Paper,*
       234–245.

314   "unacknowledged and uncollected translations": Horace E. Scudder, ed., *The Com-*

plete Poetical Works of Longfellow (Cambridge: Riverside Press/Houghton Mifflin, 1886); the sonnet, "Art and Nature," is on page 652.

315 "Dear Sir": HWL letter to an unidentified correspondent, April 27, 1877, *Letters,* vol. 6, 267. In a footnote, Andrew Hilen cites Henry's "letter calendar" for that date as giving the name "Henry S. Stone" for the recipient.

315 "I have learned": Jill Lepore, "How Longfellow Woke the Dead," *American Scholar,* vol. 80, no. 2 (Spring 2011), 33–46. For full text of the Bertha Shaffer letter to Henry, and others he received from a wide variety of admirers, see Christoph Irmscher, *Public Poet,* 131–152. See also Sydelle Pearl, *Dear Mr. Longfellow: Letters to and from the Children's Poet* (Amherst, NY: Prometheus Books, 2012).

315 "The dissolution": HWL Journal, Feb. 15, 1861.

315 "after the 4th of March": FEAL to EAW, Feb. 12, 1861, FEAL-B3-F12-I4.

315 Hawthorne's dedication to Pierce: Publisher James T. Fields would characterize Hawthorne's "determination at all hazards to dedicate a book to his friend" as a "beautiful incident," especially since Pierce's politics "at present shut him away from the faith of patriots." But Hawthorne, he added, "has loved him since college days and will not relent." James T. Fields journal, Feb. 11, 1863, quoted in M. A. DeWolfe Howe, *Memoirs of a Hostess,* 14–15.

316 "And so the War": HWL Journal, April 12, 1861.

316 "It has a far-off": Ibid., April 23, 1861.

316 "I was glad": Ibid., April 28, 1861.

316 "The word May": Ibid., May 1, 1861.

316 "looks death": Ibid., May 4, 1861.

316 "*dolce far niente*": Ibid., May 17, 1861.

316 "Nothing alive": Ibid., May 8, 1861.

317 "Ticknor looks": Ibid., May 18, 1861.

317 "If one": Ibid., June 19, 1867.

317 "We seem": Ibid., June 26, 1867.

317 "a grand time . . . sun-burnt": Ibid., July 5, 6, 7, 1861.

318 "Edith's hair": HWL Family Papers, filed as "separated items removed from Edith Longfellow Dana Papers (box 57, folder 12); personal materials," 5 envelopes, box 12, folder 34 (10-14).

319 Victorians and hair relics: See Deborah Lutz, "The Dead Still Among Us: Victorian Secular Relics, Hair Jewelry, and Death Culture," *Victorian Literature and Culture,* vol. 39, no. 1 (2011), 127–142; Deborah Lutz, "Relics and Death Culture in *Wuthering Heights,*" *Novel: A Forum on Fiction,* vol. 45, no. 3 (Fall 2012), 389–408.

319 "one of the commonest": Wilkie Collins, *Hide and Seek: or, the Mystery of Mary Grace* (London: Chatto and Windus, 1875 edition), 208.

319 "This literary fascination": Elizabeth G. Gitter, "The Power of Women's Hair in the Victorian Imagination," *PMLA,* vol. 99, no. 5 (Oct. 1984), 936–954.

319 red leather pouch: Initials H.W.L., Feb. 27, 1877, a lock of white hair, with a valentine inscribed, "Hair of the poet Longfellow cut by Rose Fay Xmas 1876," HL, MS Am 1340 (231).

319 Houghton locks of hair and poem "Two Locks of Hair": The locks are dated, in Henry's hand, Sept. 11, 1848, and July 10, 1861, HL, MS Am 1340 (51).

320 "You are lucky": FEAL letter to Ernest Longfellow, July 7, 1861, FEAL-B3-F12-I12.

320 "As I was stepping": Ernest Longfellow, 69.

321   Playing with matches: Charles C. Calhoun, in *A Rediscovered Life* (215–218), cites a memorandum written in 1908 by Richard Henry Dana III, the husband of Edith Longfellow, in which Annie Allegra is said to have acknowledged responsibility for what happened in the mishap, although the memory of a traumatized five-year-old, related half a century after the fact and passed on through a third party, has to be weighed accordingly. The memorandum is in the collections of the Massachusetts Historical Society.

321   "This was before . . . martyred saint": Skinner, 8–17.

322   "There was nothing . . . the happiest": Charles Eliot Norton to Mrs. Gaskell, Aug. 12, 1861, in Norton, *Letters*, 238–241.

322   "trembled to look": William Dean Howells, "The White Mr. Longfellow," *Harper's New Monthly Magazine,* Aug. 1, 1896.

323   John Lothrop Motley and the Civil War: See William Peterfield Trent, ed., *A History of American Literature*, vol. 2 (New York: G. P. Putnam's Sons, 1919), 123–147.

323   *The History of the United Netherlands*: John Lothrop Motley, 1861, Longfellow House copy, LONG 10084, 12037-9.

323   "There is something": Motley, 173–174.

324   "almost daily holocaust": *The Lancet* (London), Oct. 27, 1859.

324   "that inflated absurdity . . . Suicide by Crinoline": *Punch* (London), March 22, 1862; April 23, 1862; May 3, 1862.

324   "crinoline accidents" . . . intense suffering: *The Examiner* (London), Jan. 4, 1862; Jan. 18, 1862.

325   "Every means": *The Spectator* (London), July 29, 1861.

325   "most piteous and agonizing": *Harper's Weekly,* Sept. 28, 1861, under the headline "Shocking Occurrence at Philadelphia," accompanied by an artist's rendering of the horror that took place two weeks earlier, on Sept. 14.

325   "the dresses of ballet girls": *Scientific American,* vol. 5, no. 13 (new series), Sept. 28, 1861.

326   "I remember": Ernest Longfellow, 69.

327   "Dearest Longfellow . . . God bless you.": Letters from CS to HWL, July 11 and July 21, 1861, in Pierce, vol. 4, 37.

327   "What is there": Julia Ward Howe to HWL, July 14, 1861, Houghton bMS Am 1340.2 (2864).

328   "How does Longfellow bear": Nathaniel Hawthorne letter to James T. Fields, July 14, 1861, Huntington Library, quoted in Mellow, 545.

328   "your terrific disaster": Thomas Buchanan Read to HWL, Aug. 20, 1861, HL, bMS Am 1340.2 (4601).

328   "I feel that only you": HWL to MAM, Aug. 18, 1861, *Letters*, vol. 4, 241–243.

329   "many thousand hearts": GWC to TGA, July 17, FEAL Misc. Correspondence 1861 07-17.

329   "dark valley . . . such things": GWC to HWL, Sept. 7, 1861, HL, bMS Am 1340.2 (1395).

330   "affectionate and touching": HWL to GWC, Sept. 28, 1861, *Letters*, vol. 4, 245.

330   "Henry is jealous": FEAL to EAW, Dec. 12, 1849, in two parts, FEAL-B3-F13-I76, FEAL-B3-F14-I22. Fanny's copy of *Shirley* (New York: Harper & Brothers, 1859), LONG 8153.

330   "Your letters": HWL to EAW, Oct. 17, 1861, HL, Am 1340.12 (12). The letter was

transcribed by Kathryn Hanson Plass, archives and collections specialist at Longfellow House—Washington's Headquarters National Historic Site.

331   "I am sorry": HWL to James T. Fields, Nov. 8, 1861, in *Letters,* vol. 4, 250.

331   "So closes": HWL Journal, single entry for August 1861.

17 · PERFECT PEACE

332   Lethe and Eunöe: In *Purgatorio,* the converging rivers at the peak of the earthly mountain upon reaching the Garden of Eden, through which penitents must wade and cleanse themselves of evil memory before entering Paradise; it is here, in the final canto of the canticle, that Dante is greeted by Beatrice.

332   "infant Hercules": FEAL to ALP, Aug. 7, 1845, FEAL-B2-F15-I18.

333   Peter Piper and Little Merrythought: See Irmscher, *Public Poet,* 66–76.

333   children's drawings: See Robert Arbour, " 'Not from the Grand Old Masters': The Art of Henry and Ernest Longfellow," in Irmscher and Arbour, 159–176, and Diana Korzenik, " 'That Is Best Which Liest Nearest': Longfellow Family Art, 1804–1924," in *New England Quarterly,* vol. 80, no. 3 (Sept. 2007), 491–501. The originals are kept in LONG 19588–19590 and 19617–19618.

334   letter to Santa Claus: Quoted in Andrew Hilen, "Charley Longfellow Goes to War," in *Harvard Library Bulletin,* vol. 14 (1960), issue 1, 59–81, and issue 2, 283–303.

334   "On Tuesday": HWL Journal, March 14, 1863.

334   "Dear Papa": CAL to HWL, undated, quoted by Hilen in "Charley Longfellow Goes to War," 59.

334   "Your motive": HWL to CAL, March 14, 1863, *Letters,* vol. 5, 313–314.

334   "I did not consider": Capt. W. H. McCartney to HWL, March 12, 1863, in Hilen, "Charley Longfellow Goes to War," 61–62.

335   "I expect to hear": HWL to CS, March 24, 1863, *Letters,* vol. 5, 317.

335   checklist: Henry spent about $800 outfitting his son for service in the Union Army.

335   "If I had taken my pick": CAL letter to his family, in Hilen, "Charley Longfellow Goes to War," 65.

335   "They may talk": Ibid., 285.

336   "A letter . . . it is finished": HWL Journal, March 16, 1863.

336   "In weariness of spirit": Ibid., Feb. 1, 1853. See Christian Dupont, "Longfellow and Dante," Kathleen Verdun, "Grace of Action: Dante in the Life of Longfellow," and Christoph Irmscher, "Reading for Our Delight," in Lansing, *Dante Studies.*

336   "I write a few lines": HWL to Catherine Eliot Norton, March 21, 1843, *Letters,* vol. 2, 521.

336   "thick warm fog": FEAL letter to EAW, Feb. 7, 1840, FEAL-B2-F10-I7.

336   "Let us, like": FEAL to MAM, July 18, 1853, FEAL-B3-F3-I13.

337   "Henry has gone to college": FEAL to EAW, March 15, 1847, FEAL-B2-F16-I32. The engraving of the Ary Scheffer painting of Paolo and Francesca, by Luigi Calamatta, *Françoise de Rimini,* LONG 4694.

337   "It is tempting": Irmscher, *Public Poet,* 156.

338   "I am reading along": FEAL to EAW, March 15, 1847, FEAL-B2-F16-I32.

338   "the great drama": Henry Wadsworth Longfellow Dana and Christian Y. Dupont, "Longfellow and Dante," *Dante Studies, with the Annual Report of the Dante Society,* no. 128 (2010), 239.

338 "I am like": quoted in Parke Godwin, *A Biography of William Cullen Bryant, with Extracts from His Private Correspondence* (New York: D. Appleton, 1883), vol. 2, 249–251.

338 "Of what I have been through": HWL to Ferdinand Freiligrath, May 24, 1867, *Letters,* vol. 5, 140–141.

338 "Translated the beautiful": HWL Journal, Feb. 10, 1862.

338 "Another week": Ibid., March 25, 1862.

339 "With all that he wrote": Unpublished manuscript of Longfellow's Harvard lectures on Dante, dated March 22, 1838, HL, MS Am 1340 (106). My gratitude to the Cambridge author Matthew Pearl for sharing with me his transcriptions of these lectures; the honors thesis Pearl wrote as a Harvard College undergraduate, "The Dante Club: A Re-assessment of the Emergence of Dante in Nineteenth Century America" (March 19, 1997), Harvard College Archives HU 89.808.1314), suggested to him the premise for his best-selling novel *The Dante Club* (New York: Random House, 2003). See my profile of Pearl in *Fine Books & Collections,* Summer 2016.

339 "Waiting, waiting, waiting": HWL Journal, Sept. 15, 1862.

340 "Write a little upon": Ibid., Oct. 11, 1862.

340 "a delicious . . . Boston westward": Ibid., Oct. 31, 1862.

341 "Everybody": HWL to James Ticknor, Aug. 29, 1863, *Letters,* vol. 4, 355. Following the publication of Henry's poem, the inn reopened for business under the new name "Longfellow's Wayside Inn," and has been designated a National Historic Landmark.

341 "all the characters": HWL to GWG, Dec. 28, 1863, *Letters,* vol. 4, 376–377.

341 "inherited a penchant": Hilen, in *Letters,* vol. 3, 76, fn. 3. See also John J. Appel, "Henry Wadsworth Longfellow's Presentation of the Spanish Jews," in *Publications of the American Jewish Historical Society,* vol. 45, no. 1 (September 1955), 20–34. Longfellow did two *Wayside Inn* sequels featuring the same cast of characters; the second appeared in 1870, the third two years after that. For a full discussion of the real-life narrators, see Van Schaick, 37–47.

341 "Fifteen thousand copies": HWL Journal, Nov. 25, 1863.

341 Nathan Appleton Jr. (1843–1906): the eldest son of Nathan Appleton and his second wife, Harriot Sumner Appleton, and though only two years older than Charley, was his mother Fanny's half-brother, and thus technically his uncle. Like Charley, he joined the Union Army in 1863 as a lieutenant, served honorably in several campaigns, and was with General Grant at Appomattox for the surrender of General Lee. His papers are divided between the Longfellow House—Washington's Headquarters National Historic Site and the Massachusetts Historical Society.

341 "We drank the health": Ibid., Nov. 26, 1863.

341 "camp fever": See Chapter III, "Camp Fevers," in Joseph J. Woodward, *Outlines of the Chief Camp Diseases of the United States Armies as Observed During the Present War* (Philadelphia: J. B. Lippincott, 1863), 74–161. Also Margaret Humphreys, "A Stranger to Our Camps: Typhus in American History," *Bulletin of the History of Medicine,* vol. 80, no. 2, 269–290.

342 "Yesterday": HWL to Ernest Longfellow, June 22, 1863, *Letters,* vol. 4, 342–343.

343 "bathing without clothes": Ernest Longfellow, 76–77; also Hilen, *Charley Goes to War,* 80–81.

343 "An Enfield bullet": HWL to GWG, Dec. 18, 1863, *Letters,* vol. 4, 372.

344 "I was not of age": Ernest Longfellow, 52.

344 Charley in Japan: See Laidlaw, passim, an annotated selection of the journals Charley kept during his residence in Japan in the early years of the Meiji period. My thanks to David R. Daly, curator at Longfellow House, for his insights on Charley, of whom he is the resident authority.

345 "Shall I put you down": HWL to CAL, dated "Xmas 1869," *Letters*, vol. 5, 311; Charley's response is quoted in a footnote.

347 "a lark": Charley's original cable from England to his father is lost; other materials relating to the crossing are in the Charles Appleton Longfellow Papers, BX1, FLDR4.

347 Civil War uniform: Two of Charley's cavalry hats have been preserved, both with crossed-sabers insignia, one an oval with the numeral 1, LONG 14050 and LONG 14051. His field jacket, LONG 14047.

347 "Lowell, Norton, and myself": HWL Journal, Oct. 15, 1865.

347 Dante Club meetings: See J. Chesley Mathews, "Mr. Longfellow's Dante Club," in *Annual Report of the Dante Society, with Accompanying Papers,* no. 76 (1958), 23–35.

348 "to consider": Charles Eliot Norton letter to Aubrey de Vere, Cambridge, March 25, 1867, in Sarah Norton, *Letters of Charles Eliot Norton*, vol. 1, 294.

348 "When Longfellow read": Howells, *Literary Friends,* 183–184.

349 "The supper": Ibid., 184–185. In all the meetings he attended of the Dante Club, Howells could recall only one instance of unpleasantness; it fell on a night immediately after Christmas, when holiday decorations were still strung about Craigie House. As the group came out from the evening's reading, cuttings of holly and pine wreathed about the chandelier above the supper table caught fire from the gas flame. "Longfellow ran forward and caught the burning garlands down and bore them out. No one could speak for thinking what he must be thinking of when the ineffable calamity of his home befell it" (195).

350 "priceless fidelity": Attributed to James Merrill (1926–1995) by his literary executor, J. D. McClatchy, editor of the 2001 Library of America edition of Longfellow's poetry, in an interview with Matthew Pearl, author of *The Dante Club* and editor of a Modern Library edition of Longfellow's translation of the *Inferno*.

350 "In translating Dante": HWL Journal, May 7, 1864.

350 "I shall always read": George Ticknor to HWL, June 1, 1867, HL, bMS Am 1340.2 (5546). See Patricia Roylance, "Longfellow's Dante: Literary Achievement in a Transatlantic Culture of Print," in Lansing, 135–48.

351 "Longfellow is a superb lyric poet": Harold Bloom, *Best Poems of the English Language: From Chaucer Through Frost* (New York: HarperCollins, 2007). The four Longfellow poems he selected for inclusion: "Snow Flakes," "The Cross of Snow," "The Tide Rises, the Tide Falls," "The Bells of San Blas," 512–515. Bloom writes this of Longfellow's place in the firmament: "Longfellow is not, like Whitman and Dickinson, a great original, and he compares poorly with the rugged Emerson in what Emerson called 'meter-making argument.' But he remains a permanent poet, replete with grace and his own chastened mode of cognitive music."

351 "*all* the current versions": Harold Bloom, author interview, March 30, 2016.

351 "The only merit": HWL to Robert Ferguson, May 8, 1867, in *Letters*, vol. 5, 134.

351 earlier sonnets: "Mezzo Cammin," 1842; "Dante," 1845; "The Evening Star," 1845; "On Mrs. Kemble's Readings from Shakespeare," 1848. See Greenslet, *The Sonnets of Henry Wadsworth Longfellow,* xi–xviii. In his critical examination, Newton Arvin wrote that the "late flowering of the form" that "took hold" of Longfellow toward

the end of his life had striking results: "Longfellow revealed himself to be the most accomplished writer of sonnets in the American nineteenth century" (304–305).

352   "all done": HWL Journal, May 6, 1867.

352   Dickens in Boston: See Payne, *Dickens Days in Boston*, passim, and Henry Wadsworth Longfellow Dana, "Longfellow and Dickens: The Story of a Trans-Atlantic Friendship," in Proceedings of the *Cambridge Historical Society,* vol. 28 (1942), 55–104. Also, George Curry, "Charles Dickens and Annie Fields," in *Huntington Library Quarterly*, vol. 51, no. 1 (Winter 1988), 1–71.

352   "It was right pleasant": HWL Journal, Nov. 20, 1867.

352   "triumph for Dickens": Ibid., Dec. 2, 1867.

352   "I took it into my head": Charles Dickens to Wilkie Collins, Jan. 12, 1868, in *Charles Dickens: Letters and Speeches* (London: Chapman & Hall, 1908), vol. 2, 332–333.

353   "I can think of nothing": HWL Journal, June 14, 1870.

353   "I suppose you don't": Charles Dickens to his eldest son, also named Charles Dickens, Nov. 30, 1867, in *Charles Dickens: Letters and Speeches*, vol. 2, 215–216.

18 · DAYBREAK EVERYWHERE

355   *Departure of Hiawatha*: Painting by Albert Bierstadt, presented to HWL in London, 1869, Longfellow House Museum Collection, LONG 4138.

355   Photograph: Henry later reported that the picture Queen Victoria presented to him had been "purloined" from an album he kept by a "French governess we once had in the house," along with several other valuable items "before her pilferings were discovered." HWL to Edith Stuart Appleton, Jan. 7, 1873, *Letters*, vol. 5, 644.

356   Prince Albert biography: Theodore Martin: *The Life of His Royal Highness the Prince Consort,* 5 vols. (London: Smith, Elder & Co., 1875–1880).

356   "I wished for you": Austin, 348.

357   Julia Margaret Cameron: Lord Tennyson personally took Henry to Cameron's studio for the portrait, and introduced them with these words. "I have brought you a great man, who will let you immortalize him. This is Longfellow; you know him by name, now you know him in the flesh. I will leave you now. Longfellow, you'll have to do whatever she tells you. I'll come back soon and see what is left of you." Raymond Blathwayt, "How Celebrities Have Been Photographed," in *The Windsor Magazine,* vol. 2 (July–Dec. 1895) (London: Ward, Lock & Bowden, 1895), 639–648.

357   "I have in my brain": HWL to John Forster, July 20, 1868, *Letters,* vol. 5, 252.

357   "but Longfellow, alas": quoted by Dana Gioia, in Parini, 65. See also Anthony Trollope, "Henry Wadsworth Longfellow," in *The North American Review*, vol. 132, no. 293 (Apr. 1881), 383–406, published a year before Henry's death.

357   "currency in Europe": Quoted in Annie Adams Fields, 17–18.

358   "Ever since I reached": HWL to GWG, Feb. 7, 1869, *Letters,* vol. 5, 276–277.

358   G. P. A. Healy portraits in Longfellow House: Fanny Appleton, 1834, Museum Collection, LONG 4437; Mary Appleton, 1834, LONG 4137. For more on Healy and his years in Europe, see McCullough, passim.

358   Healy portrait of Henry and Edith: Displayed for many years in the home of Edith Longfellow Thorp, it passed on to her heirs in 1915 and is now among the permanent collections of the Worcester Art Museum, a gift from one of her granddaughters.

358 "I had recently . . . pleasure to Longfellow": George P. A. Healy, *Reminiscences of a Portrait Painter* (Chicago: A. C. McClurg, 1894), 219–221. For more on the Healy painting— "one of the two best portraits of Liszt ever executed"—see Edward N. Waters, "A Letter from Liszt to Longfellow," in *Quarterly Journal of Current Acquisitions*, vol. 12, no. 1 (Nov. 1954), 1–13. It has the Longfellow House designation LONG 4134.

359 "Your portrait": HWL to Franz Liszt, Oct. 18, 1872, *Letters*, vol. 5, 603.

360 "Allow me to": Franz Liszt to HWL, Nov. 22, 1874, quoted in Edward N. Waters, "A Letter from Liszt," with his translation.

360 "I am heartily tired": HWL to CAL, May 30, 1869, *Letters*, vol. 5, 284–285.

361 "He wrote that he could not go": [Horace P. Chandler], "Longfellow's First Wife and Early Friends," in *Every Other Saturday*, vol. 1, no. 2, Jan. 19, 1884, 20–21. Chandler's mother, Martha Ann Cleaveland Chandler, was the daughter of Parker Cleaveland; Henry stayed in the Cleaveland House during his return trip to Bowdoin for his fiftieth class reunion. Henry later wrote a sonnet, "Parker Cleaveland: Written on Revisiting Brunswick in the Summer of 1875," which he sent to Martha Chandler on Feb. 25, 1876. See Hilen, *Letters*, vol. 6, Feb. 25, 1876, 105–106.

361 "I am rejoiced": Joshua L. Chamberlain to HWL, March 22, 1875, HL, bMS 1340.2-1340.7 (1035).

361 Longfellow weeping: Alice Rains Trulock, *In the Hands of Providence: Joshua Chamberlain and the American Civil War* (Chapel Hill, NC: University of North Carolina Press, 1992), 349.

362 Bowdoin class of 1825: Horatio Bridge was especially close to Nathaniel Hawthorne and was instrumental in helping launch his career. He wrote at length about their years at Bowdoin, including concise profiles of his high-achieving classmates, in *Personal Recollections of Nathaniel Hawthorne* (New York: Harper & Brothers, 1893).

362 "from the advance sheets": *The New York Times*, July 6, 1875.

362 "indescribably affecting": Quoted in Underwood, 222–225.

362 *Bowdoin Orient*: (Brunswick, ME), vol. 5, no. 6, July 14, 1875, copy in Henry Wadsworth Longfellow Collection M112, George J. Mitchell Department of Special Collections, Hawthorne-Longfellow Library, Bowdoin College.

363 "non clamor sed amor": The motto was discovered by Henry in a four-line verse that he had found, without any author's name, in one of his books, and had translated to read: "Not voice but vow, / Not harp-string but heart-string, / Not clamor but love, / Sounds in the ear of God." See Samuel Longfellow, *Final Memorials*, 440.

363 "evidence of the diversity": Hilen, in *Letters*, vol. 5, 315–316.

363 "bought a copy": *Life*, vol. 3, 276. The book, Plutarch's *Vitae*, published in 1496, remains in the collections, catalog number LONG 2650.

364 "Even closets": Annie Adams Fields, 26–27.

364 "The Exequy": For a superb discussion of this poem, and these lines in particular, see Donald Hall, "The Poetry of Death," in *The New Yorker*, Sept. 12. 2017.

364 "most intimate friends": Ibid.

365 "no catalogue was ever": Alice Longfellow, "Longfellow in Home Life," *The Cambridge Magazine*, vol. 1 (new series), no. 2 (March 1896), 73–83.

365 final months: Charley returned from a trip abroad in March 1892, according to a clipped obituary in the Charles Appleton Longfellow Papers at Longfellow House (box 18, folder 10), and died on April 13, 1893, after having been "ill for over a year."

His half-uncle and occasional travel companion, Nathan Appleton Jr., wrote in *Russian Life and Society* (Boston: privately published, 1904), that Charley "had a sudden stroke of paralysis from which he never recovered" following a trip to Tahiti a year earlier (159).

365   "In this same old house": Alice M. Longfellow, "Longfellow in Home Life."

366   Fanny sketch of Henry: Dated 1847, framed, in the study, on bookcase shelf, LH Museum Collection, LONG 4154 HWL.

366   Henry sketch of Fanny: Dated in Henry's hand, "January 31, 1847, Sunday afternoon."

366   Eastman Johnson portraits in Craigie House: Study: Charles Sumner, LONG 545; Henry Wadsworth Longfellow, LONG 544; Cornelius Conway Felton, LONG 543; Nathaniel Hawthorne, LONG 542; Ralph Waldo Emerson, LONG 541. Dining room: Anne Longfellow Pierce, LONG 4419; Mary Longfellow Greenleaf, LONG 4418.

367   "Here Vassall": George Washington Greene, "Longfellow House and Library," *The Aldine*, vol. 5, no. 5 (May 1872), 100–103.

367   "He is my oldest": HWL Journal, March 10, 1877.

368   "He was inclined": Annie Adams Fields, 58–59.

368   Accounts of the exposition: Frank H. Norton and Frank Leslie, *Frank Leslie's Illustrated Historical Register of the United States Centennial Exposition, 1876* (New York: Frank Leslie's Publishing House, 1876), LONG 2674; Frank H. Norton, *Illustrated Historical Register of the Centennial Exhibition, Philadelphia, 1876, and of the Exposition Universelle, Paris, 1878* (New York: American News Company, 1879), LONG 2925.

368   "a charming vacation": HWL Journal, May 16–21, 1876.

369   "series of illustrations": Thomas Moran to HWL, June 5, 1876, HL, bMS Am 1340.2 (3960).

369   *Mountain of the Holy Cross*: See Wilkins, *Thomas Moran,* 95–107. The original oil painting displayed at the Centennial Exposition is now in the permanent collections of the Autry Museum of the American West in Los Angeles, Object ID 91 221 49.

370   "The principal peak": *Picturesque America, or the Land We Live In,* 2 vols., issued in parts, ed. William Cullen Bryant; "the main literary work on this publication was done by Oliver B. Bunce" (New York: D. Appleton & Co., 1872–74), part 25, 502. HL copy f*58-1462.

370   "a hearty, genial": HWL Journal, June 10, 1876.

370   Sarah Bernhardt: Ernest Longfellow, 43. "Of the actresses," Ernest wrote of the many celebrities who visited Craigie House, "first place should be given Mrs. Kemble, whose wonderful reading of Shakespeare enthralled us when we were young."

371   "In personal contact": Anthony Trollope, *North American Review* (April 1881).

371   breakfast: Oscar Wilde said privately to a friend afterwards that "Longfellow was himself a beautiful poem, more beautiful than anything he ever wrote." After Henry's death a few weeks later, he professed a different view, saying at a public lecture in Boston that "the lips of Longfellow are still musical for us though his dust be turning into the flowers which he loved." See Richard Ellmann, *Oscar Wilde* (New York: Alfred A. Knopf, 1988), 180–181.

371   "Day by day": Annie Adams Fields, 31.

371   "As I was standing": HWL Journal, Aug. 22, 1879.

371 "and asked": Ibid., Oct. 22, 1866.

371 Unexpected visitors: Fanny once described for Emmeline the unending parade of admirers who came calling "at all hours" on Henry: "One day a lantern-jawed Kentuckian with son and daughters all greatly desiring autographs—another day some Italian or German refugee hoping for a little advice about their future," the two being "just a specimen of the odd varieties" they continually received: "Henry seems to be considered a kind of Helper General to all nations and his good nature always encourages the idea." FEAL to EAW, Aug. 22, 1851, FEAL-B3-F1-I32.

372 "Next to Mount Vernon": David Millar, *Measured Drawings of Some Colonial and Georgian Houses* (New York: Architectural Book Publishing Co., 1916), 3.

372 Magnolia: Numerous replicas of Craigie House still stand throughout the country, a number constructed before the Sears Roebuck copy, including one built in 1906 in Minneapolis that now serves as an information center for the Minneapolis Park System. An even earlier replica was created for the 1895 Cotton States and International Expositions in Atlanta. See "The Next Best-known House in America and Its Replicas," in *Longfellow House Bulletin,* vol. 3, no. 2 (December 1999), and John Hebble, "The Vassall-Craigie-Longfellow House of 1759: From Colonial America to the Colonial Revival and Beyond," a thesis submitted for the degree of Master of Arts at Virginia Commonwealth University, Richmond, VA, 2010.

373 "He has made": FEAL to MAM, June 19, 1854, FEAL-B3-F4-I8. The Samuel Laurence portrait of Longfellow: LONG 2896.

373 Alexander Longfellow: See Richard Shain Cohen, *The Forgotten Longfellow* (West Yarmouth, MA: Artship Publishing, 2009), a consideration of the career of the poet's younger brother, a cartographer and explorer who lived much of his life in Henry's shadow.

374 "I told you": FEAL to EAW, a fragment from August or September 1857, FEAL-B3-F14-I15. The portrait of Annie and Edith: LONG 2897.

374 "The Cross of Snow": First appearance in print, *Life,* vol. 2, 372–373.

374 "Rowse began": HWL Journal, March 3, 1858.

375 Saint Benedict, Monte Cassino, and the first monastic scriptorium: See my book *Patience & Fortitude,* 93–99.

375 "Mezzo Cammin": Three versions of the sonnet, written in Germany during the 1842 "water cure," one of them a fair copy, are in HL, MS Am 1370 (72).

377 420 poems: See "a chronological list of Mr. Longfellow's poems" in Horace E. Scudder, ed., *The Complete Poetical Works of Longfellow* (Cambridge: The Riverside Press/Houghton Mifflin, 1886), 676–679.

377 sonnets: See the introduction by Ferris Greenslet in *The Sonnets of Henry Wadsworth Longfellow* (Boston: Houghton Mifflin, 1907).

377 Longfellow's death: Henry's funeral was a small affair, attended by family and a few close friends, with a light snow falling outside Craigie House. William Dean Howells wrote that after viewing the body in the library, a by then very feeble Ralph Waldo Emerson remarked: "The gentleman we have just been burying was a sweet and beautiful soul; but I forget his name."

377 "Typical Journeys and Country Life": [W. H. Bishop], *Harper's New Monthly Magazine,* vol. 64 (Dec. 1881–May 1882), 537–553.

377 "Book of Suggestions": HL, MS Am 1340 (51).

378 "My slight sketch": William Henry Bishop, *Old Mexico and Her Lost Provinces* (New York: Harper & Brothers, 1883), 291.

378   "with a special force": Arvin, 316. For more on Newton Arvin, and how an egregious invasion of his personal life led him to write this superb critical treatment of Longfellow's poetry, see Barry Werth, *The Scarlet Professor: Newton Arvin, a Literary Life Shattered by Scandal* (New York: Nan Talese/Doubleday, 2001).

380   coda: Harold Bloom, in *Till I End My Song* (New York: HarperCollins, 2010), an anthology of "last poems," includes a "remarkable" poem Longfellow wrote in the final year of his life, "Elegiac Verse," and praises him as a "wonderful lyric poet, once famous and then neglected," who "merits revival and begins to receive it" (125).

Bibliography

Abdo, Joseph C. *The Quiet Radical: The Biography of Samuel Longfellow.* Lisbon, Portugal: Tenth Island Editions, 2007.

Arvin, Newton. *Longfellow: His Life and Work.* Boston: Atlantic Monthly Press/Little, Brown, 1962.

Austin, George Lowell. *Henry Wadsworth Longfellow: His Life, His Works, His Friendships.* Boston: Lee and Shepard, 1882.

Babin, John William, and Allan M. Levinsky. *Henry Wadsworth Longfellow in Portland: The Fireside Poet of Maine.* Charleston, SC: The History Press, 2015.

Basbanes, Nicholas A. *A Gentle Madness: Bibliophiles, Bibliomanes, and the Eternal Passion for Books.* New York: Henry Holt, 1995.

———. *Every Book Its Reader: The Power of the Printed Word to Stir the World.* New York: HarperCollins, 2005.

———. *On Paper: The Everything of Its Two-Thousand-Year History.* New York: Alfred A. Knopf, 2013.

———. *Patience & Fortitude: A Roving Chronicle of Book People, Book Places, and Book Culture.* New York: HarperCollins, 2001.

———. *A Splendor of Letters: The Permanence of Books in an Impermanent World.* New York: HarperCollins, 2004.

Bell, J. L. *George Washington's Headquarters and Home—Cambridge, Massachusetts.* Historic Resource Study. Washington: US Department of the Interior, National Park Service, 2012.

Bridge, Horatio. *Personal Recollections of Nathaniel Hawthorne.* New York: Harper & Brothers, 1893.

Bruccoli, Matthew J. *The Profession of Authorship in America, 1800 to 1870: The Papers of William Charvat.* Foreword by Howard Mumford Jones. Columbus, OH: Ohio State University Press, 1968.

Burt, Stephen, and David Mikics. *The Art of the Sonnet.* Cambridge, MA: The Belknap Press/Harvard University Press, 2010.

Busch, Jason T., Christopher Monkhouse, and Janet L. Whitmore. *Currents of Change: Art and Life Along the Mississippi 1850–1861.* Minneapolis: The Minneapolis Institute of Art, 2004.

Calhoun, Charles C. *Longfellow: A Rediscovered Life.* Boston: Beacon Press, 2004.

Cary, Edward. *George William Curtis.* Boston: Houghton Mifflin, 1894.

Cifelli, Edward M. *Longfellow in Love: Passion and Tragedy in the Life of the Poet.* Jefferson, NC: McFarland, 2018.

Crawford, Mary Caroline. *Romantic Days in Old Boston: The Story of the City and Its People During the Nineteenth Century.* Boston: Little, Brown & Co., 1910.

Crowninshield, Clara. *The Diary of Clara Crowninshield: A European Tour with Longfellow, 1835–1836.* Edited by Andrew Hilen. Seattle: University of Washington Press, 1956.

Curtis, George William. *Lotus-Eating.* London: Richard Bentley, 1852.

———. *Prue and I.* Introduction by M. A. DeWolfe. New York: Crowell, 1899 [first Harper Bros. edition 1856].

Damon-Bach, Lucinda, and Victoria Clements, eds. *Catharine Maria Sedgwick: Critical Perspectives.* Foreword by Mary Kelley. Boston: Northeastern University Press, 2003.

Donald, David. *Charles Sumner and the Coming of the Civil War.* New York: Alfred A. Knopf, 1960.

Elliott, Maud Howe. *Uncle Sam Ward and His Circle.* New York: The Macmillan Company, 1938.

Fields, Mrs. James T. [Annie Adams Fields]. *Authors and Friends.* Boston: Houghton Mifflin, 1897.

Fisher, Marion Hall, and Howard T. Fisher. *Frances Calderón de la Barca née Frances Erskine Inglis.* Edited by Alan H. Fisher. Bloomington, IN: Xlibris Corp., 2016.

Freidel, Frank. *Francis Lieber: Nineteenth-Century Liberal.* Baton Rouge, LA: Louisiana State University Press, 1947.

Friedman, David M. *Wilde in America.* New York: W. W. Norton and Co., 2014.

Gale, Robert L. *A Henry Wadsworth Longfellow Companion.* Westport, CT: Greenwood Press, 2003.

Gollin, Rita K. *Annie Adams Fields: Woman of Letters.* Amherst, MA: University of Massachusetts Press, 2002.

Goodman, Susan, and Carl Dawson. *William Dean Howells: A Writer's Life.* Berkeley and Los Angeles: University of California Press, 2005.

Gorman, Herbert S. *A Victorian American: Henry Wadsworth Longfellow.* Port Washington, NY: Kennikat Press, 1967 [reissue of the 1926 edition].

Gregory, Frances W. *Nathan Appleton: Merchant and Entrepreneur, 1779–1861.* Charlottesville, VA: University Press of Virginia, 1975.

Hatfield, James Taft. *New Light on Longfellow.* New York: Gordian Press, 1970 [reprint of the 1933 Houghton Mifflin edition].

Henry, Madeleine M. *Prisoner of History: Aspasia of Miletus and Her Biographical Tradition.* New York and Oxford: Oxford University Press, 1995.

Higginson, Thomas W. *Henry Wadsworth Longfellow.* Boston: Houghton Mifflin Co., 1902.

Hilen, Andrew. *Longfellow and Scandinavia: A Study of the Poet's Relationship with the Northern Languages and Literatures.* New Haven, CT: Yale University Press, 1947 [Yale Studies in English, vol. 107; reprinted in an unaltered and unabridged edition by Archon Books, 1970].

Hillard, George, ed. *Life, Letters & Journals of George Ticknor.* Boston: Houghton Mifflin, 1909.

Historic Furnishings Report: The Longfellow National Historic Site. Vol. 1: Administrative and Historical Information. Harpers Ferry Center: Division of Historic Furnishings, National Park Service, 1999.

Homes of American Authors, Comprising Anecdotal, Personal, and Descriptive Sketches, by Various Writers. New York: G. P. Putnam, 1853.

Howe, M. A. DeWolfe. *Memories of a Hostess: A Chronicle of Eminent Friendships Drawn Chiefly from the Diaries of Mrs. James T. Fields.* Boston: The Atlantic Monthly Press, 1922.

Horton, James Oliver, and Lois E. Horton. *Black Bostonians: Family Life and Community Struggle in the Antebellum North.* New York and London: Holmes & Meier, 1999 [revised edition].

Howells, William Dean. *Literary Friends and Acquaintance: A Personal Retrospect of American Authorship.* New York: Harper & Brothers, 1911.

Irmscher, Christoph. *Longfellow Redux.* Urbana and Chicago: University of Illinois Press, 2002.

———. *Public Poet, Private Man: Henry Wadsworth Longfellow at 200.* Amherst, MA: University of Massachusetts Press, 2009.

———. *Louis Agassiz: Creator of American Science.* Boston: Houghton Mifflin, 2013.

———, and Robert Arbour, eds. *Reconsidering Longfellow.* Madison, NJ: Fairleigh Dickinson University Press, 2014.

Jacob, Kathryn Allamong. *King of the Lobby: The Life and Times of Sam Ward, Man-About-Washington in the Gilded Age.* Baltimore: The Johns Hopkins University Press, 2010.

Jakšić, Iván. *The Hispanic World and American Intellectual Life, 1820–1980.* New York: Palgrave Macmillan, 2007.

James, Henry, ed. *William Wetmore Story and His Friends from Letters Diaries, and Recollections.* Two volumes. Edinburgh and London: William Blackwood and Sons, 1903.

Johnson, Carl L. *Professor Longfellow of Harvard.* Studies in Literature and Philology, no. 5, April 1944. Eugene, OR: The University Press, 1944.

Laidlaw, Christine Wallace, ed. *Charles Appleton Longfellow: Twenty Months in Japan.* Cambridge, MA: Friends of the Longfellow House, 1998.

Lansing, Richard, ed. in chief. *Dante Studies, with the Annual Report of the Dante Society.* Cambridge, MA/The Bronx, NY: Dante Society of America/Fordham University Press, 2010 [issue devoted to "Longfellow and Dante"].

Lawrence, Robert Means. *Old Park Street and Its Vicinity.* Boston: Houghton Mifflin, 1922.

Long, Orie William. *Literary Pioneers: Early American Explorers of European Culture.* Cambridge, MA: Harvard University Press, 1935.

Longfellow, Ernest Wadsworth. *Random Memories.* Boston: Houghton Mifflin, 1922.

Longfellow, Henry Wadsworth. *The Letters of Henry Wadsworth Longfellow.* Edited by Andrew Hilen. 6 vols. Cambridge, MA: Belknap Press/Harvard University Press, 1968–1982.

———. *The Sonnets of Henry Wadsworth Longfellow.* Arranged and with an introduction by Ferris Greenslet. Boston: Houghton Mifflin, 1907.

Longfellow, Samuel. *Life of Henry Wadsworth Longfellow, with Extracts from His Journals and Correspondence.* 2 vols. Boston: Ticknor and Company, 1886 (third edition).

———. *Final Memorials of Henry Wadsworth Longfellow.* Boston: Ticknor and Company, 1887 [incorporated as vol. 3 in later editions of *Life of Henry Wadsworth Longfellow*].

Maine Historical Society. *Longfellow's Portland and Portland's Longfellow.* Essays by Daniel Aaron, "The Legacy of Henry Wadsworth Longfellow"; Joyce Butler, "The Wadsworths: A Portland Family" and "The Longfellows: Another Portland Family." Portland, ME: Maine Historical Society, 1987.

Marshall, Megan. *The Peabody Sisters: Three Women Who Ignited American Romanticism.* Boston: Houghton Mifflin, 2005.

Mathias, Christopher R., and Kenneth C. Turino. *Nahant.* Charleston, SC: Arcadia Publishing Co., 1999.

McCullough, David. *The Greater Journey: Americans in Paris.* New York: Simon & Schuster, 2011.

McFarland, Philip. *Sea Dangers: The Affair of the Somers.* New York: Schocken, 1985.

McFarland, Ron. *The Long Life of "Evangeline": A History of the Longfellow Poem in Print, in Adaptation and in Popular Culture.* Jefferson, NC: McFarland Publishing Co., 2010.

Mellow, James R. *Nathaniel Hawthorne in His Times.* Boston: Houghton Mifflin, 1980.

Morison, Samuel Eliot. *Harrison Gray Otis, 1765–1848: The Urbane Federalist.* Boston: Houghton Mifflin, 1969.

Morris, Timothy. *Becoming Canonical in American Poetry.* Urbana and Chicago: University of Illinois Press, 1995.

Moss, Sidney P. *Poe's Literary Battles: The Critic in the Context of His Literary Milieu.* Durham, NC: Duke University Press, 1963.

National Park Service. *Papers Presented at the Longfellow Commemorative Conference, April 1–3, 1982.* Coordinated by the National Park Service, Longfellow National Historic Site. Washington: US Government Printing Office, 1982 [full text available online].

Norton, Sarah, and M. A. DeWolfe Howe. *Letters of Charles Eliot Norton, with a Biographical Comment.* 2 vols. Boston: Houghton Mifflin, 1913.

O'Connor, Thomas H. *Lords of the Loom: The Cotton Whigs and the Coming of the Civil War.* New York: Charles Scribner's Sons, 1968.

Parini, Jay, ed., and Brett C. Miller, associate ed. *The Columbia History of American Poetry.* New York: Columbia University Press, 1993. Includes Dana Gioia, "Longfellow in the Aftermath of Modernism," 64–96.

Paterson, Stanley, and Carl G. Seaburg. *Nahant on the Rocks.* Nahant, MA: Nahant Historical Society, 1991.

Payne, Edward F. *Dickens' Days in Boston: A Record of Daily Events.* Boston: Houghton Mifflin, 1927.

Pierce, Edward Little, ed. *Memoir and Letters of Charles Sumner.* Four vols. Boston: Roberts and Brothers, 1878–1893.

Pinsky, Robert, trans. and ed. *The Inferno of Dante. Bilingual edition.* New York: The Noonday Press/Farrar, Straus & Giroux, 1994.

Pratt, William Haven. *The Craigies: A Footnote to the History of the Revolution.* Cambridge, MA: The Cambridge Historical Society, 1942.

Roman, Judith A. *Annie Adams Fields: The Spirit of Charles Street.* Bloomington and Indianapolis: Indiana University Press, 1990.

Ronda, Bruce A., ed. *Letters of Elizabeth Palmer Peabody: American Renaissance Woman.* Middletown, CT: Wesleyan University Press, 1984.

Sedgwick, John. *In My Blood: Six Generations of Madness & Desire in an American Family.* New York: HarperCollins, 2007.

Shand-Tucci, Douglass. *Built in Boston: City and Suburb, 1800–1950.* Foreword by Walter Muir Whitehill. Boston: New York Graphic Society, 1978.

Shepard, Odell, ed. *Henry Wadsworth Longfellow: Representative Selections, with Introduction, Bibliography, and Notes.* New York: American Book Company, 1934.

Sherwood, M. E. W. [Mary Elizabeth Wilson]. *An Epistle to Posterity: Being Rambling Recollections of Many Years of My Life.* New York: Harper & Brothers, 1897.

Showalter, Elaine. *A Jury of Her Peers: American Women Writers from Anne Bradstreet to Annie Proulx.* London: Virago Press, 2009.

———. *The Civil Wars of Julia Ward Howe: A Biography.* New York: Simon & Schuster, 2016.

Silverman, Kenneth. *Edgar A. Poe: Mournful and Never-ending Remembrance.* New York: HarperCollins, 1991.

Skinner, Henrietta Dana. *An Echo from Parnassus: Girlhood Memories of Longfellow and His Circle.* New York: H. Sears & Co., 1928.

Sumner, Charles. *The Selected Letters of Charles Sumner.* Edited by Beverly Wilson Palmer. 2 vols. Boston: Northeastern University Press, 1990.

———. *The Grandeur of Nations: An Oration.* London: William Smith, 1846.

Tharp, Louise Hall. *The Appletons of Beacon Hill.* Boston: Little, Brown, 1975.

Thompson, Lawrance. *Young Longfellow (1807–1843).* New York: The Macmillan Company, 1938.

Trachtenberg, Alan. *Shades of Hiawatha: Staging Indians, Making Americans, 1880–1930.* New York: Hill and Wang, 2004.

Tryon, Warren Stenson. *Parnassus Corner: A Life of James T. Fields, Publisher to the Victorians.* Boston: Houghton Mifflin, 1963.

Tyack, David B. *George Ticknor and the Boston Brahmins.* Cambridge, MA: Harvard University Press, 1967.

Underwood, Francis H. *Henry Wadsworth Longfellow: A Biographical Sketch.* Boston: James R. Osgood, 1882.

Van Schaick, John Jr. *The Characters in "Tales of a Wayside Inn."* Boston: The Universalist Publishing House, 1939 [reprinted by Haskell House Publishers, New York, 1974].

Wadsworth, Horace Andrew. *Two Hundred and Fifty Years of the Wadsworth Family in America.* Lawrence, MA: Privately printed at the Eagle Steam Job Printing Rooms, 1883.

Wagenknecht, Edward. *Henry Wadsworth Longfellow: His Poetry and Prose.* New York: Ungar Publishing Co., 1986.

———. *Longfellow: A Full-Length Portrait.* New York: Longmans, Green & Co., 1955.

———. *Henry Wadsworth Longfellow: Portrait of an American Humanist.* New York: Oxford University Press, 1966.

Wagenknecht, Edward, ed. *Mrs. Longfellow: Selected Letters and Journals of Fanny Appleton Longfellow.* New York: Longmans, Green and Co., 1956.

Whitehill, Walter Muir. *Boston: A Topographical History.* Cambridge, MA: Belknap Press/ Harvard University Press, 1968 [second edition, enlarged].

Whitman, Iris. *Longfellow and Spain.* New York: Instituto de las Españas en los Estados Unidos, 1927.

Wilkins, Thurman. *Thomas Moran: Artist of the Mountains.* Norman, OK: University of Oklahoma Press, 1966.

Williams, Gary. *Hungry Heart: The Literary Emergence of Julia Ward Howe.* Amherst, MA: University of Massachusetts Press, 1999.

Willis, William. *History of Portland, from 1632 to 1864.* Portland, ME: Bailey and Noyes, 1865.

Wineapple, Brenda. *Hawthorne: A Life*. New York: Alfred A. Knopf, 2003.

Winter, William. *Old Friends: Being Literary Recollections of Other Days*. New York: Moffat, Yard, and Co., 1909.

Winthrop, Robert C. *Memoir of the Hon. Nathan Appleton, LL.D.* Boston: John Wilson and Son, 1861 [first published in *Proceedings of the Massachusetts Historical Society*, vol. 5 (1860–1862), 229–308].

Index

Note: Page numbers in *italics* refer to illustrations.

ILLUSTRATION CREDITS

A NOTE ON THE TYPE

This book was set in Adobe Garamond. Designed for the Adobe Corporation by Robert Slimbach, the fonts are based on types first cut by Claude Garamond (ca. 1480–1561). Garamond was a pupil of Geoffroy Tory and is believed to have followed the Venetian models. He gave to his letters a certain elegance and feeling of movement that won their creator an immediate reputation.

Composed by North Market Street Graphics,
Lancaster, Pennsylvania

Printed and bound by Berryville Graphics,
Berryville, Virginia

Designed by Cassandra J. Pappas

Photocomposition Interligne

Impression réalisée sur CAMERON
par BRODARD ET TAUPIN
La Flèche
en décembre 2004

Imprimé en France
Dépôt légal : décembre 2004
N° d'édition : 61205/40 – N° d'impression : 27461

VIEW OF PART